The Political Economy of Full Employment

The Political Economy of Full Employment

Conservatism, Corporatism
and Institutional Change

Edited by
Philip Arestis and Mike Marshall
Department of Applied Economics,
University of East London

Edward Elgar

© Philip Arestis, Mike Marshall 1995

Published by
Edward Elgar Publishing Limited
Gower House
Croft Road
Aldershot
Hants GU11 3HR
England

Edward Elgar Publishing Company
Old Post Road
Brookfield
Vermont 05036
USA

British Library Cataloguing in Publication Data
Political Economy of Full Employment:
Conservatism, Corporatism and
Institutional Change
    I. Arestis, P. II. Marshall, Michael
    339.5

Library of Congress Cataloguing in Publication Data
The political economy of full employment: conservatism, corporatism,
    and institutional change / Philip Arestis & Mike Marshall, editors.
        p. cm.
    Includes bibliographical references and index.
    1. Full employment policies. 2. Employment (Economic theory)
    I. Arestis, Philip, 1941– . II. Marshall, Mike, 1947– .
    HD5701.5.P65   1995
    339.5—dc20   94–29162
                                                       CIP

ISBN   1 85278 880 1

Printed and bound in Great Britain by
Hartnolls Limited, Bodmin, Cornwall

Contents

Figures

Tables

Notes on the contributors

Eileen Appelbaum joined the Economic Policy Institute in Washington D.C., as Associate Research Director in 1991. Formerly she was Professor in Economics at Temple University and spent several summers as a Guest Research Fellow in the Labour Markets and Employment section of the Wissenschaftszentrum Berlin. Dr Appelbaum has acted as consultant to the office of Technology Assessment of the US Congress on several volumes, including *Programmable Automation Technologies in Manufacturing* (1985) and *Trade in Services* (1988) and is co-editor of *Labour Market Adjustments to Structural Change and Technological Progress* (1990). She has studied and written about employee participation, and is co-author of *Job Saving Strategies: Worker Buyouts and QWL* (1988), and *The New American Workplace,* and a forthcoming book on high performance work systems in the US (1994). She has published numerous articles on employment and labour market issues and on developments in the service sector of the economy. She has also published extensively on the labour market experiences of women, including the effects of technology on women's jobs and the reasons for the expansion of part-time and contingent work arrangements in the US. Her current research focuses on (1) high performance work systems in the apparel industry and (2) an international comparison of common and diverging trends in employment developments in the industrialized economies. Dr Appelbaum received her PhD in Economics from the University of Pennsylvania in 1973.

Philip Arestis is Professor of Economics and Head of Department of Applied Economics, University of East London. He has also taught at the Universities of Surrey and Cambridge (Department of Extra-Mural Studies) and Greenwich University (where he was Head of Economics Division). He was editor of the *British Review of Economic Issues* and joint editor of the *Thames Papers in Political Economy,* and is on the editorial board of a number of journals and a member of the Council of the Royal Economic Society. His publications include *Post-Keynesian Monetary Economics: New Approaches to Financial Modelling* (Edward Elgar, 1988) and he is the co-author of *Introducing Macroeconomic Modelling: An Econometric Study of the United Kingdom* (Macmillan, 1982), and of *Post-Keynesian Economic Theory: A Challenge to Neo-Classical Economics* (Wheatsheaf, 1984). His most recent book is entitled *the Post-Keynesian Approach to Economics: An Alternative Analysis of Economic*

Theory and Policy (Edward Elgar, 1992). He has published articles on macro-economics, monetary economics and applied econometrics.

Keith Bain is a Principal Lecturer in the Department of Applied Economics at the University of East London, having taught previously in both Australia and Papua New Guinea. He studied at the University of Queensland in Australia. He has co-authored a number of books, the most recent being *Financial Markets and Institutions* (with Peter Howells, 1991), and has contributed articles in journals on international trade, international monetary systems and monetary economics.

Harald Hagemann has the Chair for Economic Theory at the University of Hohenheim in Stuttgart, Germany. He has been Professor of Economics at the University of Bremen (1982–88), Visiting Professor of Economic Theory and Political Economy at the Free University of Berlin (1980–81) and Assistant Professor at the University of Kiel (1977–80) where he got his PhD in Economics in 1977. He was a Fullbright Visiting Professor at the Graduate Faculty of the New School for Social Research in New York in 1986 and Visiting Professor at the University of Cambridge in 1989–90 where he also became a Life Member of Clare Hall. His main areas of research are macroeconomic theory and policy, technological change and employment, and the history of economic thought. Harald Hagemann is managing editor of *Structural Change and Economic Dynamics,* a member of the editorial board of *The European Journal of the History of Economic Thought* and of the advisory board of other international journals.

Joseph Halevi was educated mostly in Rome, where, after starting university in the faculty of engineering, he moved to mathematics and eventually ended up studying political economy and philosophy. From 1975 until 1979 he taught at the New School of Social Research in New York and at Rutgers University. In 1979 he started teaching at the University of Sydney while periodically holding visiting appointments at a number of universities in the US and France. Since 1989 he has been a member of the editorial board of *Economie Appliquée* in Paris. His publications are heavily oriented towards Marxian themes in an attempt to combine them with the theory of effective demand and with structural analyses of production. He has published in the *Annals of Public and Cooperative Economy* (1975), *Banca Nazionale del Lavoro Quarterly Review* (1978, 1981), *Economie Appliquée* (1984, 1988, 1991), *Social Research* (1979, 1983), and *Monthly Review* (1992). With David Laibman and Edward Nell he edited the book *Beyond the Steady States*, published by Macmillan in 1992.

Andrew Henley is Lecturer in Economics at the University of Kent at Canterbury. He is author of *Wages and Profits in the Capitalist Economy* (Edward Elgar, 1990) and co-author with Euclid Tsakalotos of *Corporatism and Economic Performance* (Edward Elgar, 1993). He has published widely in academic journals on labour economics, industrial economics and the economics of consumer behaviour.

Peter Kriesler obtained his Bachelor's and Master's degrees from the University of Sydney, and his PhD from the University of Cambridge. He has written and taught in a number of areas including the history of economic thought and economic methodology, but the bulk of his work has been on Kaleckian analysis and its application to contemporary circumstances, and the Australian economy. He is the author of a book on Kalecki's microanalysis and has edited two books on the Australian economy. He is currently working with Bruce McFarlane and Jan Toporowski on Kalecki's biography.

Mike Marshall is Senior Lecturer at the University of East London. He has given numerous conference papers covering a wide range of topics from the classical economists to the British economy in the 1920s. He has recently published articles on contemporary economic and social policy-making in *Journal of Economic Issues, International Journal of Applied Economics,* and *Review of Social Economy.* He is also a contributor to Philip Arestis and Malcolm Sawyer (eds), *The Elgar Companion to Radical Political Economy* (Edward Elgar, 1994).

Thomas R. Michl is Associate Professor of Economics at Colgate University, Hamilton, New York. He received his BA from Oberlin College and his MSc. and PhD from the New School for Social Research. He has published articles in the *Journal of Post Keynesian Economics, Review of Economics and Statistics, Review of Radical Political Economy, Cambridge Journal of Economics, International Review of Applied Economics, Monthly Review,* and *Dollars & Sense.*

Michael Perelman is a Professor of Economics at California State University, Chico. He has been a visiting professor at Stanford University and a visiting Scholar at the University of Paris. He has published the *Pathology of the US Economy: The Costs of a Low Wage System* (1993), *Information, Social Relations, and the Economics of High Technology* (1991), *Keynes, Investment Theory and the Economic Slowdown: The Role of Replacement Investment and q-Ratios* (1989), *Karl Marx's Crisis Theory: Labour, Scarcity and Fictitious Capital* (1987), *Classical Political Economy, Primitive Accumulation, and the Social Division of Labour* (1984), and *Farming for Profit in a Hungry World: Capital and the Crisis in Agriculture* (1977).

Peter Andrew Riach was educated at the Universities of Melbourne and London, and after teaching at Monash and Melbourne Universities he became Head of the Department of Economics, De Montfort University in 1989. He has published articles in *Kyklos, Australian Economics Papers, Public Administration, Journal of Industrial Relations, Cambridge Journal of Economics* and the *Journal of Post Keynesian Economics.* His most recent publications include: 'Testing for Sexual Discrimination in the Labour Market', *Cambridge Journal of Economics* (1987), and 'Measuring Discrimination by Direct Experimental Methods: Seeking Gunsmoke', *Journal of Post Keynesian Economics*, (1991/1992), both with Judith Rich.

Malcolm Sawyer is Professor of Economics and Head of the Economics Division at the University of Leeds and formerly Professor of Economics at the University of York. He is the author of several books including *Macroeconomics in Question* (Harvester-Wheatsheaf and M.E. Sharpe, 1982), *The Economics of Michal Kalecki* (Macmillan and M.E. Sharpe, 1985) and *The Challenge of Radical Political Economy* (Harvester-Wheatsheaf and Barnes and Noble, 1989). He is the managing editor of *International Review of Applied Economics,* joint editor of the recently launched *International Papers in Political Economy*, and editor of the series *New Directions in Modern Economics* published by Edward Elgar. He has recently co-edited *The Biographical Dictionary of Dissenting Economists* and *The Elgar Companion to Radical Political Economy* (Edward Elgar, 1994). He has published widely in journals and books in the areas of industrial economics, macroeconomics and political economy. His current research interests include the theory of industrial policy and the conceptualization of competition and markets in economic theory, the causes and cures for unemployment; he also continues to work on post-Keynesian macroeconomics.

Ronald Schettkat was at Technical University Berlin between 1979 and 1981 as a lecturer in statistics for economists. In 1981 he began a five-year stay at the Wissenschaftszentrum Berlin. He joined the Institute of Economic Change and Employment as a Senior Research Fellow in 1986, during which time (1986–88) he was elected chairman of the Assembly of Fellows of Wissenschaftszentrum Berlin. He has lectured in Economics at the University of Bremen and the Netherlands Institute for Advanced Studies, and he has been Visiting Researcher at the University of California at Berkeley, the Science Policy Research Unit at the University of Sussex, the Swedish Institute for Social Research, University of Stockholm, and Stanford University. He has also been a consultant to the Brookings Institution; Economic Policy Institute, Washington D.C.; and the Institute of Industrial Relations, University of California. Recent work with Eileen Appelbaum published in English has included their contribution to Matzner, Egon and Streeck, Wolfgang (eds), *Beyond Keynesianism: The Socio-Economics of Production and Full Employment* (Edward Elgar, 1991).

Frank Skuse is Principal Lecturer at the University of East London where he is the Director of Undergraduate Programmes in Economics. He has also taught economics at Monash University in Australia, IUT Dijon in France and the Civil Service College, London. He has worked as an economist in the Department of Transport. Recently he has, *inter alia*, co-authored papers with Philip Arestis in *Economie Appliquée* and *Economie et Société* and published a review article in *International Journal of Applied Economics*.

Euclid Tsakalotos was Lecturer in Economics at the University of Kent at Canterbury before his appointment as Assistant Professor at the Athens Economics University. He is the author of *Alternative Economic Strategies: The Case of Greece* (Avebury, 1991), co-author with Andrew Henley of *Corporatism and Economic Performance* (Edward Elgar, 1993) and co-editor with Heather Gibson of *Economic Integration and Financial Liberalization: Prospects for Southern Europe* (Macmillan, 1992). He has published widely in academic journals on macroeconomics, European economics and political economy.

John Wells is University Lecturer in the Faculty of Economics and Politics, University of Cambridge. He co-authored (with Bob Rowthorn) *De-industrialization and Foreign Trade* (Cambridge University Press, 1987). Recent work includes: 'Britain in the 1990s: the legacy of "Thatcherism"' in John Cornwall (ed.), *The Capitalist Economies: Prospects for the 1990s* (Edward Elgar, 1993), 'The Economy after Ten Years; Weaker or Stronger' in Nigel Healey (ed.), *Britain's Economic Miracle: Myth or Reality?* (Routledge, 1993) and 'De-industrialization' in Philip Arestis and Malcolm Sawyer (eds), *The Elgar Companion to Radical Political Economy* (Edward Elgar, 1994).

Introduction: obstacles to, and strategies for, the achievement of full employment

Philip Arestis and Mike Marshall

It has been clear for some time now that the period of the 1950s and 1960s constituted not, as was thought at the time, the ushering in of a new regime of unbroken prosperity in the West, but rather a 'Golden Age' interposed between two recessionary eras. The business cycle, it would seem, was not after all one of the casualties of the Second World War, and stagnationist theories retain a force and relevance in a post-1970 world economy in which the growth rates of the major economies halved compared with those of the previous two decades and two large-scale recessions were separated by a recovery period that still left unemployment rates in many economies at unacceptably high levels.

The conditions that generated the 'Golden Age' clearly broke down some time in the 1970s, although the precise timing and causation of the breakdown is the subject of considerable controversy. Both internal and international forces played a part in the prosperity of the 'Golden Age' and in its collapse. Indeed it has been most persuasively argued that all historical epochs must be understood as a set of interlocking institutions and that it is the *interaction* of complementary institutions and forces that is the key to both success and failure. Taking this perspective, of course, means rejecting the idea that one set of factors in isolation produces growth or retardation.

If the timing and causation of the end of the period of prosperity after the Second World War are subject to considerable dispute, however, there is an apparently overwhelming consensus that the obstacles to the achievement and maintenance of full employment, that were thought to have been removed or permanently weakened after the war, are strong and intractable.

Malcolm Sawyer discusses these constraints in Chapter 1. Four groups of obstacles to the achievement of full employment are identified. First, the social and political forces which would lose (at least in relative terms) from full employment will resist full employment. Second, the difficulties which decentralized market economies generally have in sustaining a level of effective demand high enough for full employment. The third group arises from the view that there are significant economic, social and political forces which generate and reinforce disparities and inequalities, whether between individuals, regions or countries. The fourth group of obstacles is a collection of barriers: the inflation barrier, the international trade constraint and the work effort constraint.

The central argument of this chapter is that full employment, defined as a situation in which there is a balance between those seeking work and the vacancies which enterprises are seeking to fill, is not an impossible dream. However, its creation and maintenance require fundamental changes in conventional economic thinking and, more importantly, in the institutional and political arrangements under which market economies operate.

The achievement of full employment demands the creation of policies and institutions which will overcome the obstacles referred to. Further, since unemployment is seen to play certain systemic roles (e.g. imposing worker discipline, constraining inflation), alternatives to unemployment for those roles need to be found. Worker discipline is not desirable *per se* but rather is a mechanism for promoting acceptable levels of productivity, and alternative forms of work organization which foster productivity are needed. For inflation, alternative wage- and price-setting arrangements would have to be made. The sustaining of full employment may require a long-term government budget deficit to overcome a tendency in the private sector to underspend. A broad-ranging industrial strategy to promote industrial competitiveness, to reduce regional imbalances and to provide training and skill acquisition is necessary. Such a strategy, it is argued, would help lift balance of trade constraints and reduce other obstacles to the economy operating at a high level of demand without running into inflationary pressures. These policies would involve substantial intervention by government and a shift of direction away from an unfettered market economy.

In contemporary political and economic discourse technological advance is probably the factor most referred to in explaining why a return to full employment as it was understood during the 'Golden Age' is unlikely or impossible. Certainly the so-called microeconomics revolution has evoked the spectre of technological unemployment once again, and the complex issues raised here are the subject of Chapter 2.

Here Harald Hagemann shows that many of the issues which are now at the forefront of the debate on the employment consequences of technological change were already key issues in earlier discussions. In fact, technological change has enjoyed a rich history in the development of economic thought since the time of Adam Smith and Ricardo's analysis of the machinery problem. Looking at the post-Ricardian literature, Hagemann distinguishes between the compensation school, which asserts that free market mechanisms will lead to the re-employment of those workers who have been displaced from their jobs by technological change, and the displacement school, which denies the existence of a self-regulating mechanism that achieves full compensation automatically.

Hagemann discusses the pros and cons of the classical compensation arguments. It is shown that the extent of compensatory employment depends on the degree to which substitution between capital and labour is possible in the economy and on the flexibility of prices. Thus the harmonistic result of automatic self-correction of all temporary distortions of the full employment level follows from dropping two classical premises: the given level of real wages and the fixed coefficients of production.

The employment consequences of new technologies can differ in the short and long run. Thus the replacement of labour by better machines may cause temporary unemployment which sooner or later may be absorbed by increased accumulation. It is, Hagemann argues, Ricardo's lasting merit to have emphasized that additional savings and investment are necessary to ensure that displaced workers are re-employed. Characteristically Hicks and Lowe, the two pioneers in the modern analysis of the traverse, start their investigation from Ricardo's machinery chapter. They show that the decisive problem resulting from the technological change is the inappropriateness of the capital stock, since the necessary adjustments are costly and time-consuming. This holds for a *horizontal* model, as developed by Leontief, Sraffa and von Neumann, which concentrates on the circular flow of mutually dependent economic activities as well as within a *vertical* model of economic structure in the Austrian tradition. Hagemann concludes by indicating some directions for more satisfying empirical research on the displacement and reabsorption effects at the macroeconomic level.

The long-term pattern of Western industrialized economies, it is unremarkable to say, has been one of cyclical movement. Periods of expansion have given way to ones of crisis and restructuring. Only when restructuring has been successfully achieved have the conditions for continued profitable accumulation and growth been re-established.

In the US and the UK 'social democratic' governments were left fatally wounded by the economic difficulties of the 1970s and in both countries radical New Right-inspired governments dominated in the 1980s, introducing free market-based attempts to restructure their economies. This meant a significant break with the so-called Keynesian consensus. Consequently therefore this led to the initiation of an era of economic policy making which was avowedly anti-Keynesian in its orientation and inspiration.

In particular, control of inflation became the key target of macroeconomic policy; the use of fiscal policy to manipulate aggregate demand was eschewed. There was a clear switch, especially initially, to severe deflationary monetarist policies, and reductions in marginal tax rates were utilized to achieve 'incentivist' supply-side results. Chapters 3–6 below deal with key issues relating to the changes of objectives and policy in the UK and the US in the 1980s and early 1990s.

Chapter 3 by Tom Michl addresses the issue of whether the costs of inflation justify a policy of combating inflation through unemployment, or one of tolerating high unemployment out of fear of inflation. It summarizes much of the state of economic knowledge on the costs of inflation and unemployment, starting with the cost of reducing inflation as measured by the excess unemployment that must be endured. In the US, this sacrifice ratio has been shown to be quite high, suggesting there is no painless way to disinflate.

A central distinction is made between the unavoidable and avoidable costs of inflation. The costs which are most difficult to avoid through indexation include menu costs (the costs of changing prices) and costs associated with economizing on money holdings during inflations: these are shown to be small for moderate inflations. In theory, they are sometimes used to justify a target of zero (or negative) inflation, but the argument has been shown to break down in several cases. By contrast, the avoidable costs of inflation, such as the tendency for non-indexed taxes on capital income to rise during inflations, are practically significant. These costs fall heavily on the wealthiest households, creating a powerful anti-inflation lobby in influential circles. Moreover, the costs of unanticipated increases in inflation also fall heavily on wealth. These findings recommend policies to adapt to inflation, such as indexing the financial and tax systems.

The usual case against inflation – that high inflation creates uncertainty – is, Michl argues, theoretically and empirically flawed. Several explanations suggest that high inflation and uncertainty are caused by a common third factor, calling into question the causal relationship between inflation and uncertainty.

The chapter concludes with the observation that because the costs of disinflation are borne by low-income households while the benefits accrue to the wealthiest, the policy of disinflation does not stand up to a standard cost–benefit analysis. Unemployment is extremely regressive in incidence. Moreover, there are health effects, psychological effects and other human costs of joblessness that seriously undermine the argument that unemployment represents a temporary sacrifice in exchange for a permanent reduction in inflation. The policy implication is that measures to adapt to inflation are preferable to outright disinflation.

Frank Skuse in Chapter 4 concentrates on Thatcherism and the impact of the Conservative governments since 1979 on the UK economy. After suggesting that the change of administration in 1979 marked a clear break with the consensus approach to employment of the 1950s and 1960s, he looks at the behaviour of unemployment between 1979 and 1993 and identifies its key features. This discussion supports the idea of a significant change over the period since 1979, the most worrying aspects being the upward drift in the number of long-term or core unemployed and the damage caused by the rapid decline in the manufacturing sector. He also points to the evening out of regional disparities in terms of unemployment rates in the recession of the early 1990s. This section is followed by an overview of government policy during the period, considering both the intellectual underpinnings of the 'New Right' approach and the particular policy initiatives that were followed. The clear picture is of a government which has all but removed the objective of full employment from its agenda. To the extent that its policies are couched in terms of employment objectives, they are entirely concerned with supply-side actions. It is also suggested that they are based on an untenable view of the institutions and functioning of the UK economy. The chapter concludes with a discussion of the possibility of returning to full employment and argues that any policy designed to move towards this objective will have to embody a combination of supply-side and demand-side measures. It will also require a new spirit of partnership between the government and the private sector, particularly in connection with investment and control of inflationary factors. Further, it is important that it is understood as a policy based on a long-term move towards permanently higher levels of employment. Short-term measures will simply be insufficient to solve the problem of core unemployment and the factors leading to it.

Unlike in the US, UK unemployment was very slow to fall in the recovery from the early 1980s recession. This, plus the constant changes in the method of calculating the official unemployment figures, meant that the nature and scale of unemployment has remained a very controversial issue – and one which John Wells takes up in Chapter 5. Here Wells closely examines the official measure in relation to its accuracy as a measure of unemployment and as regards its sensitivity to changes in labour market conditions. It is concluded that the level of unemployment in 1993, properly measured, was nearly four million, as opposed to the official figure of just under three million.

After dealing with these measurement issues, Wells then moves on to a discussion of job creation and job destruction. Job destruction in goods-producing sectors experiencing rapid productivity growth has been accompanied by job creation in services. However, the latter, although on a truly massive scale, has been insufficient to counteract job shedding and the expansionary demographic factors feeding the growth of the working-age population as well as increases in female participation. Insufficient job creation in expanding sectors has been the result of the slow growth of GDP overall – the consequence principally of the weak international competitive performance and, hence, slow output growth of the internationally exposed or traded sector of the economy, principally manufacturing.

Wells argues that the consensus of forecasts for UK GDP in the medium term of at most 2.5 to 3 per cent, combined with estimates of underlying productivity growth of 2 to 2.5 per cent, does not suggest that very great inroads will be made into unemployment via the normal route of market forces operating under the stimulus of economic recovery. Wells concludes that mass unemployment on the scale currently being experienced by the UK and other European countries is a true 'crisis of capitalism', at both national and international levels, which requires, as in the 1930s, new forms of public intervention for its alleviation. He suggests that nationally an important part of the answer lies in the adoption of special employment and training measures, some of which would be designed to strengthen the economy's capacity to compete internationally, while others would aim to increase the supply of labour-intensive services provided collectively.

As Keynesianism became discredited in the US in the 1970s, neo-classicism, in a variety of forms, increased its influence. As it did so the much vaunted strategy of greater 'flexibility', largely a renewed promulgation of the gospel of unfettered market forces in the New Right formulation, came to the fore. In the US the neo-conservative backlash fairly quickly resulted in the triumph of a supply-side economic ideology. *Inter alia*, the claims of the supply-siders are examined by Mike Marshall in Chapter 6. In this chapter the incentivist effects of supply-side policies are critically assessed, important labour market changes are examined, and Reaganomics' distributional impact, and also its value as a modernization/restructuring project, is evaluated.

In the late 1970s and early 1980s the 'Labour Accord' in the US was considerably unravelled. Employers faced a growing need to boost profitability and improve their relative competitive position, especially with Far East producers and both they and New Right theorists started to refer to the need to achieve greater 'flexibility' in the labour market. With the encouragement of the government and the assistance of a slack labour market, US employers undertook a restructuring of the labour market that contributed towards a faster and more complete introduction of new technology, and important changes in payment and working systems. The upshot of all this was a downward pressure on unit labour costs and an increase in labour productivity in manufacturing. These labour market changes, it is argued, are likely to have had a greater impact on productivity than the fiscal changes.

If the fiscal changes had poor incentivist results, their impact on the distribution of income was much clearer and stronger. Aided by a patchy recovery and the state of the labour market, the fiscal changes helped stimulate an increase in income inequality and a rise in poverty and low pay.

What is abundantly clear from the experience of the 1980s is that the conservative economic policy making of that decade did not constitute a coherent, successful or acceptable attempt to create non-inflationary growth. Supply-side claims have not been validated by the evidence of the 1980s. The supply-side 'softball' strategy for a painless adjustment to higher productivity is not well founded either empirically or theoretically. In terms of raising the productivity of the majority of the working population, reducing marginal tax rates does not appear to be a very strong candidate. In fact, in the supply-side literature the emphasis is largely on the *top* rates of tax and therefore on the role and position of the rich rather than on the mass of working people.

Productivity miracles are not performed by simply reducing the top rates of income tax. Moreover, while the New Right in Europe might have pointed to the allegedly superior (i.e. more 'flexible') labour market conditions in the US leading to a better job-creation performance, in fact many, too many, of the new jobs that were created were part-time or low-wage, low-skill, low-productivity jobs.

The New Right strategy of labour market deregulation and 'increased flexibility', such that workers price themselves back into work via real wage cuts, is examined in Chapter 7. Here Michael Perelman attacks this conventional wisdom in the US, which he dubs the 'Haitian road to economic progress', and he supports his conclusion that high wages can be economically beneficial through a long-term perspective on the debate about the merits and demerits of high wages.

Perelman rejects the contemporary view held by business and political leaders throughout the developed capitalist world that those economies where labour is bought more cheaply inevitably hold a competitive advantage *vis à vis* the rest of the world. Perelman argues that high wages give firms a strong incentive to invest in productivity-enhancing capital goods (a line of reasoning consistent with conventional neo-classical economic theory) and also stimulate workers to exert themselves more enthusiastically. The literature on efficiency wages has recently rediscovered some of the pathways through which high wages stimulate productivity.

In enhancing productivity in highly advanced technological systems emphasis is placed on the need to tap workers' creativity and goodwill. Unfortunately too many employers prefer to adopt coercive labour management regimes thereby limiting the workers' creative participation in production and undermining cooperation. This Perelman contrasts with the Japanese approach which, however, is not novel and, Perelman argues, is the approach foreign observers identified with the US.

Perelman shows that during the nineteenth and early twentieth centuries economists commonly attributed the success of the US economy to the influence of high wages. Visitors from abroad such as Tocqueville, and Adam Smith, agreed that high wages contributed to the success of the US. Perelman concurs with this view, arguing that until the end of the era of high wages. which occurred around the end of the 1960s, the US represented a case study in which relatively high wages exerted a positive influence on a major economy.

Peter Riach in Chapter 8 looks at wage-employment determination in a more formal theoretical framework. Many conservative politicians and neo-classical economists have sought to explain high levels of unemployment in terms of the alleged emergence of a 'real wage gap' (the increase in real wages relative to labour productivity) with unemployment being generated simply because entrepreneurs substitute away from labour for *cost* reasons. In contrast, Keynesian theory has long emphasized the *income* effect of an increased wage share: a redistribution of income from profits to wages boosting aggregate demand and employment.

In the *General Theory of Employment Interest and Money* the quantity of employment is determined by the propensity to consume and invest in the commodity market, but Keynes retained the marginal product relationship to establish the real wage which corresponds to any employment level so determined. In contrast to neo-classical theory wage increases are a *consequence*, rather than a *cause*, of decreases in employment in the *General Theory*. Keynes broke out of the neo-classical price-theoretic mould dominated by substitution effects and determined quantity from *without* price-quantity space; however the retention of the marginal product relationship involved the determination of price *within* that space.

Post-Keynesians, Riach suggests, differ from Keynes in determining both employment and the real wage from without price-quantity space, and any relationship between them becomes the result of income, rather than substitution, effects. In post-Keynesian theory, both consumption and investment are dependent on the distribution between wages and profit: an increase in the wage share raises aggregate consumption but deters investment. Consequently the net result, for employment, of an increase in the wage share and real wages can be either positive or negative, but is reliant on income rather than substitution effects. The post-Keynesian rejection of diminishing returns removes the link between price and quantity: instead of price and quantity being the simultaneous outcome of the Marshallian scissors, real wages and employment are determined by separate forces – the degree of monopoly and aggregate commodity demand.

The main practical alternative to the neo-conservative socioeconomic project has been corporatism. Corporatism means different things to different people. In particular, there have been different usages in the economics and political science literature. Moreover, corporatist ideas have a long lineage, especially in Catholic social thought, and one, unfortunately, that clearly includes fascism in the interwar years. This book, however, refers to corporatism after the Second World War (M2), in which individual interests are collectively represented through organized groups and in which there is tripartite consultation in economic policy implementation. Coordination of economic activity takes place neither through pure market forces nor central dictat. Institutional features figure large in producing compromise, facilitating consensus, and mobilizing mutual understanding about problems, ends and means. Societies with such features thus clearly possess some of the key characteristics of what has been referred to as a 'negotiated economy'.

A central defining feature of a corporatist economy has been taken to be a strong centralized wage-bargaining system. The evidence on the relative economic performance of corporatist economies is reviewed in Chapters 9 and 10 and is impressive.

As regards unemployment, Chapter 9 by Andrew Henley and Euclid Tsakalotos reviews the unemployment performance of the industrialized economies since the end of the postwar 'Golden Age' and finds diversity in that performance. It argues that this diversity has much to do with the different institutional arrangements for collective bargaining and, more widely, with the establishment of economic consensus about macroeconomic strategy.

Within the economics literature the importance of corporatism has been viewed in terms of short-term macroeconomic analysis. The focus has been on the effects of corporatist structures on the labour market and in particular on their influence on the responsiveness of wages to employment. The particular structural feature of the labour market that most analysts have stressed is the degree of centralization in wage bargaining. Corporatist arrangements may serve to draw the attention of wage bargainers to the macroeconomic implications of bargaining outcomes. They can also help reduce uncertainty about the wider implications of the wage-setting process.

While economists have predominantly focused on corporatism as an institution which reduces uncertainty and enhances coordination in the labour market, political scientists and political economists tend to view the effects of corporatism in terms of conflict reduction. This difference of emphasis leads to an assessment of corporatism that is both longer-term and broader in scope, picking up on the possible relationship between corporatism and investment and growth.

In neo-liberal economic regimes unemployment effectively acts as a labour-disciplining device or control mechanism. Conflict is suppressed through the fear of unemployment. As Henley and Tsakalotos point out, however, if corporatist institutions can regulate conflict and allow the achievement of cooperative, non-inflationary solutions to the wage/investment determination process, then corporatist bargaining can be seen as an alternative mechanism to unemployment for suppressing inflationary distributional conflict.

In addressing the question of what within the corporatist institutional arrangements actually explains superior economic performance, therefore, Henley and Tsakalotos argue that corporatism appears to work both as a means to reduce the uncertainty that agents face about the macroeconomic consequences of their actions, and as a successful conflict-resolution mechanism.

Corporatist strategies have not, of course, been uniformly successful and even the best have faltered (along with every other approach and style of economy – including Japan) in recent years. Chapter 10 by Mike Marshall looks, *inter alia*, at the main features of, and the key changes in, one of the most successful of the modern corporatist strategies, the Swedish model.

Despite its undoubted successes, however, it is clear that the 'Swedish model' came under increasing strain in the 1970s and 1980s and certain fundamental modifications had to be made to the model. In particular, there has been a breakdown of the key feature of centralized bargaining, with employers showing a growing unwillingness to depart from local pay settlements. Moreover, the trade unions have displayed a reluctance to restrain wage claims despite a deteriorating economic situation. Further, the solidaristic wage strategy has been significantly compromised as workers' pay rises have increasingly reflected the profitability of their firms via local productivity deals and profit sharing. There is no doubt that the move to local bargaining has been accompanied by widening wage differentials. Moreover, the socialization of investment project has been abandoned.

Thus it does seem as though some of the most central features of the 'Swedish model' have been fundamentally restructured – dismantled, some would say – in the face of a complex confluence of socioeconomic and political changes in the 1980s and early 1990s. This, however, is not to suggest that lessons cannot be learned from the Swedish experience or that all corporatist arrangements are doomed to failure. As has been seen, the evidence of the period after the Second World War suggests that corporatist institutions can improve macroeconomic performance and produce progressive distributional changes. For a long period corporatist arrangements proved successful in improving the wage–unemployment trade-off and they seem to have done this largely by reducing 'insider' influences on wage levels. As Marshall emphasizes, another obvious lesson that can be drawn from examining the Swedish experience relates to the advantages of an active labour market policy and the social benefits to be obtained from operating a 'right to work' system. Certainly the advantage of spending money on training and maintaining people in work over paying huge sums in unemployment benefits seems fairly clear. Moreover, the wage-earner funds, while a political failure, are defended as a potentially very valuable extension of classic corporatist arrangements.

Halevi and Kriesler in Chapter 11 argue that the attempt to consciously 'import' the main features of the Swedish model was unsuited to Australian conditions and therefore proved unsuccessful. Their work also, however, points to a flaw in the Australian government's perception of the fundamental strengths of corporatist arrangements since at the heart of the failure of the Australian corporatist experiment seems to have been a short-termism by government and a failure to encourage investment and stimulate an active involvement by capital.

Kriesler and Halevi argue that, instead of focusing on long-run relationships and performance, the government remained instead preoccupied with short-term macro performance and electoral success. With no investment policy there was no change in the structure or underlying performance of the economy.

The failure of the corporatist policies to produce the necessary restructuring of the Australian economy, Halevi and Kriesler argue, meant that such policies also failed in terms of their major goal: to keep unemployment low. Unemployment rose rapidly in the latter part of the 1980s, reaching its highest level since the Second World War. This deterioration is blamed on contractionary government policy specifically aimed at alleviating growing current account problems. The key difficulty facing the Australian economy in the 1980s, and continuing in the 1990s, the authors argue, is the inadequacy of the industrial base. The declining world importance of raw materials, the traditional base of Australian prosperity, has forced the growth of other sectors. These emerging sectors have been heavily service-oriented and thus, Halevi and Kriesler argue, have undermined the basis of corporatism which required a dominant trade union movement.

They conclude that the post-1983 corporatist policies of the Labour government had little impact on the underlying structure of the Australian economy which remained susceptible to the same international forces that have always played a dominant part in the economic development of Australia.

Eileen Appelbaum and Ronald Schettkat in Chapter 12 present an endogenous explanation for the secular increase in unemployment in the industrialized economies over the last two decades. While recognizing the importance of exogenous shocks and misguided deflationary policies in exacerbating the difficulties facing the industrialized economies, the analytical model presented situates the shift from full employment to unemployment in the development process itself. The model developed is a simple, two-sector framework which the authors nevertheless believe is sufficient to capture the main facts of economic development in the industrialized economies.

Appelbaum and Schettkat's main argument is that, in the process of economic development, the price elasticity of demand for many consumer durables has declined over time in the industrialized economies as the accumulation by households of these durable goods grew over time. They argue that national institutions had little impact in the 25 years following the end of the Second World War, when productivity growth, employment and wages all followed favourable trends and labour markets operated near their full-employment equilibria. However, labour market institutions and national economic policies did become more important in influencing aggregate employment developments when industries in the technologically progressive sector began to reduce employment.

The chapter analyses the diverging employment developments among the industrialized economies in the last several decades, and concludes with a discussion of the principal policies which their analysis suggests can be effective in restoring full employment: policies for raising living standards and developing markets in less industrialized economies; policies that promote product and process innovations and that facilitate the development of new technologies to address articulated but unmet human needs (like medical and environmental technologies); and policies to expand public investment and collective consumption.

What Appelbaum and Schettkat's model does not support, however, is the idea that downward flexibility of wages is a promising method of stimulating employment. Price-inelastic demand produces only moderate quantity reactions following from price reductions occasioned by cuts in wages. They argue that technological progress in industries on the price-inelastic part of the demand curve leads to reductions in employment even as prices fall and output increases.

Keith Bain in the final chapter considers the impact on unemployment in peripheral regions/countries of monetary integration in Europe and examines the implications for these areas of having to meet the Maastricht convergence conditions. He argues that slow growth will be necessary to overcome current account deficits and thus avoid expectations of exchange-rate depreciation. In the absence of institutional change produced by increased anti-inflation credibility of peripheral governments, strongly deflationary policies will also be needed to meet the inflation and interest rate conditions. This will, in any case, follow from the attempt to meet the very stringent fiscal policy conditions. The net effect will be high unemployment in peripheral countries and very uneven rates of unemployment across the EU countries.

This latter issue is then addressed on the assumption of a 'one-speed Europe' (one in which all EU members are also members of EMU). A strongly sceptical view is taken of the conventional argument that regional imbalances will be overcome by the flow of private capital towards capital-scarce regions. Rather, Bain supports 'core/periphery' views of the economy which suggest that capital flows are more likely to be *towards* the core countries, increasing regional imbalance. The difficulties for peripheral countries associated with the idea of a 'two-speed Europe' are considered, with the suggestion that it will be difficult for countries which do not join EMU at the outset to do so at a later date.

The chapter continues by looking at the specifically financial problems associated both with the European single market and European monetary integration, raising the possibility that the financial fragility of the peripheral countries will be much increased, adding yet further to their problems.

Finally the likely policies of the European central bank and the particular problems associated with the free market framework for the central bank which was proposed at Maastricht are examined. A sceptical view of the possibility of a one-speed European union based upon an independent central bank with the dominating objective of maintaining low inflation is taken. Peripheral countries, Bain argues, will either not be allowed to join or will, in the push to join, cause such damage to their real economies and financial structures that the gap between core and periphery will have been enlarged and will continue to grow.

Since the collapse of the 'Golden Age' of economic performance of the advanced capitalist countries there has been a growing awareness, even amongst Keynesians themselves, that expansionary macroeconomic policies on their own are not likely easily or unproblematically to generate and maintain a high level of employment. As is pointed out in this volume, deflationary policies can exacerbate the problems of employment and income growth, but expansionary policies may be no longer sufficient to jump start the economy and achieve acceptable income and employment outcomes. This is particularly likely to be the case in economies like the UK's which faces a severe and continuing balance of payments constraint. New approaches seem to be necessary. The main new approach that emerged in the 1980s was that inspired by supply-side economics.

The supply-side perspective that became dominant in the US was a classic example of a simplistic, reductionist, stimulus-response model that conceptualized only one type of 'flexibility' – unfettered response to market signals. It was an inadequate theory and therefore produced a simplistic policy prescription that was doomed to failure. Reaganomics did create conditions under which growth of the US economy was re-established. However, it did so, albeit inadvertently, via a Keynesian demand stimulus to the economy. Reaganomics, ironically, created conditions under which an essentially Keynesian macroeconomic structure could function. Apart from the fiscal boost to aggregate demand, the main feature of Reaganomics that had significant effects was the resurrection of the fear of unemployment to discipline labour, raise productivity and hold wages in check. The increasing threat and cost of unemployment helped lead to changes in working conditions and practices, both in the US and the UK, that seem to have paid off in terms of increasing productivity. However, this is neither a desirable nor necessary means of stimulating productivity growth.

Despite the fact that neither Reaganomics nor Thatcherism constitute an economically effective or socially desirable restructuring project, it has increasingly been accepted by non-orthodox economists that there is a need for a so-called 'two-handed' approach, focusing on both demand and supply. Much discussion here has been devoted to the need for a proper socio-institutional perspective on the supply-side to counteract the dominant New Right views which seek to dismantle whatever socioeconomic institutions exceed the minimum necessary for the operation of free, deregulated markets.

The experience of corporatist arrangements highlights the positive contribution that institutions which limit competition and mediate market pressures can make to prompting cooperation, reducing uncertainty and conflict and thereby promoting investment and economic and employment growth.

Within the literature on the institutional conditions likely to promote employment growth, much attention has been given to corporatist arrangements concerning the labour market and industrial relations – particularly those that have been adopted in Sweden.

As has already been said, corporatist arrangements are neither permanent nor perfect. However, while corporatist arrangements, particularly in Sweden. have undergone major transformation and appear under threat, they have in the past been multidimensional and have evolved over time in the face of changing economic and political circumstances. The problem of unemployment, at the time of writing, remains endemic to *all* industrialized economies. The general message of this book is that a movement back towards full employment lies not in deregulation and the attempt to re-establish a free market economy. What is needed is government intervention that clearly addresses the social and economic obstacles to the achievement of full employment. There are no easy, bespoke, ready-to-wear solutions that can be imported from Sweden or elsewhere; careful institutional design with detailed attention to specific socioeconomic forces and problems is necessary. However, practical and satisfactory resolutions to the full-employment challenge are more likely to spring from the principles and experience of corporatist social democracy than from New Right conservatism.

Special thanks must go to the contributors for their willingness to respond to our suggestions and comments with forbearance and good humour. Thanks also to June Daniels and Christine Nisbett – both of the Department of Applied Economics, UEL – for their faultless secretarial assistance and, above all, for their ability to unscramble and standardize the various word-processed files we received! Finally, thanks must also be extended to Edward Elgar, Julie Leppard and Jo Perkins who, as always, have been excellent commissioning editor, editor and editorial assistant respectively. We are grateful for their strong support throughout the period this book was being written and compiled.

1. Obstacles to full employment in capitalist economies

Malcolm Sawyer

The central argument in this chapter is that full employment is not an impossible dream but its creation and maintenance require a different conception of the nature and purpose of economic analysis from the current orthodoxy. More importantly changes are needed in the institutional and political arrangements under which market economies operate. Indeed, the institutional changes and the related policy measures sketched out below would lead many to argue that if these policies were to be adopted, the economy could no longer be labelled a market one in that what could be seen as market forces would be severely modified by institutional changes and government intervention. However, this chapter is more concerned with seeking solutions for unemployment than engaging in debates over what is meant by a market economy. Nevertheless it should be noted that all market economies involve a variety of institutional arrangements (including markets themselves) and government intervention and hence it is a question of which arrangements and interventions are or should be adopted and not whether there should be any such arrangements. Further, it is argued here that an unfettered market economy would exhibit substantial unemployment, and that in a sense unemployment is inevitable in such an economy, and hence some interventions are required to underpin full employment.

There are two underlying themes, one of which will be elaborated below. The other can only be touched upon briefly here. It is that unemployment not only represents an under-utilization of available resources but has numerous other detrimental effects. For not only does unemployment cause clear hardship and waste; there is a much wider range of detrimental effects – psychological well-being, occurrence of stress-related disease and suicide. There is evidence of substantial social costs of unemployment, e.g. suicide rates (Shapiro and Ahlburg, 1983) and mental illness and crime (Brenner, 1979); for a recent overview see Burchell (1992). Further, it is because unemployment is unequally distributed that it is such a social as well as an economic problem. If unemployment were equally distributed so that everyone worked say 20 per cent fewer hours than they wished rather than 15 per cent with no job, others worked fewer hours than desired whilst the rest worked as many or more hours than they wished, unemployment would be of much less concern. The undoubted adverse social and psychological impacts of unemployment would still arise if everyone were working 20 per cent less than they wished.

It is difficult to define precisely what is meant by a market economy (see Sawyer, 1992a for further elaboration). Those economies which are generally labelled market ones involve very substantial government intervention, often significant trade union activities, agreements between firms etc., none of which would appear in a 'pure' market economy.[1] The observation that most such 'market' economies exhibit in most periods significant levels of unemployment is the starting point for many of the arguments below,[2] and there are reasons to think that unemployment will be a general feature of such economies. Further, unemployment does not arise as a result of imperfections in existing market economies (as compared with some hypothetical market situation as, for example, under perfect competition). Instead, unemployment is seen to arise as a control mechanism, albeit a socially and economically inefficient one. 'Thus it is reasserted here that unemployment is the most powerful of all economic controls. The ideal is to replace the arbitrary undemocratic "control" of unemployment by conscious controls, operated democratically in the public interest' (Oxford University Institute of Statistics, 1944, p. 15). In order to understand the forms of institutional and other changes necessary for the achievement of full employment, some elaboration of the ways in which market economies actually work is needed.

Before coming to the central concerns of the chapter, there are two particular arguments which I wish to address. The first is that full employment is no longer possible because of technological advances and the accompanying high levels of productivity. Without seeking to minimize the effects which technical change has on the disruption of employment in specific sectors and regions (arising from the 'perennial gale of creative destruction', to use Schumpeter's phrase) I would argue that technology has not made the achievement of full employment an impossible objective. To say that it has is tantamount to saying that all our material needs and desires have been satisfied for it would imply that technology permits the production (at full employment) of more goods and services than people can absorb.[3] It can readily be recognized that the fulfilment of material needs does not necessarily bring human happiness and that many current desires have been inflated by advertising. Nevertheless, it is difficult to believe that most people's material needs have been satisfied. There is simply too much poverty and homelessness in this country, and too much hunger and want in third world countries to make that a tenable position. Thus there remain needs to be satisfied, and people willing to work, and hence unemployment is not an inevitable consequence of technology.

The second argument is that full employment can no longer be unambiguously defined. There is some strength in this argument, as socioeconomic and demographic changes have meant that full employment can no longer (if it ever could) be identified as the employment on a full-time basis of men and single women in the working age range. Allowance has obviously to be made for the desire to undertake paid work for less than the standard full-time working week[4] and for decisions to delay entry into and to advance exit from the workforce. A working definition of full employment (which I recognize is not as precise as I would like) would be as follows. Full employment would be a balance between those seeking work and the vacancies which enterprises are seeking to fill (subject to the proviso that no-one remains unemployed for more than say six months). In putting forward this definition, it is recognized that 'those seeking work' is socially conditioned and changes over time (influenced by economic and social developments). The prevailing social and individual attitudes towards the participation of married women and those over 65 years of age has clearly changed dramatically in the past 50 years in most countries.

The idea that there can be a well defined concept of full employment which does not change over time may itself reflect the dominance of the neo-classical mind-set. Full employment is taken as the fullest possible use of resources subject to some individuals being temporarily without work as they move jobs. But the post-Keynesian approach would emphasize that the available resources will be influenced by the path followed by the economy as well as general sociopolitical factors. For example, low levels of demand and corresponding levels of employment will discourage people from entering the workforce and may push people back into the home. Thus the labour supply (both in terms of quantity and quality) available at a particular time will be influenced by the past and present levels of aggregate demand as well as many other factors such as training and education provision.

UNEMPLOYMENT AND ECONOMIC ANALYSIS

The conventional economic analysis of a market economy (which finds its highest expression in general equilibrium analysis) suggests that market-clearing equilibrium, involving a balance between demand and supply in each market, will ensure the full employment of labour. There are, of course, many caveats to the translation from that analysis through to the operation of markets in the real world (and also a general equilibrium can only be shown to exist under some rather severe conditions). There may be lags in the adjustment process with consequent disequilibrium trading, as in the temporary equilibrium literature arising from the reappraisal of Keynesian economics undertaken by Clower, (1965) and Leijonhufvud (1968). The way in which wages and prices are set and changed by economic agents in practice does not generally conform to that envisaged in the analysis (where prices change in response to excess demand)

and rather are set by economic agents in pursuit of their own interests (e.g. for efficiency wage considerations: Weiss, 1990). But the demand and supply analysis of the market takes centre stage, and it is difficult to deny the working out of forces leading to markets clearing: if demand exceeds supply price will sooner or later rise to bring about market-clearing equilibrium (and conversely price will fall when supply exceeds demand). Full employment is then reached sooner or later through the operation of 'market forces'.

Neo-classical economics is organized around the concept of scarcity following the definition of the scope of economics given by Robbins as 'the science which studies human behaviour as a relationship between ends and scarce means which have alternative uses' and thereby economic analysis 'focuses attention on a particular aspect of behaviour, the form imposed by the influence of scarcity' (Robbins, 1932). As Joan Robinson remarked (Robinson, 1972, p. l), 1932 was not the most appropriate time to make this definition since the main economic problem of the time was not the scarcity of resources but rather a scarcity of demand for those resources: 'it was just a coincidence that the book appeared when means for any end at all had rarely been less scarce'. Both the major theoretical advances in the 1930s involve demand as the limiting factor. The theory of imperfect competition suggests the expansion of the firm as constrained by demand, with the firm operating subject to decreasing unit costs, and of course the macroeconomics of Kalecki and Keynes suggests that firms collectively are demand-constrained. It is difficult for neo-classical economics to cope with the phenomena of unemployment and excess capacity which clearly involve the under-utilization and waste of resources when its subject matter is defined as the use of scarce resources. Thus a broader view of the subject matter of economic analysis is required, which does not find unemployment as inconsistent with its definition of its own subject matter. This would be one which 'emphasises features such as the distribution of income, the dynamic rather than static nature of capitalist economies, capital accumulation and the generation and uses of an economic surplus' (Sawyer, 1989, p. 3, seeking to define radical political economy), out of which (as suggested below) would come explanations for the existence and persistence of unemployment.

The starting point of the analysis here is the postulate that unemployment may perform a variety of functions, and the reduction of unemployment requires the development of institutions and policy instruments which would perform those functions instead. Unfettered market economies tend (by observation and for reasons discussed below) to exhibit unemployment. Further, the research agenda is changed from one in which full employment is viewed as the norm and deviations from that are to be explained to one in which unemployment is regarded as the usual situation and times of full employment require special explanation.

OBSTACLES TO FULL EMPLOYMENT

The obstacles to the achievement of full employment can be usefully divided into four types, three of which are examined here in detail. The first obstacle, in brief, is the social and political forces which would lose (at least in relative terms) from full employment. The balance of power between employer and employee is influenced by unemployment, and employers are in a much stronger relative position when unemployment is high. It would be naive to think that correct economic analyses of the causes of unemployment and of the conditions for full employment will lead to full employment, or even to the implementation of policies designed to achieve it. For such there clearly has to be a political will arising from sociopolitical forces pushing for full employment (Kalecki, 1943). The experience of the last 20 years suggests that those forces are relatively weak, as substantial unemployment has been suffered by many countries. Clearly those sociopolitical forces which favour the reduction of inflation over unemployment have been in the ascendant.

The second obstacle is derived from the simple Keynesian (and Kaleckian) point that in a decentralized monetary economy there is no automatic market mechanism which ensures that aggregate demand is sufficient to purchase full employment aggregate supply (*even* in the absence of other constraints such as balance of trade, or insufficient capital equipment). Thus inadequate aggregate demand may prevent the achievement of full employment. The problems of coordination between aggregate demand and potential aggregate supply can be viewed as an inevitable consequence of a decentralized monetary economy, even if some of the problems can be reduced by appropriate policies and institutional arrangements. There are benefits from the existence of money and of exchange, but there are also some inevitable costs, arising from failures of coordination in a decentralized economy.

This basic Keynesian idea of the importance of aggregate demand operates in a range of ways additional to those analysed by Keynes, most notably that the supply side (of labour and of capital equipment) is influenced over the long term by the demand side. For not only are additions to the stock of capital equipment (investment) influenced by the general level of demand, but also the effective supply of labour is likely to be influenced by the demand for it. High levels of demand for labour draw people into the workforce, whilst low levels of demand push people out of the measured workforce, back into the home, into early retirement and so on. Thus it is not only ratios such as the rate of unemployment and capacity utilization which are influenced by aggregate demand, but also the scale of the economy (labour force, capital stock).

The third obstacle arises from the view that there are significant economic, social and political forces which generate and reinforce disparities and inequalities, whether between individuals, regions or countries. This is an application of the notion that 'success breeds success' and the corollary 'failure breeds failure': and that '[f]or to everyone who has will more be given, and he will have abundance but from him who has not even what he has will be taken away' (St Matthew 25:29). In the economic sphere, the operation of market forces (by which I mean here the spontaneous interaction of individuals) generates cumulative causation (Myrdal, 1957) and centrapetalism (Cowling, 1987; 1990). An economically successful region generates profits which enable further investment; it can attract mobile, often highly skilled, labour from other regions; it can benefit from static and dynamic economies of scale (which feature heavily in the work of Kaldor, e.g. Kaldor, 1972). Other forces also arise: for example, local government revenue depends on local prosperity enabling more prosperous areas to enjoy better public services. Whilst the prosperous regions and groups benefit from growth, prestige and so on, the less prosperous do not, and the resources of the less prosperous are under-utilized (for further discussion see Sawyer, 1989 Ch. 13; Sawyer, 1991). Unemployment and low wages are both characteristics of relatively less prosperous regions. Full employment in the more prosperous regions would still entail unemployment in the less prosperous regions. Any further attempts to reduce unemployment through demand stimulation is likely to cause problems of insufficient capacity, shortages of skills and inflationary pressures in the more prosperous regions.

The forces of cumulative causation tend to widen disparities between regions. There are other forces which may tend to reduce disparities, for example low wages can attract inward investment, thereby tending to push up economic activity and wages. The relative strengths of the two sets of forces may well vary over time so that sometimes a relatively backward region can catch up, but at other times such a region may slip further behind. There are clear examples of the former (the outstanding cases at the national level being Japan and South Korea) but also of the latter (most African countries). However, many would ascribe the economic success of Japan and South Korea to the role of the state in fostering economic and industrial development (e.g. Amsden, 1989 Johnson, 1982; Chang, 1993). After the war market forces would have led Japan, for example, to concentrate on labour-intensive industries such as textiles in which it held a comparative advantage. But if Japan had

> chosen to specialise in this kind of industry, it would almost permanently have been unable to break away from the Asian pattern of stagnation and poverty ... The Ministry of International Trade and Industry decided to establish industries which require intensive employment of capital and technology ... From a short-run, static viewpoint, encouragement of such industries would seem to conflict with economic rationalism. But, from a long-range point of view, these are precisely the industries where income elasticity of demand is high, technological progress is rapid and labour productivity rises fast ('the words of a high level MITI official; quoted by Scott, 1984, from OECC, 1972).

Disparities between regions and between nations do not show any strong tendency to close.[5] One part of the significance of the forces of cumulative causation is that the relatively backward regions will experience not only lower levels of *per capita* income but also face higher levels of unemployment and severe constraints on their ability to grow. The consequence of this general view is that, while there are forces for convergence between regions and countries, there are also strong forces for divergence. Regions which are relatively backward will display both lower levels of per capita income and higher levels of unemployment, and find considerable difficulty in catching up with more prosperous regions. Further, individuals can become trapped in a cycle of relatively low wages, poor employment prospects and so on.

Another aspect of this general view concerns international trade. In a world of primary products it is reasonable to argue that international trade will (or should) be governed by comparative advantage, arising from the endowments of nature. But in a world of manufactured goods and of services, where new products are being continuously developed, where economies of scale, dynamic as well as static, operate and in which investment in equipment, research and people is recognized as important for economic success, *competitive* advantage (Porter, 1990) comes to the fore. The notion of competitive advantage contains a strong element of cumulative causation, for clearly success in one time period generates the surplus which can be used to build success in subsequent periods. The availability of that surplus does not guarantee that it will be used to build future success. It can be used in other ways ranging from high levels of luxury and conspicuous consumption through to military expenditure (and the UK and US have tended recently to indulge in both), which may eventually lead to economic and political decline (Kennedy, 1988). But the availability of a surplus is a prerequisite for growth and competitive success. Competitive advantage can to some degree be created (as is clear from the Japanese economic success over the past 50 years) whereas comparative advantage is given by nature. This line of argument also interacts with our next group of obstacles in that a lack of competitive advantage shows up as a balance of trade constraint on growth.

The fourth obstacle to the achievement of full employment is a collection of constraints which arise in a decentralized economy. Those focused on here are the inflation barrier, the international trade constraint and the work effort constraint. It could first be noted that these constraints would not exist in a neoclassical world and hence in a sense they can only be identified by adopting a different perspective on how market economies operate.[6]

The inflation barrier simply suggests that at or near full employment there is likely to be substantial inflationary pressure. This is not to subscribe to any simple-minded trade-off between inflation and unemployment, for as I have argued elsewhere (Henry, Sawyer and Smith, 1976; Sawyer, 1987), that view should be rejected on both theoretical and empirical grounds (though those who do subscribe to such a view do arrive at estimates of around 9 or 10 per cent for the rate of unemployment at which inflation would be constant). In many respects it is difficult to say what would happen to inflation at full employment in light of the fact that it is over 20 years since there was full employment and many institutional changes have occurred in the interim. But I suggest that there are reasons to think that full employment would involve considerable inflationary pressures. The 'elasticity' of the stock of money arising from the ease with which money is created through credit and the impossibility of control over it by the state would mean that any inflationary pressures would be little constrained by the stock of money which can evolve in response to price and wage changes. Thus, even if limiting the growth of the stock of money constrained inflation (rather than reduce output), such a monetary policy is no longer available to the British government in a deregulated internationalized monetary system (see also Michl, Chapter 3 in this volume).

The balance of trade constraint has a level and a growth dimension. A difference between imports and exports has to be covered by borrowing from overseas, and hence creates obligations for future interest payments.[7] persistent excess of imports over exports (i.e. trade deficit) would involve a growing current account deficit as the interest payments on borrowing build up. However, provided that the growth of the domestic economy exceeds the rate of interest on foreign borrowing, the ratio of liabilities to domestic income (and hence the interest payments to income) would eventually stabilize. The algebra for this is essentially the same as that for a budget deficit which is given in note 15. However, the condition of the domestic growth rate exceeding the rate of interest may not be met, leading to a debt trap.

The growth aspect of the balance of trade constraint arises if there is a tendency for the growth of imports to exceed the growth of exports. Thirlwall (1978; 1979) and Thirlwall and Gibson (1992, Ch. 12) among others have seen this as a problem confronting the British economy in particular. Simply, when the (domestic) income elasticity of demand for imports is greater than the (world) income elasticity of demand for the country's exports, the maintenance of a non-exploding trade deficit requires the domestic growth rate to be sufficiently below the world growth rate so that actual imports and exports grow in line with one another.

Clearly the balance of trade constraint is not one which affects all countries, simply because while some countries run trade deficits, others must run trade surpluses. Further, the constraint can be eased by devaluation of the currency, though such a route is often resisted because of its perceived effect on inflation and the reduction of domestic living standards (not to mention national pride).[8]

The attainment of high levels of productivity requires an appropriate work intensity and commitment of the labour force as well as the provision of relevant capital equipment, training, skills and management. Unemployment (and more particularly the threat of it) serves under present conditions as a significant mechanism to ensure a high work intensity. The level of unemployment is, of course, not something which is chosen by the firms but it provides the background against which the firms operate. In this way, unemployment is seen as playing a systemic function (of aiding the disciplining of workers). This is not to argue that unemployment is *necessary* to ensure work effort; indeed unemployment heightens fear and brings demoralization which serves to undermine work effort. Instead, I would argue that a sustained high level of employment requires the development of other mechanisms to underpin high levels of productivity. These mechanisms are likely to include forms of worker involvement and participation in effective decision making, job enrichment and so on.

A (perhaps *the*) distinguishing characteristic of a market economy (in contrast to a planned one) is that it involves the unconscious coordination of the actions of numerous individuals. In contrast, of course, a planned economy uses conscious coordination. It has often been pointed out that in what are generally labelled market economies there are many forms of coordination, some unconscious and some conscious. Implicit and explicit rules govern behaviour so that individuals' actions are more or less coordinated, perhaps the simplest example being the use of roads. There is (often incomplete) conscious coordination within organizations, most notably within, though not limited to, firms. In contrast to the neo–classical paradigm much of the coordination between firms is conscious and is not mediated through parametric prices. Firms may collude, undertake joint ventures, have long-term (if implicit) trading agreements and so on. An understanding of actual market economies has to incorporate these other means of coordination, and indeed the (perhaps implicit) argument below is that certain forms of institutions are needed as a more efficient mode of coordination.

The coordination which has attracted the attention of economists has been that concerned with the allocation of resources, and the efficiency or otherwise of a market economy has been judged in these terms. The allocative efficiency of a market economy is not our prime concern here but I do not fully share the view of Keynes that 'it is in determining the volume, not the direction, of actual employment that the existing system has broken down' (Keynes, 1936, p. 379). Instead our focus is on three important aspects of economic performance. First, there is the question of the full utilization of resources, of which the generation of sufficient aggregate demand is an important though not the only, factor. A further requirement would be a lack of inflationary pressures at full employment.[9] Second is the creation of new resources including those created through investment in human and non-human capital, and in new knowledge and skills. This, again, has numerous aspects of which we highlight two. The first of these is the tendency for market economies to under-invest in training and education because of the difficulties which employers have in capturing the benefits of training even if they pay for its provision. The second is the short-termism of financial markets which imposes a short-term perspective on industry.[10] The third aspect of economic performance is the creation of the institutional and organizational conditions which ensure that productive efficiency is at an acceptable level.

CONDITIONS FOR FULL EMPLOYMENT

The creation of full employment in Britain (and more widely within the European Community) will require many conditions to be met, some of which are set out in this section. The discussion will largely relate to technical economic considerations but two other points should be borne in mind. First, full employment involves some large-scale distributional shifts as compared with significant unemployment. The balance of power at the workplace is tilted away from the employer; and work is more evenly spread among the population generally to the benefit of the lower-skilled workers (since unemployment is generally concentrated among the less skilled). The wages of the lower-paid are likely to improve (relative to those of the better-paid). There are other shifts implicit in what is written below. But I want to make the point that those who lose *relatively* (if not absolutely) from these distributional changes are politically powerful and are likely to oppose the changes (or at least some of their manifestations). As Kalecki (1943; 1971, pp. 140–41) wrote, the maintenance of full employment 'would cause social and political changes which would give a new impetus to the opposition of business leaders. Indeed, under a regime of permanent full employment, the "sack" would cease to play its role as a disciplinary measure. The social position of the boss would be undermined and the self assurance and class consciousness of the working class would grow'.

Second, the concept of hysteresis has attracted considerable attention especially in the literature on the relationship between inflation and unemployment.[12.]The general idea of hysteresis is that the path taken by an economy influences its destination (in contrast to the assumption within comparative static analysis that it does not), and specifically that prolonged periods of unemployment affect people's attachment to the workforce, their usable skills and employability. The idea of hysteresis can be applied rather more generally. Unemployment will not only affect those directly experiencing it, but persistent unemployment will influence the general culture. The work ethic is unlikely to have much appeal to those who cannot find work, and who can see that their neighbours also cannot find work. When employment is not available, people have to find other activities to fill their time, with the development of alternative non-working cultures. These other activities can range from idleness and apathy through drug dependency and crime. A return to full employment will, in effect, have to reverse those hysteresis effects of prolonged unemployment: for example, the work ethic may have been lost in many communities and would have to be gradually restored.

The starting-point for the discussion is the view that both demand-side and supply-side considerations are relevant to the achievement of full employment. Making a distinction between demand-side and supply-side factors does not imply that they are in any sense independent of each other but rather the distinction is used as a convenient form of categoriziation. The stimulation of aggregate demand is necessary but not sufficient for reaching full employment. It is necessary since we reject Say's Law that supply will create its own demand. But it is not sufficient in that an inadequate supply side may mean that high levels of demand provoke a massive trade imbalance, generate inflation, or reveal a mismatch between the demand and supply of different types of labour. Similarly, supply-side policies to ensure a well-functioning industrial base are necessary but not sufficient (see Arestis, 1992, Ch. 10).

The demand-side considerations can be usefully analysed in two related stages. First, it is argued that government does have the ability to manipulate aggregate demand and thus aid the achievement of full employment.[13] There are, of course, limits on this ability, many of which arise from constraints on the supply side of the economy, which are discussed further below. There are, though, sociopolitical forces which militate against the use of budget deficits to sustain full employment, as can be seen from the experience of the past 20 years or so. As Kalecki wrote in 1943, '[t]he social function of the doctrine of "sound finance" is to make the level of employment dependent on the "state of confidence"' (p.325). There can however, be limits on the size of the budget deficit, though not as severe as usually imagined. Consider a primary budget deficit which is defined as the difference between government expenditure and taxation, excluding any effect of interest payments,[14] which bears a constant ratio with GDP. The overall budget deficit including interest payments will grow over time, but provided that the rate of economic growth exceeds the post-tax real rate of interest, the public debt to national income ratio will eventually stabilize. In other words, a permanent budget deficit under these conditions would not lead to an exploding debt to income ratio.[15] However, this ratio may be regarded as high alongside a substantial volume of interest payments and this may suggest limits on the size of a politically sustainable budget deficit (and we may also wish to take note of the distributional aspects of the interest payments by government which tend to accrue to the relatively wealthy: Michl, 1991).[16]

It will have been noted that the condition for the stability of the debt to income ratio is that the rate of growth exceeds the post-tax real rate of interest. At the time of writing in late 1993 this condition is not met, and this observation adds some strength to the arguments for the reduction of the level of interest rates.

In national accounting terms, the counterpart of a budget deficit is some combination of net private savings (excess of private savings over investment expenditure) and foreign trade deficit.[17] Since this is an identity it always holds, but the key question concerns the mechanisms by which the equality is ensured. The Keynesian view would, of course, be that in a decentralized economy the adjustment occurs predominantly through changes in the level of income, rather than through, say, changes in the rate of interest. It is necessary to broaden the analysis and acknowledge that there can, for example, be sharp changes in savings behaviour. In the second half of the 1980s, personal savings in the UK dropped sharply under the impact of a credit boom (since going into debt counts as negative savings), and the counterpart of that fall in savings was a move of government budget into surplus and the opening up of a large trade deficit. Conversely, in the early 1990s, savings rose (in part in response to the overhang of debt from the 1980s) and investment fell, to which the counterpart has been budget deficit and (relatively small) improvements on the trade balance.

When a budget deficit arises through an imbalance between private savings and investment, the alternative policy approach is clear (though difficult to implement). The alternative is the reduction of the savings propensity and/or the stimulation of investment. In a similar vein, the reduction of imports and/or the increase in exports would have the same type of effect. Whereas attempts to reduce a budget deficit by raising taxation or reducing public expenditure are deflationary, the alternative route of stimulating investment and exports and/or of reducing savings and imports is usually reflationary.

Further domestic and international financial arrangements should not have deflationary biases. It is clear, for example, that the operations of the European Exchange Rate Mechanism (ERM) and the proposals under the Maastricht agreement[18] had significant deflationary biases. The former placed pressure on countries to defend their exchange rate through high interest rates and to focus policy attention on inflation rather than employment levels. Indeed unemployment rose substantially as countries strove to stay within the ERM and to bring their inflation rate into line with the German rate. The latter sought to place limits on government budget deficits which would have meant, for example, a cut in public expenditure equivalent to 5 per cent of GDP in the UK in 1993.[19] It has often been observed that since fixed exchange rate mechanisms require some means by which deficit countries can reduce their deficit, this is likely to lead to deflationary pressures on those countries to bring about such a reduction but without any compensating reflationary pressures in the surplus countries.[20] A flexible exchange rate system does not entirely overcome these problems, and it also imposes a volatility of exchange rates. Deflationary pressures can still apply: for example, countries are pressured by falling exchange rates to take deflationary measures to reassure the exchange markets.

I therefore suggest that there are two requirements for an acceptable international monetary system. The first is that it should ensure a degree of stability in exchange rates which encourages trade. This would rule out a flexible exchange rate system with the considerable volatility of exchange rates observed during the late 1970s and the 1980s. On the other hand, a rigid fixed exchange rate system generates pressures which ultimately blow it apart (as illustrated by the experience of the ERM in the early 1990s).[21] This suggests an adjustable peg system with arrangements for deficit countries to overcome their deficit position without deflationary biases.[22] The main aim for any international monetary system in the context of the pursuit of full employment is to avoid deflationary biases, and countries must be able to adjust to trade deficits without reducing demand. A further aim is that the system should serve the demands of trade rather than encourage financial flows which themselves tend to increase the volatility of exchange rates.

The role of domestic financial institutions should be viewed as serving the needs of production, for it is from production that income and wealth are generated. Specifically, institutional arrangements and regulations are needed which channel savings into productive investment and which ensure that the fragile financial system does not become unstable, with adverse effects on the productive economy. This may require, for example, the imposition of lending ratios to prevent the over-expansion of credit, as happened in the UK in the late 1980s, especially where the rapid growth of credit spills over mainly into asset price inflation (rather than any stimulation of production).

The problem which lies at the heart of financial arrangements, whether domestic or international, is that the creation of money can help finance an expansion of real output or an increase in prices. Similarly, the provision of finance for countries experiencing trade deficits can be used to make changes in the economy which will lead to improved international competitiveness or it can be used for (unsustainable levels of) consumption.

On the supply side, we first consider the problem of inflation.[23] It is, of course, the case that an economic agent is as well-off with a 2 per cent increase in the price received for services when prices in general are stationary as with a 22 per cent increase when prices in general are rising at 20 per cent per annum. There is then a coordination problem: if there is a coordination of expectations at low levels of inflation then inflation is likely to be low. Further, inflationary pressures can arise from distributional conflicts.[24] For example, an attempt by firms in general to raise profit margins will show up as a rise in prices and adversely affect real wages. Workers may well respond by seeking to raise money wages to defend living standards. In so far as both were successful, a price–wage spiral would be initiated. There are a number of ways to restrain inflationary pressures, some of which are more socially acceptable than others. One is to generate low levels of demand which limit the ability of firms to raise prices and workers to increase wages, but that would, of course, conflict with the aim of full employment. Another is to generate a consensus over the distribution of income.

The worsening of inequality which has been particularly apparent in the UK and US since the late 1970s has made the prospects for the creation of a consensus on the distribution of income (which would include the division between wages and profits and relative earnings) more difficult. A consensus is obviously not something that can be switched on and off. Thus policy proposals in this direction have to focus more on institutional arrangements which minimize the inflationary consequences of pay and price determination. Other chapters in this volume (Chs. 9 and 10) discuss aspects of this in some detail.

There is no particular reason to think that decentralized wage determination with an emphasis on performance-related pay would be non-inflationary at or near full employment. If atomistic bargaining involves frequent price and wage adjustments, then it is likely to speed up the inflationary process, whereas a degree of institutional rigidity places some brake on upward price and wage adjustments. Further, the more negotiating units there are, the less attention each one pays to the overall impact of their own settlement, and the less effect will any call for wage restraint have.

The literature on the impact of institutional arrangements (including wage bargaining structures) on economic performance has focused on the effects on unemployment (e.g. Calmfors and Driffill, 1988; Calmfors, 1993; Henley and Tsakalotos, 1993). The picture there is a complex one as reflected in the conclusion reached by Calmfors when he wrote that

> [t]he diversity of effects discussed in the paper makes it hard to arrive at unambiguous policy conclusions ... It may, however, not be very meaningful to formulate the question as whether bargaining ought to be centralised or decentralised. Rather it may be more fruitful to discuss how features of centralisation and decentralisation can be combined in a well-functioning wage-setting system ... It is unrealistic to expect *one* universally optimal set-up of bargaining institutions to exist for all countries (Calmfors, 1993 p. 39)

The concern here is a little different, namely whether the wage- and price-setting arrangements are consistent with the absence of inflationary pressures at full employment.[25] We suggest that some degree of centralization and of coordination of pay setting will be needed.

A second aspect of the supply side arises from the requirement for something approaching a balance on the overseas current account at an acceptable level of unemployment which for a country such as the UK means an ability to compete in (relatively) high technology sectors. The current account requirement means that roughly speaking the growth of imports and of exports must be aligned. The growth of the domestic economy is then set by the growth of the world economy, and the relative (marginal) propensities to import by the UK and the rest of the world. A relatively high propensity to import by the UK and/or a low propensity to import (from the UK) by the rest of world generates a low growth rate in the UK (relative to the rest of the world). Further, if that growth rate is below the growth of productivity in the UK then rising unemployment will be the consequence. While there appears to have been some improvement in the relative attractiveness of British-produced goods during the 1980s there remains considerable doubt as to whether that has been sufficient to permit enough growth to support full employment.

The growth of exports obviously requires a growth in the demand for them and in the capability of producing them. The growth of export demand will in turn be influenced by the attractiveness of the goods and services produced and, in particular, by general growth of demand for the products concerned. It is plausible to think that relatively fast-growing demand will be concentrated in some service products and in new manufactured products. The former do not feature greatly in international trade while the latter tend to be associated with the new technologies and especially, of course, with the development of new and improved products. The development of new products and processes requires not only investment in research and development but also the formation of linkages between companies to develop the whole production system. In other words, an industrial strategy is needed.

The essence of an industrial strategy is a commitment by government to the support of industrial development. It springs from the view that government can play a key strategic role in fostering such development. What is needed is not detailed central planning but rather the working out of an overall coherent strategy, so that decisions on, for example, support of research and development can be made on an informed basis. It is well known that economic activities such as provision of training and skills, or the undertaking of research and development are likely to be underprovided by an unfettered market. While the case for an industrial strategy would draw on such arguments, it involves more than correcting 'market failures'. It provides a framework for decision making by government and by private enterprise, and commits the government to a developmental role in economic policy.[26] An industrial strategy can take many forms and be organized and implemented in ways which are thoroughly undemocratic. The type of strategy which is advocated here is rather along the lines proposed by Cowling and Sugden (1993b) where they see

the concentration of decision-making within these organizations [large and dominating corporations] that shapes the character of the market. To remedy defects in the free-market economy we must seek to change the nature of strategic decision-making within the modern corporation and, in the longer-term, seek to displace its dominance within the market system. It is this process whereby a concentrated structure of decision making within the industrial economy is progressively replaced by a democratic structure that constitutes the essence of industrial strategy-making.

The final aspect of supply-side policies to be considered is that of the organization of work. The point has been made above that unemployment serves as a control mechanism on workers to enforce work intensity, and that full employment would require the development of alternative 'control mechanisms'. There is substantial evidence that worker participation in decision making enhances productivity.[27] Further, many enterprises have used various forms of worker involvement in the search for higher levels of productivity. But this is not universally the case, for other enterprises have no such involvement and make undisguised use of the threat of job loss. Whatever mechanism an enterprise uses (and a combination may be used and/or different ones may be used for different types of workers), it does so against a background of unemployment. It remains an open question whether there has to be some external pressures on workers to ensure work intensity. This external pressure may be exercised through the threat which competition from other firms poses for the survival of the workers' own firm. Competition will always involve winners and losers, and those who lose most will be the workers in the firm which does not survive. Temporary unemployment for the individual will remain a feature of any dynamic economy in which there is competition between independent firms.

The challenge raised here is to find ways of organizing work such that the economic system does not require unemployment as a 'back-up' threat. The participation of workers in decision-making and a drive to eliminate 'dirty' and uninteresting jobs through technological change may help in this regard. At relatively high levels of productivity, degrees of technical inefficiency may be a price worth paying for full employment. But the view expressed here is that the development of a range of ways which encourage technical efficiency is necessary if unemployment is to be removed.

CONCLUSIONS

Unemployment involves the waste of resources and inflicts suffering on many. At the same time as people are unemployed, there are also many unfulfilled human needs. Seeking the solutions for unemployment by use of the neo-classical paradigm is unlikely ever to succeed simply because that paradigm is locked into a market-clearing approach which finds it difficult to explain why unemployment should arise and persist. I have advanced some tentative reasons why unemployment exists in market economies; it has been argued that attention must be paid to the demand and supply sides if full employment is to be secured on a long-term basis. On the demand side, there is the need for a commitment to use macroeconomic policies (broadly conceived) in pursuit of full employment. On the supply side, there is a need for a wide range of institutional and policy changes.

NOTES

1. A 'pure' market economy could be seen as one which involves only an arms-length parametric price relationship between economic agents as exemplified in the Walrasian general equilibrium analysis (Sawyer, 1992a). As many have observed, firms would not exist in such an economy, and the many forms of relationship between firms which we observe would be seen as (at best) market imperfections.
2. For example, it has been remarked that an 'exceptional and equally beneficial phenomenon was the achievement in the 1960s of full employment, at least in the north-western part of the area [Europe]. This was an unprecedented success for industrial societies. Bouts of full employment for the urban labour force had occurred at cyclical peaks in the past, but a prolonged period of peace-time full employment, including the virtual disappearance of underemployment on the land, was something which the more cyclically sensitive and agriculturally dependent prewar economies had not experienced' (Boltho, 1982, pp. 1–2).
3. Even if too much would be produced with the available workforce fully employed, that still leaves open the possibilities of sharing out the unemployment through, for example, a reduction in working hours or a shortening of the working lifetime.
4. This should not obscure the fact that many may work part-time through force of circumstance (e.g. unavailability of full-time work, lack of child-care facilities) rather than by choice.
5. For a brief discussion on inequality between regions see Sawyer (1989) p. 425. There has been a considerable debate over whether there has been convergence between countries in terms of level of economic development. Baumol (1986) observed convergence of income levels among the richest group of countries but divergence within the poorest group which also fell behind the rest. Amable (1993) finds 'a general pattern of divergence rather than convergence in productivity levels [among 59 countries over the period 1960–85]'. During the 1980s, low-income countries grew (in terms of GNP per capita) at an annual average rate of 1.0 per cent (excluding India and China which averaged 5.6 per cent), lower-middle-income countries declined by an average of 0.1 per cent per annum, upper-middle-income countries grew at 0.6 per cent and high-income countries at 2.3 per cent. The world average was 1.2 per cent (Source: World Bank, 1993).
6. In a neo-classical world, inflation is governed by the rate of increase of the money supply, which is itself determined by government or central bank, and the real side of the economy can be analysed independently of the financial side of the economy. Any international trade difficulties can be solved by an appropriate exchange rate, and indeed with market-determined exchange rates, the rate would move to clear the market. There would not be any binding trade constraint though a country may have to experience a low or declining exchange rate. Production is assumed to be undertaken in a technically efficient manner. Neo-classical economists would no doubt point to lags of adjustment to recent developments (e.g. the idea of principal agent) which would modify these views somewhat.
7. If the borrowing takes the form of financing inward direct investment, future obligations to pay dividends to foreigners are created. The borrowing may take the form of a run-down of assets rather than a build-up of liabilities but the same basic argument applies.
8. The effects of devaluation are more complex than suggested in the text. For example, devaluation can stimulate exports and hence production, often leading to lower unit Costs; importers need not respond to devaluation by raising price (in terms of the domestic currency) as they strive to maintain market shares. See Arestis and Milberg (1993), Cowling and Sugden (1989).

9. I would argue that the achievement of full employment should be a much more important objective of policy than inflation (and than it has been over the past two decades). But it would seem that many people are concerned over inflation, and those concerns may limit economic policy. How far this is concern with inflation *per se*, and how much concern over changes which may accompany inflation, is debatable. Further, it is often argued that inflation will evolve into hyperinflation, which leads to a breakdown of the monetary system. That may suggest that there should be concern if inflation moves into the range of over say 50 per cent per annum but hardly suggests concern over inflation of the order of 5 to 10 per cent per annum.

10. Financial markets are often seen as a good example of competitive markets in which prices change frequently and in which there is exchange of pre-existing assets. In contrast production involves the creation of assets and different time-scales than exchange.

11. There are many reasons to think that enterprises will never operate in a technically efficient manner, in part for the reason analysed by Leibenstein (1966) and the inevitable conflict of interests between employer and employee, between owner and manager and so on.

12. For a general discussion of hysteresis see Isaac (1994); for work specifically related to unemployment and inflation see Cross (1988).

13. The response of many orthodox economists would be to argue that there is a crowding-out problem whereby public expenditure directly or indirectly reduces private expenditure. The crowding-out argument requires that there is some constraint on overall real expenditure which is operative. In the orthodox approach this would be full employment with the assumption (often implicit) that the economy is operating at full employment.

14. That is, interest payments are excluded from government expenditure and the taxation paid on those interest payments is also excluded .

15. Let the outstanding public sector debt be D, and then the budget deficit is dD/dt and is equal to $G + rD - T$ where r is the post-tax rate of interest on public debt, G is government expenditure (other than that based on receipt of interest from government). With Y as national income, we have:

$$d\,(D/Y)\,/\,dt = (1/Y)\,dD/dt - (D/Y)\,(1/Y).\,dY/dt = (G + rDT)\,/\,Y - (D/Y)g$$

where g is the growth of national income. The debt to income ratio rises if $(G - T)\,/\,Y > (D/Y)\,(g - r)$.

From this simple manipulation, the following can be concluded:

(i) In the case when there is a constant deficit (excluding interest payments) to income ratio, provided that the rate of growth exceeds the post-tax real rate of interest, then the debt to income ratio will stabilize at the deficit to income ratio divided by $(g - r)$. Since $(g - r)$ is likely to be small (i.e. of the order of 0.01 or 0.02), this can imply a high debt to income ratio (i.e. of the order of 50 or 100 times the deficit to income ratio). In turn this would entail very substantial interest payments (especially when seen in pre-tax terms). For example, suppose $(G - T)/Y$ is 0.03, $(g - r) = 0.01$, then D/Y would stabilize at 3; With a real rate of interest of 0.03 and zero inflation, interest payments would be at the equivalent of 0.09 of national income.

(ii) In the case when there is a constant deficit (including interest payments) then the debt to income ratio will stabilize at the deficit to income ratio divided to g. This would be much lower than in case (i).

16. But it should be noted that the government is in effect permitting the savings to occur by running a deficit and absorbing those savings. If investment were higher, thereby reducing the need for public expenditure, savings would again occur and profits flow to the wealthy.

17. The equation government expenditure minus taxation equals private savings minus investment plus imports minus exports must hold; it can be restated as government budget deficit equals net private savings plus trade deficit.

18. Specifically the conditions that budget deficits should not exceed 3 per cent of GDP and that government debt should not exceed the equivalent of 60 per cent of GDP.

19. The budget deficit in the UK for 1993/94 was forecast at the equivalent of 8 cent of GDP, against the Maastricht condition of 3 per cent. A reduction of public expenditure (or the imposition of taxation) to meet that condition would thus be at least 5 per cent of GDP even without any consideration of the subsequent downward multiplier effects of such changes on GDP.

20. It then appears paradoxical that the quarter of a century from 1948 to 1973 was characterized (at least in the OECD area) by the fastest economic growth ever recorded and (for most of the period) a fixed exchange rate regime. The fears expressed by some over the Bretton Woods system were not justified. But for much of the period the US was prepared to run deficits and in effect supply the world with dollars. Further, there were no substantial differences in national inflation rates as between the main OECD economies. The refusal of France to continue to accept dollars and the divergence of inflation rates undermined the Bretton Woods system in the late 1960s.

21. A sustainable fixed exchange rate system requires a very close similarity in economic performance in terms of, for example, inflation, trade performances and so on. It is assumed here that such strong convergence is unlikely to occur in the forseeable future.

22. For some further discussion by post-Keynesians see for example Davidson (1992) (on the international monetary system) and Arestis (1994) (on a European monetary system).

23. It may be necessary to say why we regard inflation as a supply-side rather than a demand-side issue. We would reject any monetarist analysis of inflation on the basis that money is created by the banking system in response to changes in production and prices rather than the reverse causation suggested by the monetarist to the effect that changes in the money stock lead to changes in prices. High levels of (and changes in) demand may stimulate inflation in the presence of inadequate supply conditions and institutional arrangements for price and wage determination. We see the underlying problem to be the inadequate supply-side and institutional arrangements acting as a constraint rather than the high levels of demand which may trigger off the inflation.

24. For further discussion and empirical evidence see Arestis and Skott (1993).

25. The absence of inflationary pressures is taken here to mean a lack of any tendency for inflation to increase.

26. For further discussion see Cowling and Sugden (1990; 1993a; 1993b); Sawyer (1992b; 1994).

27. For a brief view of evidence see Sawyer (1989) pp. 66–73.

REFERENCES

Amable, B. (1993), 'Catch-up and convergence: a model of cumulative growth', *International Review of Applied Economics*, vol. 7.

Amsden, A. (1989), *Asia's Next Giant*, New York: Oxford University Press.

Arestis, P. (1992), *The Post-Keynesian Approach to Economics*, Aldershot: Edward Elgar.

Arestis, P. and Milberg, W. (1993), 'Degree of monopoly, pricing and flexible exchange rates', *Journal of Post Keynesian Economics*, vol. 16.

Arestis, P. (1994), 'An independent European central bank: a Post Keynesian perspective', paper delivered at the 1993 *Keynes Conference* on *Keynes and the Post Keynesians* held at University of Kent, 17 November 1993, forthcoming in the proceedings of the conference to be published by Macmillan, London.

Arestis, P. and Skott, P. (1993), 'Conflict, wage relativities and hysteresis in U.K. wage determination', *Journal of Post Keynesian Economics*, vol. 15.

Baumol, W. (1986), 'Productivity growth, convergence and welfare: what the long-run data show', *American Economic Review*, vol. 76.

Boltho, A. (1982), 'Growth' in A. Boltho (ed.) *The European Economy: Growth and Crisis*, Oxford: Oxford University Press.

Brenner, H. (1979), 'Influence of social environment on social pathology: the historical perspective' in James E. Barrett et al. (eds), *Stress and Mental Disorder*, New York: Raven Press (for American Psychopathological Association).

Burchell, B. (1992), 'Changes in the labour market and the psychological health of the nation' in J. Michie (ed.), *The Economic Legacy, 1979–1992*, London: Academic Press.

Calmfors, L. (1993), 'Centralisation of wage bargaining and macroeconomic performance: a survey', *OECD Economics Department Working Papers*, no 131.

Calmfors, L. and Driffill, J. (1988), 'Bargaining structure, corporatism and macroeconomic performance', *Economic Policy*, no. 6.

Chang, H.-J. (1993), 'The political economy of industrial policy in Korea', *Cambridge Journal of Economics*, vol. 17.

Clower, R. (1965), 'The Keynesian counter revolution' in F. Hahn and F. Brechling (eds), *The Theory of Interest Rates*, London: Macmillan.

Cowling, K. (1987), 'An industrial strategy for Britain', *International Review of Applied Economics*, vol. 1.

Cowling, K. (1990), 'The strategic approach to economic and industrial policy' in K. Cowling and R. Sugden (eds), *A New Economic Policy for Britain*, Manchester: Manchester University Press.

Cowling, K. and Sugden, R. (1989), 'Exchange rate adjustment and oligopoly pricing behaviour', *Cambridge Journal of Economics*, vol. 13.

Cowling, K. and Sugden, R. (1990) (eds), *A New Economic Policy for Britain: Essays on the Development of Industry*, Manchester: Manchester University Press.

Cowling, K. and Sugden, R. (1993a), 'A strategy for industrial development as a basis for regulation' in R. Sugden (ed.), *Industrial Economic Regulation: A Framework and Exploration*, London: Routledge.

Cowling, K. and Sugden, R. (1993b), 'Industrial strategy: a missing link in British economic policy', *Oxford Review of Economic Policy*, vol. 9.

Cross, R. (1988), (ed.), *Unemployment, Hysteresis and the Natural Rate of Unemployment*, Oxford: Basil Blackwell.

Davidson, P. (1992), 'Reforming the world's money', *Journal of Post Keynesian Economics*, vol. 15.

Henley, A. and Tsakalotos, E. (1993), *Corporatism and Economic Performance*, Aldershot: Edward Elgar.

Henry, S.G.B., Sawyer, M. and Smith, P. (1976), 'Models of Inflation in the U.K.: An Evaluation', *National Institute Economic Review*, no. 76.

Isaac, A. (1994), 'Hysteresis' in P. Arestis and M. Sawyer (eds), *The Elgar Companion to Radical Political Economy*, Aldershot: Edward Elgar.

Johnson, C. (1982), *MITI and the Japanese Miracle*, Stanford: Stanford University Press.

Kaldor, N. (1972), 'The irrelevance of equilibrium economics', *Economic Journal*, vol. 82.

Kalecki, M. (1943), 'Political aspects of full employment', *Political Quarterly*, vol. 14.

Kalecki, M. (1971), *Selected Essays on the Dynamics of the Capitalist Economy*, Cambridge: Cambridge University Press.

Kennedy, P. (1988), *The Rise and Fall of Nations*, New York: Vintage.

Keynes, J.M. (1936), *The General Theory of Employment, Interest and Money*, London: Macmillan.

Leibenstein, H. (1966), 'Allocative efficiency vs. X-Efficiency', *American Economic Review*, vol. 56.

Leijonhufvud, A. (1968), *On Keynesian Economics and the Economics of Keynes: a Study in Monetary Theory*, London: Oxford University Press.

Michl, T. (1991), 'Debt, deficits and the distribution of income', *Journal of Post Keynesian Economics,* vol. 13.

Myrdal, G. (1957), *Economic Theory and Underdeveloped Regions*, London: Duckworth.

Organisation for Economic Co-operation and Development (1972), *Industrial Policy in Japan*, Paris: OECD.

Oxford University Institute of Statistics (1944), *The Economics of Full Employment*, Oxford: Blackwell.

Pasinetti, L. (1974), *Growth and Income Distribution*, Cambridge: Cambridge University Press.

Porter, M. (1990), *The Competitive Advantage of Nations*, London: Macmillan.

Robbins, L. (1932), *An Essay on the Nature and Significance of Economic Science*, London: Macmillan.

Robinson, J. (1972), 'The second crisis of economic theory', *American Economic Review*, vol. 62.

Sawyer, M. (1987), 'The political economy of the Phillips curve', *Thames Papers in Political Economy*, Summer.

Sawyer, M. (1989), *The Challenge of Radical Political Economy*, Hemel Hempstead: Harvester Wheatsheaf.

Sawyer, M. (1991), 'Analysing the operation of market economies in the spirit of Kaldor and Kalecki', in J. Michie (ed.), *The Economics of Restructuring and Intervention*, Aldershot: Edward Elgar.

Sawyer, M. (1992a), 'The nature and role of the market', *Social Concept*, vol. 6, no. 2 (a slightly revised version appeared in C. Pitelis (ed.), *Transaction Costs, Markets and Hierarchies*, Oxford: Blackwell, 1993).

Sawyer, M. (1992b), 'Reflections on the nature and role of industrial policy', *Metroeconomica*, vol. 52.

Sawyer, M. (1994), 'Industrial strategy and employment in Europe' in J. Grieve Smith and J. Michie (eds), *Unemployment in Europe – Policies for Growth*, London: Academic Press.

Scott, B.R. (1984), 'National strategy for stronger US competitiveness', *Harvard Business Review*, vol. 52.

Shapiro, M. and Ahlburg, D (1983), 'Suicide: the ultimate cost of unemployment', *Journal of Post Keynesian Economics*, vol. 5.

Thirwall, A.P. (1978), 'The UK's economic problem: a balance of payments constraint', *National Westminster Bank Quarterly Review*, February.

Thirlwall, A.P. (1979), 'The balance of payments constraint as an explanation of international growth rate differences', *Banca Nazionale del Lavoro Quarterly Review*, March.

Thirlwall, A.P. and Gibson, H.D. (1992), *Balance-of-payments Theory and the United Kingdom Experience*, fourth ed., London: Macmillan.

Weiss, A. (1990), *Efficiency Wages,* Princeton: Princeton University Press.

World Bank (1993), *World Development Report, 1993*, Oxford: Oxford University Press.

2. Technological unemployment

Harald Hagemann

Shortly before his death Schumpeter pronounced the long debate on the employment effects of technological change to be 'dead and buried' (1954, p. 684). However, in recent years not only has Schumpeter's own work experienced a renaissance but, against the background of the microelectronics revolution, there has also been a revival in the old controversy between labour displacement pessimism and compensation optimism. The spectre of technological unemployment has come centre stage again. Technological changes are both heroes and villains in modern legend. Some regard the modernization of the economy, the development and diffusion of new technology, and rapid structural change as the most efficient strategies for fighting high rates of unemployment. Others, however, fear that new technologies, whether already installed or yet to be introduced, will eventually lead to a further reduction in the number of available jobs thus aggravating unemployment and also threatening to displace skilled labour in all sectors of the economy. The diverging expectations on the employment consequences of new technologies mirror the ambiguous character of technological change which both creates jobs and eliminates them. This double-sided nature of new technologies raises two important questions: Does technology create more jobs than it destroys? Does technology create more higher-skilled jobs than it destroys?

DISPLACEMENT AND COMPENSATION EFFECTS OF NEW TECHNOLOGIES

It is interesting to note that many of the issues now at the forefront of the debate on the effects of technological change on employment were also key issues in earlier discussions. Adam Smith, for example, gave a pessimistic answer to the second question posed above but an optimistic one to the first. Smith did not recognize the problem of technological unemployment in his analysis of technical progress. Progressive division of labour is the root of rising productivity, but 'the division of labour is limited by the extent of the market' (1976, p. 31) which itself is dependent on capital accumulation. Capital accumulation thus figures as the *conditio sine qua non* of technical progress which is at the same time cause and effect of economic growth. Investment leads to an extension of the market, and hence to an increase in the division of labour via the production–income nexus. The rate of growth in productivity is governed by the rate of growth of aggregate demand.[1] For Smith it was fundamental that technological change was designed to raise the output per man in response to growing demand. The issue of reabsorbing displaced workers never came up because he took it for granted that output expansion and cost reductions due to the introduction of new machinery were inseparably linked. Essentially, Smith looked upon capital as a complement of rather than a substitute for labour. The growing market makes possible the introduction of new technologies which in turn, by attracting labour, help the market to grow.

However, the division of labour has its drawbacks as well as its virtues. Whereas Smith was entirely optimistic concerning the quantitative employment effects of new technologies, he saw, on the other hand, that an increased efficiency due to a growing division of labour had its price.

> In the progress of the division of labour, the employment ... of the great body of the people comes to be confined to a 'few very' simple operations; ... The man whose whole life is spent in performing a few simple operations ... has no occasion to exert his understanding. ... He naturally loses, therefore, the habit of such exertion, and generally becomes as stupid and ignorant as it is possible for a human creature to become. (1976, p. 782)

Smith thus looked upon the growing horizontal and vertical division of labour as a historical process which had an economic as well as an important social dimension. Especially in the course of a growing vertical division of labour less skilled workers are required at the various stages of the manufacturing process. Smith's opinion that there was a tendency to deskilling was subsequently taken up and developed by Marx when he discussed the degradation, alienation and pauperization of the labouring class. Marx deeply appreciated the special dialectics of Smith's analysis where creativity of the common people declines while that of society as a whole grows as a result of a growing division of labour.[2]

The possibility of a *temporary* technological unemployment as a consequence of the *sudden* introduction of a new technology has already been pointed out, nine years before the publication of the *Wealth of Nations*, by James Steuart who dedicated a whole chapter[3] to the machinery problem.

> It is hardly possible *suddenly* to increase the smallest innovation into the political oeconomy of a state, let it be ever so reasonable, nay ever so profitable, without incurring some inconveniences. A room cannot be swept without raising dust, one cannot walk abroad without dirtying one's shoes; neither can a machine, which abridges the labour of men, be introduced *all at once* into an extensive manufacture, without throwing many people into idleness. (1966, pp. 121–2)

However, these disadvantages have to be balanced with the advantages. Steuart in particular pointed out the cost- and price-reducing effect of the introduction of new machinery and its consequences for the international competitiveness of the innovating economy. The increase in exports was the main argument for Steuart to favour new technologies and to see the long-run advantages clearly dominating the short-run inconveniences:

> Upon the whole, daily experience shews the advantage and improvement acquired by the introduction of machines. Let the inconveniences complained of be ever so sensibly felt, let a statesman be ever so careless in relieving those who are forced to be idle, *all these inconveniences are only temporary; the advantage is permanent*, and the necessity of introducing every method of abridging labour and expence, in order to supply the wants of luxurious mankind, is absolutely indispensable, according to modern policy, according to experience, and according to reason. (1966, p. 125; my emphasis.)

The question of whether and under what conditions technological change will lead to persistent unemployment became the central theme in the new Chapter 31, 'On Machinery', in the third edition of Ricardo's *Principles*, published in 1821. In this chapter, which according to Sraffa marked 'the most revolutionary change in edition 3' (Sraffa, 1951, p. lvii), Ricardo retracted his previous opinion that the introduction of machinery is beneficial to all the different classes of society and instead came to the conclusion '[t]hat the opinion entertained by the labouring class, that the employment of machinery is frequently detrimental to their interests, is not founded on prejudice and error, but is conformable to the correct principles of political economy' (Ricardo, 1951, p. 392) By taking note of the labour-displacing effects of new machinery, confidence in the steady growth of aggregate output and employment was lost. Ricardo thus removed the cornerstone from Smith's theoretical edifice.

Since Ricardo, we distinguish between the labour-displacement effect arising from certain technological changes and the conditions required to assure the eventual absorption ('compensation') of the displaced workers. The advocates of the *compensation theory* believe in the operation of free market mechanisms whereby those who have been displaced from their jobs by technological change are re-employed. The advocates of the *displacement theory*, on the other hand, believe that the conditions for compensation are not fulfilled sufficiently, if at all. To be precise: the main issue in the controversy between the compensation school and the displacement school of thought is not whether technological unemployment, once it occurs, can be absorbed at all. In principle, compensation is possible. The question in dispute is whether the market provides for an endogenous mechanism that ensures compensation within the Marshallian short period – as it was maintained by Ricardo's contemporary McCulloch – or whether some degree of public intervention might be necessary to counter destabilizing tendencies of an uncontrolled market. In denying the existence of a self-regulating mechanism capable of achieving automatic compensation, Ricardo fundamentally questioned the ability of a free market system to bring about full employment through the operation of its spontaneous forces. Ricardo's analysis of the problem of technological unemployment, from today's point of view, can be regarded as an early and rude type of traverse analysis containing a capital shortage theory of temporary technological unemployment. Although it is a characteristic feature of Ricardo's numerical example that it abstracts from capital accumulation, i.e. the time paths of employment and output the economy takes after the introduction of new machinery are largely left in the dark, Ricardo's analysis nevertheless has everlasting merit for emphasizing that a process of additional saving and investing is necessary to assure the compensation of displaced workers.

The re-employment of displaced workers in the construction of the new machines is often mentioned as the first compensating factor (see, e.g., Say, 1821, p. 87) Against this '*machinery production argument*' Marx raised his 'infallible law' according to which '[t]he new labour spent on the instruments of labour, on the machinery, on the coal, and so on, must necessarily be less than the labour displaced by the use of the machinery; otherwise the products of the machine would be as dear, or dearer, than the products of the manual labour' (Marx, 1954, p. 417). The machinery production argument undoubtedly contains an important element of truth. Even process innovations involve in most cases the introduction of new capital goods. This implies that a faster rate of diffusion of new technologies presupposes an increased investment demand which may even increase employment in the short run. However, the basic problem remains that a *short-run* effect (more employment in the industries producing capital goods in the construction phase of new machines) is set off against a *long-run* effect (displacement of labour during the utilization phase of new machines). This means that speeding up accumulation may even overcompensate displaced labour in the short run. On the other hand, long-run employment problems will be aggravated if investment demand is only expanded temporarily.

The case for capital shortage found a new protagonist in Marx, but contrary to Ricardo and other predecessors it was no longer a deficiency of circulating capital in the form of a wage fund but a shortage of fixed capital that caused the trouble. Overcoming the bottleneck of capital formation is a necessary but not a sufficient condition for reabsorbing displaced workers. Neisser threw light on this problem when, in discussing the Marxian analysis of Ricardo's chapter on machinery, he coined the famous phrase of 'the capitalistic process as a race between displacement of labor through technological progress and reabsorption of labor through accumulation' whose outcome 'is impossible to predict ... on purely theoretical grounds' (Neisser, 1942, p. 70). Thus there is a special dialectics at work. An increase in the rate of accumulation (per time unit) might increase the demand for labour, but accompanying changes in technology which would lead to an increase in the amount of capital per worker could neutralize this favourable effect. Neisser's conclusion therefore is clear: there exists no mechanism which would secure the full compensation of displaced workers. The outcome of the 'race' is open and it may differ with changing times and between various countries.

There is another endogenous compensating factor operating in the economy. Technological progress leads to cost reductions which manifest themselves either in falling prices or in rising profits, i.e. additional real purchasing power is created either in the hands of consumers and/or in those of the Schumpeterian pioneers. This will increase aggregate demand. Thus displaced workers will find new jobs in the production of commodities to satisfy the additional aggregate demand. According to the so called *'classical compensation principle'*, in the case of perfect competition, prices fall *uno actu* with cost reductions.[4] This means that lower costs of production are transmitted without delay or curtailment to consumers whose real incomes increase; this in turn stimulates the demand for goods. The price elasticities of consumer demand decide whether an increased demand for labour compensates the initial displacement of workers in the same industry (or industries) where technological progress takes place or in other industries of the economy. If demand is unresponsive to lower prices, purchasing power in the hands of consumers is freed for spending on other goods.

However, the introduction of more productive technologies does not necessarily increase the total *purchasing* power, but only the *productive* power of an economy. If labour displacement occurs, the loss of the purchasing power of those displaced may be compensated by the increase in purchasing power of those still working. But the additional productive capacity may not be absorbed. It was John Stuart Mill who first denied that aggregate purchasing power could be raised in this manner and who instead emphasized that '[d]emand for commodities is *not* demand for labour' (Mill 1976, p. 79; my emphasis). What Mill was driving at was the basic idea that production and employment possibilities are limited by the existing stock of real capital. Thus, if capital formation is insufficient, the fall in prices and the increase in real incomes caused by technical progress will be inadequate to ensure the re-employment of all redundant workers. They will assure only that no secondary displacement effects (i.e. no negative employment multipliers) occur.

More recently some authors have argued that '[t]he existence of extensive networks of unemployment benefits in most of the Western industrialised economies has contributed to an automatic adaptation of the purchasing power to the production power of the economy' (Blattner 1981, pp. 444–5). Although there can be no doubt that the widespread existence of unemployment benefits represents an important compensation mechanism, a fundamental methodological objection has to be raised. This specific compensation mechanism is not of an endogenous nature provided by the market but itself the result of public intervention.

The extent of compensatory employment also depends on the degree to which substitution between labour and capital is possible in the economy. If proportions are *fixed*, the degree of capital accumulation determines the demand for labour. If *substitution* is possible, the amount of labour employed in equilibrium depends on the ratio between the wage rate and the rate of profit. Contrary to the view of classical economists that compensation depends on accumulating additional fixed capital, neo-classical economists such as J.B. Clark argued that the stock of fixed capital as it exists at any moment in time offers, at least in principle, unlimited employment opportunities. This optimistic conclusion follows from dropping two classical premises, namely the given level of real wages and the fixed coefficients of production. According to the marginal productivity theorem, varying quantities of labour can be combined with any quantity of fixed capital, if only money wages are flexible enough and if real wages thereby adjust to changes in the marginal productivity of labour. In the extreme world of the neo-classical parable, in which the only good 'jelly' is malleable, the adjustment process requires neither costs nor time, and compensation is automatic.

The neo-classical solution is applicable only under quite specific and largely unrealistic conditions, as has already been shown by Neisser (1942), and in practice the marginal productivity mechanism may not achieve compensation for a long time. The discussion, however, shows the decisive influence two major modelling decisions have on the results when we are analysing the impact of new technologies on employment. The first concerns the *production-theoretic basis*, i.e. fixed coefficients or substitution. The second concerns the question *how prices react to disequilibrium*. If one specifies, in a Walrasian manner, that prices react instantaneously to notional disequilibria, i.e. prices are perfectly flexible, then there will be no unemployment resulting from technological change. Therefore, in the framework of the new classical macroeconomics, the introduction of new technologies creates no involuntary unemployment, for the labour market always clears. However, we are away from the natural rate of unemployment during the whole transition period in which expected prices are adjusting to the new equilibrium prices. If, due to a rational expectations mechanism, expected prices adjust with infinite speed, the economy would jump directly from the old equilibrium to the new one and would always be at the natural rate of unemployment. So again some price rigidity is required – here inflexibility in price expectations – if new technologies are to create a disequilibrium in the labour market.

According to neo-classical theory there is only one reason for the existence of persistent unemployment: real wages are too high and too inflexible downwards.

This would lead to *capital shortage unemployment* in the medium run and *technological unemployment* in the long run. That displaced workers 'cannot remain unemployed unless we are prepared to violate the assumption that perfect competition and unlimited flexibility of wages prevail' has been emphasized already by Schumpeter (1954, p. 683) who, like Marx, started his analysis of the question whether and under what conditions technological change will lead to persistent unemployment from Ricardo's investigation of the machinery problem. While Marx elaborated Ricardo's arguments in favour of displacement, Schumpeter concentrated on those that favoured compensation.[5] Schumpeter (1954) also criticized the classical economists, especially Ricardo, for their inability 'to understand substitution (both of factors and of products) in its full importance' (p. 680). The possibility of substitution between the factors of production affects the extent to which a drop in wages can act as a compensating factor. The diminished demand for labour brought about by mechanization can depress wages. When some capital can be replaced by labour, the displaced workers are re-employed and the negative impact of new machines lies not in unemployment but in lower wages. This was already the core of Wicksell's basic objection to Ricardo's analysis.[6] Wicksell criticized Ricardo for neglecting the effects of wage reductions caused by the diminished demand for labour after the introduction of new machinery: these would bring about the reabsorption of displaced workers. In Ricardo's analysis, a fall in the real wage is considered neither a necessary consequence of, nor an effective remedy for, the displacement of workers. Wicksell's argument illustrates the importance of the principle of substitution in connection with a drop in wages. However, Wicksell neither described explicitly the long-run equilibrium level of wages after the introduction of new machinery, nor recognized that the return to old and more labour-intensive methods of production in reaction to wage reductions could imply a sacrifice of the investment incurred to introduce the new machinery, and thus involve heavy losses for the entrepreneurs. Instead he considered a special case characterized by a decrease in the marginal productivity of labour.[7]

The old controversy between labour-displacement pessimism and compensation optimism is itself submitted to long waves and, naturally, very much intensified in times of mass unemployment. No wonder that rapid labour-saving technical progress was identified as a key factor in explaining the severity of the employment problems during the Great Depression, as Lederer (1938) did in his theory of structural unemployment. Gourvitch's survey (1940) on the relationship between technological change and employment also has to be seen against the background of the debates taking place in the 1930s. Kähler's study (1933) on the displacement of workers by machinery is important because his pioneering analysis was based on a very advanced embryo of a closed input–output model, applied to the intersectoral shifts required for capital formation. Kähler analysed the displacement and reabsorption effects within a multisectoral model comprising eight sectors, and thus an 8×8 matrix of inter-industry coefficients, a vector of final demand and a vector of sectoral labour inputs.

BEYOND THE STEADY STATE: TRAVERSE ANALYSIS AND STRUCTURAL CHANGE

Within the analysis of growth theory, emphasis in recent years has shifted to problems of structural change and technological unemployment.[8] Here the analysis of the *traverse* is particularly relevant. This is the study of the macro-economic consequences of technological change and of the necessary conditions for bringing an economy back to an equilibrium growth path. Hicks (1973) and Lowe (1976), the two pioneers in the field of traverse analysis, have shown that the decisive problem that the economy faces after technological change is the inappropriateness of its capital stock, since the necessary adjustments are costly and time-consuming. Characteristically, both authors started their investigation from Ricardo's analysis of the machinery problem. However, they used alternative notions of economic activities, namely '*horizontally*' integrated and '*vertically*' integrated models of economic structure.

Hicks based his traverse analysis on the concept of a neo-Austrian, vertically integrated production process, in which a stream of labour inputs is transformed into a stream of consumption good outputs. It is a significant property of his model that the intertemporal complementarities in the productive process are put into sharp focus. Hicks's Austrian representation of production structures does lead immediately to a 'stages' analysis of the adjustment process. For the investigation of the traverse Hicks employs a type of 'scenario' analysis, i.e. different macro-behavioural assumptions are made (fixwage or full employment) and their implications are studied. Hicks concentrates on the short-run and medium-run effects of an innovation, the 'early phase', and plays down the problem of convergence of the traverse to a new steady-state path which can be assured only under very special conditions.[9] Hicks, whose fixwage model contains almost an exact replica of Ricardo's assumptions, came to the defence of what he regarded as the central message of Ricardo's analysis of the machinery question:[10] namely that there are important cases in which the introduction of a new type of machinery might reduce both real output and employment in the short run. The harmful effects might persist for quite a time, but the constantly increasing investment of the higher profits (due to the greater efficiency of the new production process) should eventually lead to a path of output and employment which is above that which could have been achieved with the old production process, thereby offsetting technological unemployment.[11]

There is no process interdependence in Hicks's vertical representation of production structures, i.e. capital goods are regarded as intermediate products. By treating fixed capital as if it were working capital Hicks does not recognize the need for a special machine-tools sector. An important consequence of this procedure is that the neo-Austrian approach does not show the effects of innovation on industrial structures. However, the assumption was deliberately made by Hicks who saw the decisive advantage of the Austrian method in its ability to cope with the important fact that process innovations nearly always involve the introduction of *new* capital goods, Hicks (1977) thus thought it

> undesirable that these goods should be physically specified, since there is no way of establishing a physical relation between the capital goods that are required in the one technique and those that are required in the other. The only relation that can be established runs in terms of costs, and of capacity to produce final output: and this is precisely what is preserved in an Austrian theory. (p. 193)

The elaboration of the impact of process innovations on industrial structures, on the other hand, is the strength of the circular view of production or the horizontal model, as developed by Leontief, Sraffa and von Neumann. Lowe's scheme of industrial production comprises not only three sectors but also four successive stages within each sector that lead up to the finished goods. The fact that all sectors are divided into stages representing the successive maturing of natural resources into final goods with the help of labour and fixed capital goods brings into light the often neglected role of working capital goods as goods in process. However, in contrast to the (neo-) Austrian model there is full circularity in that capital goods are already applied in the first stage of the production process. Lowe's 'tripartite' division of the economy into three vertically integrated sectors implies a definite hierarchy of sectors, from 1 via 2 to 3 ('machines' $\rightarrow$ 'tractors' $\rightarrow$ 'corn'). This characteristic leads to a definite intertemporal complementarity during the traverse.[12] A central idea is the perception that there exists a group of fixed capital goods, classified as 'machine-tools', which have the capacity for physical self-reproduction and therefore hold the strategic position in any industrial system similar to seed corn in agricultural production. Lowe's analysis emphasizes the role of sectoral interrelationships and of physical bottlenecks which become relevant when structural change occurs, rendering the inherited structure of the stock of fixed capital goods inappropriate. The existing stock of machines is the bottleneck that any process of rapid expansion and even the introduction of new process technologies must overcome.

Lowe's analysis shows nicely the precedence patterns of the interrelationship of sectors and the analogy between compensation of technological unemployment and the traverse of an economy adapting to an increase in the rate of growth of labour supply in order to achieve the macro-goal of full employment. However, the behavioural and motivational patterns that will set the economy on a goal-adequate traverse will be quite different. Another important result of Lowe's investigation is the demonstration that a compensation problem not only exists in the case of labour-displacing innovations but also in the case of a pure capital-displacing innovation. For example, a capital-displacing innovation in the production of corn in sector 3 reduces the outputs as well as the inputs in both capital-producing sectors. As a consequence of this secondary effect a compensation problem for displaced workers in sectors 1 and 2 exists, although these sectors are not directly affected by technological change.

However, a circular approach encounters some difficulties when the effects of innovation to be studied involve the introduction of new types of capital goods. No wonder that the phasing of the adjustment path in Lowe's model is not as refined as in Hicks's neo-Austrian model. As a consequence, the initial phase in which the building and instalment of new technology takes place is largely left in the dark. Lowe also does not show the side-by-side existence of different processes/technologies in the course of the traverse; this heterogeneity is an important feature of a traverse.[13] Since both approaches of economic structure, the horizontal and the vertical model, enjoy comparative advantages in the analysis of traverses a complementary (or synthetic) perspective should be followed.[14]

Recent research work also has been stimulated by Pasinetti's important study *Structural Change and Economic Growth* (1981). The author's main aim is to develop a theory of structural change which is a characteristic of every industrial system in the long-run development. In contrast to Hicks and Lowe, Pasinetti does not elaborate traverse analysis but concentrates on the (restrictive) conditions which have to be fulfilled in order for the economy to develop through time with full employment and full capacity utilization, if it is subject to dynamic impulses such as technological change, a growing population (changes in the ratio of active to total population or in the ratio of working hours to total time), and changes in consumers' preferences according to Engel's law. The equilibrium path through time is no 'steady state' with constant structural proportions but one where permanent changes in some basic magnitudes, such as the national product, total consumption and investment or overall employment, are associated with changes in their composition. The dynamic movements of productivity, labour supply and structure of demand are typical features of any industrial system, independent of its institutional set-up.

As time goes by, the various vertically integrated sectors experience a structural dynamics of both their production and their costs (and thus equilibrium prices) which has important consequences for the development of the demand for labour, i.e. it generates a certain *structural dynamics of employment*. If, with a constant labour supply, labour productivity in sector i grows with the rate δ_i and demand for good i grows with the rate r_i, the sectoral demand for labour would only be constant in the special but unlikely case $\delta_i = r_i$. If r_i exceeds (is smaller than) δ_i, sector i will expand (reduce) its demand for labour. With different rates of productivity growth and different sectoral rates of growth of demand, apart from the very special case where in every single sector demand grows at exactly the same rate as labour productivity, a reallocation of labour between the sectors will be necessary. Thus a high level of employment can be kept only with an appropriate mobility of labour between sectors (and regions). Pasinetti's theoretical framework allows both expanding and declining industries in the process of structural change. When in some sectors the introduction of new technologies causes high rates of growth of productivity which cannot be matched by a proportional increase of demand because some saturation is reached, then a fall of employment in these sectors cannot be avoided.

With a growing population, the economy must also enlarge its overall productive capacity continuously whereby in each sector a very definite relation between the rate of growth of sectoral demand and the amount of new investment has to be fulfilled. In order to maintain full employment through time an effective demand condition *and* a capital accumulation condition must be satisfied. It is therefore very probable that, even if the economy starts from an equilibrium position with full employment of the labour force and full utilization of productive capacities, the structural dynamics which cause that position to change will not lead to the maintenance of full employment by the endogenous mechanisms of the market system. Pasinetti thus comes to the conclusion

> that the structural dynamics of the economic system inevitably tend to generate ... *technological* unemployment. At the same time, the very same structural dynamics produce counter-balancing movements ..., *but not automatically*. There is nothing in the structural evolution of technical coefficients on the one side and of per-capita demand on the other, as such, that will ensure ... the maintenance of full employment. Therefore, if full employment is to be kept through time, it will have to be actively pursued as an explicit aim of economic policy. (p. 90)

In order to sustain full employment over time, society has to choose one of the following strategies or combination of them:

- a Keynesian-type policy which will raise per capita demand for existing goods;
- the promotion of research and development for new goods. Since technical progress does not only lead to an increase in productivity but also to product innovations with a high potential for an increase in demand, investment and employment, a more supply-side-oriented policy of this kind aims at strengthening this second tendency to compensate the first one;
- a policy of shortening the working time or reducing the participation rate. Within certain boundaries, technical progress gives society the option of choosing between the production of more and/or better goods and enjoying more leisure.

It is the main merit of Pasinetti's investigation to have shown so clearly that overall full employment will only be maintained if the economy is able to implement a continuous process of structural reallocation of labour between the sectors, in accordance with the twofold effect of technical progress on labour productivity and the evolution of demand. The structural dynamics of employment causes serious problems for firms and individuals, because it requires a very special pattern of investment behaviour and training as well as mobility between sectors (and regions) over time.

The integration of the demand aspect of technological change into the theoretical framework is another advantage of Pasinetti's analysis of structural change. The factor ultimately responsible for structural change is technical progress as a result of learning. Increases in productivity lead to increases in per capita income. With increases in real income consumers do not expand their demand for each existing commodity proportionally. Moreover, with technical progress new products emerge. This generalization of Engel's empirical law, i.e. the integration of structural dynamics of demand, plays an important role in the analysis of Pasinetti who emphasizes 'that, in the *long* run, it is the level of real income – not the price structure – that becomes the relevant and crucial variable' (p. 78). It certainly is one of Pasinetti's most innovative achievements to have shown so clearly the two facets of technological change on the supply side *and* on the demand side and the interaction between the two.

However, one problem remains: Pasinetti makes the assumption that the different rates of productivity growth in the various vertically integrated sectors are exogenously given. In order to do so he had to give up the general model containing basics in favour of a special model in which, even in its 'more complex' version (involving capital goods for the production of capital goods) no basic products exist and, therefore, the production process is not circular. Even if one takes into consideration that diffusion of new technologies is often dependent on the existence of industries interrelated from the technological point of view, this procedure eliminates one important aspect of technological change: the industry-specific nature which in the general case implies that, contrary to Pasinetti's assumption, rates of productivity growth in the different vertically integrated sectors cannot be thought of as being independent of each other. This important characteristic that technological change takes place at the industry level, and in the case of basic products indirectly affects all other sectors, is washed out in vertically integrated sectors but is at the very centre of input–output models.

SOME RECENT STUDIES

Up to the present, *empirical* research work has not yet succeeded in capturing all the discussed phenomena in a satisfactory way. One reason for this may be seen in the fact that the basis for judgements on the employment consequences of technological change has often been narrowed down to case studies and the inappropriate generalization of results from these studies. On the other hand, in investigations concerning the economy as a whole there has been a lack of unambiguous criteria to determine the distinct impact of technological change on employment. In order to study displacement and reabsorption effects at the *macro*economic level, an appropriate analytical framework has to be developed. First, a *multisectoral* or inter-industry model is indispensable to take account of the secondary as well as the primary consequences of technological change on output and employment. Second, a *dynamic* analysis is required because in the diffusion process of a new technology time matters. Third, an *endogenization of final demand* becomes necessary since basic factors compensating for the initial displacement effect apply to different components of final demand such as

- increased investment demand in order to implement the new technology;
- increased consumption demand due to higher real incomes resulting from reduced prices and costs and/or higher wages increasing with productivity;
- increased export demand resulting from a higher price and non-price international competitiveness.

Especially for a computation of the indirect effects of technological change an input–output model is essential. A fruitful course in this direction was followed by the authors of the study on the application, diffusion and effects of microelectronics on the Austrian economy.[15] The core of this investigation consists of a combination of a *static* input–output model with an econometric demand model which is combined with a demographical and an educational model. Technological data were systematically collected, evaluated and transformed into hypotheses concerning the development of inter-industry – and labour – coefficients. The authors use the scenario technique in which the different rates of productivity growth depend on the different speeds of the diffusion process which characterize the alternative scenarios developed. The model makes it possible to attribute changes in the number of jobs to three additive components: the *productivity effect* which expresses the (negative) employment effects resulting from the reduced labour coefficients; the *input effect* which covers the employment effects of different inter-industry coefficients; and the *demand effect* which represents the employment effects of technologically induced changes in the level and structure of final demand. Private consumption is the only component of final demand which is endogenized as a linear function of disposable income. Since the study assumes that wages per hour are increasing with productivity and the diffusion speed of microelectronics, one of the compensation effects discussed in the literature – increased consumption demand due to higher wages increasing with productivity – is placed into the foreground.

However, the result of the study is that this effect does not suffice to compensate the displacement effect due to the additional productivity gain, so that a further reduction in working time becomes necessary to limit unemployment, although this would limit the wage increase too. The Austrian study has many fruitful elements which should be incorporated and developed in future analytical frameworks to estimate the innovation-induced displacement and compensation effects. Among these elements are the combination of an input–output model with an econometric demand model, the piecing together of particular case studies and often differing expert opinion into a coherent *macroeconomic* perspective, the working with the scenario technique and the endogenization of private consumption. Compared to an ideal study, however, the Austrian one still has some weaknesses. In particular the modelling of the development of final demand is unsatisfactory. The sectoral composition of final demand is assumed to be constant during the time of the forecast, which contradicts previous empirical evidence and excludes the structural dynamics of production which are at the heart of the analysis of Pasinetti (1981). The treatment of investment demand as exogenous is another major weakness. Since the new technologies are mainly embodied in new capital goods, investment demand has to be endogenized.

The most advanced study in the field is Leontief and Duchin's analysis of *The Future Impact of Automation on Workers* (1986) in which a *dynamic* input–output model is developed to study the effects on labour requirements in the US between 1963 and 2000. The main novelty of this study, which comprises 89 sectors and 53 different occupations, consists in the treatment of investment demand, making use of some version of the capital stock adjustment principle. The endogenization of private investment demand is a decisive advantage of this study which thus takes into consideration the machinery production argument associated with the diffusion of new technologies. On the other hand, even this model still has some shortcomings because it does not allow for declining industries, which are often an important aspect of structural change. Moreover, it does not endogenize export demand and private consumption demand and thereby neglects changes in the composition of consumption demand which often go hand in hand with an increase in per capita income due to technical progress. Since it is an important result of the investigation that the subsequent effects of automation are different for different occupations, the assumption of a constant structural composition of demand is a major weakness. However, despite these deficiencies there can be no doubt that the Leontief–Duchin study can give much inspiration for future research on the employment consequences of technological change.

The fruitfulness of the Leontief–Duchin study has already been displayed in the intensive research efforts which were made in Germany in the late 1980s to investigate the direct and indirect employment effects of the introduction and use of modern technologies at different levels of the economy.[16] For example, a modified model was used to investigate the quantitative employment effects and the changing skill requirements of the introduction of industrial robots (see Edler, 1990). The dynamic analysis of the spread of industrial robots has shown that the negative direct employment effects in the use of the robots are partly offset by the positive employment effects on the side of the producers, i.e. in the construction of the robots. In the early phase the positive employment effect dominates whereas in the longer run, when more and more industrial robots are in their utilization phase, the negative user effect outweighs the producer effect. The higher the rate of capital accumulation in industrial robots the greater is the weight of the compensation effect. The study reveals that the development of overall employment also depends on the impact of cost and price reductions on the expansion of output and changes in the structural composition of demand (which were outside the scope of the study).

The effects of the diffusion of microelectronic-based new technologies on the volume and structure of employment in the West German economy were also studied in the framework of a dynamic input–output analysis. The model incorporates a determination of investment demand which is different from the Leontief–Duchin study and also allows declining industries.[17] With the help of the scenario technique different transition paths from the old to the new technique are investigated which are characterized by a different speed of diffusion of the new 'best-practice technique'. The different time paths of employment of the diffusion scenarios are then compared with the employment path of the reference scenario which is characterized by a constant technique. The study yields very interesting results but still suffers from some weaknesses, especially concerning the endogenization of final demand which is so important for quantifying the compensation effects. The authors were not able to estimate the impact of technological change on the export and import (substitution) performance of the West German economy (a shortcoming which due to the higher shares of exports and imports is more severe than in the Leontief–Duchin study for the US). The model also does not adequately deal with (relative) prices and income distribution, and thus with the role of wage flexibility in order to equilibrate supply and demand in the labour market. Two important compensation arguments therefore are not fully investigated: the increased export demand resulting from a higher price and non-price international competitiveness of the innovating economy and the neo-classical factor-substitution argument.

CONCLUSION

Even the most advanced empirical studies demonstrate how difficult it is to quantify the employment consequences of new technologies for a dynamic open economy which will always experience a loss of jobs compensated simultaneously to some degree by new employment opportunities in the process of economic growth and structural change. Short-run employment effects have to be distinguished from long-run effects, just as effects at the micro-level from those at the macro-level or direct from indirect effects. In contrast to direct effects which can be observed (especially at the micro-level), it is extremely difficult and methodologically complex to quantify the indirect effects for the economy as a whole.[18] It is precisely these indirect effects of the introduction of new technologies, of course, which are so important and which have been at the centre of the compensation controversy since Ricardo's analysis of the machinery problem. However, no economist of any stature should suggest that the compensation mechanism always operates in a painless and automatic manner.

NOTES

1. Smith's analysis sounds remarkably modern in this respect, since it refers to Verdoorn's law. Even more, the very nature of the underlying cumulative causation mechanism causes us to think that output, employment and productivity growth may be jointly determined.
2. See Smith (1976, pp. 783–4).
3. Chapter XIX 'Is the Introduction of Machines into Manufactures prejudicial to the Interest of a State, or hurtful to Population?' (Steuart, 1966, pp. 121–5).
4. The theory that technological unemployment is at best a 'transient evil', because innovations bring about price reductions and the expansion of output, i.e. under perfect competition compensatory adjustment processes are automatically generated, has been clearly stated for the first time by Say (1821, Ch. VII) and McCulloch (1821, see also 1864, Part I, Ch. VII).
5. For a more detailed comparison see Kalmbach and Kurz (1986).
6. See the section on 'The influence of technical inventions on rent and wages' in Wicksell (1934, pp. 133–44).
7. For a critical evaluation of Wicksell's basic objection to Ricardo's analysis see Neisser (1990, pp. 150–63).
8. See the contributions in Baranzini and Scazzieri (1990) and Halevi, Laibman and Nell (1992).
9. For an analysis of the 'late phase' of the traverse and the problem of convergence see Nardini (1990; 1993).
10. For a more detailed discussion of Hicks's investigation of the Ricardo machinery effect see Hagemann (1994).
11. See Hicks (1973, Ch. VIII).
12. See Lowe (1976) and Hagemann (1992) for a precise inspection of the traverse.
13. Lowe's and Hicks's emphasis was on the rigidities which existing capital structures and work in process flows impose on the dynamics of transformation. A similarly important theme is the explicit specification of the rigidities and potentialities of a given stock of human capabilities; skill structures and the resource- and time-consuming process of transforming existing and evolving new skills impose a similar rigidity constraint on the transformation of a productive system as a given stock of capital goods; the difference, however, is the inherent ability of the same human producer to acquire new skills and thus advance the productive potential of the productive system. Capital goods, on the other hand, have to be exchanged with new capital goods or at least combined with new complementary production elements to achieve a similar result.
14. For greater details see Hagemann (1990, pp. 164–7) and Baranzini and Scazzieri (1990, pp. 227–324).
15. See Austrian Institute of Economic Research (1981).
16. See the survey on the 'Meta Study' project given by Matzner, Schettkat and Wagner (1990).

17. See Kalmbach and Kurz (1990).
18. See also Cooper and Clark (1982), OECD (1982) and Whitley and Wilson (1982).

REFERENCES

Austrian Institute of Economic Research (1981), *Mikroelektronik, Anwendungen, Verbreitung und Auswirkungen am Beispiel Österreichs*, Vienna and New York: Springer-Verlag.
Baranzini, M. and Scazzieri, R. (1990) (eds), *The economic theory of structure and change*, Cambridge: Cambridge University Press.
Blattner, N. (1981), 'Labour Displacement by Technological Change? A Preliminary Survey of the Case of Microelectronics', *Rivista Internazionale di Scienze Economiche e Commerciali*, vol. 28, pp. 422–48.
Cooper, C.M. and Clark, J. (1982), *Employment, Economics and Technology: The Impact of Technical Change on the Labour Market*, Brighton: Wheatsheaf.
Edler, D. (1990), *Ein dynamisches Input-Output-Modell zur Abschätzung der Auswirkungen ausgewählter neuer Technologien auf die Beschäftigung in der Bundesrepublik Deutschland*, Berlin: Duncker and Humblot.
Gourvitch, A. (1940), *Survey of Economic Theory on Technological Change and Employment*, Philadelphia, reprint, New York 1966: Augustus M. Kelley.
Hagemann, H. (1990), 'The structural theory of economic growth', in Baranzini and Scazzieri, pp. 144–71.
Hagemann, H. (1992) 'Traverse Analysis in a Post-Classical Model', in Halevi, Laibman and Nell, pp. 235–63.
Hagemann, H. (1994), 'Employment and Machinery', in H. Hagemann and O.F. Hamouda (eds), *The Legacy of Hicks*, London: Routledge, pp. 200–224.
Halevi, J., Laibman, D. and Nell, E.J. (1992) (eds), *Beyond the Steady State. A Revival of Growth Theory*, London: Macmillan.
Hicks, J. (1973), *Capital and Time*, Oxford: Clarendon Press.
Hicks, J. (1977), *Economic Perspectives. Further Essays on Money and Growth*, Oxford: Clarendon Press.
Kähler, A. (1933), *Die Theorie der Arbeiterfreisetzung durch die Maschine*, Greifswald: Julius Abel.
Kalmbach, P. and Kurz, H.D. (1986), 'Economic Dynamics and Innovation: Ricardo, Marx and Schumpeter on Technological Change and Unemployment', in H.J. Wagener and J.W. Drukker (eds), *The Economic Law of Motion of Modern Society. A Marx-Keynes-Schumpeter Centennial*, Cambridge: Cambridge University Press, pp. 71–92.
Kalmbach, P. and Kurz, H.D. (1990), 'Micro-Electronics and Employment: A Dynamic Input-Output Study of the West German Economy', *Structural Change and Economic Dynamics*, vol. 1, pp. 371–86.
Lederer, E. (1938), *Technical Progress and Unemployment. An enquiry into the obstacles to economic expansion.* Geneva: International Labour Office.
Leontief, W. and Duchin, F. (1986), *The Future Impact of Automation on Workers*, Oxford and New York: Oxford University Press.
Lowe, A. (1976), *The Path of Economic Growth*, Cambridge: Cambridge University Press.
Marx, K. (1869), *Capital, Vol. I*, London 1954: Lawrence & Wishart.
Matzner, E., Schettkat, R. and Wagner, M. (1990), 'Labour Market Effects of New Technology', *Futures*, vol. 22, pp. 687–709.

McCulloch, J.R. (1821), 'The Opinions of Messrs. Say, Sismondi and Malthus on the Effects of Machinery and Accumulation, Stated and Examined' in *Edinburgh Review*, vol. 79, pp. 102–23.

McCulloch, J.R. (1864), *The Principles of Political Economy*, 5th ed., Edinburgh: Adam and Charles Black, reprinted New York 1965: Augustus M. Kelley.

Mill, J. S. (1848), *Principles of Political Economy*, reprint 1976, Fairfield: Augustus M. Kelley.

Nardini, F. (1990), 'Cycle-Trend Dynamics in a Fixwage Neo-Austrian Model of Traverse', *Structural Change and Economic Dynamics*, vol. 1, pp. 165–94.

Nardini, F. (1993), 'Traverse and Convergence in the Neo-Austrian Model: The case of a Distributive Shock', *Structural Change and Economic Dynamics*, vol. 4, pp. 105–25.

Neisser, H. (1942),. '"Permanent" Technological Unemployment', *American Economic Review*, vol. 32, pp. 50–71.

Neisser, H. (1990), 'The Wage Rate and Employment in Market Equilibrium', *Structural Change and Economic Dynamics*, vol. 1, pp. 141–63.

OECD (1982), *Micro-Electronics, Robotics and Jobs*, Paris: OECD.

Pasinetti, L.L. (1981), *Structural Change and Economic Growth. A Theoretical Essay on the Dynamics of the Wealth of Nations*, Cambridge: Cambridge University Press.

Ricardo, D. (1951), *On the Principles of Political Economy and Taxation* (first ed. 1817; third ed. 1821), Vol. I of *Works and Correspondence of David Ricardo*, edited by P. Sraffa with the collaboration of M. Dobb, Cambridge: Cambridge University Press.

Say, J.-B. (1821), *A Treatise on Political Economy or the Production, Distribution and Consumption of Wealth*, reprint New York 1971: Augustus M. Kelley.

Schumpeter, J.A. (1954), *History of Economic Analysis*, London: Allen & Unwin.

Smith, A. (1776), *An Inquiry into the Nature and Causes of the Wealth of Nations*, Oxford 1976: Oxford University Press.

Sraffa, P. (1951), 'Introduction' in *The Works and Correspondence of David Ricardo*, vol. I, Cambridge: Cambridge University Press, pp. xiii–lxii.

Steuart, J. (1767), *An Inquiry into the Principles of Political Oeconomy*, Vol. I, ed. by A.S. Skinner, Edinburgh and London 1966: Oliver & Boyd.

Stoneman, P. (1983), *The Economic Analysis of Technological Change*, Oxford: Oxford University Press.

Whitley, J.D. and Wilson R.A. (1982), 'Quantifying the Employment Effects of Microelectronics', *Futures*, vol. 14, pp. 486–95.

Wicksell, K. (1906), *Lectures on Political Economy*, vol. I, London 1934: Routledge & Kegan Paul.

3. Assessing the costs of inflation and unemployment

Thomas R. Michl*

> Our strategy continues to be centered on moving toward, and ultimately reaching, stable prices, that is, price levels sufficiently stable so that expectations of change do not become major factors in key economic decisions.
>
> Alan Greenspan, in Testimony to the House Committee on Banking, Finance, and Urban Affairs, 24 January 1989.

From 1979 to 1983, as monetary policy tightened and the unemployment rate in the US climbed from 5.8 per cent to 9.5 per cent, Paul Volker, the Chairman of the Federal Reserve Board, explained that the need to resist inflation after a second round of OPEC price increases necessitated this pain. Margaret Thatcher invoked the cost of inflation in similar fashion in the UK where, by the mid-1980s the unemployment rate rose to nearly 11 per cent, up from 4.0 per cent in 1979. In the US, over 10 million workers were idle in 1982; in the UK, over 3 million were without work by 1986.[1] The sheer number of people involved compel the question, was the game worth the candle?

This chapter examines the benefits of reducing the inflation rate from a range of 9–15 per cent (where it stood in the US and UK in 1979) to a lower range of 4–6 per cent (where it stood by 1990).[2] Even though these disinflations now lie in the distant past, they are the benchmarks used by central bankers, politicians and economists to justify current policies devoted to preventing inflation from rising to the levels of the 1970s. The danger of inflation is perhaps the most common excuse for policies which shrink from aggressively reducing unemployment. Many now believe that such timidity on the part of the monetary authorities (and perhaps the desire to drive inflation toward zero evident in the quotation above) contributed to the depth and length of the US recession in 1990–91 (Walsh, 1993).

* The author wishes to thank Philip Arestis, Elizabeth Lewis and Mike Marshall for their helpful suggestions, but accepts responsibility for all errors.

THE MODERN THEORY OF INFLATION AND UNEMPLOYMENT

Economists measure the cost of reducing inflation (as opposed to the cost of the inflation itself) by the sacrifice ratio, which is simply the extra unemployment that must be endured to cut inflation by one percentage point.

The sacrifice ratio is generally calculated from estimates of the expectations-augmented Phillips curve which forms the basis for modern theories of inflation and unemployment.

The Phillips curve relates the rate of inflation to the rate of unemployment, the expected rate of inflation, and the long-run equilibrium[3] rate of unemployment. According to this equation, given people's forecasts of the inflation rate, an increase in the unemployment rate will reduce the inflation rate. The standard Keynesian explanation is that lower demand for goods and labour creates disinflationary pressure. However, in the long run, people's forecasts of inflation will eventually be right and the economy will return to its equilibrium level of employment. Thus, the appropriate 'thought experiment' would start at a high-inflation equilibrium, with inflation perfectly anticipated. A restrictive monetary policy would then put the system through a period of disinflation, during which unemployment rises and inflationary expectations are readjusting. The experiment would end at a new equilibrium with low, anticipated inflation.

Economists find it useful to distinguish between the costs of anticipated and unanticipated inflation. From the Phillips curve model, it is clear that the costs of the anticipated inflation experienced in long-run equilibria are central to the policy debate.

Most researchers agree that the magnitude of the sacrifice ratio implied by the Phillips curve is around two or three in the US, meaning it takes about two or three 'point-years' of excess unemployment to eliminate each percentage point of inflation. (One 'point-year' occurs when the unemployment rate stays one percentage point above its long-run equilibrium for one year, or stays one-half percentage point above for two years, and so on.) This range is consistent with the Volker disinflation. Benjamin Friedman has calculated that from 1980 to 1987, the US economy cumulated 14.2 point years of excess unemployment, which created enough slack to lower inflation from 9.0 in 1980 to 3.2 in 1987 (Friedman, 1988, Table 3). Thus the sacrifice ratio, 2.4, falls comfortably within the consensus range.

Calculating a similar sacrifice ratio for the UK economy is complicated by the presence of hysteresis effects, which raise the equilibrium rate of unemployment (whether temporarily or permanently is in dispute) during the period of disinflation. One recent study of Phillips curves by three leading specialists (Layard et al., 1991) suggests that the sacrifice ratio is of the same order of magnitude in the UK as in the US, and that for both countries it is considerably higher than for comparable nations.[4] They also find the UK (but not the US) to be plagued by hysteresis effects which help explain why British inflation stubbornly refused to fall during the 1980s despite very high unemployment rates.[5]

Therefore, we must conclude that wringing inflation out of the system, (a towel metaphor much favoured by bankers and economists) is painful. While economists have speculated about a painless, cold-turkey disinflation, the actual experience confirms that this is not likely.

The question we can now state more precisely is, assuming that there exists a unique long run equilibrium rate of unemployment,[6] do the benefits of reducing the inflation rate by a specific amount justify the social costs of excess unemployment which must be endured throughout the disinflationary period? An allied question is whether the costs of inflation justify a conservative approach to job creation during economic downturns. Because most writers have used 10 per cent inflation as a standard of comparison, and because policy discussions treat the high inflation of the 1970s as unacceptably high, it remains relevant to ask what price we should stand ready to pay to avoid a return to the bad old days when inflation was this high.

THE UNAVOIDABLE COSTS OF INFLATION

Many of the most significant costs result from a failure to adapt financial institutions and tax codes to inflation; these costs are, in principle, avoidable. There is some merit, therefore, in starting with the costs of inflation which are hardest to avoid. These unavoidable costs are best studied at a high level of abstraction in an ideal economy with complete indexation of financial contracts and tax codes.[7]

The two most important unavoidable costs of inflation are shoe leather costs and menu costs. Shoe leather costs are associated with the added financial transactions that agents in a high-inflation setting undertake. One candidate theory for the demand for money, the Tobin–Baumol inventory theory, is particularly clear on this point. In this theory, the cost of holding money is the nominal interest foregone (that money earns no interest is in fact a critical assumption to the shoe leather argument). People deposit their pay cheques in an interest-bearing account and make regular trips to the bank to extract money over the pay period. They use the frequency of these trips to economize on cash; more frequent trips permit them to keep a larger average balance in an interest-bearing account. Higher inflation and interest rates will therefore induce more frequent trips to the bank, which is the source of that curious term, shoe leather costs.

More precisely, suppose that the long run rate of inflation rises (say because the authorities accommodate a supply shock), and that money is superneutral[8] with respect to the real interest rate, which is simply the nominal interest rate minus the inflation rate. The nominal interest rate will therefore rise by exactly the increase in the inflation rate. Higher inflation will induce more frequent trips to the bank, and we can measure its costs by the inconvenience this imposes upon society.

More generally, the demand for money arises from other useful services of money besides the means of payment function; money, for example, is a store of value. As Martin J. Bailey (1956) showed, the costs of inflation can be measured from the demand curve for money, using the microeconomic theory of consumer surplus. The change in the area under the demand curve for money when interest and inflation rates drop approximates this welfare gain, and because of its geometric shape economists speak of the 'money triangle' and the triangle costs of inflation.[9]

If we assume a constant elasticity of demand for money, we can generate a back-of-the-envelope calculation of triangle costs. The Tobin–Baumol model predicts an elasticity of 0.5; most estimates in the US put the elasticity of demand for highly liquid monetary aggregates (like M1 and its components) in a range of 0.15 to 0.25 (Goldfield, 1976). An appropriate monetary aggregate for estimates of the 'triangle costs' under the demand curve is the stock of high-powered money consisting of currency and bank reserves. In 1990, this stock stood at $293 billion in the US. Using 0.25 for the elasticity of money demand, the cost of a 10 per cent inflation comes out to be $7.28 billion, or around 0.13 per cent of the $5.5 trillion GDP.[10]

Many economists have been impressed by the magnitude of the triangle costs of inflation. For example, noted MIT economist Stanley Fischer calculates the welfare loss associated with 10 per cent inflation to be 0.3 per cent of GDP[11] in 1980, and comments that compared to other inefficiencies 'the money triangle at a ten per cent inflation rate is large in the distortions league' (Fischer, 1981a). Similar calculations for the US lie in the same region. Garfinkel (1989), using a broader monetary aggregate, M1, estimates the burden of a 5 per cent inflation rate at 0.38 of GDP. Lucas comes up with 0.9 per cent of GDP (for 15 per cent inflation), and observes that 'as deadweight losses go. [this] is a sizeable number' (Lucas, 1981).

For the UK, Minford and Hilliard calculate a range of welfare costs from 0.78 per cent of GDP for a 10 per cent inflation to 5.28 per cent of GDP for a 30 per cent inflation (Minford and Hilliard, 1978 p. 114). Aside from their similarity to the US figures, these numbers put the shoe leather costs into a common sense perspective. Even at rates of inflation as high as 10 per cent, these costs, while non-negligible, seem quite small. Only at very high rates of inflation do people become sensitive to the loss in purchasing power that befalls any cash they may own, and take costly steps to minimize its use.

According to the logic of using the consumer surplus to measure the costs of inflation, the optimal rate of inflation is that which brings the nominal interest rate to zero. Only then will the area under the demand curve for money be at its maximum. With a constant real interest rate, r, the optimal rate of inflation will simply be $-r$. Milton Friedman (1969) is credited with this observation.

Friedman's theory that the optimal rate of inflation is negative considers only the benefits of holding more money, but there are also costs associated with the loss of the inflation tax. Because the government enjoys a monopoly on the creation of money, it can finance part of its operations through seigniorage. An important part of seigniorage is the inflation tax, or the loss in purchasing power that befalls non-interest-bearing money. A reduction in inflation therefore forces the government to make up the lost revenue by using other taxes. In a bold argument, Edmund Phelps (1973) proposes that the inflation tax may under some conditions turn out to be more efficient (less distorting) than the taxes used to replace it. By this reasoning, the government's optimal mix of taxes should include an inflation tax, and the optimal rate of inflation need not be negative or even zero. Attempts to measure the efficiency of competing taxes, however, do not generally support this position. An argument in the same spirit is that the inflation tax might prove useful as a way to tax the underground economy.

The second unavoidable cost of inflation results from the fact that there are costs associated with changing prices at regular intervals. These menu costs are harder to quantify than are shoe leather costs, but they are generally thought to be small. Indeed, in modern New Keynesian models, it is precisely because these costs are small that they are thought to have such large real effects: firms do not bother changing prices when demand changes but when all firms operate this way, the economy becomes sensitive to small demand shocks. Unemployment (a large social cost) can thus be attributed to small menu costs.

Menu costs are surely important in very high and hyperinflations that lie outside the limitations of this chapter. Consider, for example, the inconvenience of having pay phones rendered inoperative by inflation-induced changes in the coinage, as is said to have occurred in Mexico during the 1980s. But for the moderate inflations under consideration here these costs are unimpressive.

Since menu costs are incurred with any change in prices, they militate against Friedman's argument that the optimal rate of inflation is negative. But, even more interestingly, menu costs form the basis of an argument by Leif Danziger (1988) that the optimal rate of inflation is positive. Monopolistic firms that have fixed costs of adjusting prices will not change prices continuously in an inflation, but rather will set prices above their target real price, and then let inflation erode the real price until this cycle begins again. Let the price firms would choose with no inflation be Z. Recall that under monopolistic conditions, this price will result in monopolistic profits and economic inefficiency. Under moderate inflation, firms set price at S (above Z) and let inflation erode it to s. Because profits in the future are discounted, the extra profits during the first part of the pricing period (for example, $S - Z$) will be exceeded by the reduced profits earned in the last part, $Z - s$. Therefore, on average the real price will be below Z. Moderate inflation thus acts as a monopoly abatement programme, and it actually increases social welfare.

Several central banks, for instance those of New Zealand and Canada, have adopted an official target of zero inflation, but they are not necessarily on solid theoretical ground. For both menu and shoe leather costs, economic theory does not jump to the conclusion that the optimal rate of inflation must be zero just because it is costly to change prices.[12]

These unavoidable costs of inflation must seem abstract to the average citizen. Yet they are relevant to inflationary policy, for a society with a moderate rate of inflation has a choice between disinflating and adapting its financial institutions to inflation, through indexation for example. The argument against adaptation hinges on the unavoidable costs of inflation.

There are at least three important qualifications that limit how seriously we should regard the welfare calculations on offer. First, the analysis is strictly 'partial equilibrium', assuming that money is superneutral in every respect but its effect on money demand for example. But if there are general equilibrium effects, it is likely that other real variables, notably the real interest rate, would also change. So the calculation must be taken as purely illustrative, not definitive. Second, the analysis of shoe leather costs assumes that interest is not paid on money, yet there is no inherent reason why it cannot. Indeed, a host of financial innovations (such as credit cards and interest-bearing cheque accounts) have allowed consumers to economize on their use of cash. Third, the analysis of menu costs assumes that there are no ways to overcome the costs of price changes, yet this is clearly false. Firms could post price rules rather than the prices themselves, as is done, for example, by music stores when they put coded letters on their CDs and tapes.[13]

If we ended here, it would be hard to explain why anyone should care whether the inflation rate were 2 or 12 per cent. Indeed, the terms shoe leather and menu costs are sometimes all it takes for a skilful lecturer to mock the argument against inflation. But there are other, more impressive costs to inflation, which are apparent in the imperfectly indexed economies that we in the real world inhabit.

AVOIDABLE COSTS OF STEADY, ANTICIPATED INFLATIONS

The most important costs of inflation in practice are those associated with the failure of governments and financial institutions to adapt fully. Some important economic institutions have adapted well to inflation. Trade unions in the US, for example, began to include cost-of-living escalators in their contracts with greater frequency as the inflation rate rose after 1960. But many economic institutions are not so easy to inflation-proof, notably the tax system and mortgage loans.

The most obvious effect of inflation on taxes occurs when a progressive tax system lacks indexation. Inflation pushes everyone into a higher tax bracket, even though their real before-tax income stays constant. In the US prior to the Tax Reform Act of 1986, this process of 'bracket creep' was suppressed by a series of sporadic tax cuts, beginning with the Kennedy/Johnson round in 1964. But the Tax Reform Act of 1986 indexed the rate structure automatically.

The Tax Reform Act left standing several holdovers from non-inflationary times. The most important interactions of inflation with the tax code are the taxation of nominal (rather than real) interest income and capital gains, the deductibility of interest for income and corporate taxes, and the use by corporations of historical accounting for inventories and depreciation allowances.

The taxation of nominal interest affects both the after-tax returns to savers and the after-tax cost of funds to borrowers. When the before-tax real interest rate, r, is constant, the effective tax on real interest income rises as the rate of inflation rises. To see this, consider the formula for the real after-tax rate of return on saving, r_a, with an average tax rate t, or

$$r_a = i\,(1 - t) - \pi$$

If real interest were taxed, by contrast, the part of the nominal interest rate equal to inflation would be exempt on grounds that it simply keeps the principal balance from eroding with inflation.[14]

An individual in the 28 per cent tax bracket earning nominal interest at 6 per cent under a 3 per cent inflation rate will earn an after-tax rate equal to 1.32 per cent. In the absence of inflation the same individual earns 2.16 per cent (holding constant the before-tax real rate), or roughly two-thirds more.

The macroeconomic effects of this relationship are not clear. There have been attempts, notably by Martin Feldstein (1983), to explain the decline in the US saving rate during the 1970s as a response to the inflation-induced rise in effective tax rates on capital income. Yet most studies of saving in the US have concluded that the interest-sensitivity of personal saving is negligible (cf. Hausman and Poterba, 1987).

Even if saving is interest-inelastic, this inflation-induced increase in taxation can have welfare effects, as Stanley Fischer (1981a) has argued. He considers a simple two-period life cycle model. People work in period one, save out of their wages, and live off savings in period two. A decline in the return (after tax) on saving thus reduces their consumption in period two. Fischer calculates that the welfare costs of this reduction in the living standards of retirees would be around 0.7 per cent of GDP for a 10 per cent inflation. His calculations assume that the period is 20 years, and that the tax distortions are permanent over the entire period (meaning that no changes in the tax code occur). Thus, it is not clear whether this calculation is an argument against inflation or in favour of rewriting the tax code to remove the distortion.[15] It is clear that this putative cost is not on a par with the triangle costs, which are not so easily avoided.

A similar distortion arises from the taxation of nominal, rather than real, capital gains. Someone whose stock- (share-)holdings have doubled in value over a period when the price level has also doubled would pay tax on the capital gain, even though it represents no real change in net worth. Someone whose stock doubled in value in one year would (assuming low inflation) experience a substantial increase in net worth, and would quite rightly pay tax on it.[16]

On the other side of this coin, inflation reduces the cost of borrowed funds when, as in the US, interest expenses are deductible from taxable income. In this case, the formula above measures the after-tax cost of funds. By this means, inflation makes home ownership more desirable. (Deductibility of interest also affects the rate of taxation of corporate income, as we discuss below.)

Nonetheless, home owners are hurt by inflation under the prevailing mortgage instrument with level payments. Inflation obviously erodes the real value of a level nominal payment over time. To compensate for this, lenders must set the payment at a high level, so that it gives them the appropriate real payment on average over the life of the mortgage. This tendency for inflation to tilt the real payment stream toward the present makes home ownership more difficult. For example, fewer first-time buyers will qualify for mortgage loans under the standard procedures used by banks, such as maximum payment–income ratios. Again, this cost of inflation can be attenuated by changing the features of the financial instrument. Graduated payment mortgages, in which payments rise over time, take some of the pressure off home owners in the early years of ownership.

Thus for home owners, inflation has offsetting effects. While it reduces the after-tax cost of funds, it also increases the real payment in the early years of home ownership. Some evidence drawn from the inflationary decade from 1970 to 1980 has concluded that on balance, inflation tends to depress the housing industry, dampening the construction of new residential housing (cf. Hibbs, 1987, pp. 111–17).[17]

Inflation affects the returns to equity ownership of corporate capital in complex ways. The corporate income tax is paid on profits after nominal interest expenses have been deducted; this tends to favour corporate capital income for the same reason that it favours home owners. On the other hand, profits are often calculated by deducting expenses of depreciation and materials using historical cost accounting. Historical accounting methods ignore the rise in the value of capital stock and warehoused inputs during inflations; they understate costs and overstate taxable income. Some of this distortion is built into the tax codes, such as their failure to permit corporations to adjust depreciation expense for inflation. Some of the distortion seems to be the result of corporate accounting practices themselves, such as the surprisingly extensive use of FIFO rather than LIFO methods for inventories in the US.[18] During the inflationary 1970s, not surprisingly, corporations shifted toward use of LIFO. Yet by 1982, only 35 per cent of manufacturing firms reported using LIFO (US Department of Commerce, 1986, Table 2-3c).

The effect of inflation on stockholders can be understood with the help of a model. Suppose that every extra percentage point of inflation raises taxable profits per dollar of capital stock by x, and thus reduces after-tax profits by t, the statutory tax rate, times x. Further, suppose that each share represents ownership of one dollar worth of capital stock, measured at its true replacement cost. In addition, let the corporation hold debts equal to b dollars per dollar of capital, with an interest rate i, and non-interest-bearing monetary assets equal to c dollars per dollar of capital. Inflation reduces the value of both liabilities and assets. Thus, profits distributed to shareholders form the base for their after-tax rate of return, p_a, given by

$$p_a = (1 - t)\, p_b - (1 - t)bi - tx\pi + (b - c)\, \pi$$

where p_b is the before-tax rate of profit on corporate capital and π is inflation. Differentiating with respect to inflation, and assuming that both the before-tax profit rate and the real rate of interest are constant (so $di/d\pi = 1$), we get

$$dp_a/d\pi = (tb - c) - tx$$

Thus the direction of the effect of inflation on shareholders' returns cannot be specified *a priori*; it depends on the size of three parameters, of which x is the toughest to pin down. In 1992, non-financial corporations in the US had a capital stock of $4693 billion, debt of $2330 billion, and monetary assets of $152 billion (Board of Governors, 1993). Assuming a corporate tax rate of 35 per cent, $dp_a/d\pi = 0.141 - 0.35x$. Thus, x must exceed 0.40 for inflation to erode the returns to shareholders. Otherwise, the advantages that inflation bestows upon debtors will dominate, and inflation will actually benefit the owners of corporations. Some calculations of x for the 1970s place it in a range from 0.46 to 0.53 (Feldstein, 1982, p. 158), just large enough to make inflation a nuisance to shareholders. A 10 per cent inflation would reduce the rate of return on equity by a modest 0.2–0.4 percentage points. But during the 1970s, when corporate debt was much smaller (b equalled 0.30 in 1977 compared to 0.50 in 1992), the bite taken out of the returns to equity by inflation was more substantial.

The significance of this distortion in the returns to capital caused by inflation would clearly be that by reducing the incentive to save and invest, inflation might retard the long-run growth of an economy. Fender (1990, pp. 58–64) provides an excellent survey of the theoretical relationship between inflation, saving and investment. We shall return to the claim that inflation generally reduces investment when we examine the empirical evidence concerning the long-run effects of inflation.

To conclude this section, we have seen that inflation does indeed have widespread costs which arise from the nature of the tax system and the financial system. It is not then surprising that despite the fairly small costs of inflation at the highest level of abstraction (namely, in the last section), public opinion polls and surveys routinely show the average person to be highly averse to inflation.[19]

We can also see that these costs are not spread evenly over the population but rather are focused on the wealthiest segments of society. Inflation, in brief, creates a natural lobby for disinflationary policy because of its interactions with the tax system. To the extent that the wealthiest citizens, who depend on interest and capital income substantially more than the average citizen, are also disproportionately represented in the political process (and who would seriously dispute that?), this creates a very strong bias toward disinflationary economic policies. Precisely because disinflation is painful (with the non-wealthy suffering the most, as we shall see), we are persuaded of the wisdom of a tax code which indexes interest income, interest expenses and capital gains.

UNANTICIPATED CHANGES IN THE INFLATION RATE

When the inflation rate changes unexpectedly, it imposes costs and bestows benefits upon parties to contracts that were premised on the erroneous forecast. Since there are winners and losers, the costs of unanticipated inflation are private, not social. However, uncertainty about the inflation rate will alter people's behaviour as they try to avoid being caught by surprise. The social costs associated with these alterations are discussed in the next section.

When the inflation rate changes unexpectedly after wages and salaries have been set, that obviously reduces purchasing power. To protect against these reductions, union contracts in the US frequently contain cost-of-living allowances (COLAs), although these rarely provide complete protection because they rely on a 'pennies per point of inflation' formula. Because of COLAs and because of the frequency with which wages are set, unexpected changes in inflation impose few costs on workers in the US. It is also possible for an unanticipated wage-push inflation to surprise employers and squeeze profits, as appeared to happen in many industrial nations during the late 1960s and early 1970s (cf. Armstrong et al., 1991).

People on fixed (non-indexed) incomes, such as recipients of welfare, social security and pensions, are often said to suffer most from inflation. Over the last two decades, the main welfare systems in the US, AFDC (Aid to Families with Dependent Children) and Food Stamps, have indeed failed to keep abreast of inflation, and real benefits have fallen. But it is not clear that this can be classified as a cost of inflation, since it reflects a conscious policy choice by legislators who have neglected to raise nominal benefits. Social security benefits, by contrast, have been indexed to the Consumer Price Index since the early 1970s, and have not suffered erosion by inflation.

Private pension plans are slightly more complex. For defined-contribution plans, pension benefits are a form of capital income, and the earlier discussion would apply. For defined-benefit plans (which appear to be the majority) benefits are tied to earnings in the last several years of service. Thus these plans are effectively indexed up until retirement (since wages generally adjust to inflation), but then become vulnerable to unexpected inflations. While some pension sponsors have experimented with increases to cover inflation, most pensions are fixed at retirement.

Probably the most significant effect of unanticipated inflation is that it erodes the value of liabilities, redistributing wealth from creditors (lenders) to debtors (borrowers). A one-year debt contracted under the assumption of zero inflation will have its real value reduced by inflation. One dollar borrowed today will only be worth $(1 - \pi)$ dollars in one year; borrowers gain by paying off their debt with cheaper dollars. If inflation is expected, the terms of the loan will include an inflation premium to compensate the lender for the inflation-induced erosion of principal.

Measuring the social cost or benefit of a redistribution of wealth, such as one caused by inflation, lies outside the limits of conventional welfare theory, which can say little about redistributions induced by unanticipated inflations, or about policy efforts to reverse them.

Studies of the effects of inflation on the distribution of income and wealth in the US have established the size of many of the effects discussed in this and previous sections. On balance the costs of inflation appear to fall preponderantly on the wealthiest households. One oft-cited study by Joseph Minarik (1979) uses the Brookings Institutions MERGE data set to conduct simulation studies of the effects of inflation on income, benefits and taxes in the 1970s. Minarik reports simulations for a comprehensive income measure which includes the all-important balance sheet changes. The lowest incomes actually grow slightly because, for example, of gains associated with home ownership. For high income earners in the top 20 per cent of the population, by contrast, inflation generates substantial losses. A modest 2 per cent inflation causes a 17 per cent reduction in income for those in the $200–500 000 range (the upper 1 per cent of households). Minarik finds that the losses to inflation for middle income households were offset by the benefits of mortgaged home ownership discussed earlier. If this study were repeated for the 1990s, it would need to incorporate such changes as the indexation of the income tax and the growing use of adjustable rate mortgages, which reduce the redistribution of wealth between lenders and borrowers. While other studies, notably Bach and Stephenson (1974) have reached different conclusions about the effects of inflation on the poorest, all have found that wealthy households experience substantial losses from inflation.

Arthur Burns, former Chairman of the Federal Reserve Board, was therefore wrong when he said that 'there can be little doubt that poor people, or people of modest means generally, are the chief sufferers of inflation.' Quite the contrary, inflation hurts the wealthy, especially if it is unanticipated. It is not surprising that in opinion polls, aversion to inflation tends to rise with income, a fact stressed by Hibbs (1987). While we cannot ignore the innocent bystanders like pensioners, it does not help the cause of good policy to deny who benefits from disinflation.

THE COSTS OF UNCERTAINTY ABOUT INFLATION

Uncertainty over the rate of inflation itself and inflation-induced uncertainty about relative prices[20] are both potentially costly to society. The claim that high inflation is inherently more uncertain has been advanced by the monetarist Milton Friedman (1977) in his Nobel Laureate address and by the Keynesian economist Arthur Okun (1971), an indication of broad support. Okun points out that there is a strong correlation across industrial countries between the inflation rate and the standard deviation of the inflation rate. Subsequent research both qualified his finding (it has been shown to be less strong in the 1950s than the 1960s) and confirmed it (some recent evidence is presented below). Much controversy has centred on whether more variable inflation is indeed more uncertain, and on whether causality runs from inflation to variability (as Okun and Friedman maintain), from variability to inflation, or from some common third factor to both inflation and its variability.

Showing that variable inflation is more unpredictable has proved surprisingly difficult. Okun's correlation merely establishes that high inflation tends to be variable, but not that economic agents have more difficulty predicting a high variable rate than a low steady one. What is clearly needed is some method for separating the variability of inflation into its predictable and unpredictable components.

One method for doing this has been to use the variation in inflation forecasts over time across respondents in surveys. Cukierman (1984), using the Livingston survey of inflationary expectations and the Michigan Survey Research Center's consumer survey, found that there is indeed a significant positive correlation between the variance of inflation in the US (measured as a moving variance) and the variance of these cross-sectional forecasts. Again, one can question whether the amount of disagreement among forecasters measures the uncertainty that they each perceive.

It is also possible to question why the cross-sectional variance in surveys correlates with the variance of the inflation rate. Batchelor and Orr (1991) use the Gallup Poll survey of consumers in the UK, and find that inflation uncertainty is indeed correlated with inflation variability, with an $r^2 = 0.69$. They then estimate an econometric model of the determinants of inflation uncertainty, and find that inflation variability plays 'little or no part in the explanation of movements in inflation uncertainty over time' (p. 1393) controlling for other factors. The factors which do affect uncertainty turn out to be policy-related variables (the composition of government) or exogenous variables (notably oil price shocks). Thus the high correlation must be due to the presence of a factor common to inflation uncertainty and variability.

Another set of studies uses the forecast error from a model of inflation as a proxy for the degree of inflation uncertainty. The obvious objection to these studies is that they are only valid assuming people are using that particular model of inflation to generate their forecasts. Most of these studies have found that inflation uncertainty does not increase with the mean inflation rate; for a representative example, see Jansen (1989).

The burden of proof appears to lie with those who insist that high inflation is inherently more uncertain. Nonetheless, even conceding that high inflation is more unpredictable, several alternative explanations could compete for our attention. For example, the association could be due to policy responses to exogenous price shocks or it could be caused endogenously by the 'time consistent' behaviour of the central bank itself. Only in the latter case could a causal relationship between inflation and uncertainty be said to obtain.

Taylor (1981) proposes a model of the first type, in which inflation results from exogenous supply shocks which are partially accommodated by the monetary authority. His model introduces a nominal rigidity – overlapping two-year wage and price contracts – into an otherwise quite classical macroeconomic model with rational expectations. Because of the exogenous shocks, there is a trade-off between output stability and price stability. Thus a central bank which is reluctant to accept the declines in output and employment that result from an exogenous price shock could follow a more accommodating policy. In this case, the variation in the exogenous price would be mirrored by inflation. Countries which value low and stable unemployment would typically show both a high and variable rate of inflation. Owing to the inherently unpredictable nature of exogenous price shocks, the variability of inflation would be hard to forecast, which would account for the tendency for survey respondents to disagree more when the inflation rate is high. Note that in this model greater uncertainty about inflation creates a benefit, in the form of more stable employment.

An alternative approach to uncertainty develops Milton Friedman's point that high inflation creates a temptation for policy makers to reverse course. This notion has been formalized by Ball (1992) in a game-theoretic model of 'time-consistent' inflation. In this type of model, inflation arises because there is a social welfare gain associated with reducing unemployment below its equilibrium level. In other words, there remains some involuntary unemployment even at the equilibrium unemployment rate. The central bank is unwilling to resist the temptation to reduce unemployment, even for only one year, by means of a temporary burst of inflation. Once the public realizes this, it will come to expect inflation. This type of inflation is labelled 'time-consistent' because the central bank is operating in a consistent way over time.

Ball's model adds two types of policy makers: Conservatives (C) who hate inflation and do not care about unemployment, and Liberals (L) who care about both. Moreover, the public does not know whether C or L are in power. When inflation is low, both C and L try to keep it low. But when inflation is high (due to exogenous shocks to the demand for money), C tries to disinflate while L is unwilling to suffer a recession. Thus 'high inflation creates uncertainty because the policy makers respond differently to the disinflation dilemma and the public does not know who will be in charge.' (Ball, 1992, pp. 372–73)

Within the stylized two period life-cycle model discussed earlier, an increase in uncertainty reduces the effective return on nominal assets, and this reduces the demand for consumption during retirement (which is financed out of savings accumulated during the first period). Fischer (1981a) estimates the welfare cost of a 10 per cent inflation rate using such a stylized model to be around 1 per cent of the relevant nominal assets. The relevant base should be an aggregate of 'outside assets' somewhere between the stock of high-powered money and the national debt. In 1981, Fischer observed that these stocks were $150 billion and $800 billion, implying a welfare loss from inflation of from $1.5 to $8 billion. These numbers range from 0.05 per cent to 0.26 per cent of GDP; recalculating the range for 1990 pushes the upper limit to 0.44 per cent. Minford and Hilliard's (1978) estimates for the UK differ in method but agree that a 10 per cent inflation imposes a cost of 0.25 per cent of GDP through uncertainty. While these estimates are in the same range as the unavoidable costs discussed earlier, they must be discounted because of the ambiguity we have seen surrounding the relationship between inflation and uncertainty.

THE PROOF OF THE PUDDING

A strong anti-inflation case would clearly be at hand if it could be shown that inflation retards economic growth. A recent feature article in *The Economist*, recognizing that rounding up the usual academic suspects like shoe leather costs is unpersuasive, goes on to emphasize that a main effect of inflation is uncertainty, 'the enemy of investment and growth' (*The Economist*, 1992, p. 23).

One might expect, then, to find a clear relationship between growth and either the level or the variance of inflation across countries. But, as *The Economist* concedes, the relationship is not particularly strong. In fact, for the period 1955–73, there is a positive correlation between inflation and growth in their sample of mainly industrialized countries. This difficulty in establishing that inflation is truly the enemy of growth comes as no surprise once one recalls that there are several episodes in which countries (including Japan, South Korea, Israel, Brazil and Turkey) have grown rapidly with relatively high inflation.

Economists have generated a vast literature on this subject, using cross-country regressions to establish a link between growth and a variety of factors related to policy, including inflation. Several studies have found that high inflation reduces growth, notably Kormendi and Meguire (1985) and DeGregorio (1992).

These studies have recently been scrutinized in a series of papers by Levine and Renelt (1992), Levine and Zervos (1993), and Stanners (1993). Table 3.1 sets out the relevant correlation coefficients from the former study, Which includes 119 countries over 1969–89. Recall that the correlation coefficient measures the degree of linear association between two variables, and has theoretical limits of zero (no correlation) and one (perfect correlation). The ambiguity of the relationship between inflation and growth seen above comes as no surprise in the light of the low correlations evident in Table 3.1. Further, it is clear from the strong and statistically significant relationship between inflation and its standard deviation that high inflation is indeed more variable, as discussed above. And it is also clear from the significant relationship between investment and growth that if uncertainty created by high inflation mattered as much as the inflation hawks assert, it could reduce the growth of output. But the correlations between inflation or its standard deviation and the investment share turn out to be the lowest values in the table. Levine and Renelt (1992) and Levine and Zervos (1993) evaluate the claim that inflation effects are strong in the context of a multivariate regression, with growth of per capita income the dependent variable, and any of several policy and control variables on the right-hand side. They use a technique called Extreme Bounds Analysis to examine if the asserted linkages are robust; that is, whether they remain statistically significant in a broad range of theoretically reasonable specifications.

Table 3.1   Correlations between inflation and growth

	Growth rate of GDP per capita	Investment share in GDP	Inflation rate	Standard deviation of inflation
Growth rate of GDP per capita	1.00	0.58[*]	–0.16	–0.14
Investment share in GDP		1.00	–0.04	–0.01
Inflation rate			1.00	0.97[*]
Standard deviation of inflation				1.00

Notes: [*] indicates significantly different from zero at 0.05 level. See text and original source for further description of underlying data.

Source: Levine and Renelt (1992), Table 4, p. 949.

A fragile relationship will thus not withstand a change in other policy variables (called Z variables) included in the regression. In both studies, inflation fails this test; any significant relation to growth is idiosyncratic. As Levine and Zervos sum up, their analysis

> ... shows that inflation is not significantly negatively correlated with long-run growth. More impressively, we could not find a combination of the Z variables that produced a significant negative association between growth and average inflation over the 1960–1989 period. Given the uncharacteristically unified view among economists and policy analysts that countries with high inflation rates should adopt policies to lower inflation in order to promote prosperity, the inability to find simple cross-country regressions supporting this contention is both surprising and troubling. (pp. 428–9)

If low inflation does not generate long-term growth, then the arguments in its favour must be based on its effects on the level of economic welfare recounted in the previous sections.

DO THE BENEFITS OF LOW INFLATION JUSTIFY THE COSTS OF ACHIEVING IT?

Recall that the level effects of inflation were seen to be small (less than 1 per cent of GDP for a 10 per cent inflation). For the US, the sacrifice ratio of around 2.5 point-years of unemployment for every one percentage point of inflation translates into a sacrifice of around 6 per cent of GDP per point of inflation.[21] Sticking to round numbers, let us consider a five-year plan for lowering inflation by 10 per cent. In each year, we must endure 5 per cent extra unemployment, sacrificing 12.5 per cent of GDP. Clearly, these sacrifices are an order of magnitude greater than the benefits of reducing inflation.

One could argue that the benefits of reduced inflation last indefinitely while the costs, in terms of sacrificed output, are temporary. To illustrate, assume that the cost of 10 per cent inflation is 0.5 per cent of GDP. Since the stream of benefits lasts indefinitely, it can be evaluated like a consol or a perpetuity. With GDP in the US at roughly $6 trillion, the present value of this stream at a discount rate of 2 per cent would amount to around $1.5 trillion, or 25 per cent of GDP.[22] With small changes in the estimated cost of inflation and a different discount rate (say, 0.75 and 1 per cent) we could easily justify disinflation as a sound social investment.

However, this calculation ignores the fact that the chief beneficiaries are future generations yet unborn while the sacrifices are being made by the living who might well ask what posterity ever did for them. Economists lack a convincing framework for handling this sort of intergenerational transfer. It is not clear what discount rate would be appropriate, or even if discounting can be defended on ethical grounds.

A more straightforward approach would be to tally up the costs and benefits to the generation making the sacrifice. Consider, for example, an average family in the US, with a median income of around $36 000, an average age near 35 and life expectancy of 75. Applying the output sacrifice ratio above, this household would have to forego about $22 500 in income over the five-year plan. The benefit to the family heads of wiping out a 10 per cent inflation for the rest of their lives discounts to a present value[23] of around $5000, hardly enough to justify the pain. Even using the more favourable assumptions (0.75 and 1 per cent for the cost of inflation and discount rate), and the present value of the benefit, $8900, falls well short of the sacrifice. At this discount rate the cost of 10 per cent inflation would need to approach 2 per cent of GDP (somewhat outside the range of the estimates reviewed above) before the disease becomes worse than the cure.

But how representative is this household? The calculation ignores the unequal incidence of the costs and benefits. We have already seen that the most significant benefits of inflation reduction accrue to the wealthiest households. What can be said about the incidence of unemployment and sacrificed income?

THE COSTS OF UNEMPLOYMENT

It is well known that unemployment falls heavily on a minority among the unemployed, who suffer long-term joblessness (Clark and Summers, 1979). More recently, Henry Farber (1993) has studied the incidence of job loss (lay-offs, plant closures, and other involuntary separations) in the last two recessions in the US (1982–83 and 1990–91). The average rate of job loss for men with less than 12 years of education (10.8 per cent) is well over twice that of men with 16 or more years (4.3 per cent). Similarly, young workers face substantially higher job loss rates than older workers. And among young men (under 40), the rate of job loss for non-whites is a third higher than that for whites.

Farber also shows that while unemployment continues to fall disproportionately on the young and poorly educated, the most recent recession in the US saw an increasing tendency for both older and more educated workers to suffer job loss compared to the earlier 1982 recession. College graduates were about 15 per cent more likely to lose their jobs in the 1990–91 period than in the 1982–83 period (Farber, 1993, p. 94). Most of this hardship was concentrated among older (40+) college-educated workers, whose chances of job loss went from about 4 in a 100 to 5 in a 100. There is some reality to the popular conception in the US that recessions have become more 'white-collar' affairs, but unemployment still falls harder on the least well off.

But while the incidence of unemployment is highly regressive, it is possible that the burden, in terms of lost income, is shared sufficiently to make the household above representative. If unemployment insurance (UI) and other social programmes replaced most of the lost income of the jobless, then everyone would share in the burden through the taxes that support these benefits. In the UK, the amount of lost income replaced by UI (the replacement ratio) is around 36 per cent, while in the US it is about 50 per cent (Layard et al., 1991, Table 1.5). But in the US, the replacement ratio overstates the degree to which the burdens are shared because only about one-third of the jobless receive UI. Many unemployed are new entrants, for example, who do not qualify for benefits. Even more disturbing, the coverage ratio has fallen dramatically during the 1980s because of tightened eligibility requirements for UI. In 1970, 99 per cent of job losers received UI, as opposed to only 72 per cent in 1991 (US President, 1993, Tables B-39 and B-40).

One way of measuring the degree to which the burden of unemployment is shared is to compare the fiscal cost of unemployment to the total output loss. The fiscal cost of unemployment refers to the increased spending and lost tax revenues which must be financed by taxes on the employed population. In the US, the Congressional Budget Office uses the rule of thumb that each 1 per cent rise in the unemployment rate sustained for five years raises cumulative spending by \$56 billion and reduces tax collections by \$201 billion (Congressional Budget Office, 1992, p. 110). Thus a sustained rise of 5 per cent unemployment would have a cumulative fiscal cost of \$1285 billion, which is only about one-third of the cumulative loss of output discussed above. This calculation suggests that two-thirds of the burden of unemployment is shouldered by the small minority who experience joblessness. Dawson (1992, p. 86) reports that about the same proportion of the output loss in the UK is borne by the unemployed.

Farber (1993) shows that the losses experienced by displaced workers extend beyond the direct loss of income during a spell of joblessness. Displaced workers are more likely to be re-employed part-time or at reduced hours, and even if they are fortunate enough to find a full-time replacement job, they tend to earn substantially less than in their previous job. Farber compares a sample of workers who have suffered displacement in the previous two years with a control group of workers not displaced. He finds that displaced workers' weekly earnings are about 11 per cent less than those of their counterparts, and that this income loss applies across the board to different age, demographic and educational groups.

All these patterns are reflected in the way unemployment and inflation affect the distribution of income. Using historical data in the US, Blank and Blinder (1986) estimate the effect of a sustained one point rise in either the unemployment or the inflation rate on the share of income going to each quintile of the population. A sustained 1 point rise in the inflation rate increases the share of income going to the bottom three quintiles by about 0.06 percentage points. A 1 per cent rise in unemployment reduces the share of income accruing to the lowest three quintiles by about 0.3 percentage points, with the poorest quintile shouldering about half this loss (p. 186).

Another dimension to the problem is that unemployment reduces well-being by adversely affecting public health. Harvey Brenner (1976) has observed that increases in the unemployment rate bring with them increased morbidity and mortality rates in the US. He estimates that a 1 per cent increase in the unemployment rate will lead to 37 000 deaths (20 000 from cardiovascular disease alone) if sustained over six years.

While Brenner's results have been widely cited, they have also been challenged; see the survey by Wagstaff (1985). In particular, his use of time-series regressions of mortality rates on unemployment has been criticized for inattention to the problem of non-stationarity (Søgaard 1992). Time-series regressions on data which are not stationary often reveal spurious correlations, which give the appearance of statistical significance. However, these criticisms do not establish that unemployment is not linked to health status. Significantly, studies employing other methodologies have found a causal link between joblessness and poor health. Westin et al. (1989), for example, follow a group of workers after a plant closing in Norway, comparing their experience to a control group at a sister plant nearby. The laid-off workers were granted medical disability pensions at over three times the rate of the control group up to a decade after the closure.

In the face of such uncertainty among medical experts about the health effects of unemployment, economic theory recommends that policy makers respond to the expected value of these costs. This suggests only that Brenner's estimates need to be discounted, not ignored. The findings of medical experts that joblessness causes poor health point a ghastly and reproachful finger at those who assume that the unemployment costs of disinflations are temporary.

Two other human costs of unemployment are the psychological costs stressed by Jahoda (1982) and the costs of increased crime. Jahoda's central argument is that employment performs the latent function of satisfying our need for social interaction, the deprivation of which reduces psychological well-being. While others have criticized her for 'romanticizing employment' (Ezzy, 1993, p. 45), and ignoring the alienating, unrewarding character of many jobs, few would gainsay that abrupt termination of employment can be disruptive or even devastating. The literature on crime appears to suffer from somewhat more ambiguity, and Dawson (1992, p. 96) flatly concludes that 'no causal connection between unemployment and crime has been established.'

Perhaps the most fitting conclusion would be to quote Lord William Beveridge, who fifty years ago wrote words no less true today:

> The greatest evil of unemployment is not the loss of additional material wealth which we might have with full employment. There are two greater evils: first, that unemployment makes men [sic] seem useless, not wanted, without a country; second, that unemployment makes men [sic] live in fear and that from fear springs hate. (Beveridge, 1944, p. 248)

These considerations render dubious the proposition that the sacrifice of jobs, income and security justifies the benefits of lower inflation to those who are called up as foot soldiers in the war on inflation. Indeed, one is tempted to turn the question around, and ask how much inflation it would take to negate the benefits of lowering the unemployment rate, even if only temporarily.

CONCLUSIONS

The conclusion that the game isn't worth the candle, toward which this chapter has driven, is not meant to gainsay the costs of inflation. Those costs associated with distortions of the tax system and nominal financial institutions in particular are enormously important. But the fact that these costs are avoidable, through indexation for example, recommends adaptation rather than disinflation. Moreover, these costs fall on households in proportion to their wealth. This creates a powerful interest group for anti-inflationary policies among the financial élites which has prejudiced the case for disinflation over adaptation.[24] The substantive costs of inflation turn out to be indirect, measured by income and jobs lost by those who can least afford it in periodic crusades against inflation, rather than the direct costs so assiduously researched by economists. To the extent that we can minimize the direct costs through adaptation, we create the political conditions for reducing the indirect costs.

NOTES

1. The unemployment and inflation rates (in the next paragraph) are taken from Layard et al. (1991). The numbers of unemployed in the US are from US President (1993), and in the UK from OECD (1991).
2. The costs of very high inflations, such as Latin American nations experience, and hyperinflations, such as Germany experienced after the First World War, are actually special topics in their own right, and will not be pursued here. For a more in-depth discussion of inflation and unemployment, see Dawson (1992).
3. Whether this equilibrium rate of unemployment (u^*) represents full employment, in the sense that no unemployment is involuntary, remains hotly debated. Moreover, whether there is a unique long-run equilibrium is open to question. Most economists now believe that for European economies, at least, the long-run equilibrium tends to be affected by the history of the economy; a period of high unemployment tends to leave a lasting impression by raising the value of u^*. Whether this effect (which is known as hysteresis) is permanent or temporary is under debate. For more discussion of the Phillips curve and hysteresis, see Layard et al. (1991) or Carlin and Soskice (1990)
4. Layard et al. (1991) estimate a sacrifice ratio of only 0.8 for the US and 0.7 for the UK. Their value for the US is considerably below the range mentioned in the text, probably because they restrict their equation in order to be able to apply it in many different countries. Representative values for other countries are France (0.2), Germany (0.49), Japan (0.05) and Italy (0.14).
5. For a useful discussion of UK inflation in this period, see Michie and Wilkinson (1992).
6. While textbooks routinely teach that there is one unique equilibrium rate of unemployment (in other words, that the long-run Phillips curve is vertical), this should by no means go unchallenged. For example, David M. Gordon (1988) has shown that under some specifications, the data reject the hypothesis that the US Phillips curve is vertical in the long run.
7. This expositional strategy follows that of Fischer and Modigliani (1978), one of the most oft-cited contributions in the literature on the costs of inflation.
8. Money is neutral if an increase in the money supply merely increases all prices in proportion, without affecting any real variable. Money is superneutral if an increase in its rate of growth merely raises the inflation rate proportionately, without affecting any real variables. If inflation is costly, then money cannot be considered superneutral.
9. Because inflation acts as a tax on money balances, a reduction of the inflation rate will require consumers to pay additional taxes. These taxes must be subtracted from the conventional consumers surplus. When this is done, we are left with the 'money triangle'. For a reasonably clear exposition of this point, see Fischer (1981a) or Bailey (1956).
10. This calculation involves writing the demand curve for money with a constant elasticity, η, as $L = Ai^{-\eta}$ and assuming a constant real interest rate, r. The welfare gain, G, of moving from

inflation at a rate π to zero inflation is the added utility created by the rise in money holdings from $L(r + \pi)$ to $L(r)$, or

$$G = \int_{L(r+\pi)}^{L(r)} (A^{1/\eta} L^{-1/\eta}) dL.$$

11. Fischer does not state precisely how he arrived at this figure, but using the numbers he does report and the methodology in the previous footnote, I have calculated a welfare loss equal to \$4.45 billion, or only about 0.17 per cent of GDP.

12. There are at least two other worthy arguments against a zero inflation target. First, a moderate inflation lets workers and firms cut their real wages and relative prices without having to cut nominal wages or prices (which people find hard to countenance), and therefore it contributes to the smooth functioning of market mechanisms. Second, a moderate inflation gives monetary authorities the desirable option of running negative short-term interest rates during really severe recessions.

13. These points are elaborated by Frank Hahn who observes that 'It is a paradox of both the present political and professional economists' scene that very many people who explicitly or implicitly postulate unique long-run equilibrium and economies which most of the time are in such an equilibrium also profess themselves most worried about the price level and the money supply. In such a world they do not matter a fig' (Hahn, 1990, p. 17).

14. In this case, the formula for the real after-tax rate of return would be

$$r_a = r(1 - t) = (i - \pi)(1 - t).$$

With a constant real interest rate before tax, inflation would not affect the return to saving.

15. In the debates surrounding the Tax Reform Act of 1986, a proposal to tax real interest income was part of the Treasury I plan, but it did not survive even the first round of revisions, and the Treasury II plan that emerged six months later was without indexing interest income or interest expenses.

16. Indexation of capital gains was also part of the Treasury I proposal in the run-up to the 1986 tax reform, and it made it to the Treasury II plan before being dropped in the House Ways and Means Committee.

17. One reason that inflation-induced declines in the cost of funds may not have stimulated demand for housing in the 1970s was that interest rate ceilings on bank deposits (Regulation Q) in place up until 1980 caused banks to ration loans. These restrictions were eliminated by the Depository Institutions Deregulation and Monetary Control Act of 1980. For the opposing view that tax and monetary policies have unduly favoured residential capital formation in the US, see Feldstein (1982).

18. Last In First Out (LIFO) accounting values the cost of an input by its current price. First In First Out (FIFO) accounting values the cost of an input by the price actually paid in the past. The US is unique among industrial nations in allowing firms a choice of LIFO or one of several historical cost accounting systems (mainly FIFO), on condition that the same system is used for tax and financial purposes.

19. As Fischer and Huizinga (1982) have shown, people usually appear to care more about inflation than unemployment in polls. Moreover, inflation aversion is spread widely throughout the population. However, on the question that really matters, public opinion polls show that people are unwilling to fight inflation by creating unemployment!

20. Space limitations prevent discussion of uncertainty about relative prices, for which the reader is referred to Fischer (1981b).

21. According to Okun's Law, it takes about 2.5 per cent growth of GDP to lower the unemployment rate by 1 per cent in the US. So multiplying the sacrifice ratio by 2.5 gives the output sacrifice ratio.

22. The present value of a perpetual stream of income, B, at a discount rate of r is simply B/r. A consol paying B per year is worth B/r when the interest rate is r.

23. These estimates derive from the general formula for the present value, *V*, of a constant stream of benefits, *B*, at discount rate *r*, or,

$$V = B \int_{t=0}^{T} e^{-rt}dt = B\left(\frac{1-e^{-rT}}{r}\right).$$

Note that when *T* is infinity, this reduces to the formula for the value of a consol, *B/r*.

24. For a highly readable account of monetary policy in the US along these lines, see Greider (1987). For a similar assessment of the direct and indirect costs of inflation, see Hibbs (1987).

REFERENCES

Armstrong, Phillip, Glyn, Andrew and Harrison, John (1991), *Capitalism Since 1945*, London: Basil Blackwell.

Bach, G. and Stephenson, J. (1974), 'Inflation and the distribution of wealth', *Review of Economics and Statistics*, vol. 56, no. 1, February.

Bailey, Martin J. (1956), 'The welfare cost of inflationary finance', *Journal of Political Economy*, vol. 64 no. 2, April.

Ball, Lawrence (1992), 'Why does high inflation raise inflation uncertainty?', *Journal of Monetary Economics*, vol. 29 no. 3, June.

Batchelor, Roy and Orr, Adrian (1991), 'Inflation uncertainty, inflationary shocks and the credibility of counter inflationary policy', *European Economic Review*, vol. 35, October.

Beveridge, W.H. (1944), *Full Employment in a Free Society*, London: Allen and Unwin.

Blank, Rebecca M., and Blinder, Alan S. (1986) 'Macroeconomics, Income Distribution, and Poverty', in Sheldon, Danziger (ed.), *Fighting Poverty: What Works and What Does Not*, Cambridge Mass.: Harvard University Press.

Board of Governors of the Federal Reserve System (1993), *Balance Sheets for the US Economy. 1945–92*, Washington: Federal Reserve Board.

Brenner, Harvey (1976), *Estimating the Social Costs of National Economic Policy: Implications for Mental and Physical Health and Clinical Aggression*, Report to the Joint Economic Committee of the US Congress, Washington: GPO.

Carlin, Wendy and Soskice, David (1990), *Macroeconomics and the Wage Bargain: A Modern Approach to Employment, Inflation, and the Exchange Rate*, Oxford: Oxford University Press.

Clark, Kim B. and Summers, Lawrence H. (1979), 'Labor market dynamics and unemployment: a reconsideration', *Brookings Papers on Economic Activity*, no. 1.

Congressional Budget Office (1993), *The Economic and Budget Outlook: Fiscal Years 1994–1998*, Washington: GPO.

Cukierman, Alex (1984), *Inflation, Stagflation, Relative Prices, and Imperfect Information*, Cambridge: Cambridge University Press.

Danziger, Leif (1988), 'Costs of price adjustment and the welfare economics of inflation and disinflation', *American Economic Review*, vol. 78 no. 4, September.

Dawson, Graham (1992), *Inflation and Unemployment: Causes Consequences and Cures*, Aldershot: Edward Elgar.

DeGregorio, Jose (1992), 'The effects of inflation on economic growth: lessons from Latin America', *European Economic Review*, vol. 36, April.

Economist (1992), 'Zero inflation', *The Economist*, vol. 325, 7 November.

Ezzy, Douglas (1993), 'Unemployment and mental health: a critical review', *Social Science and Medicine*, vol. 27 no. 1, 41–52.

Farber, Henry (1993), 'The incidence and costs of job loss: 1982-1991', *Brookings Papers on Economic Activity Microeconomics*, no. 1.

Feldstein, Martin (1982), 'Inflation, capital taxation, and monetary policy', in R.E. Hall, (ed.), *Inflation: Causes and Effects*, Chicago: University of Chicago Press.

Feldstein, Martin (1983), *Inflation. Tax Rules and Capital Formation*, Chicago: University of Chicago Press.

Fender, John (1990), *Inflation: Welfare Costs. Positive Theory, and Policy Options*, Ann Arbor: University of Michigan Press.

Fischer, Stanley (1981a), 'Toward an understanding of the costs of inflation: II' in K. Brunner, and A. Meltzer (eds), T*he Costs and Consequences of Inflation*, Carnegie–Rochester Conference Series on Public Policies, vol. 15.

Fischer, Stanley (1981b), 'Relative shocks, relative price variability, and inflation', *Brookings Papers on Economic Activity*, no. 2.

Fischer, Stanley and Huizinga, John (1982), 'Inflation, unemployment, and public opinion polls', *Journal of Money, Credit. and Banking*, vol. 14 no. 1, February.

Fischer, Stanley and Modigliani, Franco (1978), 'Toward an understanding of the real effects and costs of inflation', *Weltwirtschaftliches Archiv*, vol. 114.

Friedman, Benjamin (1988), 'Lessons in monetary policy from the 1980s', *Journal of Economic Perspectives*, vol. 2 no. 3, Summer.

Friedman, Milton (1969), *The Optimum Quantity of Money and Other Essays*, Chicago: Aldine.

Friedman, Milton (1977), 'Nobel lecture: inflation and unemployment', *Journal of Political Economy*, vol. 85 no. 3, June.

Garfinkel, Michelle R. (1989), 'What is an "acceptable" rate of inflation? – a review of the issues', *Federal Reserve Bank of St. Louis Review*, vol. 71 no. 4, July–August.

Goldfield, Michael (1976), 'The case of the missing money', *Brookings Papers on Economic Activity*, no. 3.

Gordon, David M. (1988), 'The un-natural rate of unemployment: an econometric critique of the NAIRU hypothesis', *American Economic Review*, vol. 78 no. 2, May.

Greider, William (1987), *Secrets of the Temple*, New York: Simon and Schuster.

Hahn, Frank (1990), 'On inflation', *Oxford Review of Economic Policy*, vol. 6 no. 4.

Hausman, Jerry A. and Poterba, James A. (1987), 'Household behavior and the tax reform act of 1986', *Journal of Economic Perspectives*, Summer.

Hibbs, Douglas A., Jr (1987), *The American Political Economy: Macroeconomics and Electoral Politics*, Cambridge, Mass.: Harvard University Press.

Jahoda, Marie (1982), *Employment and Unemployment: a Social-psychological Analysis*, Cambridge, UK: Cambridge University Press.

Jansen, Dennis (1989), 'Does inflation uncertainty affect output growth?', *Federal Reserve Bank of St. Louis Review*, vol. 71 no. 4, July–August.

Kormendi, R.C. and Meguire, P.G. (1985), 'Macroeconomic determinates of growth: cross-country evidence', *Journal of Monetary Economics*, vol. 16 no. 2, September.

Layard, Richard, Nickell, Stephen and Jackman, Richard (1991), *Unemployment: Macroeconomic Performance and the Labour Market*, Oxford: Oxford University Press.

Levine, Ross and Renelt, David (1992), 'A sensitivity analysis of cross-country growth regressions', *American Economic Review*, vol. 82 no. 4, September.

Levine, Ross and Zervos, Sara (1993), 'What have we learned about policy and growth from cross-country regressions?' *American Economic Review*, vol. 83 no. 2, May.

Lucas, Robert E., Jr (1981), 'Discussion of Stanley Fischer' in Brunner, K. and Meltzer, A. (eds), *The Costs and Consequences of Inflation*, Carnegie–Rochester Conference Series on Public Policies, vol. 15.

Michie, Jonathan and Wilkinson, Frank (1992), 'Inflation policy and the restructuring of labor markets' in Michie, J. (ed.), *The Economic Legacy 1979–1992*, London: Academic Press.

Minarik, J. (1979), 'The size distribution of income during inflations', *Review of Income and Wealth*, December.

Minford, A.P.L. and Hilliard, G.W. (1978), 'The costs of variable inflation', in M.J. Artis and A.R. Nobay (eds), *Contemporary Economic Analysis*, London: Croom Helm.

OECD (1991), *OECD Economic Surveys: UK*, Paris: OECD.

Okun, Arthur (1971), 'The mirage of steady inflation', *Brookings Papers on Economic Activity*, no. 1.

Phelps, Edmund S. (1973), 'Inflation in the theory of public finance', *Swedish Journal of Economics*, vol. 75.

Søgaard, Jes (1992), 'Econometric critique of the economic change model of mortality', *Social Science and Medicine*, vol. 34 no. 9.

Stanners, W. (1993), 'Is low inflation an important condition for high growth?', *Cambridge Journal of Economics*, vol. 17 no. 1, March.

Taylor, John B. (1981), 'On the relation between the variability of inflation and the average inflation rate', in K. Brunner and A. Meltzer (eds), *The Costs and Consequences of Inflation*, Carnegie–Rochester Conference Series on Public Policies, vol. 15.

US Department of Commerce, Bureau of the Census (1986), *General Summary, 1982. Census of Manufacture*, Washington: GPO.

US President (1993), *The Economic Report of the President, 1993*, Washington: GPO.

Wagstaff, Adam (1985), 'Time series analysis of the relationship between unemployment and mortality: a survey of econometric critiques and replication of Brenner's studies', *Social Science and Medicine*, vol. 21 no. 9.

Walsh, Carl (1993), 'What caused the 1990–1991 recession?' *Federal Reserve Bank of San Francisco Economic Review*, no. 2.

Westin, S., Schlesselman, J., and Korper, M. (1989), 'Long-term effects of factory closure: unemployment and disability during ten years' follow-up', *Journal of Clinical Epidemiology*, vol. 42 no. 5.

4. Thatcherism and unemployment in the UK

Frank Skuse

There have been two large-scale shifts in UK policy over the question of employment levels in the last 50 years. The publication of the White Paper on Employment Policy in 1944 had a major impact in that governments of both political persuasions accepted a commitment to economic policies that encouraged the attainment of full or near to full employment. This period of consensus, based in part at least on the insights of Keynes's *General Theory*, lasted until the 1970s. During it there was an explicit use of demand management to engineer changes in aggregate demand with the aim of controlling unemployment levels. On many occasions, often due to balance of payment pressures, this required periodic contractions in aggregate demand, leading the approach to become known as 'stop–go' policies. The result nevertheless was to produce low levels of unemployment, accompanied by low and acceptable levels of inflation.

The 1970s saw this consensus approach start to crumble, with the appearance in the political sphere of a different view of the relationship between government and the economy associated with the emergence of the 'New Right'. This was mirrored by developments in economics as economists found the Keynesian model increasingly difficult to apply in a world in which high and rising levels of unemployment were associated with high and rising levels of inflation. The phenomenon of stagflation threatened the tenability of the Phillips curve trade-off, causing it to be re-examined and throwing it into serious doubt. The Labour prime minister, Mr Callaghan, observed in a speech to the 1977 Labour Party conference that the time had passed when governments could spend their way to high levels of activity and employment. This was echoed by Sir Keith Joseph, a leading proponent of 'New Right' views within the Conservative Party, in a 1978 speech to the Bow Group in which he said, 'Full employment is not in the gift of governments. It should not be promised and it cannot be provided' (Quoted in Johnson, 1991, p. 219).

The replacement of Callaghan's government with the Thatcher administration in 1979 signalled the second significant change in the last 50 years concerning policy on unemployment. Despite using the slogan 'Labour isn't working', accompanied by a picture purporting to be a dole queue, in its campaign, the new government effectively had no policy on unemployment at all. As Johnson (1991) points out, the Conservative election manifesto of 1979 contained no reference to measures to control unemployment. The government was elected on a platform which gave priority to the fight against inflation. At best, control of unemployment was an afterthought to the main target of bringing down the rate of price increases, and by a mechanism that was not always made explicit, reductions in unemployment were held to follow from success in limiting wage demands as part of the anti-inflationary stance. At worst, the pursuit of full employment effectively dropped off the agenda completely. The 1980s thus saw a policy approach which deliberately turned its back on the mainte- nance of high employment levels in the interests of the fight against inflation. The result was a decade in which higher levels of unemployment than at any stage since the 1930s became a feature of the UK economic landscape.

In the following sections changes in the level and pattern of unemployment in the UK over the period since 1979 are discussed. In doing so an attempt is made to draw out the key elements and suggest important trends. This is followed by a section which examines the implications of the observed trends for the prospects of a return to lower levels of unemployment on a long-term basis.

UNEMPLOYMENT IN THE 1980s[1]

The pattern of unemployment during the 1980s and 1990s shows a number of key features which, it is argued, distinguish the period from previous experience in general and the 1970s in particular. In considering these changes, emphasis is placed on levels of unemployment, its duration and its composition.

The first of these concerns the rate of unemployment in relation to the workforce (see Figure 4.1). The seasonally adjusted unemployment rate for the UK rose above 4 per cent for the first time in the second quarter of 1976, peaked at 4.6 per cent in the last quarter of 1977 and then declined slowly to a low of 4 per cent in the first quarter of 1980. With the exception of the second quarter of 1980 it never again fell below 5 per cent. It rose rapidly through the recession of the early 1980s, remaining at levels of 10 per cent or greater from the beginning of 1983 to the third quarter of 1987, peaking at 11.2 per cent in 1986. The boom years of the late 1980s saw a reduction but the best figure, 5.6 per cent in the second quarter of 1989, was still nearly 50 per cent higher than the level inherited by the government in 1979. The recession that followed saw it rise again and by the last quarter of 1992 the rate was back above 10 per cent again.

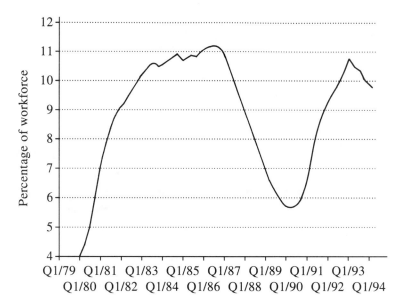

Source: Based on data from *Economic Trends* (various dates).

Figure 4.1 UK unemployment rate, 1979–94

This indicates that the 1980s represented a dramatic break with the past. Levels of unemployment which would have been considered politically disastrous in the 1950s and 1960s were accepted or at least tolerated by public opinion in the 1980s and early 1990s. Even at the peak of the output cycle in the first half of 1990, unemployment remained at 6 per cent. Growth in output during the upswing was insufficient to reduce unemployment to levels that had been attained in the previous decade. Higher levels of unemployment appear to have become a structural characteristic of the post-1979 world.

This is confirmed by the changes that can be observed in the structure of unemployment in terms of the duration of the period of unemployment (see Figure 4.2). At the beginning of the period, short-term unemployment, using the standard definition of duration of less than 26 weeks, accounted for some 60 per cent of the total unemployed. The proportion in long-term unemployment was below 30 per cent and falling, though the absolute level was stable until July 1990. The rapid growth that ensued in total unemployment up to the third quarter of 1982 was associated with a steady growth in both the absolute level of long-duration unemployment and in the proportion of total unemployment in this category. The relative stability shown by short-term unemployment levels over 1981 to 1983 was not mirrored in long-term figures which, small

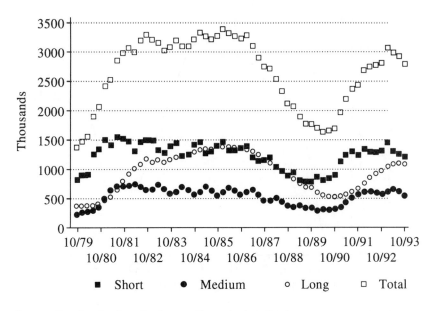

Source: Based on data from *Employment Gazette* (various dates).

*Figure 4.2   UK unemployment levels: total and composition by duration,
1979–93*

contractions in two quarters of 1983 excepted, continued to grow in absolute
terms until early 1986. In relation to total unemployment, the long-term jobless
proportion did not peak until the middle of 1987.

The total jobless figure began declining steadily from the first quarter of 1987,
and this was reflected in a parallel decline in those in long-term unemployment.
Total unemployment reached its lowest level in the middle of 1990, but short-
term unemployment bottomed out in the middle of 1989, rising steadily over
the ensuing two years. With the obvious lag, this was reflected in long-term
unemployment figures which increased again from early 1991, as those who
had been made unemployed at the start of the recession found it difficult to obtain
work and thus switched from the short-term to the long-term category. This is
reflected in the steady decrease in the proportion of short-term unemployed from
mid-1991 accompanied by a sharp rise in the proportion of long-term jobless
over the same period, the latter approaching its peak levels of the mid-1980s.

Some understanding of the composition by duration of unemployment is
important in terms of the prospects of gaining full employment as a realistic or
achievable target of economic policy. Hysteresis effects suggest that historically experienced levels of unemployment become embedded in the economy

and make movement back to higher levels of employment more problematic. If one were to talk in equilibrium terms, the 'equilibrium' level of unemployment is affected by past actual levels. Thus in an economy which has experienced higher than 'historically normal' levels of unemployment in the recent past, a return to something nearer to full employment will be that much more difficult. Hysteresis effects constitute one possible explanation of how this process operates. Whatever the precise explanation, the suggestion here is that the UK evidence over the 1980s is entirely consistent with the notion of an upward shift in the 'natural' rate of unemployment.

Absolute levels of unemployment and rates of unemployment were higher in the 1980s and early 1990s than anything that had been experienced since 1945. Of equal importance is the fact that the core of long-term unemployed remained resistant to those periods when economic activity in the UK did expand. Thus the lowest level of long-term unemployment in the 1980s, the 0.507 million recorded in the third quarter of 1990, was over 40 per cent higher than the corresponding figure for the third quarter of 1979. Similarly throughout the period the proportion of long-term unemployed remained higher than it had been at the beginning of the decade, and even as the late 1980s boom faded, and rising unemployment affected first the short-term figures, the proportion fell only to 25 per cent compared to levels of below 20 per cent in 1980. It rose sharply towards 40 per cent during 1992 and 1993 as the effects of the recession were felt.

All of this indicates a set of circumstances that make return to full employment more difficult According to the duration thesis explanation of hysteresis effects, the impact of long-term unemployment is a sufficient condition in itself to explain the difficulty. This view argues that one consequence of prolonged joblessness is to deskill workers and make it more difficult for them to gain employment. This will be particularly important in activities where technological change has occurred. There is some evidence that this has taken place, with the average age of capital equipment in the UK economy falling in the second half of the 1980s, as investment embodying newer technology occurred (*National Institute of Economic and Social Research, 1991*). It will also be significant where the composition of economic activity has changed significantly, as happened in the UK with the contraction of manufacturing industry and the growth of the service sector. Even where deskilling has not taken place, persons in long-duration unemployment may appear to be less employable. Where employers use screening devices in order to deal with information deficiencies in hiring decisions, especially when faced with large numbers of job applicants, long periods out of work may be used as such a filtering device. In addition, there is the demotivating effect of long periods of unemployment in terms of intensity of job search. The combined result of these factors is that unemployment may exhibit the characteristics of cumulative causation whereby as periods out of work lengthen, it makes it progressively more difficult to find re-employment, posing serious problems for any policy designed to move towards full or near full employment.

A third characteristic of unemployment over the period since 1979 has been the evening out in regional disparities across the UK. As Table 4.1 shows, in 1980 the North-West, Wales, Scotland, Northern Ireland and the North all had rates of unemployment that were 20 per cent or more above the national rate. The South-East and East Anglia were the only regions with a rate that was 20 per cent or more below the average. The 1980s saw a considerable convergence in the regional rates of unemployment, this being particularly noticeable in the recession of the early 1990s. The most dramatic impact has been in the traditionally favoured regions of the South, namely the South-East, South-West and East Anglia. Although the rate of unemployment in these regions rose during the recession of the early 1980s, rates were consistently below the national average, and the recovery of the late 1980s caused them to diverge further from the national rate. However the recession of the 1990s has produced a considerable ironing out of disparities as rates of unemployment have grown more rapidly in these regions than in others. The result is that by the first quarter of 1993, only one region, Northern Ireland, had an unemployment rate that diverged from the national figure by more than 20 per cent. It is clear from Table 4.1, however, that the more even distribution of unemployment rates is almost entirely due to the worsening levels in the previously favoured regions, rather than to reductions in the worst affected areas.

A fourth change to which attention should be drawn is the dramatic shift in the composition of employment and the consistent contraction in the number of persons employed in manufacturing activity (see Table 4.2). At the end of 1979, 7.05 million people worked in the manufacturing sector, 27.7 per cent of the workforce that was in employment. By the end of the third quarter of 1993, the corresponding figures were 4.19 million and 16.7 per cent. This represents a contraction of 41 per cent over the period. It clearly poses problems in the context of employment policy, in terms of overall prosperity, in terms of productivity growth potential and for the balance of payments.

The impact on employment policy is considerable. Only in two years since 1979 has the absolute level of manufacturing employment increased, a 0.4 per cent rise in 1987 and a 0.6 per cent increase in 1988. The recessions of the early 1980s and the early 1990s hit manufacturing employment particularly hard. It fell by 24 per cent over 1980–83 and a further 18 per cent over 1990–93. This has contributed to structural unemployment of a long-term kind as when expansion of economic activity has taken place, it has not led to any significant increase in manufacturing employment. Indeed there were several years in the 1980s when total employment rose but manufacturing employment continued to fall. This means that a demand-led increase in activity, such as occurred in the late 1980s, has not had any significant impact on manufactur-

Table 4.1 Regional unemployment rate as proportion of UK rate, 1980–93 (measured in fourth quarter of each year)

	North-West	Wales	Scotland	N. Ireland	North	Yorks/Humber.	East Midlands	East Anglia	South-East	South West	West Midlands
1980	1.27	1.37	1.34	1.81	1.49	1.07	0.92	0.78	0.63	0.88	1.15
1981	1.25	1.25	1.20	1.50	1.42	1.08	0.90	0.76	0.68	0.82	1.24
1982	1.27	1.25	1.18	1.52	1.39	1.09	0.89	0.79	0.71	0.82	1.23
1983	1.27	1.23	1.17	1.49	1.40	1.08	0.91	0.76	0.72	0.84	1.21
1984	1.26	1.24	1.17	1.45	1.43	1.10	0.93	0.73	0.72	0.85	1.18
1985	1.25	1.25	1.18	1.47	1.42	1.11	0.90	0.75	0.74	0.85	1.16
1986	1.23	1.20	1.23	1.59	1.37	1.14	0.91	0.77	0.74	0.85	1.15
1987	1.27	1.22	1.33	1.81	1.45	1.16	0.93	0.72	0.71	0.81	1.14
1988	1.32	1.25	1.44	2.09	1.52	1.19	0.88	0.63	0.65	0.76	1.09
1989	1.34	1.14	1.47	2.49	1.56	1.20	0.85	0.58	0.61	0.69	1.03
1990	1.27	1.12	1.32	2.28	1.47	1.18	0.88	0.68	0.70	0.78	1.00
1991	1.14	1.07	1.01	1.56	1.22	1.06	0.91	0.74	0.90	0.91	1.07
1992	1.07	1.00	0.94	1.40	1.13	1.00	0.92	0.80	0.97	0.96	1.07
1993	0.98	0.95	0.88	1.30	1.13	0.94	0.88	0.77	0.93	0.89	1.00

Unemployment rate by region

	North-West	Wales	Scotland	N. Ireland	North	Yorks/Humber.	East Midlands	East Anglia	South-East	South West	West Midlands
1980	7.5	8.1	7.9	10.7	8.8	6.3	5.4	4.6	3.7	5.2	6.8
1993	10.5	10.2	9.4	13.9	12.1	10.1	9.4	8.2	10.0	9.5	10.7

Source: *Economic Trends* (HMSO, various dates).

ing employment. Those made unemployed from this sector faced the problem that any recovery did not make it significantly easier to find employment in the manufacturing sector and this contributed to the higher levels of core long-term unemployment referred to above.

Table 4.2   Manufacturing employment, 1979–93 (all Q4, except 1993; figures are seasonally adjusted)

	Total workforce	Workforce in employment	Manufacturing employment	Annual change (%)	Manufacturing employment/total employment (%)
1979	26 673	25 485	7 053		27.7
1980	26 843	24 786	6 408	−9.1	25.9
1981	26 662	24 057	5 931	−7.4	24.7
1982	26 524	23 617	5 560	−6.3	23.5
1983	27 078	24 038	5 348	−3.8	22.2
1984	27 636	24 452	5 292	−1.0	21.6
1985	27 829	24 581	5 232	−1.1	21.3
1986	27 957	24 743	5.069	−3.1	20.5
1987	28 253	25 574	5 087	0.4	19.9
1988	28 369	26 343	5 117	0.6	19.4
1989	28 482	26 844	5 098	−0.4	19.0
1990	28 496	26 651	4 969	−2.5	18.6
1991	28 232	25 682	4 485	−9.7	17.5
1992	27 915	24 943	4 190	−6.6	16.8
1993	27 931	25 005	4 185		16.7

Source: Economic Trends (HMSO, various dates).

It could be argued that the trend downwards in manufacturing employment has been a feature of the UK economy since well before 1979, and that what has been witnessed subsequently has been simply a continuation of that trend. It is true that manufacturing employment did move downwards over the 1970s. At the end of 1971, 7.7 million (31.5 per cent of the employed workforce) were engaged in manufacturing activity. This figure slumped to just over 5 million in the first quarter of 1975, but by the end of 1978 had risen again to 7.2 million and 28 per cent of the employed workforce. Manufacturing employment thus showed a resilience that it did not reproduce over the subsequent 15 years. It is thus difficult to sustain the view that the 1980s was just a continuation of the slow downward trend of the 1970s.

The reduction in manufacturing employment after 1979 can be attributed to several factors. The first of these is a considerable improvement in productivity in manufacturing industry which took place over the 1980s. The interpretation of this improvement is disputed, some claiming it as evidence of the alleged 'Thatcher economic miracle' and arguing that it has placed the UK economy on a new growth path; others that it was a one-off improvement not so dramatically out of line with recent economic history. There seems a greater measure of agreement that a significant part of the explanation at least during the early 1980s was the recession and the severe shakeout that was associated with it. In particular, managements took advantage of the new climate to eliminate overmanning and underemployment. As one commentator put it 'This tougher attitude to manning has probably raised the national level of unemployment permanently' (Britton, 1993b, p. 48). It is also clear that the main effect of the productivity rise was to push employment levels downwards rather than result in an expansion of output and movement along a new growth path.

A second reason is to be found in the behaviour of manufacturing investment. Although the 1980s saw an increase in profit share as the balance of social power between labour and management shifted (Arestis and Skuse, 1989), this did not lead to a recovery in investment. Real gross fixed investment in 1989 in manufacturing (the peak of the decade) was only 13 per cent higher than in 1979. In only two years of the 1980s was manufacturing investment higher than 1979, and at worst (1983) had fallen to 67 per cent of that level. The comparison is marginally more flattering if extended to the whole of the 1970s, but the essential point is that the productivity improvements were not matched by growth in investment and capacity and therefore did not lead to higher levels of output and employment. The picture is probably even bleaker in that scrapping rates of old equipment were significant as investment was used to introduce new technologies, so gross investment almost certainly overestimates the impact in terms of creation of new employment opportunities.

It is clear from this discussion that after a long period of a high and relatively stable level of unemployment, 1979 marked a watershed. Throughout the 1980s and early 1990s the UK learned to live with much higher levels of unemployment, even in the period of the late 1980s known as the Lawson boom. What were the policies pursued by the government during this period, with particular reference to unemployment?

GOVERNMENT POLICY AND UNEMPLOYMENT

As indicated at the beginning, government policy towards unemployment shifted dramatically in the late 1970s, culminating with the Conservative administration of 1979. 'Initially ... the new Conservative government had no explicit policy for employment' (Maynard, 1993, p. 58). Little changed over the ensuing years, and in Britton (1993b, p. 5) remarks '... it cannot be said that full employment is now an objective of government policy'.

This important shift can be seen as the result of two influences. The first is an ideological shift, the result of a complex set of factors. It is concerned with the 'New Right' rejection of the consequences of Keynesian demand management in terms of the role of the state and interference in the market mechanism. As has been argued widely (for one example, see Arestis and Skuse, 1989) greater emphasis is placed on the efficiency of markets and their ability to clear, including the case of the labour market. Markets should be left to themselves, free from government interference. Emphasis is placed on individual decision making, with informed, rational economic agents being able to make economic decisions which best promote their own interests. Government intervention obstructs this process and is therefore to be minimized. Demand management policies, involving the deliberate use of fiscal policy to gain control over resources which could otherwise be more effectively allocated through the market, are suspect.

Coupled with this is the emphasis on the supply side of the economy and the argument that the greatest barrier to economic expansion and higher employment is restraint on enterprise and economic freedom. For both these reasons the Conservative government was committed to rolling back the frontiers of the state, to reducing taxation as an incentive to enterprise, to placing in the private sector large areas of economic activity which were then in the public domain and to relying or monetary policy to provide the parameters within which the market would make its own decisions, free from government interference. To the extent that employment was considered, the emphasis was on reforms on the supply side and reduced rigidities in the labour market. This was manifested in legislation designed to reduce what was seen as the excessive influence of organized labour and changes that restricted social security benefits available to the unemployed. This was part of an overall objective to change the balance of power in society and, behind the rhetoric of individual freedom, to restore the influence of capital and management at the expense of labour. Confrontation with the unions, culminating with the miners' strike of 1985, is the most obvious illustration of this approach.

However, the shift in attitude to unemployment cannot be placed only in the ideological sphere. New classical economics was arguing that it was impossible to engineer lasting shifts in employment levels. With the assumption of rational expectations, and assuming that all markets, including the labour market, are sufficiently flexible to allow rapid market clearing, governments are argued to be impotent in terms of using aggregate demand changes as a means of creating long-term employment. Given the existence of a vertical long-run aggregate supply curve, determined by the natural rate of output or employment, attempts to change these variables will only produce inflationary effects, with no long-term reduction in unemployment. Under the rational expectations hypothesis, all economic decision makers construct their expectations on a full understanding of the relevant economic model and are able to modify their expectations as the result of announced changes in government policy and thus fully anticipate their effects, notably in terms of prices.

The assumptions required to generate the new classical view are rather restrictive. They require a level of information on the operation of the economy on the part of *all* economic agents that it is difficult to believe exists in reality, though new classical economists protect themselves by the defence of asserting that agents behave 'as if' they possessed the relevant knowledge. Equally the approach is based on a view of market flexibility and speed of adjustment that also is at variance with the institutional structure of an economy such as that of the UK. As Arestis (1992, p. 30) suggests, '… the New Classical model attempts to bring back into the heart of economic analysis the invisible hand assumption …' (p. 30). How realistic is this assumption of the invisible hand in a world of large corporations with significant degrees of monopoly pricing power, and of labour market institutions that make for rigidities as the result of the wage bargaining process? (See Arestis and Skuse, 1991.)

However, the combination of the 'New Right' desire to roll back the frontiers of the state on ideological grounds, coupled with the arguments of the new classical school, provided a heady mixture, especially given the firm commitment of the 1979 government to make the fight against inflation its main policy objective. As Healey (1993, p. 1) indicates, the government set out with 'the [then] radical proposition that fiscal and monetary policies should be directed towards re-estab-lishing price stability, regardless of the short run costs in terms of falling output and higher unemployment'. On the evidence from the previous section, it would appear that the consequence of the policies adopted was to have more than a short-term effect on unemployment.

Consistent with the theoretical underpinning provided by new classical theory, the policy adopted by the government in the early years of the 1980s was centred on the Medium-Term Financial Strategy (MTFS). This established a rolling set of monetary aggregate targets, designed to bring down the rate of growth of sterling M3, and to signal to economic agents a commitment to a set of targets over the medium term. It was associated with a programme of austerity and cut-backs in expenditure, detailed elsewhere (see for example Arestis and Skuse, 1989 or Wells, 1993) which contributed to a severe recession and con-sequences for unemployment outlined in the previous section. The MTFS was effectively abandoned in 1983.

In addition to a relaxation in terms of expenditure that followed the demise of MTFS, greater emphasis was placed on supply-side measures and an attempt to restore incentives. The most obvious example of this was the reduction in

Table 4.3 Unemployment rates in selected countries, 1989–93 (OECD standardized rates)

	EC average	UK	Australia	Belgium	France	Germany (FR)	Eire	Netherlands	Japan	US
1989	9.0	7.2	6.1	8.0	9.4	5.6	14.7	8.3	2.3	5.2
1990	8.4	6.8	6.9	7.2	8.9	4.9	13.4	7.5	2.1	5.4
1991	8.7	8.7	9.5	7.1	9.4	4.4	14.9	7.0	2.1	6.6
1992	9.5	9.9	10.7	7.8	10.2	4.8	16.1	6.8	2.2	7.3
1993 (Sept)	10.8	10.2	10.7	9.5	11.7	5.9	16.7	8.5	2.5	6.6

Source: *Employment Gazette*, January 1994.

personal taxation. Just as important in terms of unemployment was the government's attempt to operate on it from the supply side through a systematic erosion of benefit entitlements. As Atkinson and Micklewright (1989) indicate, over the period 1979–88, there were 17 changes to the system of national insurance unemployment benefit, of which 11 worsened the position of the unemployed; of 17 changes to supplementary benefit and income support, 12 had a negative effect. This is part of a drive to increase the motivation actively to look for work, embodying the Conservative view that a significant proportion of unemployment is voluntary. In addition the government attempted to increase wage flexibility for lower-paid workers by curtailing severely the powers of wages councils in 1986. Throughout the 1980s, the government passed a series of legislative measures to restrict the powers of trade unions, with the consequence of making it increasingly difficult for them to pursue disputes at other than a local level. This weakened their power relative to employers and had the objective at least of increasing the degree of labour market flexibility. The decline in trade union influence was further enhanced by the decline in union membership which occurred over the period, encouraged by the decline of the more highly unionized manufacturing sector and growth in the less unionized services sector.

The final aspect of the supply-side approach to alleviating unemployment involved a series of government training schemes to raise skill levels, targeting particularly young entrants to the labour market and those who have been in long-term unemployment. These included the Youth Training Scheme for 16–18 year-olds, introduced in 1986, Employment Training for 18–24 year-olds in 1988 as well as such schemes as Job Splitting, Job Training Scheme etc.[2] However, as Gregg (1991) indicates, the resources devoted to such special employment measures have declined since the mid-1980s, with the government mixing encouragement to retrain with a greater element of compulsion in terms of job search and evidence of engagement with the labour market. He further argues that there is little evidence of any success. It is not clear that Employment Training succeeded in reaching those most vulnerable to long-term unemployment, i.e. those with very low initial skill levels, and the element of compulsion may just be reinforcing the vicious circle by encouraging these groups to continue seeking low pay/low skill jobs of uncertain tenure. Certainly the evidence from the previous section of the nature of long-duration unemployment is entirely consistent with this rather pessimistic view.

In line with its philosophy of disengaging the state from active participation in economic life, the Thatcher government pursued an active policy of denationalization of erstwhile public sector utilities and companies. A side-effect of this policy has been an increase in unemployment as in order to make these companies more attractive to private shareholders, significant reductions in the labour force have occurred, not only before privatization, but also subsequent to it. Water is an example of the former where over the period 1980–89, an output increase of 6 per cent was accompanied by an employment reduction of 22 per cent (see Fine and Poletti, 1992, p 319). Gas, electricity and telecommunications are examples of the latter where significant lay-offs have occurred as the industries are run on a more overtly commercial basis, leading, to cite two examples, to significant reductions in British Telecommunications middle management in 1993 and reductions in employment due to rationalization of gas showrooms in 1994.

As already suggested, there is little evidence that the supply-side-oriented approach to problems of unemployment has worked. Long-term core unemployment has in fact increased over the period 1979–93 (see Figure 4.2). The only period in which unemployment appeared to be on a downward path was in the late 1980s and this could be seen as a response to an increase in aggregate demand, rather than the consequence of improved supply-side efficiency. Britton (1993b) argues that the supply-side reforms of the 1980s did nothing to initiate a lasting reduction in the level of sustainable unemployment, and indicates that the late 1980s boom was constrained by both skilled labour and plant capacity shortages. Despite the substantial surge in activity during this period, unemployment at no stage fell below 1.6 million. When recessionary conditions returned, employment suffered, and throughout 1991 and 1992, unemployment rose sharply.

To place matters in context, it must be pointed out that the problem is not unique to the UK, and amongst its European Union partners, France and Belgium in particular experienced increases in levels of unemployment (see Table 4.3). Britain faced the problems of the 1990s against a background of a world recession. However, the poor competitive position of UK manufacturing, coupled with the contraction and low levels of investment in that sector discussed above, placed it in a weaker position than many of its trading partners, most notably Germany and Japan. The comparison with Germany is significant given UK monetary policy objectives in terms of shadowing the D-mark, and then entering the ERM at a rate which overvalued the pound sterling and made UK exports uncompetitive.

RETURN TO FULL EMPLOYMENT: REALISTIC PROSPECT OR PIPE DREAM?

Has the UK condemned itself to a situation in which the unemployment levels of the 1980s and 1990s are to become a permanent feature of the economy, or is it possible to devise policies that will move the economy back to levels that were experienced in the 1950s and 1960s? The answer to this question is far from clear and there are many factors which lead to pessimistic conclusions. Much depends on what is considered to be a socially and politically acceptable level of unemployment, both in terms of absolute numbers and of average duration. Even if the acceptable absolute level were defined as 5 per cent of the workforce, on 1993 figures this would involve unemployment remaining at 1.4 million.

Much has been made of the contrast in approach between the Thatcher years and the three decades that preceded them. It is clear that the emphasis in the earlier period was on the use of fiscal policy to operate on the demand side of the economy in order to provide conditions conducive to high levels of employment. In other words, the governments of the day accepted that the economy would need active fiscal involvement to control unemployment. The post-1979 world has eschewed such policies and placed the burden of responsibility on supply-side policies operating through encouraging people to return to work and by providing incentives to employers to undertake investment in growth that will provide the demand in the labour market.

Given the record of unemployment over the period 1979–93, it is difficult to be anything but sceptical about the impact of a supply-side approach. The evidence indicates that unemployment has not been reduced in any long-term way and that the underlying trend is upwards, with an obstinate refusal of long-duration unemployment to approach pre-1979 levels except for a very short period. Medium-term unemployment has exhibited a similar resilience. Despite an increase in the workforce from approximately 26.5 million in 1979 to nearly 28 million by the end of 1993, the workforce in employment has actually fallen marginally, indicating a failure of the supply-side policy to create conditions appropriate to using more fully the human resources available. Further, one is entitled to query the quality of the jobs that have been created: at the end of 1986, 7.5 per cent of male jobs and 44 per cent of female jobs were part-time. By the third quarter of 1993 this had risen to 10.8 per cent for males, with a much more modest increase to 46 per cent for females. At the same time the number of people self-employed has risen from 2.5 million in 1986 to 2.9 million in 1993, having peaked at 3.2 million at the end of 1989. Both these factors suggest a failure of the labour market to create adequate opportunities.

The problem of unemployment is sufficiently complex that neither reliance on the application of traditional Keynesian demand management methods, nor dogmatic insistence on the efficacy of supply-side measures, can provide self-contained solutions by themselves. What is required is a mixture of both approaches: merely making people more willing to work does not help if there are no jobs available; and expanding demand will do little other than generate inflation and cause balance of payments problems if the labour skills and the capacity to produce the goods required are not available.

There can be little doubt that the level of investment that the UK has experienced over the last 14 years, most particularly the poor levels of manufacturing investment, have left production capacity in a poor position to respond to any increases in demand. As Blackaby and Hunt (1993, p 111) argue, a sound manufacturing base is usually seen as the 'key to growth and transformation of the economy' and a decade or more of poor performance in manufacturing investment and employment have left the economy in a weak position. Given that over the period since 1979, levels of profitability have been restored from the low levels of the 1970s, this failure of investment within the UK economy is a serious concern. One aspect of any policy to regain lower levels of unemployment on a long-term basis must therefore be to raise levels of industrial investment. Whether this means a policy, advocated by some post-Keynesians (see, for example, Arestis, 1992), of socialization of investment is something that may be argued. It undoubtedly means, however, a greater degree of partnership between the government and industry than has been the practice in the UK since 1979. The evidence is that the market, left to itself, will not be capable of curing the deep-seated problems that are associated with high and enduring levels of unemployment. If markets have shown by experience that they do not achieve these results, then a greater degree of state involvement is essential. If there is an understanding that markets are systematically and inherently incapable of generating near-full employment then governments have no alternative but to play a greater role in key economic decisions The danger is that the impact of over a decade of Conservative rule and distrust of government involvement in industrial decision making may have created a climate in which it is difficult to establish a partnership between government and industry. The dismantling of organized labour's role in any consultative process concerning government policy is but one example of this. Employers and management too have seen such processes fall into desuetude and may well regard government involvement with distaste after 15 years of the ability to impose 'the right to manage' over 'the right to work'.

A significant concern of any policy to use demand measures and investment to recreate an appropriate industrial base must clearly pay attention to the question of inflation. As Britton (1993b, p. 11) comments, the systematic attack on union power in the 1980s which has made 'hiring and firing' easier and more flexible 'does not seem to have made a lower average level of unemployment compatible with price stability' and the danger must be that expanding demand will have the consequence of rekindling inflation.

Can some form of incomes policy be avoided? This hardly constitutes a radical or a new approach, but if the inflationary process is to be contained, it may be a necessary concomitant of any attempt to move investment on to a sustainable higher growth path. If inflationary pressure is inherent in the conflict between corporations and labour over relative shares of profit and wage income, an incomes policy is preferable to reliance on market forces and bargaining strength. An explicit incomes policy would have the advantage of being open, unlike the process based more on subterfuge and threat, using public sector pay settlements as a signalling device which seems to be the approach of the current Conservative government. Such a policy would take account of the reality of price and wage setting in an economy such as the UK (see Arestis and Skuse, 1991) rather than modelling it through competitive markets and treating wages as somehow based on marginal productivity and determined, as any other price, by the market. Ironically, one further consequence of the Conservative legislation on trade unions has been to make the operation of an incomes policy more difficult as it has made for more fragmented bargaining over wages, making the operationalization of pay norms much more difficult. However, if the consequence of accepting some limitation on pay growth is accepted, and here the possibility is that labour's expectations may have been fundamentally changed, the chance to raise the level of aggregate demand and move towards a reduction of unemployment is real.

It is, however, clear that demand-side factors cannot by themselves be the only elements of policy to limit unemployment. Measures on the supply side must also play their part. Productivity increases and working habits that are conducive to flexible working are essential. As indicated above, UK productivity did increase during the 1980s, though this may have been due to a significant extent to elimination of overmanning and the consequences of the 1981–82 recession. It is less clear that it has led to an increase in long-term productivity growth, in which case an opportunity has been missed. However if a return towards fuller levels of employment is to be sustained the UK must be in a position to supply expanding demand from domestic production and therefore to remain competitive with its major trading partners. As Wells (1993) suggests, the experience of UK industry in the 1980s in withstanding imported competition was very poor: the traded goods sector was simply unable to compete effectively with imports. This is of particular significance given the concern expressed by Britton (1993b) that broad-based measures to tackle unemployment in a long-term context may have the initial impact of exerting upward pressure on jobless figures, emphasizing the need for export growth as a further component of demand expansion. This can only be brought about through an expansion in the output of traded goods and their production at competitive prices. Though this is made no easier by symbolically important moves such as the sale of Austin Rover to a non-UK company, arguably scant reward for a workforce that has adapted to the requirements of more flexible practices and significant productivity increases, other parts of the same industry such as Nissan's manufacturing capacity indicate what can be done.

Many commentators have pointed to the UK's poor record in training and skilling of its workforce, placing it at a serious disadvantage compared to its trading partners and accounting in part for its poor comparative performance in productivity terms. It also goes a long way in explaining why the boom of the late 1980s came up against shortages of skilled labour despite the level of unemployment remaining at over 1.5 million. Redressing this balance is again part of a long-term strategy on the supply side, and given the public-good nature of education and training, government involvement is unavoidable. It is a strategy that must form part of the approach to the reduction of unemployment, especially to prevent further rises in the embedded core of long-term unemployment. It is an approach that has the possibility of beneficial cumulative causation, as improvements in real employment prospects make individual participation in such retraining more likely.

SUMMARY AND CONCLUSIONS

After a long period in which unemployment on a persistent scale seemed to have been eliminated, the 1980s and 1990s have witnessed its return. Full employment as a policy objective has been pushed aside in the search for a stable price level. Coupled with this has been the underlying Conservative attitude that the unemployed themselves are primarily responsible for unemployment due to lack of motivation or lack of initiative. This contrasts with at least the popular version of the Keynesian message which is that appropriate manipulation of aggregate demand can ensure high levels of employment.

Reality is far more complex than either of these somewhat bowdlerized views would suggest. The question of moving the UK economy back to a position where lower levels of unemployment are an integral feature will require a careful mix of both demand-side and supply-side oriented initiatives. Equally the solutions will not be short-term; it will take time to eliminate long-term unemployment. Nevertheless the argument here is that guarded optimism is justified, given the appropriate mix of policies and a willingness to recognize the long-term social costs of persistently high levels of unemployment.

NOTES

1. Unless otherwise indicated, all figures quoted in this and subsequent sections are taken from *Economic Trends* (HMSO, various dates) or *Employment Gazette* (Employment Department, various dates).
2. See Johnson (1991, p. 223) for a useful summary table of White Papers related to employment, legislation and special schemes over the period 1980–90.

REFERENCES

Atkinson, A. B and Micklewright, J. (1989), 'Turning the Screw: Benefits for the Unemployed, 1979–88' in A. V. Atkinson, *Poverty and Social Security*, Hemel Hempstead: Harvester Wheatsheaf.

Arestis, P. and Skuse, F.E. (1989), 'Austerity Policies and the New Right: Recent UK Experience', *Economie Appliquée*, vol. XLII, no. 1.

Arestis, P. and Skuse, F.E. (1991), 'Wage and Price Setting in a Post-Keynesian Theory of Inflation', *Economies et Sociétés*, Série 'Monnaie et Production, vol. XXV, nos 11–12.

Arestis, P. (1992), *The Post-Keynesian Approach to Economics: An Alternative Analysis of Economic Theory and Policy*, Aldershot: Edward Elgar.

Blackaby, D.H. and Hunt, L.C. (1993), 'An Assessment of Britain's Productivity Record in the 1980s: Has There Been a Miracle?' in Healey (1993).

Britton, A. (1993a), 'The Economy in the 1980s; in Healey (1993).

Britton, A. (1993b), 'Two Routes to Full Employment', *National Institute Economic Review*, no. 144, May.

Fine, B. and Poletti, C. (1992), 'Industrial Prospects in the Light of Privatisation' in Michie (1992).

Gregg, P. (1991), 'Is There a Future for Special Employment Measures in the 1990s? *National Institute Economic Review*, no. 138, November.

Healey, N.M. (1993) (ed.), *Britain's Economic Miracle: Myth or Reality?* London: Routledge.

Johnson, C. (1991), *The Economy under Mrs Thatcher*, London: Penguin.

Maynard, G. (1993), 'Britain's Economic Recovery' in Healey (1993).

Michie, J. (ed.) (1992), *The Economic Legacy, 1979–1992*, London: Academic Press.

National Institute of Economic and Social Research (1991), *Economic Review*, no. 137, August.

Wells, J. (1993), 'The Economy after Ten Years: Stronger or Weaker?' in Healey (1993).

5. Unemployment, job creation and job destruction in the UK since 1979

John Wells

Since the Conservatives came to power in 1979, mass unemployment has stalked the land on a scale not seen since the Great Depression of the 1930s. For most of the 1980s and 1990s, the most frequently quoted unemployment measure – the 'claimant' count of those unemployed and signing on for unemployment-related benefits[1] – rarely departed from around 3 million or about 10 per cent of the work force, though it did fall briefly below 2 million during the unsustainable and unsustained Lawson boom of the late 1980s. Such levels of unemployment appear to be similar to those witnessed during the depths of the Great Depression in 1931–32 – insofar as the data permit such comparisons to be made.[2]

The Conservative government elected into office in May 1979 inherited a level of unemployment from the previous Labour administration of 1.087 million (4.1 per cent of the workforce)[3] – a situation already representing a considerable departure from the full employment conditions of the 1950s and 1960s. Then, under the impact of the Thatcher–Howe twin economic shocks of savage monetary and fiscal deflation and real exchange rate appreciation during 1979–81, employment shrank and unemployment rose rapidly and, by September 1981, it had already doubled to 2.3 million (8.6 per cent). Thereafter, as output gradually recovered, employment ceased falling in early 1983 and began to rise. Despite this, claimant unemployment continued to rise, peaking at 3.1 million (11.2 per cent) in July 1986 – lagging by some five years the output recovery.[4] The Lawson boom of the late 1980s saw a rapid growth of employment and a brief reduction in unemployment, with the claimant count falling to a low of 1.6 million (5.6 per cent) in April 1990. The subsequent recession saw employment fall by 2 million and claimant unemployment rise by 1.4 million, appearing to peak at 2.972 million (10.5 per cent) in December 1992.[5] Thereafter, much to everyone's surprise, claimant unemployment declined for most of 1993 (a brief upsurge during the summer notwithstanding) – the decline totalling 226 000. This fall in claimant unemployment lagged by just six months the output recovery in the non-oil economy which began during 1992 but much exceeded any conceivable growth in employment during 1993 – in both cases breaking with well-established past relationships.

THE CLAIMANT COUNT AS A MEASURE OF THE LEVEL OF UNEMPLOYMENT

'The count inevitably reflects the administrative system on which it is based and cannot be ideal for every purpose, for example, for measuring labour slack or social hardship' (*Employment Gazette*, October 1986, p. 418).

Claimant unemployment, even at these very high levels of around 3 million or 10 per cent of the workforce, considerably understates the true level of involuntary unemployment in the UK. To demonstrate this requires a brief description of the claimant count: its history, limitations and advantages.

The claimant count was introduced on 11 November 1982, replacing the previous clerical record of those 'registered' as unemployed with the government's employment services (job centres and careers offices),[6] after registration became voluntary.[7] The claimant count is largely based on computerized records of those signing on for unemployment-related benefits at UBOs (now known as Employment Service local offices). The switch to largely computerized records resulted in improved accuracy, whilst UBOs have more up-to-date information than job centres on outflows from unemployment. The main disadvantage of the claimant count is that 'since it is the by-product of an administrative system for paying benefits',[8] it is sensitive to changes affecting the administration or coverage of the benefit system as well as those of a purely statistical kind.[9] In fact, since 1979, the official measure of unemployment has been subject to 29 changes – 24 counting from the switch to the claimant measure – all of which resulted in either a reduction or no change; although the Department of Employment (ED) only recognizes eight of these changes. Two of the main ones affected the young and the old.

In the case of the former, changes introduced in 1981 and 1983 meant that unemployed people aged 60 and over (principally men[10]) and in receipt of income support or obtaining national insurance credits were no longer required to sign on. As a result, unemployed men aged 60 and over are only included on the claimant count if in receipt of unemployment benefit. This purely administrative change has resulted in an enormous diminution in the number of unemployed men aged 60 and over included in the claimant count: from 250 000 in 1983 to just 50 000 by mid-1993 (male unemployment overall standing at a similar level at these two dates).

However, this completely misrepresents the true unemployment – and, more to the point, non-employment – situation amongst 60–64 year-old men. From information provided by the *Labour Force Survey,* unemployment, measured on an internationally agreed basis in accordance with ILO guidelines,[11] has remained roughly constant since 1983, contradicting the picture presented by the claimant count. However, even this understates the true degree of non-employment among men aged 60–64. The employment rate in this group has fallen sharply from 73.7 per cent in 1977 to 46.8 per cent in 1992. This has been reflected, partly, in increased unemployment but, to a far greater degree, in increased inactivity. This is the result, no doubt, to some degree, of voluntary early retirement but also of involuntary withdrawal from the labour market in the wake of the massive destruction of male manufacturing jobs during the 1980s. Non-employment rates (1 minus the employment rate or the unemployment plus inactivity rates) rose from 26.3 per cent in 1977 to 53.2 per cent in 1992, to the point where more than half of men aged 60–64 are no longer working.

Unemployed young workers have also virtually disappeared from the claimant count following the 1988 Social Security Act which deprived 16 and 17 year-old young men and women of eligibility for income support in most circumstances,[12] consequent upon the government's 'guarantee' to any young person not in full-time education or work to provide a place on the Youth Training Scheme. However, the government's guarantee notwithstanding, ILO unemployment amongst this group has remained high, albeit cyclical. Thus, in Winter 1992/3, while only 15 800 16 and 17 year-olds were included on the claimant count, the *Labour Force Survey* indicated that, of those young people not in full-time education, 75 000 were ILO unemployed and a further 28 000 economically inactive.[13] The failure of the government's guarantee to provide training has left these young people virtually bereft of any welfare state safety net[14] – and the resulting destitution only too visible in Britain's large cities.

Claimant Count: Back Revisions to Historical Series

The 29 changes made to the official measure of unemployment since 1979 raise the issue of how to generate an unemployment series on a consistent basis over time? The ED has attempted to solve this problem by computing and publishing periodically back revisions to the historical 'claimant' series on a basis consistent with the coverage of the benefit regime at the point of revision. What this means, in the case of a group whose eligibility to claim benefit has been withdrawn or which is no longer required to sign on, is that the numbers in that group are estimated and then subtracted from the past totals. However, the ED does not take into account in its revisions all 29 changes, only those which are judged to have a significant effect on the numbers eligible for benefit without a cor-responding change in their labour market situation.

The ED defends its procedure mainly by criticizing the alternative approach, namely attempting to assess what unemployment would be on a previous basis of measurement – for example, prior to the 29 changes.[15]

> Any attempt to assess what unemployment would now be on an old definition involves speculation about the effect of demographic and economic change and other factors. For instance ... the introduction of voluntary registration and the changes since then, including changes in the labour market and the role played by job centres make *meaningless* any attempt to estimate the number who would now be registered as unemployed on the old definition. Similarly, not least given the sharp fall in the number of young people into the early 1990s, it would be unrealistic to continue estimating unemployment on the coverage of the count prior to September 1988.[16]

These arguments are, however, far from persuasive. In the case of the second, while there is a considerable difference in practice between obtaining an historical series on 16 and 17 year-old claimants and deleting them from past totals and trying to unearth (from e.g. the *Labour Force Survey*) data on 16 and 17 year-old unemployed non-claimants, they are completely symmetrical activities. However, the former (ED) approach eliminates information and rewrites a group out of the historical record simply because of an administrative change; while the alternative forces the authorities to unearth additional information.[17]

Moreover, whatever the shortcomings of any alternative method for estimating a consistent unemployment series, the case against the ED's approach could be decisive. Namely, that this exercise in rewriting history – even if not on quite the scale of Orwell's *1984* – would, were it more widely known of among the general public, raise further doubts as to the legitimacy of the official unemployment series; more especially as it absorbs a certain volume of public resources.

Unemployment Unit (UU) Index

The Unemployment Unit (UU) uses a different approach to trying to generate an unemployment series which is consistent over time: it attempts to estimate what unemployment would be on a pre-claimant basis. The UU index is higher everywhere than the official measure of unemployment, with the gap growing absolutely and relatively over time. According to the UU index, unemployment in October 1993 stood at 4 million against the officially measured total of 2.86 million – more than 1 million or almost 40 per cent higher – a significant difference.

It is not possible to defend every aspect of the methodology used to construct the UU index which obviously involves some rather rough-and-ready, back-of-the envelope procedures. The fact that the UU index is running at a far higher level than officially measured unemployment, however, does raises an obvious question: namely, is unemployment under 3 million, as measured by the claimant count, or is it closer to 4 million, as estimated by the UU index?

Comparing Claimant and ILO Unemployment

The claimant count appears able to summon in its support the ILO measure of unemployment, based on internationally agreed guidelines[18] and estimated from information provided by the household *Labour Force Survey*.[19] Claimant unemployment and ILO unemployment coincide quite closely, at least in total and from 1986 onwards.[20] Such agreement may be a source of reassurance for some; or, alternatively, a surprise for others, given the quite distinct approaches to measuring unemployment which each embodies. The agreement between the two is even more surprising, given that they comprise such different populations.

Common to both ILO and claimant unemployment, there exists a core of people unemployed on both definitions: ILO unemployed claimants – a group which is cyclically sensitive. ILO unemployed claimants would, by general agreement, be included in any proper measure of unemployment. However, ILO unemployed claimants account for only about two-thirds of total unemployment measured under either approach – 1.82 million out of a total of 2.8 million (Summer 1993).

In addition to this common core, ILO unemployment comprises ILO unemployed non-claimants i.e. those who are unemployed according to the LO criteria but are not eligible to sign on for unemployment-related benefits and do not, therefore, appear on the claimant count. In Summer 1993, there were 1.08 million ILO unemployed non-claimants.

Claimant unemployment, on the other hand, comprises, in addition to ILO unemployed claimants, a group of claimants not considered ILO unemployed, because either in employment or economically inactive according to ILO criteria. In Summer 1993, 1 million claimants were considered not ILO unemployed.

Given the core of ILO unemployed claimants common to both measures, the fact that the number of ILO unemployed non-claimants roughly equals those claimants not ILO unemployed ensures the high degree of agreement between ILO and claimant unemployment in total. However, except arithmetically, these two groups do not offset one another in any real sense – as they comprise very different populations. In fact, the relationship between the two, it will be argued here, is, to a considerable extent, additive.

ILO Unemployed Non-claimants

This group comprises, according to the ED, 'those people who are not entitled to claim certain unemployment benefits in their own right and also those who

may not wish or consider it worthwhile to claim'.[21] In the past, women constituted the overwhelming majority of this group, for several reasons, for
example: low earnings, opting to make reduced rate contributions thereby
precluding entitlement to unemployment benefit (UB); or an inadequate contribution record; or, once any entitlement to UB is exhausted through long-duration
unemployment, women may find themselves unable to claim means-tested
income support, because their partner is either working or already claiming benefit
(see Micklewright, 1990). However, recently, men have increased rapidly
among ILO unemployed non-claimants, almost to the point of parity with
women.[22]

ILO unemployed non-claimants, after doubling with the rise of mass unemployment in the early 1980s, has shown a small trend increase since 1984, but
with no cyclical movement.[23] Nevertheless, it is clear that all 1.08 million ILO
unemployed non-claimants would, by general consent, be included among the
unemployed, properly measured – since their exclusion from the claimant count
is solely on administrative grounds.

Claimants Not ILO Unemployed

Should the 1 million unemployed claimants who are not considered ILO
unemployed – because either in employment or inactive according to the ILO
definition – be treated as part of the unemployed, properly measured?

Employed claimants
This group, whose very existence may come as a surprise to many, comprises
claimants who, according to the ILO guidelines, are regarded as employed,
because they work more than 1 hour in the reference week. In Summer 1993 –
330 000 claimants were in this position – a doubling in numbers since 1983[24]
– with virtually all of the increase occurring among men.

The ED, in its annual analysis of these figures, is always at pains to stress
that this series 'is not necessarily an indication of activity in the "black"
economy, since in some circumstances people can legitimately claim unemployment-related benefits while they also have relatively low earnings from
part-time work'.[25] Moreover, a few of these employed claimants 'will have
become unemployed or started a job part way through the reference week'.[26]

Increasing numbers of employed claimants are indicative of a growing army
of men combining low part-time, casual earnings with unemployment-related
benefits in order to survive. This must reflect the emergence of mass unemployment and the decline in male employment opportunities in the 1980s.[27] To
quote the *Employment Gazette*:

Some of the increase in 'claimant employment' in recent years may be explained by changes in the economic cycle. In a recessionary situation characterized by continually rising unemployment and diminishing job prospects, one may see an increase in 'claimant employment' as more unemployed people accept the sort of part-time jobs which, because they only generate low earnings, do not preclude job-holders from also claiming benefits.[28]

Should 'employed claimants' be counted among the unemployed, properly measured? The answer must surely be: yes. This group is technically in employment on account of breaching the ILO's very restrictive 1-hour rule; but not many hours are being worked, given the restrictions on the amount that can be earned while still receiving benefit. The 'claimant employed' must certainly be considered severely underemployed (whether measured in terms of income or hours worked) and, thus, to a large degree, unemployed as well.

Claimants not ILO unemployed because inactive

We turn, next, to those claimants not considered ILO unemployed because 'inactive', either because they were not seeking work or because they were not available: in total numbering 670 000 (470 000 men and 190 000 women) in Summer 1993. That large numbers of claimants exhibiting these characteristics should exist at all is somewhat surprising, given: (i) that 'availability' and, since 1988, 'actively seeking' are basic conditions for receiving unemployment-related benefits – with both conditions being more rigorously applied in recent years; and (ii) the unceasing drive against benefit fraud. Indeed, such is the rigour with which the benefit regime is applied that it might be suggested all 'inactive' claimants should be treated as unemployed.

However, among 'inactive' claimants, the *Labour Force Survey* finds large numbers declaring they do not wish to work (260 000 in Spring 1993); these cannot be treated as involuntarily unemployed. The principal reasons given by such people for not looking are: long-term sickness/disablement, in which case they should be transferred to alternative benefits, retirement[29] and, among women, looking after family/home. Other claimants giving 'long-term sickness/disablement' as their reason for 'inactivity' (roughly 30 000) should be on alternative benefits and also cannot be treated as unemployed.[30]

However, should some of the remaining 'inactive' claimants be treated as unemployed? In considering this question, it is worth noting that the series on 'inactive' claimants is highly cyclical, strongly suggesting *a priori* that they might be included among the (cyclical) unemployed. One explanation for this cyclical sensitivity is that the intensity of job search is a function of the economic cycle – increases in 'inactivity' reflecting 'discouragement'. The *Labour Force Survey* actually publishes a series of those ILO 'inactives' who are 'discouraged' – defined as 'those who would like work but have not looked in the past 4 weeks as they believe there are no jobs available' – some of whom are claimants[31] and others not. 'Discouraged' workers, it is clear, should be included among the unemployed, properly measured – whether they are claimants or not.

Excluding from the total of 'inactive' claimants those who do not wish to work as well as those who are long-term sick/disabled and those 'believing no jobs available' ('discouraged' workers), there remain between 250 000 and 300 000 over whom there hangs a question mark as to whether or not they should be included among the unemployed. The reasons given by the 'inactive' for failing to look for a job during the previous week include: looking after family/home, temporarily sick, on holiday, awaiting results of job application, waiting to start job already obtained, studying, not yet started looking. Considering carefully each of these reasons for failing to engage in job search, some sort of argument could be made in each case for classifying the person involved as unemployed rather than 'inactive'. For example, claimants who are temporarily sick and on that account are not engaged in job search ought surely to be treated as unemployed, since they are only temporarily outside the labour market.[32] A similar argument holds for those claimants who have not yet started looking for work. Those awaiting the results of a job application or waiting to start a job already obtained, even if not 'available', might also be classed as unemployed. So far as claimants on holiday are concerned, benefit regulations permit claimants to take a holiday, so long as they remain ' available' even if, for obvious reasons, they cannot be engaged in active job search; this must be one of the more humane aspects of the benefit regime, and taking a holiday should surely not disqualify a claimant from being counted as unemployed. Even claimants who are looking after family/home, thereby preventing job search, cannot necessarily be regarded as putting themselves beyond the job market, since the absence may be temporary (due to illness in the family or the collapse of existing care arrangements) or may reflect 'discouragement'. For all these reasons, we would argue that a high proportion of ILO 'inactive' claimants ought to be treated as unemployed, properly measured, always bearing in mind that they are all satisfying those administering the benefit regime as to their 'capability, availability and active search' for work.

Neither ILO nor claimant unemployed
The categories 'ILO unemployed' and 'claimant unemployed' do not exhaust all possibilities, since there are some unemployed people who are not 'signing on', even though in receipt of benefit (hence, not claimant unemployed), and who are 'inactive' because they are not engaged in job search (hence, not ILO unemployed). An obvious group here are men aged 60 and over in receipt of income support or national insurance credits who are no longer required to 'sign on'. Some of these, if they still express a desire to work, may be included among the 'discouraged' workers already discussed. But many of them, demoralized by the lack of employment prospects, have probably given up wanting and looking

for work (i.e. they have accepted involuntary premature retirement). They should, nonetheless, be treated as unemployed. The Unemployment Unit estimated that around 200 000 men[33] aged 60 and over were affected by dispensing with the need to 'sign on' in the early 1980s.[34]

ALTERNATIVE UNEMPLOYMENT MEASURE

Our alternative unemployment measure (see Table 5.1) starts with ILO unemployment (ILO unemployed claimants plus ILO unemployed non-claimants) adds in claimant employed plus 'discouraged' workers and those on government work-related training schemes. We then sum together 'inactive' claimants (having subtracted 'those who do not wish to work' as well as 'long-term sick/disabled') together with men aged 60 and over and not 'signing-on' and take an admittedly arbitrary figure of 50 per cent as an estimate of those unemployed.

Table 5.1   An alternative unemployment measure (Summer 1993, not seasonally adjusted, in millions)

	Total	Men	Women
Claimant unemployed (UK)	2.81	2.14	0.67
ILO unemployed claimants (GB)	1.82	1.42	0.39
+ ILO unemployed non-claimants (GB)	1.08	0.50	0.58
+ claimants: in employment (GB)	0.33	0.25	0.08
+ 'discouraged' workers of working age (incl. claimants) (GB)	0.141	0.082	0.06
+ government work-related training programmes (GB)	0.306	0.2	0.106
Claimants: other 'inactive' less claimant 'discouraged' (GB)	0.590	0.400	0.190
less 'would not like work' and 'long-term sick/disabled'	−0.300	−0.200[e]	−0.100[e]
= * other 'inactive' unemployed claimants (GB)	0.290	0.200	0.090
* men aged 60 and over not 'signing on'	0.200	0.200	0.0
+ 50 per cent of * categories	0.245	0.200	0.045
Total alternative unemployment(GB)	3.922	2.652	1.261
Total alternative unemployment (UK)	4.07	2.75	1.316

[e] estimated

Source: Labour Force Survey

Thus unemployment, properly measured, currently (early 1994) appears closer to the Unemployment Unit's total of 4 million than to the official claimant count of under 3 million.

Additional Evidence on Unemployment

Additional evidence from the *Labour Force Survey* confirms that involuntary unemployment is considerably greater than that suggested by the claimant count. Everyone not employed or unemployed and, hence, classified 'inactive' is asked in the *LFS* whether they would like a job if one were available. This reveals (in addition to almost 3 million ILO unemployed) some 2 million or more people who would like paid employment: more than 0.5 million men and roughly 1.5 million women.[35] This group further subdivides according to the strength of labour market attachment. First, 1 million people in the 1980s (two-thirds of whom were women) – falling to 800 000 in 1992 – were available but had not engaged in job search. Thus, relaxing the job search criterion for ILO unemployment, while retaining the availability condition, yields an unsatisfied demand for work in the region of 4 million. One justification for doing this is to be found in the qualification appended to the ILO unemployment definition: 'In situations where the conventional means of seeking work are of little relevance, where the labour market is largely unorganized or of limited scope, *where labour absorption is at the time inadequate,* or where the labour force is largely self-employed, the standard definition of unemployment...may be applied by relaxing the criterion of seeking work.'[36] If in addition to relaxing the 'search' criterion, the 'availability' condition is also relaxed,[37] there are a further 1 million persons who would also like paid employment if it were available – though their labour market attachment is considerably weaker.

The main characteristics of these two groups are fairly similar: married and non-married women carers looking after the family/home; and among men 'discouraged' workers, (early, possibly involuntary) retirees and long-term sick/disabled. While undoubtedly part of the economy's labour reserve, many such people could only take paid employment if, for example, greater support could be given to those caring for dependent relatives.

Disappearing Men

Further support for the view that the claimant count understates the true size of the unemployment problem by at least 1 million can be gained from the large increase in male 'inactivity' of 1.145 million between 1979–1993.

Official figures show that, during cyclical downturns, the fall in male employment is associated with a less than equal rise in ILO unemployment, and large numbers of men 'disappear' into inactivity (see *Economic Trends,* October

1993, p.64 and Dicks and Hatch, 1989). Thus, during the early 1990s recession, male employment declined by 1.3 million, while ILO unemployment rose by just 836 000; taking into account an addition to the male working-age population of 113 000, 579 000 disappeared from the statisticians' gaze into 'inactivity'. On the other hand, during cyclical recoveries, increases in employment are not fully matched by declines in ILO unemployment, since some of the new jobs are filled by men leaving 'inactivity' . Both phenomena point to the existence of a penumbra of male labour reserves around male unemployment as officially measured.

Over the economic cycle as a whole, large numbers of men have disappeared into 'inactivity'. Thus, peak-to-peak (1979–90), male employment increased slightly (+122 000), while male unemployment rose by 311 000, resulting in an increase in the 'active' male workforce of 433 000. However, expansionary demographic factors resulted in an increase in the male working-age population of 1.002 million, and male 'inactivity', therefore, rose by 566 000. Looking at the period 1979–93, male 'inactivity' rose by 1.145 million.

To conclude, at least 1 million men of working-age have left the labour force (they are neither employed nor unemployed) since 1979. Though some of this increased 'inactivity' is voluntary (reflecting early retirement and increased schooling), much the greater part must reflect involuntary unemployment, which is not reflected in official figures.

Conclusions on Claimant Count

The claimant count understates the true level of unemployment by a wide margin. It is also not a satisfactory index of changes in labour market conditions. For one thing, it is far from clear that movements in an item which is a subset of a larger variable are necessarily an accurate guide to movements in the latter. Moreover, the claimant count is necessarily sensitive to administrative action affecting both inflows and outflows. Thus the 226 000 decline in claimant unemployment during 1993 may reflect the increased success of the Employment Service at placing people from the count into jobs – possibly at the expense of new entrants and the 'inactive' – rather than an improvement in underlying labour market conditions. There are other worrying features of claimant unemployment as a measure of labour market conditions:

- the failure, during cyclical downturns, for reductions in employment to be matched by increases in claimant unemployment, implying large increases in 'inactivity';
- the changing time lag between output recovery and reductions in claimant unemployment.[38] The fact that claimant unemployment has changed from being a strongly lagging indicator in the 1980s to only a slightly lagging

indicator currently must be a cause for concern, although demographic factors feeding the growth of the working-age population are less expansionary than in the 1980s;

- and, whereas. during previous recoveries, official unemployment fell by less than the increase in employment (as people were drawn into jobs from 'inactivity'), during 1993, claimant unemployment has fallen by 226 000, and total employment has increased by at most 50 000.[39]

ACCOUNTING FOR THE EMERGENCE OF MASS UNEMPLOYMENT

Numerous explanations exist for the emergence of mass unemployment, including many microeconomic analyses which focus on, for example, the need for given (and rising) levels of unemployment to stabilize inflation, the consequences of possible labour market rigidities, the impact of the benefit system on work incentives and so on. Our aim here is not to present a review of the existing literature; rather to flesh out our own explanation, though this is not designed to be an all-encompassing theory nor one which supersedes existing approaches.

Our account focuses on the twin processes of job destruction and job creation at the sectoral level of the economy, placing them within the context of poor sectoral and overall economic performance as a result of which the UK has moved ever further from macroeconomic balance, namely from being able to reconcile the achievement of full employment with external balance. Our argument is that rapid productivity growth principally in the goods-producing sectors of the economy resulted in massive job shedding, while, simultaneously, new jobs were being generated, principally in the services. The scale of new job creation in the services, though enormous, was insufficient, given demographic factors feeding the expansion of the population of working age and increased female participation, to compensate for the rate at which jobs were being shed in goods production – the net result being a trend rise in unemployment. The reason job creation in the services was insufficient was growth in the economy as a whole was inadequate; the product, in turn, of the competitive weakness and slow rate of output growth of the internationally exposed or *traded* sector of the economy. As a consequence, the UK departed ever further from being able to reconcile full employment and external balance. While the adverse employment consequences of shortcomings in national economic performance are emphasized, the unsatisfactory performance of the international economy since the mid-1970s has made it more difficult for all participants to be able to reconcile full employment with external balance.

We begin by focusing on the process of job shedding and job creation, the sectors involved and the scale of the employment changes.

Job-shedding Sectors

The job-shedding sectors of the UK economy during the postwar period were (see Figure 5.1) the goods-producing sectors of the economy (agriculture and industry, the latter consisting of mining, manufacturing, construction and the utilities) as well as transport and communication, which is conventionally treated as part of the services.

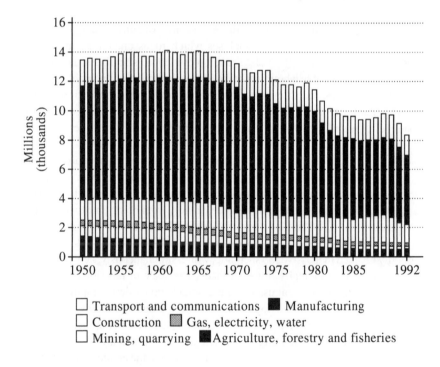

□ Transport and communications ■ Manufacturing
□ Construction ▨ Gas, electricity, water
□ Mining, quarrying ■ Agriculture, forestry and fisheries

Figure 5.1   UK sectors shedding jobs, 1950–92 (cumulative)

In the period immediately after the Second World War, employment in these sectors increased slightly in aggregate to stand at just over 14 million in the mid-1960s. However, from then onwards, employment in these job-shedding sectors declined, albeit not quite continuously, to the point where it now stands: at just under 9 million. A staggering rate of job destruction! Three of these sectors shed jobs virtually continuously between 1950 and 1992: agriculture (from 1.4 million down to 544 000), mining (from 848 000 down to 133 000) and transport and communication (from 1.8 million down to 1.5 million). On the other hand, manufacturing and public utilities both experienced rising employment up to the mid-1960s, followed by decline. Construction, meanwhile, experienced huge fluctuations in employment with peaks in the mid-1960s,1973 and during the late-1980s Lawson boom, but with a distinct downward trend over time.

Manufacturing was clearly the most important arena for job shedding in the goods-producing sectors of the economy. Manufacturing employment peaked in absolute terms in 1966. Thereafter, job shedding was, at first, a reasonably gentle affair. However, under the Tories, it became much more violent: 1 million manufacturing jobs went between 1979 and 1981, and a further 700 000 had gone by 1983. Output recovery in the late 1980s restored about 250 000 jobs between 1987 and 1989, but the early 1990s recession witnessed the loss of a further 750 000 jobs. Overall, between 1979 and 1992, one in every three manufacturing workers lost his/her job, and the sector's labour force has now declined to below 5 million. Figure 5.2 shows the respective contributions of productivity growth and output growth to manufacturing employment changes. Manufacturing employment was squeezed between, on the one hand, rapid (and, during the 1980s, accelerating) labour productivity growth and, on the other, the fact that manufacturing output since 1973, while exhibiting substantial

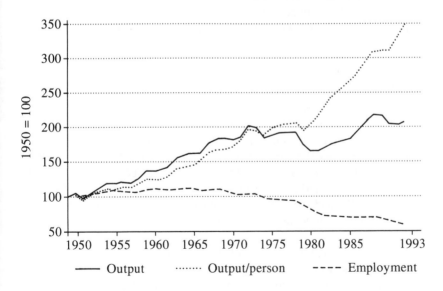

Figure 5.2   UK manufacturing: employment, output and productivity, 1950–92 (1950=100)

fluctuations, showed virtually no trend increase. If manufacturing had been more successful in international competitive, and hence output, terms, would job shedding have been any less intense? Arguably not, since a precondition for improved international competitiveness would have been an intensification of labour productivity growth.

Within transport and communication, the main areas of job shedding were: the railways (300 000 employees lost over 40 years to stand at 132 000 in 1991), passenger road transport, i.e. buses and trams (down by 120 000 over 40 years), sea transport (down by 107 000 to just 33 000 in 1991) and ports and inland water transport (down by 80 000). In road haulage, employment levels are similar to where they were in the 1950s, despite job gains up to the mid-1960s. Only air transport has recorded continuous increases in employment, while post and telecommunications, although registering an increase of 100 000 up to the mid-1970s, has since seen employment stabilized. Transport is an example of a service activity where increased self-servicing, in the form of the switch away from public transport to private car use, together with technical progress, has resulted in a net reduction in employment levels, despite a hugely increased volume of transportation activity.

Job-generating Sectors

Employment in the job-generating sectors, all service sector activities, is shown in Figure 5.3. The services saw the creation of just under 8 million new jobs between 1950 and 1992. Let us consider the main developments in each sector in turn.

Distribution, restaurants and hotels
This sector saw the creation of 1.7 million jobs,[40] from 3.4 million in 1950 to 5.1 million in 1992, despite the fact that self-employment in distribution declined in the immediate postwar decades as the supermarket revolution got underway. Wholesale distribution gained about 300 000 employees in a more or less continuous process throughout the period. Retail gained about 0.5 million employees, but all of these gains had been achieved before the mid-1960s. Employment gains during the 1980s retail boom simply compensated for losses during the 1970s and early 1980s. Restaurants, clubs, pubs and hotels registered much the largest employment gains in this sector: 580 000 in 40 years.[41]

Finance, insurance, real estate and business services
These services were the most dynamic in terms of percentage increase in employment relative to initial position: 2.34 million jobs created in 40 years (up from 0.7 million in 1950 to 3.04 million in 1992). Banking, finance and insurance generated 520 000 additional jobs for employees over this period. But

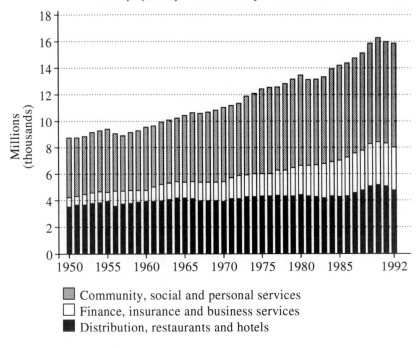

Community, social and personal services
Finance, insurance and business services
Distribution, restaurants and hotels

Figure 5.3   UK employment in job-creating sectors, 1950–92

the business services (comprising accountancy, law, real estate, advertising, market research and so on) took pride of place in terms of job creation: 1.24 million additional employees in 40 years (of which 716 000 in the 1980s).

Community, social and personal services
This sector was responsible for the largest increase in services employment in absolute numbers: 3.5 million jobs created in 40 years, up from 4.4 million in 1950 to 7.9 million in 1992, although the annual growth rate was a modest 1.4 per cent per annum. Of these additional jobs, 1 million were created in health, mostly in the National Health Service but also in the private sector and in veterinary medicine. Education was the source of a further 1.2 million new jobs between 1950 and 1991.

Insufficient Employment Growth

The 8 million jobs created in the services, a significant achievement though that was, were not sufficient, given expansionary demographic factors feeding the population of working age and increased participation among women, to prevent the emergence of mass unemployment against the background of 5 million jobs destroyed in goods production. The reason job creation in the services was inadequate lies in the unsatisfactory rate of growth of the economy as a whole. And this, in turn, can be attributed to the poor international competitive performance and slow rate of output growth of the internationally exposed or traded sector of the economy.

This primarily means manufacturing since, with a large and increasing proportion of its output traded, the sector accounts for the largest proportion of total traded output;[42] although non-manufacturing, since it failed to exhibit a compensating acceleration in output in its traded component, must bear its share of the blame.

UK-based manufacturing failed to respond adequately to the postwar challenge posed by increasingly open and competitive markets both at home and abroad, resulting from the collapse of the Empire and the liberalization of international trade in manufactures between advanced capitalist countries. The underlying factors responsible for UK-based manufacturing's poor performance (social, institutional, financial and so on) remain to be fully identified satisfactorily. But they expressed themselves in persistently low levels of investment relative to overseas competitors in fixed and human capital as well as in the R and D activities essential to the development of new processes and products, with adverse consequences for the non-price aspects of competitiveness.

Inadequate performance at the firm level was aggravated by macro-policy errors, in particular, a possible tendency to aggravate normal business cycle fluctuations resulting in the 'stop–go' cycle of excessive swings in domestic spending and interest rates and so on. The mismanagement of the North Sea energy windfall in the early 1980s further contributed to the weakening of the non-oil traded sector. Restrictive fiscal and monetary policies interacted with the growing volume of North Sea output and sterling's acquisition of petro-currency status to drive up the real £ sterling exchange rate,[43] thereby delivering an adverse shock to non-oil-traded (mainly manufacturing) competitiveness and output – to a largely avoidable degree.

Weak competitiveness resulted in a slow growth of traded output relative to the growth of domestic spending on traded goods and services that would have been associated with the level of total domestic spending required to achieve full employment and expressed itself in the form of a rapid loss of world manufacturing export share,[44] rapidly rising import penetration[45] and, most important, a worsening trade-off between unemployment and external balance.

Not that the UK is now entirely lacking in internationally competitive manufacturing businesses, it is just that there are not enough of them, given the performance of the non-manufacturing traded sector, to sustain the scale of traded output necessary to achieve macroeconomic balance. Figure 5.4 documents the worsening trade-off over time between unemployment and external balance.

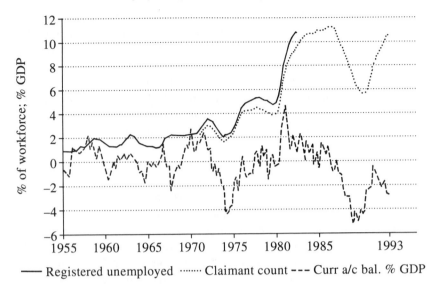

Figure 5.4   UK unemployment (% workforce) and balance of payments current account (% GDP), 1955–93: deteriorating trade-off through time

Finally, both internal performance and policy factors were aggravated by the unsatisfactory performance of the international (including European) economy from the mid-1970s onwards, characterized by deceleration in trend growth rates, possibly increased international synchronization of business cycles between advanced countries, accentuation of downturn phase of the cycle with world output actually declining in 1975, 1981 and 1992; and periods of prolonged depression and economic regression in large parts of the world (Latin America, Africa, 'transition' economies of Eastern Europe and the former Soviet Union). The deteriorating performance of the international economy made it more difficult for all participant economies to reconcile full employment with external balance, especially those whose national performance was weak.

HOW COULD FULL EMPLOYMENT HAVE BEEN MAINTAINED?

We have argued that the underperformance in the economy as a whole, resulting from the poor competitiveness of the traded sector, constrained the rate at which job-generating sectors, broadly the services, were able to create new jobs to offset those shed by the goods-producing sectors. Achieving full employment would have required both a more competitive traded sector and, hence, faster output growth overall as well as higher levels of investment to support the additional jobs which were needed in the job-generating sectors. Paradoxically, improved performance by the internationally exposed manufacturing sector was required to sustain more jobs in the sheltered services. However, to have achieved both objectives would have required a higher level of investment in both traded and non-traded sectors of the economy, and, so as to avoid excessive recourse to foreign savings, a higher level of national savings as well.

Employment During the 1980s – Total Employment Levels

The period since the Conservatives came to power in 1979 has witnessed a quite staggering roller-coaster in terms of job creation and job destruction at both aggregate (see Figure 5.5) and sectoral levels. The early 1980s economic 'shock' resulted in a net loss of 2 million jobs from 25.4 million jobs in mid-1979 to the trough in employment (23.6 million) in early 1983. At this point, economy-wide employment was no higher than in the mid-1950s – some 30 years earlier! However, as economic recovery gathered pace, total employment rose from mid-1983 onwards, and 3.5 million additional jobs (net) were created by mid-1990, of which just 1.1 million came through a reduction in 'claimant'

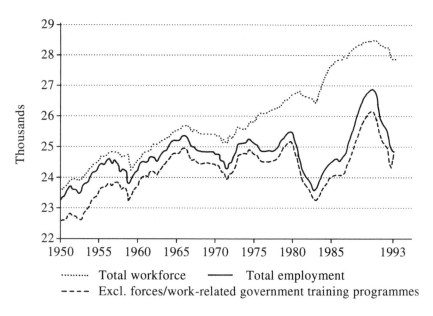

Figure 5.5   *UK employment and unemployment, 1950–93*

unemployment. At this point, total employment stood at 26.9 million – 1.5 million higher than the position the Tories inherited from Labour. The ensuing recession saw 2 million jobs destroyed and even with the recovery during 1993, total numbers employed in March 1994 (at 25.3 million) were below the 1979 level. Moreover, of this total a higher proportion consist of part-timers, so the economy is generating less employment than 14 years ago.

The intense cyclicality in UK employment totals since 1979 has been a phenomenon wholly without precedent since the Second World War and reflected the unusual intensity of the business cycle during the 1980s.[46] This is an inevitable consequence of both increased reliance on market forces and deregulation as well as a reduced role for government in stabilizing the economy, as government deliberately eschewed the use of the full range of policy instruments and, at times, openly disavowed the need for short-term demand stabilization.

Job Losses and Gains by Sector

Job-losing sectors underwent a further stage of virtually uninterrupted job shedding between 1979 and 1992: agriculture lost 122 000; mining 226 000 and public utilities 89 000. Construction underwent a particularly virulent phase of its endemic boom–bust cycle, with the early 1990s recession witnessing the loss of 383 000 jobs (21 per cent of its labour force at the peak of the Lawson boom). The manufacturing labour force shrank by 2.312 million between 1979 and 1992 – almost one in every three manufacturing workers. Job shedding continued on the railways, in passenger road transport as well as in telecommunications.

The job-generating sectors can be easily identified. Finance, insurance, real estate and business services were the most dynamic both in absolute numbers (1.4 million additional jobs peak-to-peak) and relative to its initial position (+78.8 per cent). International specialization in financial and consultancy services, growing consumer demand for financial services and the hiving-off of specialist services from goods-producing sectors (Ray, 1986) all contributed. Employment growth in the sector was quite impervious to the early 1980s recession, although about 250 000 jobs went during the early 1990s recession. Business services[47] employment increased by about 750 000 (almost doubling) in the 11 years to 1990, though about 100 000 jobs went during the early 1990s. Banking and other financial services generated 250 000 additional jobs (a rise of 57 per cent) up to 1990, but subsequently shed about 100 000. Insurance was the only part of this sector to record no job growth during the 1980s and has shed about 20 000 during the recession.

Distribution, restaurants and hotels saw a net gain of 700 000 jobs between peaks of the output cycle (1979–90), and, even after the loss of 300 000 jobs during the early 1990s recession, employment was higher than in 1979. Wholesale and retail distribution each gained about 100 000 jobs peak-to-peak; however, the early 1990s recession saw all the job gains in wholesale evaporating, while 200 000 retail jobs went. Restaurants, pubs and clubs generated a great deal of jobs during the 1980s (166 000 peak-to-peak – an increase of 30.1 per cent) as did hotels (+40 000), but both sectors have seen jobs shed during recession.

Community, social and personal services generated 1.25 million additional jobs (+ 18.8 per cent) between 1979 and 1992, somewhat surprisingly, perhaps, in view of the government's attempt to contain public spending. About 300 000 jobs have been created in medical and dental services, mainly in the NHS but also in private and veterinary medicine; about 150 000 in education, again mainly in the public sector[48] but also in private institutions such as driving schools; 100 000 in sanitary services, partly reflecting heightened concern over environmental standards; 300 000 in 'social welfare' which covers community-based personal social services (for the elderly), day nurseries and crèches and probation and after-care services. The police and criminal justice system has also experienced a modest increase in employment. Central government civil service employment declined by about 40 000 (10 per cent),[49] even taking into account the hiving-off and transfer of responsibilities, while civilian defence manpower declined by 45 000.[50] Local government administration appears[51] to have shed about 20 000 jobs in the early 1980s but, since then, employment in the sector seems to have stabilized, the apparent pressures on local authority finance notwithstanding. The conclusion seems to be that despite the Conservative government's avowed intent to contain public expenditure and a certain ideological hostility in some quarters of the Conservative party to the welfare state, employment in the public services expanded ineluctably on account of the public's aspirations for improved services and the intrinsic constraints on productivity growth in the sector.

As to private services, 'recreational and cultural services' (cinema, TV and radio, museums, sport, betting) added about 100 000 jobs during the 1980s mostly in sport and leisure centres and gambling. 'Other personal services' stagnated in employment terms around the 200 000 level; but hairdressing and beauty parlours registered increases, only to be offset by losses in laundries and dry cleaners.

Increased Part-time and Self-employment and Feminization of the Workforce

Employment developments since 1979 have exhibited three other distinctive characteristics: an increase in part-time and reduction in full-time employment, the increased feminization of the workforce, and the growth of self-employment (see Table 5.2). By September 1993, there were 3 million fewer men in full-time wage employment than in 1979, while part-time male employment rose

Table 5.2:   *UK employment composition, 1979 and 1993 compared ('000s)*

	Mid-1979	3Q 1993	Change
Male employees			
Full-time	12 663	9 651	−3 012
Part-time	728	1 226	+498
Male self-employed	1 494	2 249	+755
Female employees			
Full-time	5 646	5 647	0
Part-time	3 724	4 902	+1 178
Female self-employed	348	743	+395
Training programmes	136[a]	360	+224
Armed forces	314	267	−47

[a] 257 000 if effect of employment subsidies is included.

Source: DE, *Employment Gazette* and Unemployment Unit, *Working Brief.*

by 0.5 million; male self-employment increased by 0.75 million, but overall male employment is 1.75 million down on 1979. Female full-time employment is unchanged but part-time female employment has risen by 1.2 million. Self-employment among women more than doubled. Compared with 1979, the numbers on work-related government training programmes may hardly have changed, if jobs supported by employment subsidies in 1979 are taken into account. Overall, numbers in employment are lower than in 1979 and, since more of the jobs are part-time, fewer hours are being worked in the economy, though national income per head is some 23 per cent higher than in 1979.

The Lawson Boom: Unsustainable, Unsustained and Unrepeatable

As claimant unemployment raced towards 3 million in the wake of the destruction of 2 million jobs in the early 1990s recession, ministers attempted to reassure the public regarding future employment prospects by arguing (with reference to the Lawson boom) that: 'jobs have been created before and they can be created again', the message being that fuller levels of employment could be achieved via the normal operation of market forces in an economy undergoing cyclical recovery without new forms of government intervention.

However, the Lawson boom was not sustainable and was not, of course, sustained. Moreover, even if repeatable, boom would give way to slump as before. The two main reasons for its non-sustainability were: the strong inflationary pressures which were triggered, though inflation was accentuated by the unbalanced (regionally, sectorally) nature of economic growth; and the heavy recourse to foreign borrowing (current account deficits between 3–4 per cent of GDP between 1988 and 1990), enabling total domestic spending to be sustained at higher levels than otherwise.

High levels of domestic spending boosted employment in the sheltered or non-traded sector of the economy and brought claimant unemployment tumbling down, the construction boom in the South-East being an obvious example. However, the jobs created were, to a large degree, artificial in the sense that they depended on the traded component of the higher levels of domestic spending being satisfied, at the margin, by a high propensity to resort to increased net imports. Such high levels of dependence on foreign savings could not be sustained continuously, and, as the level of domestic spending was rapidly adjusted closer to the economy's foreign exchange earning capacity, such jobs were bound to evaporate.

A re-run of the Lawson boom and its associated jobs bonanza, since it presupposes the ability to attract substantial foreign savings, may not be an option available to the UK; but, even if it were. Prime Minister Major's government does not seem particularly keen to grasp it, to judge by its commitment to 'sustained, non-inflationary growth'.

However, the consensus forecast for UK GDP growth during the recovery phase of the current cycle is 3 per cent per annum maximum; against an underlying annual rate of productivity growth of 2 to 2.5 per cent, per annum it seems clear that really significant inroads into unemployment cannot be delivered by the normal operation of market forces, even when operating under the stimulus of economic recovery. This line of reasoning has now been accepted by the government in the person of the Chancellor of the Exchequer, along with its corollary, namely, the need for non-market interventions to bring unemployment down to socially-acceptable levels.

CONCLUSION: POLICY PRESCRIPTIONS[52]

The Tories' recommended interventions are: enhanced labour market deregulation and flexibility, resulting in British workers pricing themselves into jobs through accepting real wage-cuts. Some obvious objections to this approach are: (i) its *lack of feasibility*: the cost of reproducing labour power in late twentieth century Britain must set some sort of real wage floor below which workers refuse to work. Already many of the jobs currently on offer in job centres have wages falling below such a minimum and are being rejected as unacceptable. In some cases, this is because the worker (and his/her family) would be worse off in work than on benefit, even though the latter provides only a minimum standard of living; (ii) *social unacceptability*: additional wage cuts and/or loss of employment rights at the bottom of the earnings spectrum would produce further polarization of an income distribution which, reversing an 80-year trend, has already widened during these years of Conservative government (Atkinson, 1993); (iii) *character of jobs created:* the government's prescription presupposes the widespread reappearance of personal domestic service, with all the negative characteristics associated with such jobs as loss of personal freedom, sub-ordination to the authority of another individual, absence of social contact and so on. Such a development is unacceptable to many unemployed people, given rising aspirations and increased levels of education, as well as more broadly in society; (iv) *low wage. low tech jobs:* such a prescription implies a defensive form of adjustment to poor economic performance, whereas the only form of adjustment consistent with social and political stability in the long run is the creation of high-wage, high-productivity jobs. The low-wage adjustment path might also hold back the dynamism of the system as a whole by reducing the pressure on firms to engage in cost-reducing technical progress.

An alternative policy set involves two types of measures. The first are measures to ensure the recovery is sustained (action to improve the health of the international economy, in particular, interest rate cuts and a reversal of fiscal consolidation in Europe to ensure the UK's recovery is not foreshortened by the reappearance of balance-of-payments pressures); measures to improve the balance of the economy between private consumption spending, exports and investment (e.g. lower interest rates and enhanced investment incentives); and enhance the competitiveness of the UK traded sector (increased investment in infrastructure, skills, support for R & D relevant to the traded sector, the cost of which, it can be argued, should be born by higher levels of public borrowing).

Second are the special employment measures. Accepting that relatively small inroads into unemployment totals will be made through the normal mechanism of economic recovery augmented by the measures above, the case for special employment measures is essentially:

- the huge cost to society of unemployment in terms of output foregone and the main forms in which this is expressed; for example, the Exchequer cost (currently estimated at £9000 per annum per unemployed person in terms of increased benefit expenditure and taxes foregone[53]), the cost to the unemployed individuals themselves (in terms of reduced income, health deterioration, atrophying of skills and so on.);
- rather than paying the unemployed to do nothing, it would be better to pay them to produce socially-useful goods and services;
- there exist huge unmet demands for goods and services of all sorts.[54]

Briefly, this means examining the case for deploying some proportion of the Exchequer cost of unemployment as a labour subsidy to the private, public and voluntary sectors, so long as a means can be found of preventing substitution for existing labour; and imaginative schemes to mobilize the unemployed in special employment and training programmes designed to increase the supply of goods and services, such as home insulation, infant care and preschool education; the care of our increasingly elderly population; general environmental improvements; and the creation of leisure facilities and their operation.

Only in this way will it be possible to escape the social evils associated with the reappearance of mass unemployment, and turn the potential provided by continuing technical progress to increase the supply of goods and services.

NOTES

1. Unemployment-related benefits are: (i) Unemployment Benefit (UB), a non-means tested benefit. payable to those satisfying certain national insurance contributory conditions, currently (early 1994) available for a maximum of 12 months; (ii) Income Support (IS), a means-tested benefit, payable to those who have either exhausted their right to UB through long-duration unemployment or are unable to claim UB for other reasons (e.g. failing to satisfy UB contributory conditions, UB claim yet to be determined, UB disqualification for voluntary unemployment etc.); (iii) national insurance credits, which those unemployed but ineligible for benefit (e.g. women unable to claim means-tested IS because their partner is either employed or a claimant) can sign for voluntarily to help safeguard future entitlement to benefit. Claimants who 'sign on' are expected to be 'capable of, available for and actively seeking work'. Some claimants receive a combination of (i) and (ii), where income from UB falls below IS levels.
2. Thus Crafts (1991) adjusts interwar unemployment data (see table 41.3, p.818) in an attempt to make them comparable with 'claimant' unemployment; this yields a UK rate for 1931 of 10.2 per cent and for 1932 of 10.6 per cent – similar to that for December 1992 (the early 1990s recession peak) of 10.5 per cent. Crafts's procedure is to link the inter-war series on unemployment among insured employees (from Feinstein, 1972) with the postwar (1946–82) series on 'registered' unemployed, using correction factors linking interwar and postwar data found in Metcalf et al. (1982), and then linking up with the post-1982 'claimant' series, using the relationship between 'registrants' and 'claimants', based on the Department of Employment's (ED's) extrapolation of the 'claimant' series back to 1971 (see *Employment Gazette*, December 1982). It would be an exaggeration to claim that this attempt to produce data comparable with the 1930s is completely robust given the shortcomings of both the underlying data sets and the methodology. The ED's recent attempt to produce a 100 year unemployment series (*Employment Gazette*, December 1993) does not make any attempt to adjust the 1930s data on 'insured' employees and shows much higher unemployment for the 1930s than the 1990s.
3. All unemployment data in this paragraph refer to official 'claimant' unemployment.
4. Both male and female 'claimant' unemployment peaked during 1986, but ILO unemployment (for definition and discussion, see below) peaked, for both men and women, in 1984.
5. 'Inactivity' increased substantially during the recession: between mid-1990 to mid-1993, taking into account mildly expansionary demographic factors, by 826 600 (632 400 men and 194 200 women), using ED labour force estimates (or by 641 000 – 579 000 men and 62 000 women) using *Labour Force Survey* data – see Spence and Watson (1993).
6. Registrants were those accepted by staff of the employment or careers offices as being 'capable and available for work, whether they are entitled to unemployment benefit or not' . Many factors affected the propensity of unemployed men and women to register, including changes in regulations affecting eligibility for benefits, principally for married women. For those not eligible, other factors might apply, such as how likely they thought they would get a suitable job as a result of being on the register, see *Employment Gazette*, September 1982,

pp. 389–93. From this description, it would seem that 'registered' unemployed cannot be considered either intrinsically superior or inferior to 'claimant' unemployed.

7. This was the product of the Thatcher government's Rayner administrative economy measures, as a result of which attendance by unemployed claimants at a job centre, in addition to the Unemployment Benefit Office (UBO), was no longer mandatory.

8. *Employment Gazette*, October 1992, p. 456

9. Such as the length of time during which information relating to inflows and outflows on the reference day is allowed to accrue.

10. Women currently become eligible for the state retirement pension at age 60; but, up to the age of 65, they can choose to claim UB and defer their retirement pension by not claiming it or by electing to de-retire (see CPAG, 1993b). Thus the claimant count contains about 100 000 women aged 60 and over.

11. The ILO definition of unemployment (used for the first time in the 1984 *Labour Force Survey*) is: 'those who did not undertake more than one hour's work for pay or profit during the week prior to interview, who were available to start work in the two weeks following their LFS interview and had either looked for work in the four weeks prior to interview or were waiting to start a job they had already obtained.' The so-called LFS definition of unemployment, used in previous *Labour Force Survey* was more restrictive on the job search side (1 week as against 4 weeks) but did not contain an availability condition.

12. Small numbers of 16 and 17 year-olds remain on the claimant count even after the 1988 Social Security Act. Some of these have earned the right to UB on the basis of their national insurance contribution record. Moreover, some 16 and 17 year-olds in certain categories can claim IS through to age 18 – and some of these have to 'sign on' (see CPAG, 1993b).

13. 26 000 in full-time education were also were considered ILO unemployed; see *Employment Gazette*, July 1993, p. 308.

14. Although IS can be claimed during the so-called child benefit extension period – and afterwards; and discretionary special hardship payments are available (the number has escalated in recent years from 6500 per quarter in 1990 to 37 000 in 1993). Bridging allowances are also available at the discretion of the Employment Secretary for those between jobs and YTS (see CPAG, 1993b).

15. The Unemployment Unit's Index (for discussion see below) seeks to do precisely this.

16. See ED, *Gazette*, December 1988, p.661.

17. Which, in the case of unemployed 16 and 17 year-olds, they are obliged to do anyway simply because of public concern.

18. For definition see note 11.

19. Undertaken biannually from 1973 to 1983, annually from 1983 to 1992 and quarterly from Spring 1992 onwards.

20. The large divergences in 1979 and 1981 result from revisions to the claimant series in line with current reduced benefit coverage rather than any divergence between 'registered' unemployment reported at the time and the results of the 1979 and 1981 *Labour Force Survey*.

21. *Employment Gazette*, October 1993, p.462. Some might be on another benefit, e.g. lone parents.

22. This may reflect unemployment among formerly self-employed men, who, ineligible for UB, might be unable to claim means-tested IS on account of the £8000 private capital rule – male self-employment fell by 300 000 during the 1990s recession; and increased female participation precluding unemployed male partners from claiming means-tested benefit. Unemployed 16 and 17 year-olds (both male and female), discussed earlier, are also to be found among ILO unemployed non-claimants as are students looking for part-time and vacation work.

23. One explanation for the lack of cyclicality may be that women returnees, encouraged to enter the labour force during the late 1980s boom, would, if unable to find work but engaged in job search, have been classified as ILO unemployed – though their recent history of non-employment would have prevented their establishing a claim to UB, see *Employment Gazette*, October 1990, p. 510.

24. But with little evidence of cyclical sensitivity.

25. Quote from *Employment Gazette*, October 1993, p. 462.

26. See *Employment Gazette*, October 1985.

27. Thus, between 1979 and 1993, male employment declined by 1.18 million, while male unemployment (ILO definition) rose by 1.15 million; given an increase in the male population of working age of 1.12 million. this implied an increase in 'inactivity' (voluntary plus involuntary) of 1.15 million (estimated using population data and constant 1985 participation rates in *Employment Gazette*, April 1992).

28. See *Employment Gazette*, October 1993, p. 462.

29. In those cases where retirement is premature, 'discouragement' may be a factor (see below).

30. Though the number of sick/disabled may also be cyclically sensitive, this group being more likely to lose a job and less likely to gain one during recession.

31. See frequently-published breakdown of ILO inactive claimants by reason for not seeking work in the *Employment Gazette*, see e.g. July 1992, pp. 347–55.

32. Though they should, according to benefit regulations, be on sickness benefit.

33. See also *Employment Gazette*, July 1985, pp. 274–7.

34. Other categories of IS recipients who are not expected to 'sign on' include lone parents with dependent children, pregnant women for a period around confinement, severely disabled, those incapable of work, the unemployable as well as refugees, discharged prisoners, those affected by a trade dispute etc.; see CPAG (1993b)

35. The results of these tabulations have been published periodically in Unemployment Unit. *Unemployment Bulletin* and *Working Brief* (various). *Employment Gazette*, January 1986, pp. 21–7 also carries an article on these categories.

36. *Concepts and Definitions*, Resolution I of the 13th International Conference of Labour Statisticians (Geneva, October 1982, para 6.2).

37. Whether or not they had been engaged in job search in the past 4 weeks – though the overwhelming majority had not (see *Employment Gazette*, January 1986, p.24).

38. Theoretical considerations suggest a lag on account of a tendency for employers to respond to a recovery in demand by, initially at least, increasing output from their existing labour force; then, when employment eventually increases, jobs are filled from the 'inactive' labour reserve as well as from reductions in the claimant count.

39. Note that the replacement of one full-time job by two part-timers (which seems to be the story during 1993) increases employment by one in UK official statistics since full- and part-timers are weighted equally.

40. Jobs throughout this discussion refers to employees plus self-employed.

41. The employment gains in the sub-sectors mentioned do not sum to that for the sector as a whole since certain activities are excluded.

42. This is a reasonably robust statement, though it is by no means easy to measure, mainly because of the definition of traded output as the sum of exports plus potential exports, i.e. goods and services which could be exported but are absorbed domestically. For a recent attempt to decompose the UK Retail Prices Index (not output) between its traded and non-traded components, see Melliss (1993).

43. A process described by Lord Kaldor as 'Mrs Thatcher coming on stream at the same time as North Sea oil'.

44. Part of the decline in the UK's share of world manufactured exports (to a level in the 1980s similar to that of France and Italy, though much lower than that of the more industrialized Germany) can be explained by the disappearance of abnormal factors (e.g. imperial preference) sustaining the UK's share in the years immediately after the second World War.

45. In fact, manufacturing import-penetration in the UK, in respect of both level and rate of change, was similar to that of the other three big European economies (Germany, France and Italy); but, in the UK, the growth of domestic spending on manufactures was slower as a result of weaker overall economic performance due to the operation of the foreign exchange constraint on growth, in turn due to the poor performance of the traded sector.

46. Bill Martin's evidence to the Treasury Select Committee (1991) shows the 1979–90 cycle was unique in postwar history in terms of the length of the upswing and the intensity of both 1981 recession and 1988 boom.

47. This includes activities auxiliary to banking and finance (including stock exchanges, stock brokers, bill brokers, mortgage brokers), activities auxiliary to insurance (brokers and agents, loss adjusters); house and estate agents; legal services; accountants; architects, surveyors and

consulting engineers; advertising; computer services; management consultants; market research and public relations; TV and radio hire; self-drive car and van hire etc.

48. Despite a decline of 70 000 in core teaching-force in primary and secondary schools as declines in the school-age population (from 1974 and 1979 peaks respectively) failed to be utilized to improve teacher:pupil ratios.
49. Much of this resulted from job shedding in Inland Revenue and Customs and Excise as a result of simplification of the tax system.
50. UK defence personnel fell by 22 000 (7 per cent), 10 000 each off the Royal Navy and the Army but with the RAF and Royal Marines virtually unscathed.
51. Data for 1979–82 include police and fire service in addition to local government administration (following SIC, 1968), whereas data from 1982 onwards refer to local authority administration alone (in line with SIC, 1980).
52. This section is, for reasons of space, inevitably brief and sketchy; a proper treatment awaits further research.
53. Such calculations exclude items such as the additional burden on the NHS, police (in terms of higher crime).
54. This creates a presumption against work sharing as a solution to unemployment, except in so far as it is entered into voluntarily.

REFERENCES

Atkinson, A.B. (1993), 'What is happening to the Distribution of Income in the UK?', Cambridge: mimeo.

Child Poverty Action Group (CPAG) (1993a), *National Welfare Benefits Handbook*: 23rd edition: London: CPAG.

Child Poverty Action Group (CPAG) (1993b), *Rights guide to non-means-tested benefits: 16th edition 1993–94*, London: CPAG.

Crafts, N. (1991), 'Economics and History' in D. Greenaway, et al (eds), *Companion to Contemporary Economic Thought*, London: Routledge.

Department of Social Security (1993), *Social Security: the government's expenditure plans. 1993–4 to 1995–6*, London: HMSO (Cm 2213).

Dicks, M.J. and Hatch, N. (1989), 'The relationship between employment and unemployment', Bank of England Discussion Paper no. 39, London: Bank of England.

Employment Policy Institute (1993), 'The curious case of falling unemployment', *Economic Report*, vol. 7 no. 11, July.

Feinstein, C.H. (1972), *National Income, Expenditure and Output of the United Kingdom, 1855-1965*, Cambridge: Cambridge University Press.

Finn, D. (1993), *Unemployment and Training Rights Handbook*, London: Unemployment Unit.

Melliss, C. (1993), 'Tradable and non-tradable prices in the UK and the EC', *Bank of England Quarterly Bulletin*, vol. 33 no. 1, February, pp. 80–89.

Metcalf, D., Nickell, S.J. and Floros, N. (1982), 'Still searching for an explanation of unemployment in Inter-War Britain', *Journal of Political Economy*, vol. 90 no. 21.

Micklewright, J. (1990), 'Why do less than a quarter of the unemployed in Britain receive unemployment insurance?', *LSE Working Paper TIDI 147*, September.

Ray, G. F. (1986), 'Services for Manufacturing', *National Institute Economic Review*, vol. 117 no. 3, August pp. 30–32.

Spence, A. and Watson, M. (1993), 'Estimating employment: a comparison of household and employer-based surveys', *Employment Gazette*, October, pp. 465–70.

Treasury and Civil Service Committee (1991), *The 1991 Autumn Statement*, London: HMSO (HC 58, Session 1991–2).

6. Restructuring, flexibility and the New Right in the US: the political economy of plutocracy[1]

Mike Marshall

A so-called 'Keynesian consensus' or Keynesian social democratic state involving, *inter alia*, a commitment to the maintenance of a high level of employment via government management of the economy and an acceptance of a core level of social provision, was rather slow to develop in the US in the period after the Second World War and was less firmly established, and less extensively developed, there than in the UK.[2] This consensus was built on the bold, but at times rather contradictory, foundations of the New Deal. Keynesianism was grafted on to this tradition, but its progress was slow and limited until the 1960s and, as it turned out, its ascendancy was short-lived. As the growth of the 1960s subsided into the stagflation of the 1970s, there was a growing disillusion with Keynesianism and welfarism that undermined the consensus and laid the foundation for a neo-conservative counter-revolution.

According to orthodoxy, capitalism works when it is 'flexible' and runs into trouble when sclerosis sets in. In periods of prolonged economic crisis therefore it is usually concluded that the market mechanism has been undermined - has been prevented from working freely as an allocative and incentive system, Thus the experience of the stagflationary era led many mainstream economists to conclude that 'rigidities' and 'imperfections' in the labour market had produced excessively high wage costs, restrictive practices and a poor productivity performance. Rigidities in capital markets, allied with excessive government regulation, had discouraged investment and risk taking and, of course, high government expenditure had produced concomitant high marginal rates of tax that constituted a significant disincentive to work, save and invest. In the face of such rigidities, intervention was necessary to curb vested interests and distributional coalitions, facilitate reallocation of resources between the public and private sectors, to reorder the fiscal activities of the state, and in general restructure economic relations and the government's role in the economy. This was the New Right project of the 1980s.

As Keynesianism became discredited, then, neo-classicism, in a variety of forms, increased its influence. As it did so the much vaunted strategy of greater 'flexibility', largely a renewed promulgation of the gospel of unfettered market forces in the New Right formulation, came to the fore. In the US, the neoconservative backlash manifested itself as 'Reaganomics'. The emergence of Reaganomics was clearly of some importance not just because of the intrinsic interest of the economic, social and political changes wrought in the US itself (important and interesting as they are); but also because Reaganomics shaped the development of New Right ideas generally in the 1980s. It was clearly influential in the spread of New Right 'liberal productivist' ideas to Europe in the form of 'Euro-sclerosis' theories.[3] Moreover, the performance of the US economy, especially the job-creation record, under Reagan was successfully used to support New Right policies in Europe.

The nature and claims of this New Right project in the US therefore deserves detailed examination. In this chapter we shall offer an evaluation of Reaganomics in the 1980s, assessing its worth as a non-inflationary growth strategy, and paying particular attention to the issues of productivity, equity and job creation.

THE REAGANOMICS NEW RIGHT PROJECT[4]

With the decline in Keynesianism the way was open for opposing schools of thought to increase their influence on policy making in the new neo-conservative era. The policy goals of the Reagan administration reflected the variety of New Right doctrines that coexisted uneasily in the first years of the administration, although it is clear that, at first, the desire to curb inflation was given the highest priority.

During the first 18 months of the administration the dominant feature was the continuation of the contractionary policy initiated by the Federal Reserve Board in the Carter years, and indeed this phase has been dubbed the monetarist phase of the administration's policy-making (see e.g. Eichner, 1988). The Treasury Bill rate, M1 growth rate, and exchange rate figures in Table 6.1 all indicate the tightness of policy. The Treasury Bill rate peaked at 14.1 per cent and the dollar exchange rate appreciated over the whole 18 month period. The impact of the monetary policy on economic activity is clear, with the growth rate of GNP becoming negative in 1982 and unemployment peaking at 9.7 per cent.

The impact of the monetary contraction was unexpectedly severe, perhaps because of a drop in velocity, and the policy was reversed as the adverse consequences emerged. From late 1982 onwards, the Reagan administration increasingly adopted the mantle of a supply-side economic ideology.[5]

Table 6.1 US main economic indicators, 1979–88

Variable/ year	M1 growth rate	Treasury bill rate	Dollar exchange rate	Infla- tion rate	GNP growth rate	Unem- ployment rate	Budget deficit (US$ bn)	External trade deficit (US$ bn)	Saving rate (savings/ GNP)[a]	Invest- ment GNP (%)[b]	Produc- tivity (non- farm)[c]	Budget deficit/ GNP (%)	External trade deficit/ GNP (%)
1979	7.72	10.1	99.6	8.8	2.5	5.9	−16.1	−28.65	6.9	17.6	1.0	0.3	1.14
1980	7.49	11.6	100.0	9.1	−0.2	7.2	−61.3	−22.40	7.1	16.3	−0.3	2.00	0.08
1981	5.23	14.1	112.7	9.6	1.9	7.6	−63.8	−28.15	7.5	16.1	1.5	2.09	0.09
1982	8.65	10.7	125.9	6.4	−2.6	9.7	−145.9	−35.50	6.8	14.9	−0.4	4.60	1.12
1983	10.21	8.6	133.2	3.9	3.6	9.6	−176.0	−65.26	5.4	14.9	2.6	5.17	1.92
1984	5.28	9.6	143.7	3.7	6.8	7.5	−169.6	−110.80	6.2	15.9	2.1	4.50	2.92
1985	11.98	7.5	150.2	3.0	3.4	7.2	−196.0	−120.08	4.5	16.2	0.3	4.88	2.99
1986	15.62	6.0	122.5	2.7	2.9	7.0	−205.6	−142.70	4.1	15.9	0.5	4.85	3.37
1987	6.26	5.8	108.0	3.3	3.3	6.2	−157.8	−158.25	3.3	14.8	1.0	3.49	3.50
1988	4.30	6.7	104.2	3.5	4.3	5.5	−143.1	−128.25	4.2	14.8	1.1	2.94	2.64

Notes:
[a] Household savings only.
[b] Refers to private gross capital formation.
[c] Productivity is the rate of growth of GDP per person hour in the non-farm sector.

Source: DRI Review of the US Economy (various issues), adapted from Arestis and Marshall (1990)

The policy prescriptions which follow from the supply-side analysis, of course, are that marginal tax rates on personal and corporate income and capital gains should be substantially lowered. Moreover, since welfare payments affect the incentive to find employment, assistance through the welfare system should be kept low in relation to levels of remuneration so that the incentive to work, even at low wages, is maintained. The net result of such policies, it is argued, will produce an outward movement of the aggregate supply curve and therefore generate non-inflationary growth.

Looking at the economic record of the Reagan administration, however, it is hard to find compelling evidence to support supply-side claims (see Blanchard, 1987; Modigliani, 1988: Arestis and Marshall, 1990). The ratio of saving to GNP fell after 1981. As a proportion of GNP, personal, corporate, and in particular, total net, saving were all lower in the 1980s than in the 1960s and 1970s. Similarly total net investment, private domestic investment and residential construction were all lower in the 1980s (Boskin, 1988, p. 86). Moreover, while labour and total factor productivity rates were higher than in the depths of the slowdown of the 1970s (1973–79), judged by the standard of the rates achieved in the 1960s or by the rates achieved in the 1980s by other industrialized nations, the productivity record of the Reagan years is also rather poor (Arestis and Marshall, 1990, pp. 59–60). Further, the tax cuts certainly did not generate the extra revenue to erode the federal budget deficit which, in fact, rose to a peak in 1986 and remained extremely high thereafter (see Table 6.1).

Great claims have been made for the supply-side policies of the Reagan administration (Bartlett and Roth, 1984; Roberts, 1989; Roberts in Buchanan, 1989), but as some supply siders have stressed (no doubt at least partially to protect their creed from the assessment that it is one that has been tried and found wanting), Reaganomics was not a complete and unadulterated supply-side project. Certainly from the point of view of the hard-line supply sider there were disappointments: the three-year 30 per cent income tax cut, for example, became a four-year 25 per cent reduction, the initial tax cut was delayed, and the delay in indexation produced fiscal drag that eroded the impact of the tax cuts. Moreover, some areas of the tax reforms, for example, the corporate tax reductions have been dismissed by some supply siders as being Keynesian rather than 'incentivist'. Also even parts of the centrepiece Economic Recovery Tax Act 1981 have been criticized. In fact, only the 1986 tax changes have won the wholehearted endorsement of some supply-side purists (Miles, 1988, pp. 561–2).

Nevertheless, the Reagan administration's tax achievements, particularly in regard to the top rates of tax, must be deemed to have been significant. The top rate of tax on unearned income was lowered from 70 per cent to 50 per cent, on corporate income from 48 per cent to 34 per cent, and the highest rate of tax on personal income was reduced to 28 per cent. These top rate cuts can be seen as the over-riding concern of the administration itself and were regarded as critical by many supply-side theorists (see Chernomas, 1987, pp. 8–9). Cuts of such magnitude, if supply-side theory were well founded, should have produced significant observable changes in saving, investment and productivity. Clearly such effects were not forthcoming. The response of saving and investment was disappointing and, as will be argued below, such increases in labour productivity as did occur are more plausibly attributed to factors other than reductions in marginal rates of income tax.

In assessing the Reagan administration's achievements, supporters have tended to emphasize the following: the success in holding down the inflation rate, the sustained recovery following the early 1980s depression and the job-creation record. In the remainder of this section these areas are examined with particular reference, where appropriate, to supply-side claims.

Certainly the inflation record for the period 1983–86 was good and, although inflation edged up after 1986, the record of the entire post-1983 period is highly satisfactory compared with the 1970s. The achievement is clear; the reasons for it, however, are open to debate. The US experience in the 1980s is not supportive of the key monetarist claim regarding the relationship between the growth of the money stock and the movement of prices. Certainly the most plausible route through which the tight money policy affected inflation in the early 1980s was via higher interest rates, causing an appreciation of the currency. Also, the better inflation record of this period hardly seems likely to have been due to supply-side policies, since domestic consumption clearly outgrew domestic production and generated a growing trade deficit.

The trend of prices in this period has to be seen in the context of a number of factors: relatively high unemployment rates, significant changes in industrial relations and work practices in manufacturing industry (see below) which helped keep real earnings stable in this sector, stable real oil prices until 1986 (when oil prices fell and had an immediate impact on the general price index) and, down to 1985, a dramatically rising dollar exchange rate. The upward pressures on, largely cost-determined, industrial prices certainly tended to abate during the period.

Much has been made of the 'longest peacetime expansion on record' (see for example Roberts, 1989, p. 67), and certainly there was an unbroken increase in GNP in the US from 1983 onwards. However, it must be remembered that the growth of GDP during the 1979–88 period was *lower* than during the so-called stagflation period of 1973–79, *significantly lower* than the growth rates achieved in the 1960s, and *below* the long-term trend rate since the nineteenth century (see Arestis and Marshall, 1990, p. 61). Bearing this in mind it seems difficult to dispute Modigliani's view that the growth record of the Reagan administration was 'unimpressive' (Modigliani, 1988, p. 422).

There may have been a clear, sustained, and initially rapid, recovery from the cyclical trough of the early 1980s. When one considers the growth *trend* rather than cyclical recovery, however, the achievement of the Reagan government appears much more mundane. Further, one must also consider the nature of the depression and the likely causes of the recovery. The effects of the, delayed, first phase of tax cuts were insufficient initially to counteract the contractionary impact of higher interest rates and an appreciating dollar, given the fall in state and county expenditure in 1981 and 1982 as federal grants-in-aid declined. The supporters of the Reagan administration's policies may point to the sustained economic recovery post-1982, but it must be said that the severity of the depression itself seems to have owed much to the government's own policy (Eichner, 1988; Bowles et al., 1985).

Also, given the absence of evidence of any significant supply-side responses, the recovery itself is much more plausibly explained in Keynesian terms by the demand effects of a growing budget deficit and, to some extent, by the Federal Reserve Board's easing of monetary conditions in late Summer 1982. (See Bowles et al., 1985; Tobin, 1987; Peterson and Estensen, 1985; Peterson, 1988.) The deteriorating trade balance (see Table 6.1) certainly suggests a demand-led recovery, rather than a supply-driven one.

Reaganomics can be understood as an attempt to construct a restructured set of institutional arrangements to foster a resumption of economic growth; and the evidence of the 1980s does indeed suggest that it created conditions under which some growth of the economy was re-established. It did so, albeit inadvertently, via a Keynesian demand stimulus to the economy. Reaganomics, ironically, created conditions under which an essentially Keynesian macroeconomic structure could function (Marglin and Schor, 1990, p. 34). Admittedly it was a Keynesianism, unlike that of the 1960s, that was skewed towards the rich and the military–industrial complex; but it was Keynesian in effect nonetheless, despite the early continuation of a monetarist policy and a later adoption of a full-blown supply-side (anti-Keynesian) rhetoric.

The post-1982 recovery, of course, produced a fall in the unemployment rate. As Table 6.1 shows, unemployment fell to 5.5 per cent in 1988 from its (annual) peak of 9.7 per cent in 1982. The annual average unemployment rate for the 1980–87 period, however, was 7.7 per cent compared to 6.48 per cent for the period 1973–79. Moreover, although the unemployment rate fell after 1982, it did not fall below 7 per cent until as late as 1987 (see Table 6.1). Also comparing unemployment rates in 1989 with peak years in the business cycle since the Second World War we see that 1989 is only comparable with 1979 and higher than the unemployment rate in earlier peak years (Mishel and Frankel, 1991, Table 4.1, p. 128).

Underlying this fall in unemployment in the 1980s, of course, was a growth in job creation. Civilian employment grew at a rate of 1.68 per cent during the period 1979–88, but this much vaunted job creation was slower than during 1973–79 or 1967–73 (see Table 6.2). Moreover, the fall in unemployment in the 1980s was *not* the result of a superior job-creation rate during the period, but was due to labour force changes. The working-age population grew more slowly in the 1980s than it had done during the period 1967–79, and the labour force participation ratio levelled off, growing at only half the rate in the period 1979–88 as in the stagflationary years 1973–79. During the 1980s the growth rate of new jobs slowed down: but the growth of new workers slowed down more (see Table 6.2).

Table 6.2   The growth of employment in the US, 1967–88[a]

Period	Civilian employment	Hours of work	Full-time equivalent employment	Working-age employment	Papticipation rate[b]
1967–73	2.24	1.60	1.86	2.08	0.20
1973–79	2.50	1.80	2.28	1.90	0.48
1979–88	1.68	1.40	1.64	1.26	0.24

[a] Figures are annual percentage rates of growth.
[b] Percentage point annual growth.
Source: Adapted from Mishel and Frankel (1991), Table 4.4 p. 131.

It is also clear that part-time employment increased at a faster rate than full-time employment during this period (Loveman and Tilly, 1988, pp. 606–7). There was in fact a growth in underemployment due to people seeking full-time work having to take part-time employment. Involuntary part-time work affects the most vulnerable members of the workforce: women, teenagers and black and hispanic workers and the increase in the proportion of workers working part-time in 1979–88 was entirely due to the increased rate at which workers were working part-time *involuntarily* (Mishel and Frankel, 1991, pp. 133–5).

Moreover, although government statistics do not allow a clear or precise evaluation of the situation, surveys of major companies in the US in the 1980s indicate that employers were increasingly making use of temporary workers and showed an increased proclivity to use independent external contractors rather than expand their own workforces (Mishel and Frankel, 1991, pp. 145–9). Most members of this 'contingent workforce', of course, were typically excluded from internal promotion ladders and job structures and frequently denied the health insurance and pension coverage extended to the 'primary' internal workforce.

Furthermore, as Bluestone and Harrison (1937) and Kosters and Ross (1987) have shown, there was a substantial growth in the proportion of low paid workers in the first half of the 1980s, and there was a clear employment shift over the whole period 1979–89 to low wage sectors. This was a consequence of trade deficits, de-industrialization and stagnant or falling productivity growth in service sectors. The net gain of 18.8 million jobs over this 10 year period was produced by a fall in manufacturing and mining jobs of 1.7 million and an increase of 19.6 million jobs in the service sector. However, by far the largest overall job growth (14.4 million) was in the lowest-paying service sectors. Over the period there was a 7.7 per cent drop in the share of the workforce in high-paying industries such as manufacturing, mining, government service, transportation, communications and the utilities, while over three-quarters of the net new jobs created in the US economy over the period 1979–89 were in the two lowest-paying service sectors: retail distribution and business, personal and health services (Mishel and Frankel, 1991, pp. 104–13).

Moreover recent figures show that real hourly wages fell 9 per cent during 1980–89. Indeed the entire bottom 75 per cent of the male workforce experienced real wage reductions during the period 1979–88. Family real income fell for the lowest two quintiles, and the overall increase in family income of 7.55 per cent over the years 1979–85 for married couples was nearly all due to increased female earnings (women worked more and saw an increase in wage rates). Income growth was sluggish in the 1980s, and over the decade most US families experienced, at best, a very modest growth of real income. The trend towards part-time and temporary work, and the persistence of relatively high unemployment for certain groups and in certain areas of the country, caused severe hardship for at least a fifth of the workforce (Mishel and Frankel, 1991, pp. 37–43, 79).

Income inequality increased substantially over the decade 1979–89 as the incomes of the best-off 5 per cent of families saw their incomes rise by 25.7 per cent – some five times faster than the income growth of the bottom 80 per cent of families.[6] Poverty too increased, the expansion of low wage jobs led to an increase in the proportion of the workforce earning poverty level wages, this proportion rising from 25.7 per cent in 1979 to 31.5 per cent in 1987. The overall poverty rate rose from 11.7 per cent in 1979 to a peak of 15.2 per cent in 1983 and declined thereafter, although it was still higher in 1989 at 12.8 per cent than it had been in 1979 or indeed in 1973), (see table 6.3; see also Arestis and Marshall, 1990, Table 6, p.64.)

The recovery of the US economy in the 1980s may have created more employment, but a disturbingly large proportion of the new jobs seem to have been temporary, part-time and low paid, Moreover, while there was a small gain in real income overall, income inequalities worsened and the numbers living below the unofficial poverty line increased substantially in the first part of the 1980s and remained above the 1979 level throughout the 1980s.

RESTRUCTURING THE SOCIAL CONDITIONS OF PRODUCTIVITY

What is abundantly clear from the experience of the 1980s is that the conservative economic policy making of that decade did not constitute a coherent, successful or acceptable attempt to create non-inflationary growth. Supply-side claims have not been validated by the evidence of the 1980s. The supply-side 'softball' strategy for a painless movement to higher productivity is not well founded either empirically or theoretically, In terms of raising the productivity of the *majority* of the working population, reducing marginal tax rates does not appear to be a very strong candidate. In fact, in the supply-side literature the emphasis is largely on the *top* rates of tax and therefore on the role and position of the rich rather than on the mass of working people (Chernomas, 1987, p. 8).[7]

The main barrier to higher productivity in the US in the 1980s was not high marginal tax rates. Indeed, the key relevant relationship was not, as the supply siders claimed, that between the government as the central fiscal authority and workers, savers and entrepreneurs as taxpayers: but that between workers and employers. The central focus of analysis therefore should be on the labour market and the socioeconomic context in which it operates.

Despite the supply-side emphasis on marginal tax rates, at the heart of most neo-conservative analyses of the economic difficulties of the Western industrialized countries in the 1970s and 1980s was the belief that certain 'institutional rigidities', primarily those associated with trade union and governmental activity, were the cause of the high inflation, slow technological change and sluggish economic growth that had characterized the 1970s. Neo-classical inspired 'liberal productivist' theories emerged in the US that, directly or indirectly, emphasized the need for greater 'flexibility'. From the New Right perspective, 'flexibility' was seen exclusively in terms of removing or reducing the 'institutional rigidities' that prevented the full operation of market forces and the ability of economic agents to respond to price movements. The need for greater flexibility therefore became associated with attacks on certain vested interests (trade unions) and corporatist strategies and policies, and with support for 'freeing' labour markets, deregulation, tax and welfare cuts, and a general restriction on governmental activity. All of these, especially the 'freeing' of labour markets, seemed to find as much favour with supply siders as with other New Right groups (see e.g. Evans, 1982, pp. 222–5).

In order to better understand the labour market changes referred to in the previous section and the improvements in labour productivity that occurred during the Reagan period, it is necessary to examine the restructuring of labour relations that took place in the 1980s in the wake of the demand deflation in the early years of the decade.

The political economy of full employment

From the New Right point of view the operation of markets and government intervention are separate and contradictory phenomena. Such a viewpoint, however, is flawed, markets are not abstract asocial or ahistorical phenomena. Markets are, in fact, institutions, and conventional neo-classical analysis of them neglects the customary, legal, political and other social arrangements that are central to their operation and functioning (Hodgson, 1988, Ch. 8).

The conditions under which markets operate are fundamentally social ones: they are created by human agencies. In the period after the Second World War the state has been one of the most important of these human agencies governing market activity. The state in a number of ways, for example, influences the balance of power between different groups operating in particular markets. This is certainly true of the labour market.

After the troubled industrial relations of the interwar period and the 1940s, a so-called 'Labour Accord' developed in the US. This 'Accord' was underwritten by both employers and the government. The government through the Wagner Act of 1935 (as amended by the Taft-Hartley Act of 1947) protected the rights of workers by enabling them to be exercised in practice by outlawing discriminatory behaviour by employers against trade unions and trade unionists, and by forcing companies into collective bargaining with certified trade unions. The employers therefore were supposed to indulge in 'good faith' dealing with trade unions and some changed their style of labour management quite considerably, moving towards so-called bureaucratic control systems utilizing promotion ladders, seniority rewards and non-wage benefits (Edwards, 1979).

The degree of commitment to these arrangements by governments and employers did, of course, vary and a large number of US workers (almost two-thirds) were not unionized even in the peak years of the 'Accord'. Nevertheless, the period from the late 1940s to the end of the 1970s saw a significant increase in collective bargaining and, even in areas where firms made deliberate attempts to restrain trade union presence and hinder the development of collective bargaining, the strategies adopted by these companies, in effect, ended up guaranteeing workers rights comparable to those achieved in the union sector. The presence of the union sector was an important dynamic element in the labour market that had a positive effect on workers' rights and remuneration even in non-unionized sectors. Certainly for the first time in the US (in peacetime at least) unionism and collective bargaining came to exert an important influence on wages and conditions in US industry (Kassalow, 1988, p. 574).

In the late 1970s and early 1980s, however, the 'Labour Accord' was considerably unravelled. Employers faced a growing need to boost profitability and improve their relative competitive position, especially with Far East producers and both they and New Right theorists started to refer to the need to achieve greater 'flexibility' in the labour market (see e.g. Evans, 1982, pp. 222–5). Given the urgent stimulus of the depressed conditions of this period (which, in turn, provided the 'softer' labour market necessary for the successful implementation of their reforms), and a government sympathetic to their situation and clearly interested in a major shift of power away from labour, the employers went on the offensive and won large-scale concessions.

Increasing numbers of employers broke the law by sacking union activists. Perhaps one employee in 20 who took part in unionization in the early 1980s was illegally-dismissed (Weiler, 1983). Indeed, specialist management consultant firms advising employers how to do this most effectively mushroomed (Adams, 1989, p. 53). Many large employers pursued a policy of de-unionization by shutting down union plants altogether and shifting production to non-union ones.

Employers became more anxious to introduce elements of Japanese-style working practices so that new (often 12-hour) shift systems could be imposed. Saturday and Sunday working at normal pay rates was established in some areas and measured day work was introduced in others. Two-tier wage systems were introduced in which new employees were appointed at lower wages, and sometimes worse conditions of employment, than those enjoyed by existing staff. Lump-sum payments (not consolidated into wage structures) and wage freezes started to replace normal pay increases. The link between wages and the profits and the performance of the company or plant was strengthened; that between pay and cost of living rises weakened (Adams, 1989, p. 50). A general increase in the 'flexibility' with which labour was deployed was successfully sought (Kassalow, 1988, p. 575).

Clearly an employers' offensive of this nature constituted a great threat to trade union activity, and it must have helped further reduce the already declining percentage of US workers covered by collective bargaining. By 1988 only 17 per cent of workers belonged to a trade union compared with 25 per cent in 1980. It also helped bring about a restructuring of the labour market that contributed towards a faster and more complete introduction of new technology in some cases, and important changes in payment and working systems. The upshot of all this was a downward pressure on unit labour costs and an increase in labour productivity in manufacturing.

As a result then of increasing pressures on US employers, long-standing labour practices were changed. The focus became increasingly short-term, and the ability to adapt quickly to changed circumstances assumed much greater importance. The greater labour market segmentation, in the form of a growing proportion of 'lower-quality' jobs, was a direct result of these pressures, as was the greater hostility to trade unions, the greater intensification of work in some areas, and the growth of subcontracting in others.

The changes alluded to above were, of course, brought about directly by the employers themselves. The government's role, however, was not a neutral one. The government set an early example to private employers in 1981 with its sacking of 11 500 air traffic controllers, and it also contributed to the changes in industrial relations through its deregulation programme. Moreover, it gave tacit encouragement to the employers by being reluctant to play the 'guarantor' role of the 'Accord' years. The administration showed itself to be unwilling to protect the workers' legal rights to unionize, and the employers were tacitly encouraged to default on 'good faith' dealings and to behave illegally. The Reagan administration's desire to undermine the 'Labour Accord' seems clear. Its action in the 1980s certainly strengthened the position of capital *vis à vis* labour.

Also, the tight money policy of the early 1980s helped create the depressed conditions which undermined the ability of the workers to resist the employers' changes. Labour productivity is a phenomenon importantly affected by the ability of employers to get work effort from labour time. In this context, therefore, the experience of the high unemployment of the depression of the early 1980s, by increasing the threat of job loss, may have had an effect.

Furthermore, even as unemployment rates fell and new jobs were created, fears of unemployment no doubt persisted. In addition, the increased labour market segmentation must have accentuated the cost of job loss by increasing the likelihood that re-employment, particularly for those at a disadvantage for reasons of age, gender or race, would only be possible through the secondary labour market. Also, cuts in welfare make it even more onerous to the unemployed and therefore strengthen work discipline and increase the willingness to work for low wages and accept poor working conditions (Armstrong, Glyn and Harrison, 1984, p. 412). The perceived cost of job loss was undoubtedly increased by the sort of concerted attacks on 'welfare scroungers' and 'welfare dependency' and social provision generally that occurred during the Reagan years; and this cost of job loss variable, of course, is directly and solely under the control of the government.

Such changes were not, of course, on the declared agenda of the Reagan administration. However, given the rather weak conventional supply-side effects engendered by governmental policy, one might well conclude that the changes in industrial relations practices and systems constituted the real, 'supply-side revolution' of the Reagan years.

In terms of achieving significant and widespread increases in productivity, what is crucial is the ability to introduce new technology and more productive working methods and practices. Such changes can take place in the context of a 'Labour Accord' with firms able to introduce new technology and gain increases in productivity and reductions in unit labour costs while trade union members obtain reasonable job security and rising real wages. Usually, however, the instincts of many employers and conservative academics dispose them to think of exploiting situations in which employees willingness and ability to resist imposed changes (that, for them, imply a worsening of working conditions) is reduced. Conservatives, in fact, tend to find the industrial relations changes associated with a 'soft' labour market highly satisfactory.

A policy-induced reduction in economic activity can leave a positive impact on profitability and productivity in a number of ways. For example, to the extent that real wages can be squeezed as the bargaining strength of workers is reduced in depressed conditions, profitability can be enhanced. Furthermore, depression puts pressure on management to force through changes in working practices and rising unemployment promotes fear and reduces the ability and willingness to resist such changes (Armstrong, Glyn and Harrison, 1984, p. 408). Not surprisingly, therefore, many conservative academics and politicians believe that in such conditions the level and rate of productivity can be increased; and, as regards the US there is evidence to support such a view (Weisskopf, 1987) In the post Second World War US economy there has been something of a stop–go/confrontation–accommodation business cycle. This has tended to produce 'stop' periods in which restructuring and improvements in productivity occur, thereby laying the foundation for improvements in profitability and helping establish the conditions for further periods of expansion.

Rising unemployment may sometimes produce positive work intensity and workplace innovation effects; however, if firms rely on dismissal threats, labour markets are likely to be characterized by involuntary unemployment, labour market segmentation, discrimination and inefficient production techniques (Bulow and Summers, 1986; Krueger and Summers, 1987). Moreover, the important, and insufficiently emphasized, implication of this is that movements towards full employment will be accompanied by rising unit labour costs and falling rates of productivity growth (Rebitzer, 1989, p. 126).

Although demand deflation may be, in effect, an alternative 'hardball' productivity-enhancement strategy with some record of success in the US, it is not one that is socially desirable. It is also unlikely to be the approach capable of producing the best *long-term* results. Whilst demand deflation is more likely to have achieved better productivity results in the US in the 1980s than the supply-side strategy, it is a socially regressive approach that leaves major conflicts and contradictions intact. In particular, as and when reflation of the economy occurs, rising unit wage costs and falling rates of productivity growth are likely to be quickly encountered. This, especially in the context of the US's underlying balance of payments problem, will mean that sustained economic progress is effectively impossible to achieve.

It seems that productivity-augmenting effects of unemployment are only clearly apparent in countries where the social relations of production are conflictual and the workers lack security. On the other hand, where private and public institutions afford greater participation, security and equity, apparently low unemployment can sustain high levels and rates of growth of productivity (Weisskopf, 1987, p. 150).

CONCLUSION

In terms of its political objectives, the Reagan administration must be deemed to have been reasonably successful. It did after all increase the absolute and relative importance of defence expenditure, it redistributed income to the rich, and if the cutting edge of its attempted attack on welfare was blunted by a recalcitrant Congress, it nevertheless could still point to some real achievements here too.

The plutocratic objectives of the Reagan administration were pursued with impressive zeal and sense of purpose. The tax policy of the Reagan adminis- tration, the centrepiece of its economic policy, helped produce significant change that benefited the rich at the expense of the poor. Personal income tax became less progressive, as did corporate income taxes which declined con- siderably, while the regressive social insurance taxes went up. The overall tax system therefore became more regressive and thus exacerbated pretax income inequality.[8]

Looking at the microeconomic impact of the Reagan administration's fiscal changes it is clear that the main gainers were the inhabitants of the New England and Pacific regions (who benefited from increased defence procurement) and white male-headed families. On the other hand, those Americans who were already disadvantaged – welfare dependants, female-headed families, and those with less than average education – all benefited less or actually sustained outright income loss (Bluestone and Havens, 1986). In short, the rich got richer, and the rest, especially the disadvantaged social groups, benefited much less or, in some cases, suffered absolute losses in disposable income. There can be no doubt that Reaganomics was the political economy of plutarchy.

The sociopolitical effects of the tax cuts may have matched the administra- tion's aspirations; the so-called incentivist effects however were disappointing. A properly managed tax cut may produce, over a period of years, modest positive incentivist effects. However, such a policy also has a demand effect and this is likely to be much larger than the supply-side response – particularly in the short-run. There is no reason to believe that this was not the case in the US in the 1980s.

As was argued earlier, the evidence of the 1980s, seems to suggest that the fiscal policy of the administration had more of an impact on the demand than on the supply side of the economy. The policies pursued by the Reagan admin- istration, however, constituted a right-wing (militaristic) Keynesianism with rather unfortunate social repercussions. The administration's policies did produce economic recovery and a fall in the unemployment rate in the 1980s. Given the circumstances and scale of the administration's achievements, however, it would be foolish to conclude either that the successes were outstanding, or achieved by design rather than by accident.

Moreover, the policies pursued in the early Reagan years produced low levels of capacity utilization and high interest rates. These dampened investment and growth prospects. The high interest rates pushed up the value of the dollar and damaged US manufacturing industry. Also the rising dollar (down to 1985) and the restricted growth of capacity in the face of a rise in domestic consumption, caused a deterioration in the balance of payments.

Reaganomics was not pure supply-side of course. The entire project of Reaganomics was not completely to the liking of the supply-side theoreticians like Miles. However, given the flaws in the analysis, the weakness of incentivist responses to even quite substantial cuts in marginal tax rates, and the negative social effects of the policies carried out, more would merely have been worse. The failures were in analysis and perception of the true nature of the socio-economic problems facing the US – not in execution or degree of implementation.

The supply-side perspective that became dominant in the US was a classic example of a simplistic reductionist, stimulus-response model that conceptualized only one type of 'flexibility' - unfettered response to market signals. It was an inadequate theory and therefore produced a simplistic policy prescription that was doomed to failure. As has been seen, productivity miracles are not produced by simply reducing the top rates of income tax. Moreover, while the New Right in Europe might have pointed to allegedly superior (i.e. more 'flexible') labour market conditions in the US leading to a superior job-creation performance, as has been seen, too many of the new jobs that were created were part-time or low-wage, low-skill, low-productivity jobs.

Flexibility (interpreted as unfettered market forces) good; institutional rigidities (trade unions and government activity) bad, became the New Right liturgy. However, as Neilson has pointed out, such views are simplistic and, in particular, ignore the fact that certain 'institutional rigidities' are essential to the working of markets (Neilson, 1991, pp. 5–30). They are needed to reduce uncertainty, guide expectations and generate a necessary minimum of trust (Hodgson, 1988).

Flexibility in some areas requires stability ('rigidity') in others. The New Right would obviously not accept the experience of certain corporatist economies such as Sweden and Austria in the 1970s and 1980s as providing convincing support for this thesis. The much admired Japanese model, however, is more difficult for them to dismiss. Much Japanese success has been clearly based on 'flexible rigidities', for example, the high degree of flexibility in production that interrelates with the high degree of stability ('rigidity') in employer–employee and user–producer relationships (see Dore, 1986). Moreover, a large-scale comparative study of the US and Japan by MIT scholars (Dertouzos, Lester, and Solow, 1989) has indicated that markets in the US are too competitive and therefore, if anything, too 'free'. Consequently the study concludes that, if the US is to simulate Japanese successes, there should be a movement towards 'organized markets', the establishment of more lasting relationships between users and producers, and a strengthening of the position of workers in order to facilitate greater cooperation between employers and employees.

The macro-stimulus apart, the main feature of Reaganomics was the resurrection of the fear of unemployment to discipline labour, raise productivity and hold wages in check (Marglin and Schor, 1990, p. 35). As has been seen the increasing threat and cost of unemployment led to changes in working conditions and practices that seem to have paid off in terms of increasing productivity. However, while in the US there has been a correlation between unemployment and the rate of productivity growth, this is neither a desirable nor necessary means of stimulating productivity growth.

Reaganomics was not a successful restructuring or modernization project. The example it sets to Europe is essentially negative: what to avoid rather than what to imitate. As a 'flexibility analysis', Reaganomics is clearly inferior to the main neo-Schumpeterian, neo-Smithian and neo-Marxist alternatives (see Neilson, 1991, pp. 10–30) The crude labour market restructuring pursued in the US does not provide a satisfactory basis for the long-term growth of productivity. It does, however, emphasize the need for a reformulation of the capital–labour bargain.

NOTES

1. Parts of this chapter draw on Marshall and Arestis (1989), Arestis and Marshall (1990) and Marshall and Arestis (1991).
2. See Peterson (1987) and Heald (1983, Ch. 1) for a discussion of the Keynesian consensus and the Keynesian social democratic state.
3. On 'liberal productivism' see Jessop et al. (1991, pp. 310; 33–44), and Lipietz (1992. pp. 30–34).
4. The much discussed 'twin deficits' are not referred to below; on these topics see Arestis and Marshall (1990). For a discussion of supply-side ideas and policies see: Bartlett and Roth (1984), Wanniski (1978), Shaw (1988), Arestis and Marshall (1990), Marshall and Arestis (1991).
5. On the competing influences on policy making in the Reagan administration and the eventual triumph of the supply side see Rousseas (1982), Eichner (1988) and Marshall and Arestis (1989).
6. On the growth of income and the increasing income inequality see Mishel and Frankel (1991, Ch. 1).
7. One former eminent member of the Reagan administration, David Stockman, of course, claimed that the whole Kemp-Roth tax initiative was merely a Trojan horse to achieve tax breaks for the very rich; see Rousseas (1992, p. 102).
8. On changes in the tax structure and the impact of such changes on income distribution, see Mishel and Frankel (1991, Ch. 2).

REFERENCES

Adams, R.J. (1989), 'North American industrial relations: divergent trends in Canada and the United States', *International Labor Review*, vol. 128, no. 1, pp. 47–64.

Arestis, P. and Marshall, M.G. (1990), 'The New Right and the U.S, Economy in the 1980s: an assessment of the economic record of the Reagan Administration, *International Review of Applied Economics*, vol. 4, no. 1, pp. 45–71.

Armstrong, P., Glyn, A. and Harrison, J. (1984), *Capitalism since world war 2*, London: Fontana.

Bartlett, B. and Roth, T.P. (eds) (1984), *The supply-side solution*. London: Macmillan.

Blanchard, O.J. (1987), 'Reaganomics', *Economic Policy*, vol. 5, pp. 17–56.

Bluestone, B. and Harrison, B. (1987), 'The Grim Truth about the Jobs Miracle', *New York Times*, 1 February.

Bluestone, B. and Havens, J. (1986), 'The microeconomic impacts of macroeconomic fiscal policy, 1981–1985', *Journal of Post Keynesian Economics*, vol. 8, no. 4, Summer.

Boskin. M. (1988), 'Tax policy and economic growth: lessons from the 1980s', *Journal of Economic Perspectives*, vol. 2, no. 4, 71–97.

Buchanan, J. et al. (eds) (1989), *Reaganomics and after*, London: IEA.

Bowles, S., Gordon, D.M. and Weisskopf, T.E. (1985), *Beyond the wasteland: a democratic alternative to economic decline*, London: Verso.

Bulow, J.I. and Summers, L.H. (1986), 'A theory of dual labor markets with applications to industrial policy, discrimination. and Keynesian unemployment', *Journal of Labor Economics*, vol. 4, pp. 376–414.

Chernomas, R. (1987), 'Is supply-side economics rational for capital? *Review of Radical Political Economics*, Fall, pp. 3–17.

Dertouzos, M., Lester, R.K. and Solow, R.M. (1989), *Made in America*, Cambridge, Mass.: MIT Press.

Dore. R. (1986), *Flexible rigidities: industrial policy and structural adjustment in the Japanese economy 1970–1980*, London: Athlone Press.

Edwards. R. (1979), *Contested Terrain: The Transformation of the Workplace in the Twentieth Century*, New York: Basic Books.

Eichner. A.S. (1988), 'The Reagan record: a post keynesian view', *Journal of Post Keynesian Economics*, vol. 10, no. 4, pp. 541–56.

Evans, M.K. (1982), 'New developments in econometric modelling: supply-side tax policy', in R.H. Fink (ed.), *Supply-side economics: a critical appraisal*, Maryland: Aletheia Books.

Heald, G. (1983), *Public Expenditure*, Oxford: Martin Robertson.

Hodgson, G.M. (1988), *Economics and institutions*, London: Polity Press.

Jessop, B. et al. (eds) (1991), *The politics of flexibility: restructuring state and industry in Britain, Germany and Scandinavia*, Aldershot: Edward Elgar.

Kassalow, E.M. (1988), 'Concession bargaining: towards new roles for American unions and managers', *International Labor Review*, vol. 127, no. 5, pp. 573–92.

Kosters, M.H. and Ross, N.N. (1987), *The Distribution of Earnings and Employment Opportunities: a Re-Examination of the Evidence*, Washington DC: American Enterprise Institute for Public Policy Research.

Krueger, A.B. and Summers, L.H. (1987), 'Reflection on the inter-industry wage structure', in K. Lang and J.S. Leonard (eds), *Unemployment and the structure of labour markets*, Oxford: Basil Blackwell.

Lipietz, A. (1992), *Towards a new economic order: postfordism, Ecology and democracy*, Cambridge: Polity.

Loveman, G.W. and Tilly, C. (1988), 'Good Jobs or Bad Jobs?', *International Labor Review*, vol. 127, pp. 593–611.

Marglin, S. and Schor, J. (1990), (eds) *The golden age of capitalism: reinterpreting the postwar experience*, Oxford: Clarendon Press.

Marshall, M.G. and Arestis, P. (1989), 'Reaganomics and supply-side economics: a British view', *Journal of Economic Issues*, vol. 23, pp. 965–75.

Marshall. M.G. and Arestis, P. (1991), 'The myths and realities of conservative economics policy-making in the US', *Review of Social Economy*, vol. XLIV, no. 2, Summer, pp. 218–41.

Meltzer, A.H. (1988), 'Economic policies and actions in the Reagan Administration', *Journal of Post Keynesian Economics*, Summer, pp. 528–40.

Miles, M.A. (1988), 'An evaluation of Reagan's economic policies from an incentivist (supply-side) perspective, *Journal of Post Keynesian Economics*, Summer, pp. 559–66.

Mishel, L. and Frankel, D.M. (1991), *The state of working America*, New York: M.E. Sharpe.

Modigliani, G. (1988), 'Reagan's economic policies: a critique', *Oxford Economic Papers*, vol. 40, pp. 397–426.

Neilson, K. (1991), 'Learning to Manage the Supply-side: Flexibility and Stability in Denmark', in Jessop et al. (1991).

Peterson, W.C. and Estensen, P. (1985), 'The recovery: supply-side or keynesian?' *Journal of Post Keynesian Economics*, Summer, pp. 447–62.

Peterson, W.C. (1987), 'Macroeconomic theory and policy in an institutionalist perspective', *Journal of Economic Issues*, vol. 21, pp. 1587–621.

Peterson, W.C. (1988), 'The macroeconomic legacy of Reaganomics', *Journal of Economic Issues*, vol. 22, pp. 1–16.

Rebitzer, J.B. (1989), 'Unemployment, long-term employment relations and the determination of unit labour cost growth in US manufacturing industries', *International Review of Applied Economics*, vol. 3, no. 2, pp. 125–47.

Roberts, P.C. (1989), 'Supply-side economics: an assessment of the American experience', *National Westminister Bank Quarterly Review*, February, pp. 60–75.

Rousseas, S. (1982), *The political economy of Reaganomics*, New York: M.E. Sharpe.

Shaw, G.K., (1988), *Keynesian Economics*, Aldershot: Edward Elgar.

Solow, R. (1987), 'The conservative revolution: a roundtable discussion', *Economic Policy*, October, pp. 181–5.

Tobin, J. (1987), *Policies for prosperity: essays in a Keynesian mode*, edited by P.M. Jackson, Brighton: Wheatsheaf.

Wanniski, J. (1978), *The way the world works*, New York: Simon and Schuster.

Weiler. P. (1983), 'Promises to keep: securing workers' rights to self-organisation under the NLRA', *Harvard Law Review*, vol. 96, no. 9, pp. 1769–827.

Weisskopf, T.E. (1987), 'The effect of unemployment on labour productivity: an international comparative analysis', *International Review of Applied Economics*, vol. 1, no. 2, pp. 127–51.

7. High wages, enlightened management and economic productivity

Michael Perelman

Economists have long debated the relationship between high wages and unemployment. The most famous debate occurred during the darkest hours of the Great Depression. At the time, conventional economics held that excessive wage levels were responsible for the high level of unemployment. Keynes countered that a strategy of wage reduction would be futile, if not self-defeating, since it would also decrease demand.

This chapter deals with a less familiar theme. At least, it was less familiar until modern economists proposed the theories of efficiency wages and multiple equilibria. It was most common in the US, where people attempted to understand how employers were able to prosper even though they had to pay wages that were high by world standards.

What is argued here goes against the grain of modern economics. We repeatedly hear that high wages are the root of many of the ills of the US economy today. Presumably, our economy could prosper if only we could maintain low enough wages. Such reasoning is absolute nonsense: low wages ensure *low*, not high productivity. After all, the US historically enjoyed a high rate of productivity growth just because US wages exceeded those of the rest of the world.

The benefits of high wages are, in fact, manifold. To begin with, high wages stimulate demand. Second, the increasing demand associated with high wages helps to create economies of scale. As these economies of scale develop, firms can afford to pay higher wages, augmenting demand still more. Third, high wages encourage employers to develop improved technologies to save labour. Fourth, high wages stimulate workers to be more productive. A number of studies show that workers respond to higher wages by contributing more effort to the jobs (Akerlof and Yellen, 1986). Finally, to the extent that high wages promote investment in new technologies, workers often respond to the challenge of working with new techniques by developing their own skills and abilities. Zuboff (1988) offers dramatic examples of this response by workers in a variety of environments.

Despite the numerous economies of high wages, we must be careful not to treat the subject dogmatically. For example, high wages will not necessarily

145

create economies of scale in all economies at all times. Imagine a small country in a crowded region of the world with cheap transportation and relatively free trade, say Luxembourg. If wages rise there, employers could conceivably move to a neighbouring country to take advantage of cheaper labour costs – although, in this particular example, such an exodus has not occurred.

In addition, much of the extension of demand is likely to be dissipated in imports. In a massive nation, such as the US, which was geographically isolated from much of the rest of the industrialized world and which was largely protected from foreign competition by high tariffs and duties on imported goods, high wages have worked magnificently. To the extent that improvements in transportation and communication make the economy more open, the benefits of high wages are less assured.

Furthermore, the benefits of high wages partially depend on the ability of business to discover new labour-saving technologies, which will ultimately promote competitiveness. We have no guarantee that the new methods of production developed by business will always be so efficient that firms will be able to more than compensate for a higher level of wages.

Despite such qualifications to the theory of high wages, maintaining a healthy rate of wage growth offers a far more promising outcome than attempting to compete by depressing wages. In this chapter the case for high wages is explored through an examination of an important, but often ignored, area: the connection between incentives, labour–management relations and productivity. First, however, we look at the long debate on the US as a 'high wage economy'.

THE US AS A HIGH-WAGE ECONOMY

The historical record of the US economy suggests that business managed to create new technologies fast enough to make prices fall despite rising wages. The renowned French visitor, Alexis de Tocqueville, reported:

> I accost an American sailor, and I inquire why the ships of his country are built so as to last for a short time; he answers without hesitation that the art of navigation is every day making such a rapid progress that the finest vessel would become almost useless if it lasted beyond a certain number of years (de Tocqueville, 1848, II, p. 420)

H.J. Habakkuk wrote an entire book about the positive effect of high wages; on technical change in the US during the nineteenth century. According to Habakkuk:

> The Secretary of the Treasury reported in 1832, that the garrets and outhouses of most textile mills were crowded with discarded machinery. One Rhode Island mill built

in 1813 had by 1827 scrapped and replaced every original machine. (Habakkuk, 1962, p. 57; and the numerous references he cites)

The anticipation of early retirement of plant and equipment in the US was so pervasive that manufacturers there built their machinery from wood rather than more durable materials (Strassman, 1959, p. 88).

Throughout the nineteenth century, commentators continued to echo de Tocqueville's observation that technology in the US was designed to be short-lived (Schoenhof, 1893). For example, in the late nineteenth century, the US Secretary of State commissioned Joseph Schoenhof to inquire into the effects of high wages on the competitiveness of US business. Schoenhof concluded:

> the employer of labor is ... benefited by the inevitable results of a high rate of wages .... [T]he first object of the employer is to economize its employment. Manufacturers introducing a change in manufactures have a machine built to accomplish what in other countries would be left to hand labour to bring about. Machinery, used to the limit of its life in Europe, is cast aside in America if only partially worn (Schoenhof, 1893, pp. 33–4)

The Cornell economist, Jeremiah Jenks, asserted:

> No sooner has the capitalist fairly adopted one improved machine, than it must be thrown away for a still later and better invention, which must be purchased at a dear cost, if the manufacturer would not see himself eclipsed by his rival (Jenks, 1890, p. 254; cited in Livingston, 1986, p. 39).

This pattern of rapid capital renewal made the manufacturing capacity in the US the envy of the world. By the turn of the century, exports from the US were inundating Europe, much the same as Japanese exports are displacing US production today. Just as people in the US today try to discover the secret of Japanese ascendancy in popular books, English readers pored over alarmist books with titles such as *The American Invaders* (1901), *The Americanization of the World* (1901), or *The American Invasion* (1902) (Wright, 1990, p. 652).

By the late nineteenth century, rapid technical change had brought productivity in the US to such a high level that leading protectionists, such as David Wells, became so confident about the competitive position of the US that they called for free trade (Wells, 1885). Wells and his school were certain that the highly paid US labour force could easily out-compete what they regarded as pauper labour in the rest of the world.

Many economists at the time associated high wages with a high character of the worker. For example, Wells observed: 'High wages, then, are the normal result of low cost, and low cost is the normal result in turn of intelligence, conjoined with good machinery, applied to great resources for production' (Wells, 1885, p. 138). Wells's insight has been lost on most business people in recent decades. Today, they seem to be infatuated with the financial perspective on the complex relationship between labour and capital.

Wells noted that wages in England's cotton industry were from 30 to 50 per cent higher than in France, Belgium and Germany. He observed that an English cotton operative received more wages in a week than a Russian in a month. Yet the Continent demanded protection against English labour (Wells, 1885, p. 137). Although British wages were less than those earned in the US, they were high relative to the rest of the world. Compared with Manchester, hourly wages on the Continent ranged from less than 25 per cent as high in Prussia to 47 per cent in Rouen (Clark, 1987, p. 142). In 1911, 140 years after the first cotton mills and despite an enormous wage cost disadvantage, 40 per cent of all factory spindles were in England. Another 22 per cent were in the US and Canada. Low wage countries had only 39 per cent of all spindles worldwide (ibid., p. 143).

In 1910, one New England cotton textile worker was equivalent to 1.5 British or 2.3 German workers. Compared to lower-wage economies, the difference was phenomenal. New England textile operatives tended six times as much machinery per shift as workers in the Greek, Japanese, Indian or Chinese textile industries (ibid., p. 150).

During the period following the First World War, Wells's vision was widely shared. At the time business, especially small business, took great pains to crush unions and root out subversives, suggesting that their willingness to pay high wages was not driven by some humanitarian instinct. Business understood the wisdom of the notion that high wages could augment profits. For example, Herbert Hoover told an audience on 12 May 1926:

> The very essence of great production is high wages and low prices .... the acceptance of these ideas is obviously not universal. Not all employers ... nor has every union abandoned the fallacy of restricted effort .... But ... for both employer and employee to think in terms of the mutual interest of increased production has gained in strength. It is a long cry from the conception of the old economics (Cited in Barber, 1985, p. 30)

Hoover's reasoning was that sufficiently high wages would eliminate the appeal of unions; that high wages would make labour feel that its interests were at one with those of business. The key to the high wage policy of the 1920s was the restriction of immigration – although the restrictions drew upon xenophobic emotions as well as economic realism. Thomas Nixon Carver, a famous Harvard economist, exclaimed:

> To be alive today, in this country, and to remember the years from 1870 to 1920 is to awake from a nightmare. Those were the years when our ideas were all but obscured by floods of cheap laborers upon whose cheap labour great fortunes were made, and by floods of abuse because we were not instantaneously solving all the social and economic problems these newcomers were inflicting upon us. Those were the years

of slums and socialist agitators, of blatant demagogues and social legislation (Carver, 1925, pp. 261–2; cited in Barber, 1985, p. 30)

For both Hoover and Carver, the degree of the appeal of the socialist agitator was an excellent indicator of the level of intelligence of the worker. Limiting immigration and raising wages would expand the intelligence of the American worker, which, in turn, would increase productivity. Stripped of their racial and political biases, Carver and Hoover were correct about the outcome of cutting back on the supply of low wage workers.

The average number of immigrants fell dramatically, from 856 000 in 1910–15 to 356 000 in 1915–30. The decrease in male immigrants was even more extreme, falling from 584 000 to 217 000. This decline in such a source of unskilled labour coincided with a rise in the demand for manufactured goods (Oshima, 1984, p. 163). Standard economic theory suggests that curtailing immigration will create a shortage of unskilled workers relative to skilled workers. We should expect that the wages of unskilled workers would rise relative to the wages of skilled workers. Nothing of the kind occurred. Instead, employers invested in an enormous quantity of machines, so much so that the wages of unskilled labour fell 8 per cent compared with 3 per cent for skilled workers between 1920 and 1929 (Ibid, p. 164). In the process, output per hour of work increased by 48 per cent during this same period (Jerome, 1934, p. 5; see also Dumenil, Glick and Rangel, 1987). Given this increase in productivity, personal consumption expenditures for manufactured goods climbed from $11 billion in 1912–21, measured in 1929 dollars, to $17 billion, 1922–31, again measured in 1929 dollars (Oshima, 1984, p. 163).

Even with the onset of the Great Depression, a substantial portion of big business refrained from cutting wages. In the words of Jacob Viner:

the Hoover Administration became apostles of the ... doctrine that high wages are a guarantee and an essential of prosperity. At the beginning of the depression, Hoover pledged industry not to cut wages, and for a long time large-scale industry adhered to this pledge (Viner, 1933, p. 12; cited in O'Brien, 1989, pp. 724–5.)

Many firms, especially large firms, were in agreement with President Hoover, convinced that cutting wages would only intensify the crisis. As a result, during the early years of the Depression, wages remained surprisingly steady. In fact, hourly wages in manufacturing declined only about 2 per cent by January 1931, 17 months into the downturn (O'Brien, 1989, p. 720). Since prices were falling during the first years of the Depression, the buying power of the hourly wage was rising.

Rather than cutting wages, firms employed their workers for fewer hours; (Bernanke, 1986; Sherman, 1983). In some industries, the total number of hours worked dropped by more than 50 per cent, far more than the drop in the numbers of workers employed. Bernanke estimates that changes in the average number of hours worked per week contributed nearly as much as changes in employment to variations in the earnings of labour over the course of the Depression (Bernanke, 1986, p. 82).

Large firms' initial reluctance to cut wages substantially dampened the intensity of the initial contraction in the US. Large employers, committed to maintaining a steady level of wages, would be likely to turn to capital renewal as the obvious strategy to make their operations more efficient. Such investment helped to buffer the shock of the Depression.

By 1939, US firms had replaced one-half of all their manufacturing equipment that had existed in 1933 (Staehle, 1955, p. 127). Although the total amount of investment during the Depression was relatively small, much of that investment was directed toward modernizing existing plant and equipment. Thereafter, US business produced as much output as a decade before with 15 per cent less capital and 19 per cent less labour (Staehle, 1955, p. 133).

The pattern of intensity of R & D offers more evidence of emphasis on modernization during the depression. Although we might expect to find a curtailment of R & D during a Depression, such was not the case. Many large firms also responded to the crisis by intensifying their R & D. In fact, the value of such expenditures, adjusted for inflation, actually increased during the Great Depression and fell during the war (US Department of Labor, 1989).

Large corporations' willingness to refrain from cutting wages for a long time after the onset of the Depression was remarkable, but it was not enough to stave off the contractionary forces that eventually overwhelmed the economy. Wages began to collapse only by October of 1931. The result bore out big business's initial fear of the impact of wage cutting, since soon thereafter the Depression moved into a far more serious phase (O'Brien, 1989, p. 720).

High wages continued to work to the benefit of the US economy after the Great Depression even though economic and political leaders ceased to believe in the economy of high wages. From 1939 to 1947, average hourly wages of industrial workers in the US increased by 95 per cent, compared with only 39 per cent for the prices of machine-tools. In fact, some authors have singled out high wages as the key to the success of the Golden Age of the postwar period (see Glyn et al., 1990, p. 57).

During the Golden Age, wages rose much faster than the prices of metalworking tools, sparking a great deal of investment. Then, from 1965 to 1977, when the productivity collapse first became apparent, the average prices of metalworking tools rose by almost the same amount as wages;. During the latter part of that period, the ratio became even more unfavourable to labour. Between 1971 and 1978, wages increased by 72 per cent. In comparison, the prices of machine-tools rose by 85 per cent (Melman, 1983, pp. 3–5).

In fact, each year after 1975, the index of capital costs grew more than the index of unit labour costs (Melman, 1983, pp. 3–5 and 168). In the case of the agricultural sector, the ratio of farm labour costs to machinery costs explained a substantial portion of the rise in the investment in tractors (Kislev and Peterson, 1982).

As real wages fell in the advanced capitalist countries during the late 1960s and 1970s, business reduced the real value of the equipment with which it supplied the average worker (Schmid, 1981). From 1950 to 1965, business expanded its capital stock by two percentage points more than the growth in total hours. After 1965, the capital stock rate exceeded the rate of growth in hours by only 1 per cent (Kopcke, 1980, p. 26).

Today, business and political leaders in the US are all but unanimous in calling for an economy of low wages. They have been largely successful. Real hourly manufacturing wages in 1982 dollars fell from $8.55 in 1973 to $7.45 in 1992, at about the level they had been back in 1964 and 1965 (President of the United States, 1993, p. 396). Despite the reductions in wages, manufacturing jobs have been disappearing. In their place we find a combination of low-wage service jobs and unemployment. Of all new year-round jobs created since 1979, 36 per cent have provided workers with less than half the real income that the average worker earned in 1973 (Harrison and Bluestone, 1988, Figure 5.4).

The difficulty of earning a living in the US has become so extreme that the poorest fifth of the population must rely on transfer payments from the government for over half of their income. The bulk of these people are not welfare scroungers; over 40 per cent work, but their wages do not suffice to avoid falling back on welfare (Henwood, 1990).

Other workers only avoid welfare by holding multiple jobs. In 1979, 4.95 per cent of all workers held multiple jobs; by 1989, the level was 6.2 per cent (Tilly, 1991, p. 10). In 1977, when the conditions for labour were considerably better, more than 33 per cent of multiple job holders said that they did so out of necessity (United States Department of Labor, 1977). No doubt a higher percentage would answer similarly today.

Indeed, since the decline has begun people have been putting in more hours of work. Juliet Schor estimates in 1987 that the average person in the US worked 163 hours more than in 1969 (Schor, 1991, p. 29). She largely attributes this trend to the need to work longer hours to compensate for falling wages (ibid., pp. 79–81). She observes that production and non-supervisory workers, who make up 80 per cent of the labour force, would have to work 245 hours more each year just to maintain their 1973 standard of living (ibid., p. 81). The data on falling real wages also do not reflect the decline in the level of benefits that workers enjoy. If the wage data took account of the declining frequency of benefits such as health insurance and paid vacations, the fall in real wages would be even more dramatic.

Declining job security is another aspect of the deteriorating conditions for labour. For example, many workers cannot find full-time employment. Between 1980 and 1989, the number of contingent workers (part-time, temporary and business service workers) rose by 27.5 per cent (Belous, 1989, p. 9). Most of these part-time workers lead precarious lives. When hard times come for these workers, they have fewer and fewer resources on which to fall back.

The calamitous results of falling wages fail to dissuade proponents of the economy of low wages to reconsider their beliefs. Instead, they seem to become even more resolute in their advocacy of the low-wage road to development.

HIGH WAGES, LABOUR–MANAGEMENT RELATIONS, TRADE UNIONS AND PRODUCTIVITY

Most economists are ill-prepared to come to grips with the economies of high wages because they habitually fall into the trap of oversimplifying the multi-faceted nature of the labour–management relationship. As a first step in addressing the complexity of this relationship, we shall highlight one important dualism: the dichotomy between what we may call the financial perspective and the production perspective.

The financial perspective presumes that labour is a passive participant in the production process, indistinguishable from the other inert, raw materials that businesses purchase. Within this perspective, when employers buy labour as a commodity, the workers need only contribute their physical presence and superficial obedience.

This interpretation of the labour–management relationship reflects a world seen through the firm's account books. Indeed, business typically attempts to shore up its financial health, in part, by purchasing all inputs as cheaply as possible. In this respect, business justifiably treats labour as a commodity like any other – to be purchased as advantageously as possible.

In terms of the process of physically producing goods and services, labour takes on an entirely different appearance. On the shop floor and in the office, business must pay close attention to the specific details of labour's activities. In this respect, employers expect more than just the bodily presence and superficial obedience of their workers. Herein lies the essence of this other face of management–labour relations.

In evaluating the production process, some employers recognize that they will profit when workers feel obliged to exert themselves and perhaps even to bring creativity and ingenuity to their work. Some employers even call upon their workers to excel, but nobody exerts himself or herself to the utmost without a strong desire to do so – certainly not people who feel that their employer regards them as nothing more than a mere commodity to be bought as cheaply as possible.

How then should employers cajole or entice their workers into performing their tasks as well as possible relative to the wages that they earn? Employers have a wide range of options at their disposal for managing labour. At one extreme, business can resort to the threat of punishment for unsatisfactory work. Workers, under this sort of regime, soon realize that, if they fail to perform adequately, they will be rendered unable to feed themselves and their families. Under a regime based on strict discipline, business practices are consistent with the financial perspective. Richard Edwards refers to this system of management as simple control (Edwards, 1979, p. 19).

This method has several drawbacks. First, in a prosperous economy, workers have the option of finding alternative employment if they lose their jobs. Second, while a heightened anxiety can admittedly increase work effort, it also impairs the performance of skilled tasks (Fenoaltea, 1984). In short, this system of threats can only be effective for tasks that are easy to monitor and that require a minimum of care (ibid., 1984). Resentful workers will always find ways to withhold effort or even to sabotage the business where they work. As Genovese has shown, not even slave owners were able to achieve absolute dominance over the workplace even though the technical complexity of the slave's responsibilities was relatively limited (Genovese, 1976).

Eventually, mass production industry turned to what Edwards referred to as technological control, within which low wage workers had to adapt to a pace of work that the speed of the assembly line determined (Edwards, 1979). This attempt failed because the speed-up served to unite the workers against the employer. Later, some of the more advanced elements of US industry turned to bureaucratic control, in which relatively high paid workers advanced through artificially constructed job ladders (Edwards, 1979, p. 21). This system was somewhat more successful, but ultimately failed because its rigidity stifled creativity.

To draw the utmost from workers, business somehow has to instil a spirit of cooperation, in which workers identify with the interest of their employer. Employers have various options for eliciting this cooperation. They can reward workers financially for good work or they can appeal to the workers by offering them an exciting challenge. For example, in his award-winning book, *The Soul of a New Machine,* Tracy Kidder depicted the zeal with which engineers for Data General competed to develop a new computer (Kidder, 1981).

Most of all, if employers want to use the carrot to elicit effort, rather than to rely on the proverbial stick, they will have to treat workers with respect. We should not be surprised that sticks are more popular than carrots in management circles in the contemporary US. After all, the allure of treating labour as a commodity is self-evident. Using punishment to control the labour process is devilishly simple to administer, even though it is relatively ineffective for anything but the crudest sort of labour. In contrast, the use of incentives can be extremely effective, but incentives are exceedingly difficult to administer.

Of course, no firm relies exclusively either on threats or on positive incentives. In effect, employers choose a mix of these two seemingly contradictory sets of incentives. The employer promises to reward workers to make them perform their jobs well or even take pride in their work. They appeal to the workers' ambition and self-respect.

Because employers have no assurance that the bargain will create the desired attitude in their labour force, employers also tell the workers that they are entirely dispensable. Employers convey the message – perhaps even intentionally – that no individual worker is anything special. Should any employee fail to satisfy the employer or ask for too much money, then the employer stands ready to fire that worker and hire another, who presumably will do a better job.

In this sense, the employer's message is essentially antagonistic. Yet, in appealing to the workers to put a great deal of themselves into their work, the message conveys cooperation and a mutuality of interests.

Finding the proper mix of threat and incentive is no simple task, but the employer must somehow make these two essentially contradictory messages coherent. Coherence is all the more elusive because of the subtlety of the labour–management relationship. Workers evaluate the specific combination of signals within any employment relationship in terms of an unstated norm of 'fairness'. When workers perceive employers as fair – when they feel that they are treated with respect – they respond accordingly.

Both labour and management attempt to control the labour process. From this perspective, we see workers as active agents, with goals of their own and with the ingenuity and creativity to accomplish these goals, at least in part. If an employer violates workers' norm of fairness, the employees will seek redress by withholding their cooperation.

Such disgruntled workers often go to great lengths to exercise some control over the labour process, even when they have no expectation of wringing any concessions from management, often with dire consequences for the firm. Michael Burawoy attempted to come to grips with the depth of the tensions between labour and management by interpreting the workplace as an 'internal state' (Burawoy, 1979, p. 11). Within this state, each party, labour and management, has certain unspecified powers.

Indeed, the idea of exercising some control over their activity, even when that control is nothing more than the disruption of the labour process, can be a source of utility and even delight to workers. Those, who might not be inclined to work harder for monetary rewards, sometimes go to great lengths just to assert their independence *vis-à-vis* management. For example, Burawoy described a piecework machine shop that produced parts for truck engines, where workers transformed the incentive system into a game to relieve their boredom. Within this game, the workers developed a complex equilibrium with inspectors. If an inspector challenged them by rejecting articles with marginal tolerance, workers would retaliate by turning out scrap after the first piece was rejected, making the inspector look bad. Underlying their game was a need to relieve boredom rather than any economic motives (Burawoy, 1979, p. 89). Workers sometimes attempted to produce as much as 140 per cent of the norm. They resisted producing any more than 140 per cent only because they feared an upward revision of the norm.

These workers could have turned their creativity to making the plant more productive, but to do so would not have done much for their self-respect. When this cynical creativity becomes general, the economy as a whole will become less competitive within the world economy. Because management typically adheres to the financial perspective of labour–management relations, it is unable to comprehend how much it loses by failing to tap workers' creativity. Academic authorities, especially economists, do not offer much guidance in this regard. Burawoy rightfully charged that 'Political economy has conspired in a separation of economics and politics, never attempting to theorize a politics of production. Production has both ideological and political effects' (ibid., p. 7).

In some cases, management attacks labour in order to wring economic concessions from the workers. In others, the financial perspective leads management to display an insensitivity that can push workers to turn their creativity to disruptive ends. Shaiken writes of an incident that illustrates the importance of according adequate respect to the workers:

A familiar sight in most shops is an engineer walking in with a stack of blueprints to ask the worker if a particular job is feasible. The machinist carefully studies the prints, looks at the engineer, and says, 'Well, it can be tried like this but it will never work.' Grabbing a pencil, the machinist marks up the print and, in effect, redesigns the job based on years of experience ... [In one shop, when] management initiated a campaign to strictly enforce lunch periods and wash-up time, the judgment of some machinists began to fade. About this time a foreman dashed up to the shop with a 'hot' job ... Anxious to get the job done quickly, the foreman insisted that the machinist run the lathe at a high speed and plunge the drill through the part. Under normal circumstances the machinist would have tried to talk the foreman out of this approach but now he was only too happy to oblige what were, after all, direct orders. The part not only turned out to be scrap, but part of the lathe turned blue from the friction generated by the high speed. The disciplinary campaign was short-lived (Shaiken, 1985, pp. 19–20).

Shaiken's vignette illustrates business's dependence on labour's cooperation. Once labour withdraws this cooperative spirit, business is in trouble. Observing a similar situation, Zuboff captured the subtle ambivalence of the management–labour relationship, noting 'obedience fed by cynicism became a form of revenge' (Zuboff, 1988, p. 273).

We hear much about employers exhorting their workers to excellence, but this excellence is of a particular kind. Management expects workers to perform to their utmost according to the directives that it gives them. Workers are unlikely to display such unthinking excellence. Even if they were, it would be impossible unless the employer were able to anticipate all contingencies in advance. Shaiken's vignette suggests how difficult it would be to 'pre-programme' workers for their tasks. Instead, an efficient workforce must be able to find some satisfaction in the work it performs.

Recent experience has shown that workers who are given detailed rules and are more closely monitored experience less job satisfaction and are less motivated and place more importance on external rewards, such as compensation (Deci, Connell and Ryan, 1985; cited in Akerlof and Yellen, 1986). The famous Hawthorne experiments also seemed to indicate that workplace democracy can increase job satisfaction and work effort although some recent work has questioned these results (see Drago, 1986).

Leibenstein suggests that Japanese employers have turned this principle to good effect. He recalled:

> Recently I spent six months in Japan and visited some large firms. In all cases I inquired about the way in which employees were monitored. The managers were extremely sensitive to the idea and convinced me ... that no monitoring by superiors was attempted. Promotions, by and large were a consequence of age and duration of employment. Here we have examples of some highly ... efficient firms who did everything possible to avoid monitoring. The managers were aware that such practices were carried out in the US, but these were practices that they assiduously chose not to use, despite the fact that at some earlier period they were tried by some Japanese firms and dropped (Leibenstein, 1983, p. 838).

Unfortunately, the attitude that Leibenstein found in Japan is exceedingly rare in the US.

Of course, enlightened management on its own can, and sometimes does, take actions which improve the relations between labour and capital. However, in other cases it is the intervention of unions that is crucial by forcing improvements in labour–management relations that make labour more productive.

Unions have promoted productivity in a number of ways. To begin with, by raising wages, unions have prodded employers to devise new and improved labour-saving methods of production, just as the theory of efficiency wages suggests. The precise impact of this effect will not be obvious, since many non-union firms will also eventually adopt these new techniques. Consequently, the spread of these techniques will appear to be part of the general pattern of industrial progress.

Even so, economists consistently find that workers in unionized firms are more productive than workers in comparable non-union companies, despite the impact of union work rules. For example, Freeman and Medoff conclude that effects of union work rules on efficiency tend to be very small (Freeman and Medoff, 1984, p. 12). They provide 'striking new evidence on what unions do to productivity' (ibid., p. 163). They call their results 'striking' because they conclude, 'In sum, most studies of productivity find that unionized establishments are more productive than otherwise comparable nonunion establishments' (ibid., p. 169).

Freeman and Medoff are not alone in regarding unionization to be consistent with high productivity. For example, Allen estimates that union work rules increase typical office building costs by about 2 per cent (Allen, 1986). Allen found that union productivity, measured in square feet of floor space completed per hour worked, was at least 30 per cent higher than non-union productivity.

In projects to construct schools, union productivity was equal to non-union productivity measured by the number of workers required to build a project. Measured in terms of value added, union productivity was 20 per cent higher then non-union productivity (Allen, 1986). Allen also found that union projects produce 51 per cent more square footage per hour than non-union projects (Allen, 1988a). After reviewing the literature concerning the relationship between unions and productivity, Allen concluded that most studies find that union workers are more productive than non-union workers in comparable establishments (Allen, 1988b).

Unions even make teachers more productive. For example, students from schools with a unionized environment score about 4.7 per cent higher on their college entrance exams than their counterparts from a non-union environment (Register and Grimes, 1991). In fairness, we cannot conclude that unions necessarily cause this increase in productivity. In part, unions may be an effect, rather than a cause of high productivity. In other words, firms that are highly productive may be forcing workers to exert themselves beyond what the employees consider to be fair. Indeed, as Scitovsky noted, in the West in general, workers who felt exploited and resentful frequently turned to unionization in an attempt to create a defensive force to match the force of their employers (Scitovsky, 1990, p. 144).

Several authors have built on generalizations, such as Scitovsky's, to reach the conclusion that workers tend to join unions in situations where the work demands are high (FitzRoy and Kraft, 1985; and Duncan and Stafford, 1980). According to this line of reasoning, workers are not more productive because they belong to unions. Instead, they belong to unions because their work environment forces them to be more productive.

Freeman and Medoff also lend support to the notion that unions may be the effect, in part, rather than just the cause, of high productivity. They concluded that unionized workers in the US express less satisfaction with their jobs than non-union workers, but are less willing to quit, presumably because of their superior wages (Freeman and Medoff, 1984).

Although we cannot prove the extent to which unions are the cause or the effect of higher productivity, the superior efficiency of unionized teachers lends support to the notion that unions do indeed promote productivity. A school administration might treat teachers poorly or deny them adequate resources, but such policies would not be likely to make students learn better. We would have to stretch our imaginations to see how policies that improve students' test scores would drive teachers to join unions.

In any case, unions can be advantageous to employers for several reasons. To begin with, they can be a boon to employers, especially large-scale employers, who would otherwise have difficulty in recruiting employees to work on weekend and overtime shifts (Allen, 1987, p. 352). Besides raising wages and helping with the mobilization of the labour force, unions can benefit employers by changing workers' feelings about their situation. Freeman and Medoff build on Hirshmann's notion of the importance of voice within an organization. According to Freeman and Medoff, without unions, many workers would lack a voice in the large, faceless corporation.

With a voice, workers can take more satisfaction in knowing that they can make management know how they feel. Without a voice, workers would be reduced to making their negative feelings felt by exit, causing employers to bear the expense of costly employee turnover. Japan offers some suggestive material regarding the role of unions in giving workers a voice. Japanese unions are company unions. Japanese employers only turned to unionization after a period of intense labour militancy. Workers might be reluctant to cast their lot with company unions, which do not take a particularly adversarial position toward business. In order to make these unions more credible, Japanese firms first offered lifetime employment (Kenney and Florida, 1988, p. 128). In the process, Japanese firms soon realized that offering the workers more respect and better working conditions induces better performance (Scitovksy, 1990, p. 144).

Although Freeman and Medoff found that unions generally promoted efficiency, they do not always do so to the same extent. At times, unions can even become counterproductive. Freeman and Medoff blame these periods of a negative association between unions and productivity on shifts in labour–management relations, but they do not elaborate on this hypothesis (Freeman and Medoff, 1984, p. 168). Presumably, these authors mean that when labour–management relationships deteriorate, unions can assist workers in resisting capital.

Although many students of labour–management relations recognize the benefits of unions, business has been slow in coming to this position. Instead, it comforts itself by blaming problems on others – on the government, on foreigners, and whenever possible on unions. All the while, we allow our economy progressively to weaken.

CONCLUSION: THE NEED FOR A CO-OPERATIVE POLICY TOWARDS LABOUR

The need to tap workers' creativity is especially crucial in highly advanced technological systems, where management depends on labour for developing the best possible methods of production (see Glyn, Hughes, Lipietz, and Singh 1990, p. 89). Unfortunately, relatively few employers adequately acknowledge the degree of skill involved on the job.

Instead, employers prefer to attempt to coerce labour into absolute obedience with the threat of unemployment. By compelling obedience through coercion, management stifles the creativity which is central to the successful functioning of modern industry. This approach does serious harm to the economy. As Walton, an expert on progressive pay schemes, has observed:

> Especially in a high wage country like the US, market success depends on a superior level of performance, a level that, in return requires the deep commitment, not merely the obedience – if you could obtain it – of workers. And as painful experience shows, this commitment cannot flourish in a workplace dominated by the familiar model of control. (Walton, 1985, pp. 77–8; cited in Glyn, Hughes, Lipietz, and Singh 1990, p. 89).

In contrast to the US, Japanese firms have been extremely successful in tapping the knowledge of their workers. For example, the average worker in a Toyota plant gave 31.8 suggestions in 1983. Of these, 96 per cent were accepted (Kaplinsky, 1988, p. 460).

The Japanese approach is not novel. During the late nineteenth century foreign observers associated this approach with the US. For example, British industrialists visiting the US realized that worker involvement was an integral part of the success of that economy. An industrialist, A. Mosely, head of one of the many delegations of British industrialists that visited the US at the beginning of this century, reported:

> One point that has struck me with enormous force, as I believe it has all the delegates, is the close touch and sympathy between master and man, which is carried a step further in the enlistment of the men's good offices to improve factory methods. Suggestions are welcomed, the more so because the American manufacturer has realized that it is not the man sitting in the counting-house or private office who is best able to judge where improvements can be made in machine or method, but he who attends that machine from morning to night ... In short, the man feels that the work of his brains will handsomely benefit himself. Is it any wonder, therefore, that American machinery

is continually changing and improving, that the evolution of methods is ever and rapidly going on? ... As a rule the British employer hardly knows his men, seldom leaves his office for the workshop. (Offer, 1989, p. 124)

A cooperative labour policy can and will make an economy healthier. If the US is to regain its previous position, it will have to win the respect and the loyalty of labour.

Nonetheless, treating labour with respect and rewarding workers to encourage productivity is not a panacea which can permanently rid the economy of crises. Moreover, the inevitable extended bouts of unemployment, typical of a market economy, will work to embitter workers. Still, within the bounds of a market economy, a cooperative labour policy is about the best rule to follow. The alternative is what I have called elsewhere, 'the Haitian road to development', in which firms attempt to compete on the basis of low wages (Perelman, 1983).

REFERENCES

Akerlof, George A. and Yellen, Janet L. (1986), *Efficiency Wage Models of the Labour Market*, Cambridge: Cambridge University Press.

Allen, Steven G. (1986), 'Union Work Rules and Efficiency in the Building Trades', *Journal of Labour Economics*, vol. 4, no. 2, April, pp. 212–42.

Allen, Steven G. (1987), 'Can Union Labour Ever Cost Less?' *Quarterly Journal of Economics*, vol. 52, no. 2, May, pp. 347–73.

Allen, Steven G. (1988a), 'Further Evidence on Union Efficiency in Construction', *Industrial Relations*, vol. 27, no. 2, Spring, pp. 232–40.

Allen, Steven G. (1988b), 'Productivity Levels and Productivity Change Under Unionism', *Industrial Relations*, vol. 27, no. 1, Winter, pp. 94–113.

Barber, William J. (1985), *From New Era to New Deal: Herbert Hoover. the Economists, and American Economic Policy, 1921–1933*, Cambridge: Cambridge University Press.

Belous, Richard S. (1989) 'How Human Resource Systems Adjust to the Shift toward Contingent Workers', *Monthly Labour Review*, vol. 112, no. 3, March, pp. 7–12.

Bernanke, Ben S. (1986), 'Employment, Hours, and Earnings in the Depression: An Analysis of 8 Manufacturing Industries', *American Economic Review*, vol. 76, no. 1, March, pp. 83–109.

Burawoy, Michael (1979), *Manufacturing Consent*, Chicago: University of Chicago Press.

Carver, Thomas Nixon (1925), *The Present Economic Revolution in the United States*, Boston: Little Brown.

Chposky, James and Leonisis, Ted (1988), *Blue Magic: The People, Power and Politics Behind the IBM Personal Computer*, New York and Oxford: Facts on File Publications.

Clark, G. (1987), 'Why Isn't the Whole World Developed? Lessons from the Cotton Mills', *Journal of Economic History*, vol. 47, no. 1, March, pp. 141–73.

Deci, Edward L., Connell, James L. and Ryan, Richard M. (1985), 'Self-Determination in a Work Organization', (mimeo).

DeMarco, Tom and Lister, Timothy (1987), *Peopleware: Productive Projects and Teams*, New York: Dorset House.

Drago, Robert (1986), 'Capitalism and Efficiency: A Review and Appraisal of the Recent Discussion', *Review of Radical Political Economy*, vol. 18, no. 4, Winter, pp. 71–92.

Dumenil, Gerard, Glick, Mark and Rangel, Jose (1987), 'Theories of the Great Depression: Why Did Profitability Matter?' *Review of Radical Political Economy*, vol. 19, no. 2, Summer, pp. 16–42.

Duncan, G.C. and Stafford, F.P. (1980), 'Do Union Members Receive Compensating Wage Differentials?' *American Economic Review*, vol. 70, no. 3, June, pp. 355–71.

Edwards, Richard (1979), *Contested Terrain: The Transformation of the Workplace in the Twentieth Century*, New York: Basic Books.

Fenoaltea, Stefano (1984), 'Slavery and Supervision in Comparative Perspective: A Model', *Journal of Economic History*, vol. 44, no. 3, September, pp. 635–68.

FitzRoy, Felix R. and Kraft, Kornelius (1935), 'Unionization, Wages and Efficiency: Theories and Evidence from the U.S. and West Germany', *Kyklos*, vol. 38, no. 4, pp. 537–54.

Freeman, Richard B. and Medoff, James (1984), *What Do Unions Do?* New York: Basic Books.

Genovese, Eugene D. (1976), *Roll, Jordan, Roll: The World the Slaves Made*, New York: Vintage.

Glyn, Andrew, Hughes, Alan, Lipietz, Alain and Singh, Ajit (1990), 'The Rise and Fall of the Golden Age', in Stephen A. Marglin and Juliet B. Schor, (eds), *The Golden Age of Capitalism: Reinterpreting the Postwar Experience*, Oxford: Clarendon Press, pp. 38–125.

Habakkuk, H. J. (1962), *American and British Technology in the Nineteenth Century: The Search for Labour-Saving Inventions*, Cambridge: Cambridge University Press.

Harrison, Harrison and Bluestone, Barry (1988), *The Great U-Turn: Corporate Restructuring and the Polarizing of America*, New York: Basic Books.

Henwood, Douglas (1990), 'A Compendium of Woes', *Left Business Observer*, no. 40, 14 September, pp. 4–5.

Jenks, Jeremiah (1890), 'The Economic Outlook', *Dial*, vol. 10; cited in Livingstone (1986).

Jerome, Harry (1934), *Mechanization in Industry*, New York: National Bureau of Economic Research.

Kaplinsky, Raphael (1988), 'Restructuring the capitalist labour process: some lessons from the car industry', *Cambridge Journal of Economics*, vol. 12, no. 4, December, pp. 451–70.

Kenney, Martin and Florida, Richard (1988), 'Beyond Mass Production: Production and the Labour Process in Japan', *Politics and Society*, vol. 16, no. 1, March, pp. 121–58.

Kidder, Tracy, (1981), *The Soul of a New Machine*, Boston: Little Brown.

Kislev, Yoav and Peterson, Willis (1982), 'Prices, Technology, and Farm Size', *Journal of Political Economy*, vol. 90, no. 3, June, pp. 578–95.

Kopcke, Richard W. (1980), 'Potential Growth, Productivity, and Capital Accumulation', *New England Economic Review*, May/June, pp. 22–41.

Leibenstein, Harvey (1983), 'Property Rights and X-efficiency: Comment', *American Economic Review*, vol. 73, no. 4, September, pp. 831–42.

Livingston, James (1986), *Origins of the Federal Reserve System: Money, Class, and Corporate Capitalism, 1890–1913*, Ithaca, New York: Cornell University Press.

Melman, Seymour (1983), *Profits Without Production*, New York: Alfred A. Knopf.

O'Brien, Anthony Patrick (1989), 'A Behavioral Explanation for Nominal Wage Rigidity During the Great Depression', *Quarterly Journal of Economics*, vol. 104, no. 4, November, pp. 719–36.

Offer, Avner (1989), *The First World War: An Agrarian Interpretation*, Oxford: Clarendon Press.

Oshima, H. T. (1984), 'The Growth of U.S. Factor Productivity: The Significance of New Technologies in the Early Decades of the Twentieth Century', *Journal of Economic History*, vol. 44, no. 1, March, pp. 161–70.

Perelman, Michael (1983), *Classical Political Economy, Primitive Accumulation, and the Social Division of Labor*, Totowa, N.J.: Rowman and Allanheld.

President of the United States (1993), *Economic Report of the President*, Washington, DC: US Government Printing Office.

Register, Charles A. and Grimes, Paul W. (1991) 'Collective Bargaining, Teachers, and Student Achievement', *Journal of Labour Research*, vol. 12, no. 2, Spring, pp. 91–111.

Schmid, Gregory (1981), 'Productivity and Reindustrialization: A Dissenting View', *Challenge*, vol. 23, no. 6, January/February, pp. 24–9.

Schoenhof, Jacob (1893), *The Economy of High Wages: An Inquiry into the Cause of High Wages and their Effects on Methods and Cost of Production*, New York: G.P. Putnam's Sons.

Schor, Juliet B. (1991), *The Overworked American: The Unexpected Decline of Leisure*, New York: Basic Books.

Scitovsky, Tibor (1990), 'The Benefits of Asymmetric Markets', Journal of Economic Perspectives, vol. 4, no. 1, Winter, pp. 135–48.

Shaiken, Harley (1985), *Work Transformed: Automation and Labour in the Computer Age*, New York: Holt, Rinehart & Winston.

Sherman, Howard J. (1983), 'Cyclical Behavior of Government Fiscal Policy', *Journal of Economic Issues*, vol. 17, no. 2, June, pp. 379–88.

Staehle, Hans (1955), 'Technology, Utilization and Production', *Bulletin de l'Institut Internationale de Statistique*, vol. 34, Part 4, pp. 112–36.

Strassman, W.P. (1959), *Risk and Technological Investment*, Ithaca, NY: Cornell University Press.

Tilly, Chris (1991), 'Continuing Growth of Part-Time Employment', *Monthly Labour Review*, vol. 114, no. 3, March, pp. 10–18.

Tocqueville, Alexis de (1848), *Democracy in America*, 2 vols., tr. Henry Reeve, New York: D. Appleton, 1899.

United States Department of Labor Statistics (1977), *Handbook of Labor Statistics*, Washington, DC: US Government Printing Office.

United States Department of Labor, Bureau of Labor Statistics (1989), *Handbook of Labor Statistics*, Bulletin 2340, Washington, DC: US Government Printing Office.

Viner, Jacob (1933), *Balanced Deflation, Inflation or More Depression*. Day and Hour Series, no. 3, Minneapolis: University of Minneapolis Press.

Walton, Richard E. (1985), 'From Control to Commitment in the Workplace', *Harvard Business Review*, vol. 85, no. 2, March–April, pp. 76–84.

Wells, David A. (1885), 'The "Foreign Competitive Pauper Labor" Argument for Protection', in his *Practical Economics: A Collection of Essays Respecting Certain of the Recent Economic Experiences of the United States*, New York: G.C. Putnam; New York: Greenwood Publishers, 1968, pp. 133–52.

Wright, Gavin (1990), 'The Origins of American Industrial Success, 1870-1940', *American Economic Review*, vol. 80, no. 4, September, pp. 651–68.

Zuboff, Shoshana (1988), *In the Age of the Smart Machines: The Future of Work and Power*, New York: Basic Books.

8. Wage–employment determination in a post-Keynesian world

Peter Andrew Riach

The high, persistent levels of unemployment experienced by many industrialized countries, especially within the European Community, since the latter half of the 1970s have stimulated a search for explanations. One culprit, widely canvassed by official bodies, is excessive real wage increases:

> ... the sharp increases in real wages which have occurred in recent years but which were not justified by productivity increases, have further increased unemployment levels, through the accompanying falls in profitability. (Commission of the European Communities, 1982, p. 115)

> Studies of the effect of increases in real labour costs have shown them to exert a direct negative effect on employment in some, although not all, OECD economies. (Organization for Economic Co-operation and Development, 1984, p. 45)

Certainly, neo-classical theory has long predicted that in the short run, with perfect competition, a fixed capital stock and diminishing returns, an increase in the real wage in excess of the equilibrium level will induce a reduction in employment. When this theory is applied to a dynamic world, where the capital stock and technology are changing, a modification is required:

> According to another commonly held opinion, when techniques advance real wages cannot rise more quickly than productivity without causing a decline in employment. This opinion rests on the same theoretical basis as the former argument. If real wages increase more than productivity, it is asserted, the real cost of marginal production increases, and employment must decline so that this increased cost does not exceed the real value of the marginal product... (de Largentaye, 1979, p. 10).

Therefore when this neo-classical explanation for reduced employment levels was disinterred, a crude modification was introduced to cope with the rightwards movement of average and marginal product functions in a dynamic world where the capital stock is not constant. So the assertion became that it was an increase in real wages *relative* to labour's average product which would induce a reduction in employment. The Organization for Economic Co-operation and

Development, which was a principal proponent of this hypothesis, introduced us to the concept of 'the real wage gap', defined as: '... the difference between the growth of real wages and that *warranted* by productivity and terms of trade changes', (Organization for Economic Co-operation and Development, 1980, p. 41, n 1, emphasis added). This was a piece of obfuscation, as a 'real wage gap' is simply an increase in the wage share of output. The share of wages in output is an economic concept with a respectable lineage and not in need of re-titling, euphemistically or otherwise. The crude dynamic version of the neo-classical cost-minimizing calculus, purged of this contemporary jargon, is that an increase in the wage share will induce lower employment as profit maximizers *substitute* away from labour because of *cost* considerations.

In contrast the post-Keynesian literature has long emphasized that the *income* effect of an increase in the wage share; that is, a redistribution of macroeconomic income, away from parsimonious profit takers towards spend-thrift wage earners, boosts the aggregate consumption propensity and generates higher employment. This point can be found as long ago as 1938: 'This fall in the "degree of monopoly" results in a shift of income to wage earners and a higher average propensity to consume for the community, which results in an increased output...' (Dunlop, 1938, p. 433).

The possibility of a *positive* relationship between the wage share and employment, once the assumptions of diminishing returns and perfect competition are abandoned, and differential consumption propensities out of wages and profits are introduced, is a recurring theme in the writings of Michal Kalecki and Joan Robinson, e.g. '... the exercise of bargaining strength playing against monopolistic power raises real wages and increases employment'. (Robinson, 1960, p. 150); and '... a wage rise showing an increase in the trade union power leads – contrary to the precepts of classical economics – to an increase in employment' (Kalecki, 1971, p. 163).

THE KEYNESIAN WAGE–EMPLOYMENT RELATIONSHIP

In his *General Theory of Employment, Interest and Money* Keynes carried over from the foregoing neo-classical economists the assumptions of profit maximization, pure competition and diminishing returns, therefore he retained, within price–quantity space, the neo-classical inverse relationship between real wages and employment: '...the real wage earned by a unit of labour has a unique (inverse) correlation with the volume of employment' (Keynes, 1936, p. 17).

It is this Keynesian position which has caused such confusion in the minds of economists such as Patinkin (1965) and Meltzer (1981), who insist on interpreting this inverse relationship, derived from the production function, as an aggregate demand curve for labour. Their interpretation of Keynes is consistent with the traditional neo-classical position that price and quantity are necessarily determined *within* a price–quantity space occupied by two well-behaved functions of price, which interact via a market process, involving an invisible hand or a mythical auctioneer, to determine an equilibrium outcome. It was one of Keynes' major contributions to economic theory to break out of this price-theoretic mould, dominated by substitution effects, to explain that quantity may instead be determined from *without* under the dominant influence of income effects.

In neo-classical analysis we arrive at points on the axes of price–quantity space courtesy of an interactive market process taking place *within* that space, that is, between buyers and sellers of the good or factor plotted on the horizontal axis.

In Chapter 2 of *The General Theory* (1936) Keynes argued that the point of arrival on the quantity axis of an aggregate real wage–employment space is determined from *without*, in particular, via the activities of the buyers and sellers of commodities in establishing a point of effective demand. If W is the money wage rate, P the price level, MP_L labour's marginal product and L the quantity of labour hours, the point is as indicated in Figure 8.1.

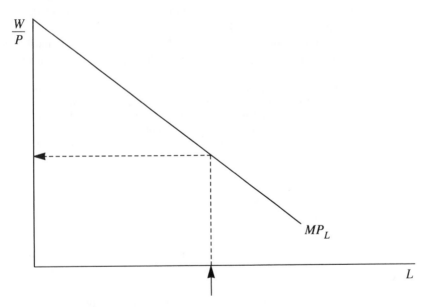

Figure 8.1   Point of arrival on quantity axis, determined from without

The point of arrival on the quantity axis of Figure 8.1 is the outcome of the expectations which entrepreneurs in aggregate have about the profitability of various output levels of consumption and investment goods:

Thus the behaviour of each individual firm in deciding its daily output will be determined by its *short-term expectations* – expectations as to the cost of output on various possible scales and expectations as to the sales-proceeds of this output; ... It is upon these various expectations that the amount of employment which the firms offer will depend ... The propensity to consume and the rate of new investment determine between them the volume of employment ... (Keynes, 1936, pp. 47, 30)

Confirmation that for Keynes, aggregate employment is a phenomenon of the commodity market comes in his definition of full employment: 'There is less-than-full employment if, the propensity to consume being unchanged an increase in investment will cause an increase in consumption' (Keynes, 1973, p. 26).

As depicted in Figure 8.1, the role of marginal product in this Keynesian system is merely to establish the real wage which corresponds to the employment level established by commodity market forces; i.e. *MP* simply transmits us from the quantity axis to the price axis – it plays no role in the quantity axis result.

Keynes reverses the neo-classical price–quantity relationship, and within wage–employment space determines only the real wage rate. Wage changes are unequivocally a *consequence* rather than a *cause*, of changes in employment: '... increasing employment must *lead* at the same time to a diminution of the marginal product and hence of the rate of wages measured in terms of this product' (Keynes, 1936, p. 18, emphasis added).

It is this unambiguous reversal of the neo-classical functional relationship between real wages and employment which has eluded mainstream economists:

The road-block for mainstream neo-classical economic analysis of real world problems of employment and inflation has been the feckless use of the first derivative of aggregate production functions to denote the demand curve for labor for entrepreneurial economies which use the institutions of money and money contracts to organize productive activities in trying to cope with a world of uncertainty. (Davidson, 1983, p. 56).

THE POST-KEYNESIAN WAGE–EMPLOYMENT RELATIONSHIP

Whilst Keynes determines, for real wage–employment space, quantity from *without*, post-Keynesians go a step further in rejecting neo-classical tools and determine the real wage also from *without*, so that price–quantity space does not perform even its Keynesian purpose of transmitting us between axes (see Figure 8.2)

Wage *OA* and employment *OX* are determined externally from this price–quantity space, and if these variables move either inversely or positively, it does not indicate a direct causal relationship between price and quantity, as is characteristic of neo-classical economics.

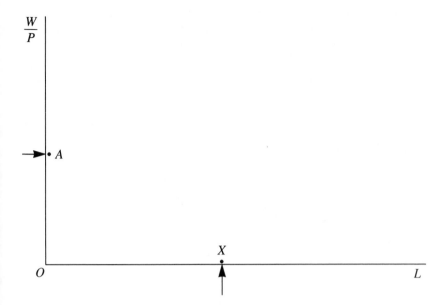

Figure 8.2   Real wage determined from without

An explicit and stylized account of the post-Keynesian income effect and how
it can produce a positive wage–employment relationship externally from this
price–quantity space is as follows: we begin with a model which accommodates
interdependence between the level and the distribution of income (Riach, 1969).
The model demonstrates the simultaneous determination of equilibrium values
for the level and the distribution of income in an approach analagous to the simultaneous determination of income and interest in Hicks' *IS–LM* model. (Hicks,
1937). The analysis is conducted within one of the sequence of short periods
which extend through time; i.e. it is recognized that eventually entrepreneurs
will have the opportunity of making a long-term response to a change in product
demand and/or input prices, but that, for the moment, they are constrained to
their existing capital capacity and technique. In this short run firms are assumed
to have the characteristics and behaviour which are standard fare of post-
Keynesian economics: i.e. constant average variable costs up to the limit of
practical capacity; mark-up pricing and quantity adjustment in an uncertain, oli-
gopolisitc world; and 'degree of monopoly'-determined mark-ups, where
'degree of monopoly' refers to a conglomeration of forces, including product
market concentration and cartelization, barriers to entry and the countervailing
power of trade unions This all adds up to the proposition that the equilibrium
wage–profit division is invariant with respect to the level of output. Therefore
in Figure 8.3, where the wage share (Z) is plotted on the vertical axis and

output (Y) is plotted on the horizontal axis, we obtain a horizontal *YD* function, this being a function which defines the equilibrium wage share corresponding to any level of output.

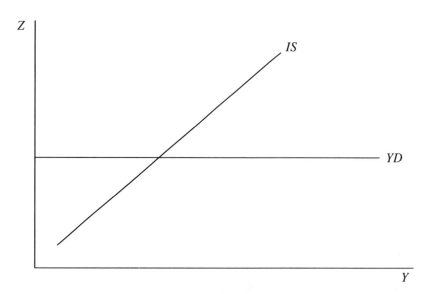

Figure 8.3   Defining the equilibrium wage share

If, instead, the degree of monopoly were related to the level of economic activity, as has been suggested by writers such as Harrod (1936) and Kalecki (1971), the *YD* function could have a positive or negative slope. Stability in this *YD* function is reliant on a reasonably constant mix of aggregate output.

This cost and pricing behaviour, which was assumed in deriving the *YD* function of Figure 8.3, is critical in distinguishing Keynes from Kalecki and the post-Keynesians:

> It is strange that Keynes who saw the deficiencies of the classical theory of employment at the macro-level so clearly, did not incorporate into his theory of a monetary production (entrepreneur) economy a realistic theory of the firm: a theory of the firm based on realistic assumptions of constant average variable cost, decreasing average total cost, *with output limited by demand*, and price set by a mark-up on prime cost in an uncertain oligopolistic market. This would have provided micro-foundations compatible with his macro theory. (Brothwell, 1986, pp. 539–40)

In post-Keynesian theory, human decisions and sociopolitical pressures predominate in the determination of income shares. It is entrepreneurial pricing decisions, the interaction between oligopolists and with governments, and the bargaining struggle with trade unions which establish the profit margin (Kalecki, 1971). This contrasts with neo-classical analysis where the determination of factor shares is dominated by technical considerations and pressures for factor substitution in the production process, and for commodity substitution in the consumption process.

The implication for labour of such mark-up pricing and quantity adjustment in the product market is that a reduction in real wages is not necessary to seduce entrepreneurs into increasing employment. Once the real wages have been determined, along with the profit margin, by the degree of monopoly forces outlined above, firms' input of labour is determined solely by aggregate demand in the product market – if it rises entrepreneurs happily extend output and employment at the existing real wage. In other words, the process of quantity adjustment feeds through into the labour market.

The *IS* function in Figure 8.3 represents a locus of points which specify saving–investment equilibria corresponding to various combinations of output and the wage share, by analogy with Hicks' *IS* function. Such a formation of the *IS* function can be found in Riach (1969) and, more recently, in Bhaduri and Marglin (1990). In Figure 8.3 the *IS* function is shown positively sloped on the assumption that investment demand is independent of the wage share, whereas, in accordance with post-Keynesian practice, it is assumed that the savings propensity out of profits exceeds that out of wages. The intersection of the *YD* and *IS* functions shows an equilibrium level of macroeconomic income which is compatible with microeconomic costs and pricing behaviour. In this sense it corresponds to the intersection of Weintraub's aggregate supply and demand functions (1958).

This model is now reproduced in the south-west quadrant of Figure 8.4. The south-east quadrant presents the short-run utilization function, which specifies the labour input necessary to satisfy product market requirements: constant returns, deriving from fixed technical coefficients of production and surplus capital capacity, up to the limit of 'practical capacity', are assumed, in conformity with post-Keynesian practice. The north-west quadrant contains a function which translates the wage share of the horizontal axis into the real wage of the vertical axis. It is obviously a positive function and its slope reflects labour productivity – an increase in labour productivity will swivel it clockwise.

The north-east quandrant is the price–quantity space characteristic of a neo-classical market, but where we arrive on the price axis depends on the degree of monopoly which determines the position of the *YD* function. The outcome for the quantity axis, on the other hand, depends on the state of aggregate commodity demand which determines the position of the *IS* function. Point *H* is, therefore, not determined *within* price–quantity space, but simply indicates a wage–employment combination arising from activity *without*, i.e. the commodity market.

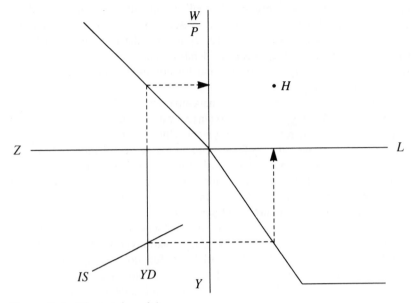

Figure 8.4   The total model

Instead of price and quantity being the simultaneous outcome of the Marshallian scissors, real wage and employment in our post-Keynesian world are
determined by separate forces – the degree of monopoly and aggregate commodity
demand. The rejection of diminishing returns effectively removes the link
between the price and quantity axes. Thus it is not meaningful to talk of a 'labour
market' in the traditional sense of an arena in which trading between buyer and
seller establishes a market-clearing equilibrium price. There is no price which
establishes a state of rest – output and employment are fluid in response to changes
in demand, without any need for a wage change (Appelbaum, 1979, p. 117).

In this post-Keynesian world a fall in the degree of monopoly, caused perhaps
by a reduction in tariffs on manufactured imports or by a removal of anti-union
legislation, will produce a lower profit share and a higher real wage. Provided
that some margin remains over variable cost there will be no adverse quantity
response in either output or employment. With constant returns, no purpose is
served in the short run by reacting to the higher real wage with a cut in
employment. Although profit per unit of output has been squeezed, it is nevertheless in firms' interests to sell as many units as customers demand, therefore
if this demand remains constant so will output and employment, regardless of
the higher real wage.

It may well be that the shift from profits to wages will itself increase the demand
for commodities, particularly through the post-Keynesian hypothesis that the

saving propensity of capitalists is higher than that of wage earners. Cowling has assessed this hypothesis against the empirical data: 'The ... empirical evidence points to the conclusion that a redistribution from wages to profits will have a depressive impact on consumption and this will be maximised when the increment of profit is retained within the corporation rather than being distributed to stockholders' (Cowling, 1982, p. 51). The hypothesis of differential savings propensities produces the positive slope of the *IS* function in Figure 8.3: with investment assumed constant, as profit margins fall, the demand for output rises under the impact of the higher consumption propensity of labour. In effect, consumption and saving are functions of the wage share in the post-Keynesian analysis.

Such an outcome is represented in Figure 8.5 where we demonstrate the possibility that, in a post-Keynesian world, entrepreneurs may seek to hire more labour at the very time its real wage is rising. In the figure the initial position is assumed to involve function *YD* and, therefore, employment *OX* and wage *OA*. This situation is disturbed by a reduction in tariff barriers, which depresses the degree of monopoly and produces a shift to *YD'*. Therefore the real wage rises to *OB* and, as consumption responds to the higher wage share, employment increases to *OV*. The outcome is point *K* in price–quantity space, which lies in a positive relationship to *H*.

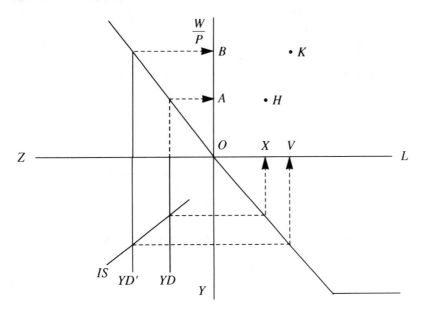

Figure 8.5   An increase in real wages accompanied by increased employment

So a simple menu of standard, and not widely unrealistic, post-Keynesian fare produces a situation where additional labour is hired in a world of higher real wages. But wages and employment are not related in the direct causal manner of a neo-classical market: firms do not hire more labour because its price has risen – no 'Veblen factor' is being mooted. Instead the impact of the higher real wage is indirect through the 'product market connection'. It is worth stressing again the point made above, that there is no Marshallian-type market linkage; instead wage and employment are controlled by independent forces, so that, while the above example produced higher wages and employment, there is no functional relationship between them and we cannot consider the move as being from one labour market equilibrium to another.

In post-Keynesian labour hiring, price may change without stimulating any associated quantity response; alternatively quantity may change without the inducement of a price variation. The foregoing example involved two separate combinations of wages and employment although this must not be envisaged as a comparison of two equilibrium positions, but rather as a process taking place over historical time. The economy is moving forward under the impetus which a reduced degree of monopoly has on human decisions and expectations of the future. As Joan Robinson pointed out in *History versus Equilibrium* (1974, p. 5) time runs at right angles to the plane of a two-dimensional diagram, and what must be recognized here is that any adjustments to wages and employment, stimulated by the reduced degree of monopoly, will probably occur at a differential temporal rate.

It is, of course, possible that a change in income distribution could also influence investment demand. In Keynes' *General Theory* investment decisions are motivated by the 'animal spirits' of entrepreneurs and are based on their expectations of future profitability. Therefore it is possible that a reduction in the profit share could react differently on investment, depending on the origin of the profit squeeze. For instance, a reduction in the degree of monopoly arising out of a reduction in tariffs is highly likely to induce pessimistic expectations of the future profitability of investment projects, as entrepreneurs face not only a squeeze on profit margins, but also the prospect of reduced sales because of a switch to imported manufactures. On the other hand, a reduction in the degree of monopoly arising from effective trade practices legislation which breaks down entry barriers, might stimulate investment activity on the part of entrants, so that the profit squeeze would be accompanied by an increased investment level. Kalecki instead argued that current profits directly impact on investment through their influence both on expectations of future profits and on the availability of internal funding for investment projects (Kalecki, 1971, Ch. 10). The relationship between investment and changes in profit in Western Europe during the 1960s was noted by Glyn and Sutcliffe (1972, p. 99). This hypothesis has been widely adopted within the post-Keynesian literature, e.g. Sawyer (1982, Ch. 5).

Once we acknowledge this possibility of an investment–profit relationship, the outcome for the *IS* function depends on the relative sensitivity of savings and investment to the profit share. If the disincentive to investment from a lower profit share exceeds the stimulus to consumption expenditure the *IS* function will have a negative slope, as in Figure 8.6 (Riach, 1969, p. 556).

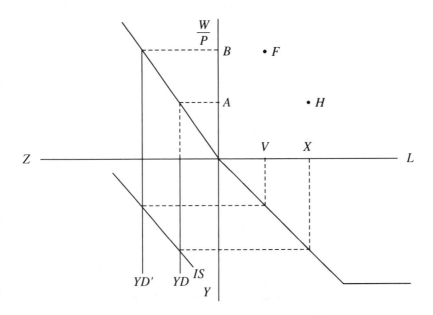

Figure 8.6   An increase in real wages accompanied by reduced employment

In this case a shift to *YD′* involves an increased real wage accompanied by reduced employment. Point *F*, which lies in a negative relationship to *H*, is, however, the result of an income effect, rather than the substitution process of neo-classical economics. Clearly such an outcome is possible and it reinforces the point made earlier, that in post-Keynesian analysis, unlike the neo-classical approach, there is no dogmatic position on the consequences for employment of higher real wages.

SUMMARY AND CONCLUSIONS

In this chapter three views of the wage–employment relationship have been presented. It has been argued that the post-Keynesian view is the most pragmatic of the three.

This accords with the general historical, humanistic approach of Keynesian economics, which is concerned with the analysis of the real world, rather than with the imaginary intellectual problems of neo-classical economics. Relevance, rather than elegance, is the objective of post-Keynesians. Turner captures well this essential characteristic of post-Keynesianism, specifically in respect of the wage-share issues discussed above: 'In the same vein, the Cambridge theory of distribution provides a general framework for behavioural study which does not rely on some predetermined notion of underlying orderlines. Indeed, there is no guarantee held out that individual decisions will produce ideal conditions, technologically, socially or otherwise' (Turner, 1966, p. 400).

REFERENCES

Appelbaum. E. (1979), 'The Labor Market', in Eichner (1979).

Bhaduri, A. and Marglin, S. (1990), 'Unemployment and the real wage: the economic basis for contesting political ideologies', *Cambridge Journal of Economics*, vol. 14, pp. 375–93.

Brothwell, J.F. (1986), '*The General Theory* after fifty years: Why are we not all Keynesians now?', *Journal of Post Keynesian Economics*, vol. 8, pp. 531–47.

Commission of the European Communities (1982), 'Annual Economic Review 1982–83', *European Economy*, no. 14.

Cowling, K. (1982), *Monopoly Capitalism*, Basingstoke: Macmillan.

Davidson, P. (1983), 'The Dubious Labor Market Analysis in Meltzer's Restatement of Keynes' Theory', *Journal of Economic Literature*, vol. 11, pp. 52–6.

de Largentaye J. (1979), 'A note on the *General Theory of Employment, Interest and Money*', *Journal of Post Keynesian Economics*, vol. 1, pp. 6–15.

Dunlop, J.T. (1938), 'The Movement of Real and Money Wage Rates', *The Economic Journal*, vol. 48, pp. 413–34.

Eichner, A.S. (ed.) (1979), *A Guide to Post-Keynesian Economics*, New York: M.E. Sharpe.

Glyn, A. and Sutcliffe, B. (1972), *British Capitalism. Workers and the Profit Squeeze*, Harmondsworth: Penguin.

Harrod, R. (1936), *The Trade Cycle*, Oxford: Oxford University Press.

Hicks, J.R. (1937), 'Mr Keynes and the "Classics"; a Suggested Interpretation', *Econometrica*, vol. 5, pp. 147–59.

Kalecki, M. (1971), *Selected Essays on the Dynamics of the Capitalist Economy 1933–1970*, Cambridge: Cambridge University Press.

Keynes, J.M. (1936), *The General Theory of Employment Interest and Money*, Macmillan, London.

Keynes, J.M. (1973), *The Collected Writings of John Maynard Keynes*. vol. 14, *The General Theory and After, Part II Defence and Development*, ed. D. Moggridge, New York: St Martin's Press.

Meltzer, A.M. (1981), 'Keynes's General Theory: a Different Perspective', *Journal of Economic Literature*, vol. 19, pp. 34–64.

Organization for Economic Co-operation and Development (1980), *Economic Outlook*, July, no. 27.

Organization for Economic Co-operation and Development (1984), *Economic Outlook*, July, no. 35.

Patinkin, D. (1965), *Money, Interest and Prices*, New York: Harper and Row.

Riach, P.A. (1969), 'A Framework for Macro-Distribution Analysis', *Kyklos*, vol. 22, pp. 542–65.

Robinson, Joan (1960), *Collected Economic Papers*, vol. 2, Oxford: Basil Blackwell.

Robinson, Joan (1974), *History Versus Equilibrium*, London: Thames Polytechnic.

Sawyer, M. (1982), *Macro-Economics in Question*, Brighton: Wheatsheaf.

Turner, M. (1966), 'Wages in the Cambridge Theory of Distribution', *Industrial and Labour Relations Review*, vol. 19, no. 3.

Weintraub, S. (1958), *An Approach to the Theory of Income Distribution*, Philadelphia: Chilton.

9. Unemployment experience and the institutional preconditions for full employment

Andrew Henley and Euclid Tsakalotos[1]

The industrialized nations have experienced a considerable diversity of unemployment performance in the two decades since the end of what has been termed the 'Golden Age' of capitalism.[2] For most countries the period since the OPEC price rise of 1973 has been one in which unemployment has been significantly higher, and the rate of unemployment has become characterized by an inexorably upward trend. Additionally the 1970s were characterized by lower rates of economic growth and considerably higher inflation. Whilst a greater measure of price stability was achieved in the 1980s, this was at the cost of rather sluggish growth and even greater unemployment. Despite this very gloomy aggregate picture some nations have appeared to weather the crisis of the 1970s and 1980s more easily than others. While suffering from the growth slowdown, they have managed, in particular, to avoid the rapid rise in unemployment that has characterized the experience of the larger nations. It is in this sense that we refer to a diversity of unemployment experience.

THE OECD UNEMPLOYMENT EXPERIENCE SINCE THE END OF THE POSTWAR 'GOLDEN AGE'

The diversity of economic performance across the industrialized world since the end of the 'Golden Age' is a subject on which a great deal has been written.[3] For present purposes we shall merely provide a short descriptive overview. Table 9.1 provides OECD standardized unemployment rate averages for the leading 19 out of 24 OECD member states between 1960 and 1990. We divide this period into four. A first period from 1960–73 covers the years from the zenith of the 'Golden Age' to the first oil shock. A second period from 1974–79 covers the 'inter-shock' period between the first and second oil shocks. The subsequent decade is divided in two at 1985 to coincide roughly with the 1980s peak in unemployment (in some countries it came earlier; in others, such as France and Japan, it came later). So the third period captures the post-'stagflationary' recession and the fourth the temporary return to growth and falling unemployment. The nations themselves are grouped into four: European Community (EC) members, European Free Trade Area (EFTA) members, non-European English-speaking countries and finally Japan which is classified on its own because of it geographical, cultural and institutional distance from the other non-European nations. It is the EFTA group of countries which contains those countries usually classified as strongly corporatist, namely Austria, Norway, Sweden and Finland (Pekkarinen et al., 1992). Switzerland is the other member, which, while it has a highly decentralized collective bargaining structure, does have some corporatist features (Soskice, 1990).

Table 9.1   Unemployment experience across the OECD since 1960

Average unemployment rate	1960–73	1974–79	1980–85	1986–90
European Community				
Belgium	2.4	6.3	11.3	9.5
Denmark	1.8	5.5	9.3	8.6
France	2.0	1.9	8.3	9.8
Germany	0.8	3.2	6.0	5.9
Ireland	5.2	7.6	12.6	16.2
Italy	3.9	4.6	6.4	7.8
Netherlands	1.5	5.1	10.1	8.8
Spain	2.5	5.3	16.6	18.7
UK	2.9	5.1	10.5	8.6
Average	2.6	5.2	10.1	10.4
EFTA				
Austria	1.4	1.5	3.0	3.4
Finland	2.0	4.4	5.1	4.3
Norway	1.9	1.8	2.6	3.5
Sweden	1.5	1.5	2.4	1.7
Switzerland	0.1	1.0	1.7	1.9
Average	1.4	2.0	2.9	3.0
North America and Australasia				
Australia	2.1	5.0	7.6	7.2
Canada	5.0	7.2	9.9	8.3
New Zealand	0.2	0.8	3.9	5.6
US	4.8	6.7	8.0	5.8
Average	3.0	4.9	7.4	6.7
Japan	1.3	1.9	2.4	2.5

Source: Computed from Layard, Nickell and Jackman (1991), Table A3, pp. 526–8.

While the growth slowdown across the OECD after 1973 is rather uniform across the four groups,[4] it is not the case that this translates into a rapid departure from full employment for all groups of countries. The table shows that before 1973 there is a good deal of uniformity in unemployment rates, in comparison with what was to come. After 1973 we begin to notice the improved relative performance of the corporatist EFTA group. Average unemployment rates doubled in the EC countries and increased by two-thirds in North America and Australasia. Yet within the EFTA between 1973 and 1979 only Finland records an average rate above 2 per cent. Outside EFTA only France and Canada stay below the 2 per cent during this 'inter-shock' period. In Austria, Sweden and Norway average unemployment rates effectively remained at the same level enjoyed in the 1960s.

Within the EC there was a further doubling in average unemployment rates between the 1970s and the first half of the 1980s, to a position where across the EC as a whole over 10 per cent of the workforce was unemployed. The large economies of France and Spain suffered particularly dramatic rises. The average rate for the North American and Australasian countries rose to over 7 per cent. Among the EFTA economies, although unemployment rates rose in the 1980s the picture was much less bleak. In the case of Switzerland and, to a lesser extent, Austria the burden of employment adjustment fell on temporary foreign workers who do not enter reported unemployment statistics. Nevertheless all the economies in this group have unemployment averages during the 1980–85 period which are lower than the best performing EC economy at the time (Germany).

Unemployment rates had peaked in nearly all industrialized nations by the second half of the 1980s, although as we now know this return to falling unemployment has been short-lived. In terms of the data in the table the late 1980s appear as a period of stabilization in unemployment. Stabilization in average unemployment occurred in the corporatist EFTA group but at a rate which is only a third of the average rate in the rest of Europe and slightly less than half that outside Europe (excluding Japan). Figure 9.1 illustrates average unemployment in the EC and EFTA groups (as defined by current membership) over the period 1960 to 1990. It shows very clearly how the latter countries have on average managed to avoid the debilitating growth in unemployment that has followed the end of the 'Golden Age'. An immediate concern is whether the EFTA economies have achieved this superior performance because they have chosen more expansionary policies with a cost in terms of higher inflation. Figure 9.2, which depicts average inflation rates for the two groups, shows this not to be the case.

One could argue that the experience of each of the EFTA countries is exceptional.[5] We have already mentioned the question of unobserved foreign worker unemployment in Switzerland and Austria. To some extent this is borne out by

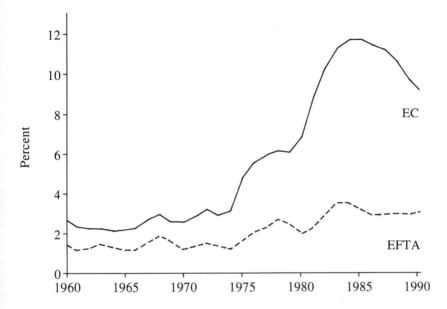

Source: Drawn from data reported in Layard, Nickell and Jackman (1991), Table A3, pp. 526–8.

Figure 9.1   Average unemployment in EC and EFTA countries, 1960–90

Table 9.2, which gives average annual rates of civilian employment growth since 1960. The table shows how employment growth weakened considerably after 1973 in nearly all countries. Within the EFTA group there is an apparent contrast between falling employment growth in Austria and Switzerland and a sustained rate of growth in employment in the Scandinavian countries. All three of the latter group managed to achieve higher average employment growth rates in the 1973–79 period than they had between 1960 and 1973. In Norway this has been the most pronounced and has in good measure resulted from the growth in the offshore oil and gas sector. After 1980 all EFTA countries were able to maintain growing civilian employment, in contrast with many other European countries. So, the smaller corporatist countries of EFTA appear to have achieved a much greater stability in their levels of employment during the economic upheaval of the 1970s and 1980s.

   This contrast suggests that while OECD economies are tied together to a certain extent with a common growth experience there is no one inevitable trajectory with respect to indicators of economic performance, such as unemployment or income distribution, which tell us how the burden of that slower growth is borne across populations. This is an important counterweight to those fatalistic or deter-

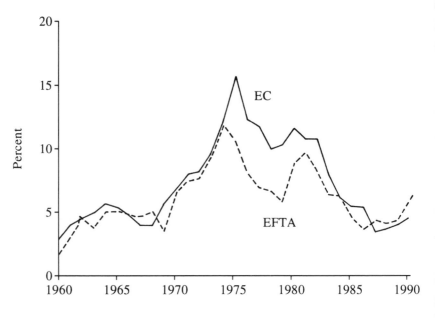

Source: As for Figure 9.1, Table A4, pp. 530–32.

Figure 9.2   Average inflation in EC and EFTA countries, 1960–90

ministic explanations of global economic performance which suggest that we
can put deteriorating economic performance down to the operation of (usually
one) inexorable force such as the introduction of new technology, the rise of
working class militancy and so on. It would suggest that 'full' employment has
not remained a solely academic concept in the last two decades, since it appears
in certain countries to have continued by and large to have been achieved. Sadly,
in terms of number and size these corporatist countries, as they are often termed,
are something of an exception rather than a rule.

   In the remainder of this chapter, we concentrate on this diversity of experience.
Our argument is that institutional diversity can go a long way in explaining
diversity in economic performance. In particular we focus on the importance
of so-called corporatist institutions. Such institutions characterize especially the
Nordic countries and certain mainland European economies, Austria being the
best example. There is no widespread agreement on what constitutes the essence
of corporatism. Indeed, certain prominent theorists have even doubted the
usefulness of the term, arguing that what is usually described as corporatism
in fact entails a wide range of institutions few of which are better understood
by merely labelling them as corporatist (Therborn, 1992). We do not take such

Table 9.2   Employment growth across the OECD since 1960

Average rate of civilian employment growth	1960–73	1974–79	1980–85	1986–90
European Community				
Belgium	0.47	0.02	–0.66	1.16
Denmark	0.92	0.39	0.58	0.89*
France	0.74	0.35	–0.31	0.73
Germany	0.35	–0.56	0.37	1.45
Ireland	0.07	1.12	–1.05	0.42*
Italy	–0.36	0.90	0.37	0.68
Netherlands	1.01	0.53	0.88	2.37†
Spain	0.53	–0.95	–1.85	3.41
UK	0.40	0.25	–0.56	1.93
Total	0.36	0.08	–0.20	1.53*
EFTA				
Austria	–0.12	–0.53	0.99	1.07
Finland	0.54	0.72	1.30	0.25
Norway	1.28	2.09	1.07	0.11
Sweden	0.81	1.26	0.47	0.96
Switzerland	2.26	–0.90	1.32	1.23
Total	0.89	0.38	0.97	0.82
N. America and Australasia				
Australia	2.76	0.85	1.70	3.22
Canada	2.86	2.90	1.31	2.30
New Zealand	2.12	1.69	0.88	1.81+
US	1.98	2.55	1.37	1.94
Total	2.10	2.47	1.37	2.41
Japan	1.38	0.69	0.97	1.48

Notes: *1985–89, †1988–90 (series rebased in 1987), +1987–89 (series rebased in 1986)
Source: Computed from OECD *Labour Statistics*, various issues

a pessimistic approach. Instead we attempt to understand how corporatist institutions have operated and the mechanisms by which superior economic performance has been achieved. In doing so, we shall see that corporatism is a multidimensional entity. This is true both through time, in that some dimensions have been more important in particular periods, and across countries, in that different economies have adopted these different dimensions to varying degrees. What these different dimensions should not obscure, however, is that there is a certain common approach in all corporatist institutions which distinguishes it from what might be called a market-liberal, deregulated or pluralist approach. Furthermore, this common approach, we believe, directly addresses some of the central problems inherent in all capitalist market economies; the two problems we focus on here are those of uncertainty and the potential for conflict. It is for this reason that corporatist institutions have been associated with better economic performance.

THE IMPORTANCE OF INSTITUTIONS

The decline of the 'Golden Age' was associated not surprisingly with important shifts in the realm of ideas. By the late 1970s, it was commonplace to discuss this shift in terms of the death of Keynesianism and end of the social democratic postwar consensus. Given the ascendancy of market-liberal ideas, there was a tendency to ignore the importance of institutions in determining economic performance. As often as not, within the market liberal approach, institutions were likely to be seen in an almost wholly negative light. The welfare state and the role of organized interests (in particular trade unions) in public policy were seen as the result of decades of giving in to special interests while ignoring the effects of this on the operation of the market. This view is particularly in evidence in the Euro-sclerosis explanation for the declining performance of European economies in the 1970s and 1980s (Giersch, 1985, Lindbeck, 1985). This explanation emphasizes 'imperfections' which provide for inflexibility in the market mechanism. It is argued that the appropriate policy response to these is to undo them through supply-side reforms to facilitate market clearing and the achievement of full employment. If economic performance is disappointing then measures should be taken to ensure that the real world becomes more like the market economy of the textbooks.

At the theoretical level, what seems to lie behind such an approach is the idea that the principles of competitive equilibrium are adequate for understanding the economic performance of modern capitalist economies. The dominant metaphor for competitive equilibrium within economics has always been that of the Walrasian system. To highlight the essentials of the system, Walras used the analogy of an auctioneer who invites all economic agents to reach agreement about all their trading decisions (both present and future). The auctioneer begins by quoting a set of prices for all commodities and asks all individuals to state their demand and supply for these commodities at this set of prices. The auctioneer keeps changing the prices until all markets clear and only when this occurs does the auctioneer allow trade to take place. This trade happens instantaneously for all goods for all time. This metaphor has been influential in all neo-classical economics, but it is only in market-liberal ideas that it comes to be seen descriptively and when it is used descriptively it suggests a world of isolated atomistic individuals whose only social interaction is through the market. Agents in this system meet only briefly to conduct the trades organized by the auctioneer. There is therefore no incentive to develop long-term trading relationships. However this metaphor is highly inadequate as a basis for understanding modern capitalist economies. It ignores two fundamental problems which are inherent in such economies: the problems of uncertainty and the potential for conflict. We shall examine these in turn.

Uncertainty

The problem of uncertainty is endemic to all market-based transactions and as a result moulds the institutional arrangements which shape those transactions. Mere observation suggests that a world of isolated atomized individuals, who only relate socially to each other through the market, misses something important about existing capitalist economies. It seems out of step with how markets are experienced in a real economy where they operate through a web of institutions: the state, employers and workers' organizations, banks and so on. Furthermore these institutions are not merely 'imperfections' in the working of the market. Indeed most of the time markets only work because of the existence of such institutions. In other words, institutions have an important role in making market exchanges possible through providing information and reducing uncertainty. Within economics this is investigated in a long-standing literature, often thought to stem from the work of Coase (1937), which examines the implications of transactions costs.

Once we relax the assumption of perfect information, transactions costs such as gathering information about potential trading partners or enforcing contracts can loom large.[6] One of the conclusions of relaxing the assumption of perfect information and introducing transactions costs is that economic agents enter into long-term commitments or relational contracts. These arrangements between firms and their suppliers or customers or their workers are important because they can reduce the uncertainty involved in spot exchanges which so often lead to conservative, or risk-averse, economic decision making. For economists such as Kay (1993) these relational contracts are the crucial element in the competitive advantage of any firm and relational contracts are equally important in labour markets. As Grahl and Teague point out:

> [i]t is costly and difficult for unemployed workers to identify potential employers and vice versa: simple wage reductions will not automatically stimulate the demand for labour because most employers, quite rationally, are involved in long-term relations

with their employees and it is again costly to disturb such relations. Whereas flexibility is built into full information markets, decentralised exchange requires a degree of inertia and internal rigidity to make it possible (Grahl and Teague, 1990, p.47)

In short, contrary to the market-liberal view, markets may work well because of the existence of certain 'imperfections', not in spite of them (Hodgson, 1988). For this reason alone, it seems unhelpful to regard organized interests in a wholly negative light. Under appropriate institutional circumstances, which we discuss below, they can on the contrary contribute to reducing the uncertainty that exists in market economies.

Conflict

As well as uncertainty, capitalist economies are also characterized by conflict. Despite this the Walrasian metaphor implicitly assumes the existence of an underlying harmony in economic actions and outcomes. But there is a fundamental problem with the assumption that market outcomes are generally accepted by all agents rather than those outcomes being in themselves a source of dissent and conflict (Goldthorpe, 1987). From the market-liberal perspective, social conflict and opposition to market outcomes would seem irrational. Economic agents are best served by the operation of the market.[7] However, as Goldthorpe argues, those who do not accept that market outcomes are fair or do not treat them as unavoidable will work to reverse them through organizing 'against the market'. It is difficult to see why this is in any sense an irrational response. How such activity is accommodated, through what institutions and with what implications for economic performance constitutes in our view a strong motivation for considering corporatist arrangements.

Corporatist institutions, in all their various forms, have tried explicitly to respond to these two fundamental problems of all market economies. We can no longer postpone giving some working definition of what we mean by corporatism. In Britain in the 1980s, the word 'corporatist' was highjacked as a term of abuse by those of the 'New Right', such as Keith Joseph, to describe a process of state control of prices and incomes which was coupled to Keynesian macroeconomic management. The word has been employed disparagingly to characterize a form of economic policy which is concerned with imposing government priorities on economic agents against the free expression of individual choice. As Gamble (1993) points out, this definition of corporatism is eccentric and is unrelated to how the concept is usually understood in the political science literature. Here the contrast between corporatism and pluralism lies in the way in which interests are represented in the policy-making process. Under pluralism, interest representation occurs through transitory alliances, with the government fulfilling the function of referee. Under corporatism, the interests of individuals are collectively represented through particular groups. These are given explicit recognition by the state in its function of reconciling competing demands on economic policy. In return, responsibilities in the process of policy implementation are conferred on those representatives. The question we address here is whether the latter strategy, by reducing uncertainty and by mitigating (or at least providing a structured framework for the expression of) conflict, leads to better economic performance.

Our definition of corporatism has been left at this stage deliberately vague. Beyond this fundamental stance towards organized interests, there are many forms of corporatist institutions. For instance, as we shall see, there are differences with respect to the stability and length of the relationships between organized interests and the state, as well as differences as to which groups are included in the dialogue. To complicate matters further, writers, beyond agreeing on the general definition of corporatism given above, have not agreed on precisely how corporatist institutions have been able to improve economic performance, and in particular employment. In other words, we need to be more specific on the exact mechanisms through which corporatist institutions operate to improve performance. We start with this latter question, before going on to look at the different forms of corporatism.

CORPORATISM AND LABOUR MARKET PERFORMANCE

Within the economics literature it is probably fair to say that the importance of corporatism has been viewed in terms of short-term macroeconomic analysis. The focus has been on the effects of corporatist structures in the labour market and in particular on their influence on the responsiveness of wages to employment (Landesmann and Vartiainen, 1992). The particular structural feature of the labour market that most analysts have stressed is the degree of centralization in wage bargaining. In this section we give a brief account of some of the insights of this literature before addressing some of its limitations.

The economics literature[8] has given more than an appreciative nod to the work of the political scientist Mancur Olson. Olson (1965, 1982) has made a seminal contribution to the understanding of how interest groups impinge on the degree of order and disorder in society and on economic performance. Overall Olson's view is that more often than not organized interests do not have a benign effect on economic performance – they may be more interested in their share of the societal 'pie' and oppose important changes or reforms that an economy may need. One of Olson's important caveats is that if organizations are encompassing enough, their objectives may extend beyond the politics of income distribution.

They may be large enough to have a real effect on the size of the 'pie' and will not be indifferent, therefore, to factors which could promote growth and long-term development. Such sentiments are echoed in the economics literature. For example, in a highly influential paper, Calmfors and Driffill state that:

> [o]rganised interests may be most harmful when they are strong enough to cause major disruptions but not sufficiently encompassing to bear any significant fraction of the costs for society of their actions in their own interests (Calmfors and Driffill, 1988, p. 15)

The economics literature has been able to examine the institutional determinants of economic performance in part by abandoning the textbook perfect competition microeconomic foundations which characterize, either explicitly or implicitly, the market-liberal analysis. A common framework in much of the debate is provided by the concept of the NAIRU (non-accelerating inflation rate of unemployment).[9] The existence of imperfect competition ensures that there are supernormal profits and thus workers and capitalists have something to bargain over – with perfect competition, bargaining seems irrational since there is no such surplus. Workers and capitalists have competing claims. If these are not compatible, with workers pushing for higher wages and employers refusing to accept cuts in profit margins and thereby increasing prices, it is intuitively straightforward to see that this could lead to an inflationary spiral.[10] The claims of workers can only be disciplined through higher unemployment. There will therefore exist some 'equilibrium' level of unemployment (the NAIRU) at which the competing claims of workers and employers become compatible and inflation stable.

A good deal of empirical investigation has been directed at identifying the factors which determine variations in level of unemployment across countries. These factors encompass unemployment benefits, labour tax structures, trade union militancy, technological factors and international competitiveness.[11] Furthermore empirical work has suggested the existence of significant variations across countries in the speed at which labour markets adjust to adverse price shocks. Corporatism, as proxied by structural characteristics such as the degree of centralization or coordination of collective bargaining, may be an important influence both on the level of unemployment and on the wage-setting process across the industrialized economies.

An important insight is that corporatist arrangements may serve to draw the attention of wage bargainers to the macroeconomic implications of bargaining outcomes. In terms of our earlier discussion, therefore, corporatist institutions can help reduce uncertainty about the wider implications of the wage-setting process. This may prevent the observed phenomenon of 'leap-frogging' in wage bargaining behaviour and reduce the lack of coordination in wagesetting between different sectors, or employers within a sector. The evidence from a number of empirical studies for the 1970s and 1980s is not only that the level of the NAIRU may be lower in corporatist economies, but also that real wages could be more responsive to unemployment and that therefore corporatist economies are better able to respond to output shocks and avoid inflation.

Table 9.3, summarizing findings from Calmfors and Driffill (1988), reports data on the level and change in unemployment, employment and the Okun index (the sum of inflation and unemployment) focusing on the impact of the post-1973 economic crises.[12] Countries are grouped into the three categories of centralized, intermediate and decentralized according to the degree of centralization of collective bargaining. It illustrates that, while decentralized countries may have achieved similar unemployment levels to centralized ones, after 1973 this has been at the expense of higher inflation (apparent as a higher Okun index). A second feature of the table, and one which has attracted a great deal of attention since the publication of Calmfors and Driffill's paper, is that the intermediate group of countries appears to have responded to economic crisis least well. This seems to imply a 'hump-shaped' relationship between unemployment and bargaining centralization, and this is confirmed by Calmfors and Driffill using rank correlations of unemployment and degree of centralization, and illustrated in Figure 9.3 also taken from Calmfors and Driffill (1988). For those countries in the intermediate position this would seem to offer a 'policy choice' of greater deregulation or the adoption of more corporatist arrangements in the labour market with, in terms of strictly economic efficiency considerations, little to choose between the two.

The rationale for this divergent performance is in terms of the differing ability of the bargaining structures to mimic the textbook competitive outcome. Under decentralization, real wage flexibility is achieved through the operation of supply and demand in competitive labour markets because trade unions are weak. Under centralized, economy-wide bargaining such more corporatist arrangements serve to reconnect wage setters to external economic conditions, by more accurately informing workers about the potential macroeconomic (employment) consequences of inflationary wage demands. With reduced uncertainty the damaging consequences of potential distributional conflict can be averted and relatively painless adjustment to adverse shocks made.

The explanation for the poorer performance of the intermediate group, where bargaining might typically occur at the industry or sector level, is usually stated in terms of its inferior mimicking of the competitive outcome. Under intermediate forms of labour market arrangements the existence of poorly coordinated monopolistic power in the labour market fails to result in the successful operation of either competitive market forces or corporatist coordination. Here trade union bargaining strength may be quite strong, because rapid labour turnover is costly to the firm in terms of wasted investment in skills. So wage setting may proceed with little attention to external conditions, i.e. what workers are being paid elsewhere. Insider bargaining power will be high. At the industry level workers will perceive that if their own wage increase results in higher product prices it will not unduly affect the aggregate price level and so their real consumption wage. Furthermore if bargaining is industry-wide no one firm will achieve a competitive advantage over the others and so, assuming that industry demand is relatively inelastic, the overall employment consequences will be slight. However, once each industry or sector has conceded a separate wage agreement the aggregate consequences will be significant, since slight output reductions and increased product prices will spill over across sectors.[13] Consequently economies with intermediate collective bargaining centralization, coupled with fairly strong trade unions, may experience particularly poor employment and inflation performance. More favourable adjustment to a nominal shock, such as an oil price increase, will occur under centralized corporatist conditions, despite strong trade unions, because unions are more likely to establish correctly the employment effects of a given wage demand designed to restore their real wage to its pre-shock level. With less centralization, but strong insider power, unions will, at least initially, underestimate the true employment consequences of an increase in nominal wages designed to restore the real consumption wage.

Table 9.3 Macroeconomic performance averages for countries grouped by degree of bargaining centralization

	Unemployment		Employment		Okun index	
	Level	Change	Level	Change	Level	Change
Centralized						
1	4.0	+2.3	72.5	+2.7	13.0	+6.1
2	4.4	+2.7	74.1	+3.8	14.2	+6.9
Intermediate	6.1	+4.8	60.9	−3.2	14.5	+8.7
Decentralized						
1	5.8	+2.9	65.8	−1.1	15.2	+7.7
2	6.7	+3.3	64.6	−0.5	17.0	+9.0

Notes: Level: 1974–85 average change: 1974–85 average minus 1963–73 average. Employment is the percentage of population between 15 and 64 in work; the Okun index is the sum of the unemployment and inflation rates.
Country groups:
  Centralized 1 – Austria, Denmark, Finland, Norway and Sweden.
  Centralized 2 – as above excluding Austria.
  Intermediate – Australia, Belgium, Germany, Netherlands and New Zealand.
  Decentralized 1 – Canada, France, Italy, Japan, Switzerland, UK and US.
  Decentralized 2 – as above except Switzerland.

Source: Calmfors and Driffill (1988)

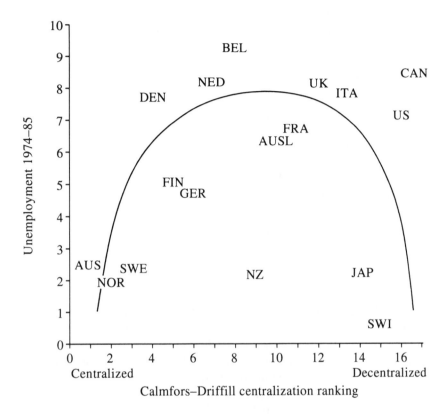

Source: Drawn from data reported in Calmfors and Driffill (1988).

Figure 9.3   Calmfors–Driffill hump

A number of studies, surveyed in Henley and Tsakalotos (1993), find that for the most corporatist countries real wage responsiveness to unemployment is highest. This is generally consistent with the argument that in corporatist countries if unions push for higher wages then they will have already taken into account the macroeconomic consequences of their actions. So they will only push for real wage increases where productivity improvements show them to be warranted. Unwarranted increases will have severe consequences for employment in such small open economies, where export reliance is high, coupled usually to a historical commitment to a high degree of exchange rate fixity.

Is the decentralization option equally attractive as corporatism, as the Calmfors–Driffill hump would appear to suggest? Convincing support for this proposition would require evidence that labour markets in economies which Calmfors and Driffill and others categorize as decentralized do in fact operate as the textbook competitive labour market model assumes. Identification of the inverted U-shaped relationship in Figure 9.3 between unemployment performance and degree of centralization rests on the presence of Switzerland and Japan alongside the US in a low centralization–low unemployment configuration. Soskice (1990) argues that Calmfors and Driffill, by focusing on the centralization dimension of corporatism underestimate the extent of corporatism, in both Switzerland and Japan. Both economies, Soskice argues, are characterized by a high degree of implicit coordination of wage setting on the part of employers through the operation of powerful employers' confederations. Such economies might be characterized as 'corporatism without labour involvement' (see Lehmbruch, 1984). Even more serious doubt about whether so-called decentralized economies follow the textbook competitive model is cast by recent disaggregated, comparative work on wage determination. Holmlund and Zetterberg (1991) model the wage setting process in Norway, Sweden, Finland, Germany and the US in order to identify the relative importance of insider bargaining power in each country. They find that compared to the others, industrial wage setting in the US is considerably less dependent on outside economy-wide influences and much more dependent on price and productivity conditions within the industry in question. In the three Scandinavian cases such insider influences on wage levels are negligible. This suggests that while in corporatist economies centralized wage determination may indeed mimic the competitive textbook, the decentralized example of the US in reality bears little resemblance to it. Decentralization in fact operates to enhance the ability of trade unions to share in product market quasi-rents. Indeed the US experience suggests that such rent sharing may be important even without formal bargaining, a phenomenon described by Okun as the 'invisible handshake' (Okun, 1981, p. 89).

CORPORATISM AS COLLECTIVE BARGAINING CENTRALIZATION

The main conclusions of the comparative literature on wage determination are readily summarized. Corporatist institutions operate on the economy through structural centralization of pay bargaining and their importance lies in the sphere of improving short-term macroeconomic adjustment. Essentially corporatism may improve the wage–unemployment trade-off. Some would argue that this improvement can also be achieved with decentralized wage bargaining, but we would argue that existing examples of decentralized labour markets do not accord closely with the textbook model. While in theory rapid real wage adjustment to adverse shocks might be achieved through decentralization, in practice the prevalence of insider bargaining power makes this rather unlikely. However, as we shall discuss in more detail shortly, the corporatism-as-centralization view has too narrow a conception of the function of corporatist arrangements.

In part the shortcomings of the economics literature stem from not dealing adequately with the potential for conflict in market economies. The NAIRU framework of competing claims does allow some consideration of this but it leaves a number of questions open. From the perspective of workers there is a suggestion that they are being asked to give their assent to the status quo and act as a sort of shock absorber in the economy. If there is a shock to the economy their choice is between wage flexibility or increased unemployment. However there are many factors which influence the level of the NAIRU aside from the stance taken by workers. If workers are to accept their part in this form of incomes policy then it seems more likely that they will demand a say in the determination of some of those factors. The distribution of income is as much about investment and aggregate demand as about bargaining power in the labour market. If wage restraint in corporatist economies is motivated by a desire on the part of employers to avoid profit squeeze then workers are likely to seek some say over the way in which those profits are invested.[14]

A further problem is the potential for conflict between subgroups of workers covered by the central wage bargain. For a strong group of workers in a dynamic sector, the temptation to abandon a centralized agreement must always be strong, and indeed it is the fragmentation of interest within the union movement that has contributed to the undermining of centralized negotiations in Sweden since the mid-1980s (Ahlen, 1989). The threat that such conflict may lead to a breakdown of agreements and an increase in the equilibrium rate of unemployment may not be telling. For what is to say that it will be the workers in the strongest groups who will be laid off?

In essence these problems highlight the difficulty of sustaining cooperative agreements in what amounts to a prisoners' dilemma-type game. Workers may receive other benefits in return for wage moderation. For example moderation may lead to higher profits and thus higher investment which, in turn, may lead to a higher growth of real wages in the future. However this line of argument also fails to confront the problem of conflict. In a pure capitalist economy investment is a decision variable of employers, and workers, once wage moderation has been adopted, will have no guarantees that such investment will occur. The promise of future real wage growth is uncertain and conditional on employers not reneging. Similarly employers have no guarantee that, once investment is committed, workers will not renege on their decision to exercise bargaining moderation.[15]

Workers may be more likely to exercise wage moderation in more corpo-ratist economies where centralized bargaining highlights with greater certainty the external consequences of their action. However such cooperative solutions or 'corporatist compromises' are more likely to be sustainable where the bargaining relationship is durable and past agreements have been seen to have worked. Thus corporatist wage moderation in the crises of the 1970s was more successful in those economies such as Austria, Norway and Sweden where a durable bargaining relationship was already well established from the 'good times' of the 1950s and 1960s. By contrast in Italy and the UK in the 1970s hastily contrived attempts at incomes policies rapidly broke down (Regini, 1984). In the successful corporatist economies negotiations over incomes policies also incorporated agreement between government, employers' confederations and trade union confederations on longer-term policies concerning investment, growth, international competitiveness and so on. The narrow focus in much of the economics literature on the wage flexibility issue seems at best a rather incomplete description of corporatist practice in many economies. A rather broader analysis is found elsewhere, and we now turn to a discussion of this.

CORPORATISM VERSUS UNEMPLOYMENT AS CONFLICT-RESOLUTION MECHANISMS

While economists have predominantly focused on corporatism as an institution which reduces uncertainty and enhances coordination in the labour market, political scientists and political economists tend to view the effects of corpo-ratism in terms of conflict reduction. This difference of emphasis leads to an assessment of corporatism that is both longer-term and broader in scope, picking up on the possible relationship between corporatism and investment and growth introduced above.

In the NAIRU framework, there is no explicit mechanism for dealing with the problem of conflict. Unemployment effectively acts as a labour-disciplin-ing device or control mechanism. Conflict is suppressed through the fear of unemployment. If corporatist institutions can manage conflict to allow the achievement of cooperative, non-inflationary solutions to the wage–investment determination game then corporatist bargaining and unemployment can been seen as alternative mechanisms for suppressing inflationary distributional conflict. A highly stylized example of such a game is presented in Figure 9.4. Workers are offered a choice between exercising wage restraint or using their full bargaining power (wage militancy). Employers have the level of their investment commitment as a decision variable. Payoffs are represented in terms of workers' utility V_i and profits P_i. Combination D in effect results in a bilateral

Workers strategies:

		Wage restraint	Wage militancy
Employers strategies:	High investment commitment	**A** Low unemployment low inflation (V_A, P_A)	**B** Low unemployment high inflation (V_B, P_B)
	Low investment commitment	**C** High unemployment low inflation (V_C, P_C)	**D** High potential inflation moderated by high unemployment (V_D, P_D)

$$V_B \geq V_A > V_D \geq V_C$$
$$P_C \geq P_A > P_D \geq P_B$$

Figure 9.4   Possible outcomes in a wage–investment prisoners' dilemma game

monopoly-type solution where workers exercise full bargaining strength but the cost-push inflationary potential of that is suppressed through high unemployment, which arises because of the low level of investment. The highest total payoff is to be achieved from combination A, where workers exercise nominal wage restraint but enjoy high employment from high investment. Employers enjoy a high level of profits resulting from high investment. A is in effect the corporatist, cooperative solution, and the only one of the four capable of delivering non-inflationary high employment. It is however not a Nash equilibrium since each party has an incentive to renege on the other in order to increase their distributional share. As both exercise this incentive, equilibrium is achieved at D. Similarly if combinations B and C are chosen in each case one party (employers in the case of B. workers in the case of C) will renege. If corporatism is to be successful it must allow either side to pre-commit themselves to the cooperative strategy or successfully rule out the adoption of the conflict strategy by either side.

Bargaining centralization, on its own, may overcome the wage bargaining coordination difficulties. However it is unlikely to result in lasting full employment because conflict is suppressed rather than resolved in the NAIRU approach. As Kalecki (1943) pointed out employers may be reluctant to tolerate lasting full employment because in due course distributional conflict will re-emerge. As he presciently predicted if lasting full employment is to be achieved, capitalism must develop social and political institutions to allow the management of distributional conflict without employers resorting once again to the weapon of unemployment. So if corporatist institutions are to be successful they need to manage that conflict over the long term. As the game represented in Figure 9.4 is repeated workers need to be sure that employers will not decide to resort to the low-investment, high-unemployment strategy. Thus, for many political scientists corporatist institutions are viewed as a response to conflict and provide a framework for the constructive management of that conflict through bargained cooperation and exchange of an inherently political nature.

POLITICAL EXCHANGE AND CONCERTATION

The concept of 'political exchange' (Pizzorno, 1978) is a description of the way in which powerful organized groups, such as trade unions, may exercise restraint in the economic sphere in exchange for other 'goods' in the political market. Pizzorno argues that workers obtain increased political influence in return for social consensus or a reduced threat of militancy. In effect therefore workers face a long-run utility maximization problem in which they seek to trade off higher short-run current incomes with the long-run benefits they might derive from current restraint. The latter might include the provision of 'goods' such as improved future employment opportunities, old age pensions, sickness insurance and so on. It is important to point out that a corporatist political exchange process will involve workers in discussions about wider economic and social objectives. Successful forms of corporatism will therefore entail durable arrangements for achieving consensus over those objectives. As Goldthorpe (1987) points out, the exchange process may be one in which workers experience a 'learning curve'. If wage restraint leads to greater investment, in due course workers may seek influence or control over the process of capital accumulation. The Swedish experience provides the clearest example of this where unions saw the proposed creation of wage-earner funds as leading to an eventual 'socialization' of investment.[16]

Critical to the success of any political exchange of this form is whether such control by workers over future provision is possible. In particular they face two problems. The first is one of preference aggregation across sectional or subgroup interests. The degree of centralization and vertical integration of the trade union movement is, therefore, important for the success of political exchange (Pekkarinen et al., 1992). The second and equally serious problem is what Pizzorno (1978) has termed the 'interpretation gap'. That is, if workers are to provide wage restraint they must be confident that it yields the promised benefits. Here the state may have a role to play as an 'honest broker', but if government is weak and there is widespread cynicism about its capacity to deliver, then the political exchange process will break down.[17] For workers the best perceived way to narrow the interpretation gap may be to seek greater political control over investment policy and the way profits are distributed, or more generally at the national level over macroeconomic policy.

For many political scientists the role of the state is critical. Indeed corporatism is often seen as model of the state in the context of organized interests. Lehmbruch (1984) sees the state's capacity to harmonize organized interests as relying on the way in which the policy-making process is conducted – the extent of 'concertation'. The role of the state is important because it may grant right of recognition and rights of national-level representation to particular organizations, such as union confederations or employers' associations, and public functions, for example responsibility for training provision, may be delegated to them. Lehmbruch identifies various levels of concertation. At the lowest level are arrangements which entail the exchange of information in order to inform a consensual approach to macroeconomic policy formulation. At this level there is no explicit *quid pro quo* between the parties but rather the aim is the creation of consensus. He cites the West German *Konzertierte Aktion* incomes policy experiment of the late 1960s as an example. At an intermediate level more explicit barter transaction takes place, in the context of more formal bargaining arrangements. Here, though, the 'interpretation gap' remains a serious hindrance. An ultimately unsuccessful attempt at such concertation might be found in the British Social Contract of the 1970s. The most developed level Lehmbruch terms 'generalized exchange' and identifies it as characterized by stable long-term relations of trust between the social partners, where exchange need not entail any immediate *quid pro quo*. Countries with this level of concertation development correspond to those usually identified as most corporatist. So, for example, in Austria there have been: 'the expectations that, thanks to the strong influence of the "social partners" on practically all aspects of economic and social policy, that national economy would be managed with the long-term interests of unions members appropriately in view' (Lehmbruch, 1984, p. 67).

Three features are associated with such durable forms of corporatist compromise. The first is one that has already appeared, namely that the process will involve a much wider policy agenda than that of a traditional incomes policy. The second is the need for widespread consensus concerning macroeconomic objectives, arising from a common understanding about how the economy works. So for example Giavazzi (1988) in his discussion of Calmfors and Driffill (1988) points out that bargaining centralization may be a necessary condition for the success of corporatist arrangements but not a sufficient one. He notes that other studies such as Newell and Symons (1987) suggest that the performance of similar labour market structures may be different from where consensus-formation is present as opposed to where it is not. The third feature is the long-term or 'relational contracting' aspect. Long-established corporatist arrangements effectively lay down institutional guidelines or codes of conduct governing the bargaining relationships. Such guidelines cannot be laid down in countries where organized interests are based on unstable and shifting coalitions.

LONGER-RUN CONSIDERATIONS

Durability in the bargaining relationship opens up the possibility for corporatists arrangements to encompass questions of long-term economic policy restructuring. The Swedish Rehn–Meidner plan, which came by many to be recognized as the epitome of corporatist arrangements, was one specifically geared towards the promotion of structural change in the Swedish economy. The centralized wage rate was explicitly seen as encouraging the decline of ailing firms and sectors and the rapid promotion of new, successful ones. Weak firms would find that the centralized wage rate was above what they would, in a decentralized situation, choose to pay and so would find profits squeezed. On the other hand successful firms would face a wage rate below what they would have the ability to pay, allowing funds to accumulate for investment purposes. It therefore operated indirectly as a form of selective industrial policy (Kenworthy, 1990). Centralized bargaining would therefore accelerate the displacement of workers and so a second key aspect of the Swedish scheme was the development of highly effective and active labour market policies to offer retraining and temporary public-sector employment. In this respect Sweden stands out, since its expenditure on active labour market policy in the 1980s was proportionately considerably higher than elsewhere.[18] Swedish labour market policy has traditionally been undertaken in a highly coordinated manner, entailing joint management by government, employers and unions. For example job placement is facilitated through a national vacancy computer. While other corporatist countries have not spent proportionately as much on labour market policy they share with Sweden a similar degree of administrative and policy coordination (OECD, 1988).

But the link between corporatist bargaining and long-term supply-side policies rests on more than the use of labour market policy. Here we return to lack of alleged equivalence between centralized and decentralized labour markets. The latter may be able to provide real wage flexibility but they have not been very successful in generating the sustained productivity growth that allows workers to enjoy sustained growth in their real 'social' wage. Weisskopf, Bowles and Gordon (1983) argue very persuasively in the US context that the social climate is of critical importance to understanding long-run productivity growth. A competitive and conflictual wage determination climate may be far less conducive to the acceptance of changing technologies and increased effort than a less uncertain climate of cooperation and negotiation, where the agenda for discussion is much wider. In this respect the US and UK are seen by some to have suffered most from the liberal strategy of decentralization and flexibility which has focused too narrowly on the problems of wage determination. Furthermore an emphasis on competitive wage flexibility may in turn avoid the immediate pressure on employers to develop strategies for innovation, since product market competitiveness can be maintained through low wage cost rather than production efficiency and quality. In the non-EC corporatist economies and in some members of the EC itself, policy makers have been reluctant to pursue the wage flexibility strategy precisely because it relieves the pressure on firms to innovate in production methods and invest in R & D.

The alternative strategy emphasizes the ability to produce a higher quality product, through the use of a wide range of non-price factors, such as product development and quality, after-sales service and so on, but requires a high-skilled, motivated and flexible workforce. A climate of corporatist compromise, particularly at a more micro-level with formal worker consultation and participation, will be a vital element. In contrast the uncertainties involved in decentralized labour markets may deter workers from thinking strategically and actively cooperating in the introduction of new technology (Grahl and Teague, 1990). Active labour market policies serve a further purpose here since training reinforces internal labour markets and helps to create a sense of long-term job security (Soskice, 1990).

A final longer-term issue that has been of importance to policy makers in corporatist countries since 1973 has been the desire to respond to economic shock while continuing to consolidate the reductions in income inequality made across the industrialized world during the long postwar 'Golden Age'. In those countries in which unemployment has risen dramatically since 1973 the trend of income inequality has made a U-turn.[19] This has been particularly pronounced where market-liberal responses have found most favour, such as in the UK and the US. The association between corporatism and social democratic government has tended to place the question of income inequality higher up the policy agenda. The desire to maintain full employment has been closely allied because it is recognized that unemployment increases inequality. Evidence on trends in inequality points to some considerable success for the corporatist economies (Green, Henley and Tsakalotos, 1992). But egalitarianism may have contributed to other aspects of economic performance in corporatist economies. It has, at least until the mid-1980s, provided a framework of social solidarity which has facilitated an adaption to economic change which avoids high unemployment or an equal sharing of the burden of adjustment. In unemployment terms corporatist institutions and policies have represented, at least until the late 1980s, a much more successful strategy for post-'Golden Age' adjustment than either narrow Keynesianism or supply-side obsessed monetarism. The former is focused too heavily on the macroeconomic manipulation of aggregate demand, while the latter fails to recognize that the NAIRU or natural rate is not merely ground out of a set of general equilibrium equations but is heavily conditioned by institutional structures. The practice of economic policy formulation in corporatist economies after 1973 appeared to recognize that the NAIRU itself is a matter for negotiation and is influenced by the longer-term bargaining strategies adopted by workers and employers. The appropriate demand-side strategies of policy makers, concerning for example, investment or tax rates, is conditional on institutional structure. The extent to which government fiscal policy can influence real output rather than be dissipated into price adjustment depends critically on the nature of the wage-bargaining process and the ability of the parties involved to think and act strategically over the long term.

CONCLUSION

Cooperative solutions tend to be unstable and, in the sense that it provides the institutional environment for such a solution, corporatism is no exception. When the cooperative strategy in corporatist economies begins to break down, the relevance of those institutions themselves is brought increasingly into question.

Corporatism is under pressure from forces both external and internal to the economies concerned. From outside the increasing internationalization of the world economy and particularly European integration has been one source of competitive pressure – one that has placed constraints on the ability of corporatist economies to pursue their own brand of more expansionary, but non-inflationary, policies against a more deflationary bias elsewhere. In addition heavy reliance by these small, open economies on transnational corporations has left them vulnerable to capital flight if employment and tax conditions are perceived to be more capital-friendly elsewhere. From within there has, in the face of two deep recessions since 1973, arisen a fragmentation of interests among both workers and employers which has seen an abandonment of centralized pay bargaining, particularly in Sweden. It has become more difficult for higher paid workers to remain convinced of continued long-term future benefits of a solidaristic wages policy which entails narrow wage differentials and high rates of marginal taxation. Under sustained global recession corporatism has, quite simply, become increasingly expensive. As corporatism has developed over time it has become apparent to employers that it entails an increasing 'socialization' of investment which they have been reluctant to sanction. In the Swedish case this came to a head in the early 1980s with employer opposition to the trade union plans for wage-earner funds. With the demise of centralized pay bargaining and the tightening of fiscal stance in the Scandinavian economies we have seen unemployment rising in the early 1990s at a similar speed to elsewhere in Europe. The rate is still lower than across much of the rest of Europe but, for example, Sweden in 1993 has unemployment of 10 per cent, a rate which for the postwar period is quite unprecedented.

It is tempting therefore to conclude, pessimistically, that corporatism is no longer able to provide the institutional basis for sustained full employment. However, while certain corporatist institutions are under threat, such institutions have always in the past been multidimensional and have evolved over time in the face of changing economic and political circumstances. The problem of unemployment and the absence of full employment, at the time of writing, remains endemic to all industrialized economies. This chapter has suggested that the only feasible solutions to this problem will be ones which entail careful institutional design. Unemployment will continue to persist while labour markets are plagued by uncertainty and conflict. The market-liberal project of the creation of a deregulated, perfectly functioning competitive global economy, where economic agents passively accept market outcomes and where there are no interest organizations to 'undermine' that process, is a chimera. Practical resolutions to the full employment challenge must therefore rely on institutional solutions such as those which have been successfully offered by the corporatist model in the past.

NOTES

1. We should like to thank Heather Gibson for comments on this chapter in draft.
2. This is a term coined by, among others, Marglin and Schor (1990) to refer to the period of exceptionally high and stable economic growth enjoyed by the developed world from the end of the Second World War to resurgence of distributional conflict which began in the late 1960s and the debilitating oil price explosions of the early 1970s.
3. Bruno and Sachs (1985) have provided one particularly influential description.
4. For the first three groups of countries average real GDP growth falls from 5 per cent per annum for the period 1960–73 to around 2.5 per cent per annum thereafter. For Japan it slightly more than halves from an average of 10 per cent per annum to about 4 per cent (see Henley and Tsakalotos, 1993, Table 1.1, p.4).
5. See Rowthorn and Glyn (1990) for a more detailed country-by-country discussion.
6. For a discussion on the importance of uncertainty and transactions costs as a basis for understanding the role of institutions, see Henley and Tsakalotos (1993, Ch. 2).
7. See the discussion in Mullard (1992).
8. For example Bruno and Sachs (1985), Newell and Symons (1987) and Calmfors and Driffill (1988).
9. Layard, Nickell and Jackman (1991) provide an extensive analysis.
10. This implies that the monetary authorities are willing to accommodate increased wage demands through expansionary monetary policies.
11. See Layard, Nickell and Jackman (1991) for a survey and recent analysis.
12. The classification of countries is that of Calmfors and Driffill. As we shall see there may be grounds for questioning its validity. To allow for the 'foreign-worker' effect on reported unemployment statistics additional averages excluding Austria and Switzerland from the relevant groupings are reported.

13. A formal model of this process, and comparisons with centralized and decentralized cases is provided by Carlin and Soskice (1990).
14. Henley and Tsakalotos (1991) provides a much more extensive discussion of this point, and empirical evidence on the effectiveness of corporatism to avoid profit squeeze and generate greater investment stability.
15. This dilemma forms the essence of what Lancaster (1973) in his theoretical presentation terms the 'dynamic inefficiency of capitalism'. Grout (1984) and van der Ploeg (1987) also provide formal presentations.
16. Pontusson (1992) provides a full description and analysis of the Swedish case.
17. Regini (1984) cites Italy in the 1970s as a case in point.
18. Over the period 1985–88 Sweden spent on average of 1.96 per cent of GDP on active labour market policies. During the same period the UK spent 0.80 per cent, Germany 0.95 per cent and the US 0.26 per cent (OECD, 1988).
19. Levy (1987) provides an excellent account of this in the US context.

REFERENCES

Ahlen, K. (1989), 'Swedish collective bargaining under pressure: inter-union rivalry and incomes policies', *British Journal of Industrial Relations*, vol. 27, no. 3, November.

Bruno, M. and Sachs, J. (1985), *The Economics of Worldwide Stagnation*, Cambridge, Mass.: Harvard University Press.

Calmfors, L. and Driffill, J. (1988), 'Bargaining structure, corporatism and macroeconomic performance', *Economic Policy*, no. 6, April.

Carlin, W. and Soskice, D. (1990), *Macroeconomics and the Wage Bargain*, Oxford: Oxford University Press.

Coase, R. H. (1937), 'The nature of the firm', *Economica*, vol. 4, no. 5, November.

Gamble, A. (1993), 'The decline of corporatism', in D. Crabtree and A.P. Thirlwall (eds), *Keynes and the Role of the State*, London: Macmillan.

Giavazzi, F. (1988), 'Discussion', *Economic Policy*, no. 6, April.

Giersch, H. (1985), 'Eurosclerosis, *Discussion Paper* no. 112, Kiel Institute for World Economics, October.

Goldthorpe, J.H. (ed.) (1984), *Order and Conflict in Contemporary Capitalism*, Oxford: Clarendon Press.

Goldthorpe, J.H. (1987), 'Problems of political economy after the post-war period', in C.S. Maier (ed.), *Changing Boundaries of the Political: essays on the evolving balance between the state and society, public and private in Europe*, Cambridge: Cambridge University Press.

Grahl, J. and Teague, P.T. (1990), *1992 – the Big Market: the future of the European Community*, London: Lawrence and Wishart.

Green. F., Henley, A. and Tsakalotos. E. (1999), 'Income inequality in corporatist and liberal economies: a comparison of trends within OECD countries', *Studies in Economics*, no. 92/13, University of Kent at Canterbury.

Grout, P.A. (1984), 'Investment and wages in the absence of legally binding labour contracts', *Econometrica*, vol. 52, no. 9, March.

Henley, A. and Tsakalotos. E. (1991), 'Corporatism, profit squeeze and investment', *Cambridge Journal of Economics*, vol. 15, no. 4, December.

Henley, A. and Tsakalotos, E. (1993), *Corporatism and Economic Performance*, Aldershot: Edward Elgar.

Hodgson, G. (1988), *Economics and Institutions*, Cambridge: Polity Press.

Holmlund, B. and Zetterberg, J. (1991), 'Insider effects in wage determination: evidence from five countries', *European Economic Review*, vol. 35, no. 5, July.

Kalecki, M. (1943), 'Political aspects of full employment', *The Political Quarterly*, vol. 14, no. 4, October/December.

Kay, J. (1993), *Foundations of Corporate Success: How Business Strategies Add Value*, Oxford: Oxford University Press.

Kenworthy, L. (1990), 'Are industrial policy and corporatism compatible?', *Journal of Public Policy*, vol. 10, no 3, July/September.

Lancaster, K. (1973), 'The dynamic inefficiency of capitalism', *Journal of Political Economy*, vol. 81, no. 5, September/October.

Landesmann, M. and Vartiainen, J. (1992), 'Social corporatism and long-term economic performance', in Pekkarinen et al. (1992).

Layard, P.R.G., Nickell, S.J. and Jackman, R. (1991), *Unemployment: Macroeconomic Performance and the Labour Market*, Oxford: Oxford University Press.

Lehmbruch, G. (1984), 'Concertation and the structure of corporatist networks', in Goldthorpe (1984).

Levy, F. (1987), *Dollars and Dreams: The Changing American Income Distribution*, New York: Basic Books.

Lindbeck, A. (1985), 'What is wrong with the West European economies?', *World Economy*, vol. 8, June.

Marglin, S. and Schor, J.B. (1990) (eds), *The Golden Age of Capitalism: Lessons for the 1990s*, Oxford: Clarendon Press.

Mullard, M. (1992), *Understanding Economic Policy*, London: Routledge.

Newell, A. and Symons, J.S.V. (1987), 'Corporatism, laissez-faire and the rise in unemployment', *European Economic Review*, vol. 31, no. 3, March.

OECD (1988), 'Profiles of labour market budgets', *OECD Employment Outlook*, September.

Okun, A.M. (1981), *Prices and Quantities: A Macroeconomic Analysis*, Washington, DC: Brookings Institution.

Olson, M. (1965), *The Logic of Collective Action*, Cambridge, MA.: Harvard University Press.

Olson, M. (1982), *The Rise and Decline of Nations*, New Haven, Conn.: Yale University Press.

Pekkarinen, J., Pohjula, M. and Rowthorn, R.E. (1992) (eds), *Social Corporatism. A Superior Economic System?*, Oxford: Clarendon Press.

Pizzorno, A. (1978), 'Political exchange and collective identity in industrial conflict', in C. Crouch and A. Pizzorno (eds), *The Resurgence of Class Conflict in Western Europe since 1968*, London: Macmillan.

Ploeg, F. van der (1987), 'Trade unions, investment and employment: a non-cooperative approach', *European Economic Review*, vol. 31, no. 8, October.

Pontusson, J. (1992), *The Limits of Social Democracy: Investment Politics in Sweden*, Ithaca, NY: Cornell University Press.

Regini M. (1984), 'The conditions for political exchange: how concertation emerged and collapsed in Italy and Great Britain', in Goldthorpe (1984).

Rowthorn, B. and Glyn, A. (1990), 'The diversity of unemployment experience', in Marglin and Schor (1990).

Soskice, D. (1990), 'Wage determination: the changing role of institutions in advanced industrialized countries', *Oxford Review of Economic Policy*, vol. 6, no. 4, Winter.

Therborn, G. (1992), 'Lessons from "corporatist" theorizations', in Pekkarinen et al. (1992).

Weisskopf, T.E. Bowles, S. and Gordon, D.M. (1983), 'Hearts and minds: a social model of US productivity growth', *Brookings Papers on Economic Activity*, no. 2.

10. Lessons from the experience of the Swedish model

Mike Marshall

Since the collapse of the post-Second World War 'Golden Age' of economic performance of the advanced capitalist countries there has been a growing awareness, even among Keynesians themselves, that expansionary macroeconomic policies are not likely easily or unproblematically to generate and maintain a high level of employment. Certainly in the UK the balance of payments constraint and the familiar 'stop–go' cycle seems to be an enduring feature of the entire postwar period, even during the 'Thatcher miracle' years (Wells, 1993). Moreover, despite the New Right rhetoric and policies in the 1980s, the economies of the UK and the US have not witnessed a genuine supply-side transformation.

Increasingly therefore the necessity of a so-called 'two-handed' approach, focusing on both demand and supply, has surfaced. Consequently, attention has been devoted to the need for a proper socio-institutional perspective on the supply side to counteract the dominant New Right views which recommend dismantling whatever socioeconomic institutions exceed the so-called 'neo-classical minimum'.

Numerous studies have highlighted the positive economic contribution that institutions which limit competition and mediate market pressures can make by prompting cooperation, reducing uncertainty and conflict and thereby encouraging investment and economic and employment growth (See e.g. Matzner and Streeck, 1991, Chs 2 and 11). Within the literature on the institutional conditions likely to promote employment growth, much attention has been given to corporatist arrangements concerning the labour market and industrial relations – particularly those that have been adopted in Sweden.

This concern with the 'Swedish model' has been especially noticeable in post-Keynesian circles. In large part this has been due to Kaleckian concerns regarding the capacity of capitalist economies to deal with the problem of income distribution under conditions of full employment. These, in turn, have provoked interest in institutional arrangements that might produce lasting social consensus on distribution and a wage-bargaining structure that is compatible with satisfactory macro-performance (Henley, 1990, Ch. 8). The post-Keynesian interest in

Swedish socioeconomic insitutional arrangements, however, has also been fuelled by the view that the 'long-term' Keynes ought to be at the heart of post-Keynesian policy formulation (Arestis and Driver, 1984). In particular, the view that the best perspective for a suitable non-neo-conservative approach to the supply side of the economy is provided by Keynes's long overlooked but now celebrated assertion that 'a somewhat comprehensive socialisation of investment will prove the only means of securing an approximation to full employment' (Keynes, 1936, p. 378) has stimulated attention and support for the wage-earner fund-supplemented 'Swedish model' (see e.g. Arestis, 1986a).

Clearly then the corporatist arrangements in Sweden are of great interest to those concerned with the achievement and maintenance of high levels of employment, especially those that reject supply-side and monetarist ideas and policies. In this chapter therefore we look at the main socioeconomic institutional features of the 'Swedish model' and assess its problems, modifications, and 'lessons' for other economies.

THE SWEDISH MODEL

The 'Swedish model' was developed by the trade union economists Rehn and Meidner after the Second World War and although it has been perceived in a variety of ways it is most usefully described as an *integrated* system of macroeconomic, pay and labour market policy geared towards the achievement of full employment and greater equality. The two key features of the traditional Swedish model have been the highly centralized wage bargaining system and the active labour market policy.

The bargaining system developed in the context of a very high unionization of manual workers and a strong trade union federation covering such workers (the LO), and the early emergence (before the First World War) of a centralized employer organization (the SAF). Centralized bargaining was not in place until the 1950s but it quickly become established as a successful way of dealing with the inflationary impact of wage pressures without open and formal governmental intervention. Indeed, a central feature of the original model was the viewpoint that the responsibility for achieving full employment and a satisfactory macroeconomic performance of the economy should rest with the government, with the trade unions left free to negotiate with the employer's associations.

The central negotiations were to yield framework agreements that set the overall level of wage cost increases and these were to be supplemented by industry contracts. The government was to play no part in this process. The trade unions, however, were to reconcile membership aspirations with the need to generate a wage structure that would avoid wage-inflationary competition between different groups of workers, and generally to align their wage demands with the requirements of social responsibility and the macroeconomic needs of the economy. The centralized collective bargaining process, to put it simply, was to be a system of centralized self-regulation: it was to function as an extra-governmental incomes policy.

The Swedish employers were the main initiators of the negotiations that yielded the first major central settlement in 1952. Their strong support for the centralized bargaining system was based on the hope that it would restrain wage inflation and ameliorate industrial conflict. Certainly it is likely that continuing employer interest in the system was stimulated by the 'peace obligation' arrangements whereby trade unions pledged themselves to forego the use of industrial action as a means of resolving disputes concerning matters covered by the settlements for the period (1–3 years) of the central agreements.

The determination of prices and wages in the 'Swedish model' was based on the so-called EFO model which was originally presented as a joint study of the central employer and employee organizations in 1970. Within this model the economy was seen as being comprised of two main sectors:[1] the competitive sector (or C sector) of tradeable goods which consists of export branches and activities working under import competition, and the sheltered sector (or S sector) which includes, as one might expect, building, retail trade, most private and public services, public administration and so on. Prices in the C sector were taken to be determined in world markets. Prices in the S sector were determined by events in the C sector and internal conditions according to the mark-up hypothesis.

A central feature of the 'Swedish model', of course, has always been the understanding and acceptance of the trade union movement of the role of wages in maintaining the international competitiveness of the industries in the C sector. This explicit understanding of what effectively amounts to restrictions on wage increases has been accompanied by a strong trade union emphasis on full employment, an objective firmly shared by the social democratic governments in the period after the Second World War. Furthermore, this non-inflationary, full employment attitude by the trade union movement has been accompanied by a strenuous attempt to maintain, indeed enhance whenever possible, their relative position in the income distribution.[2]

As mentioned above, the employers were very interested in centralized wage negotiations as a means of achieving wage restraint. The trade unions on the other hand were mainly interested in 'wage solidarity'. The aims of the LO underlying its acceptance of the centralized 'wage accord' were clearly spelt out in its 1951 report (Landsorganisationen, 1951). These aims were to obtain a fair share of the national income for labour and establish an equitable and acceptable set of wage differentials whilst preventing wage settlements from adversely affecting the inflation rate. An important aspect of the solidaristic wage policy pursued by the LO was that wage differentials should reflect skill, training and certain social criteria but *not* the profitability of the employer. This policy has been defined as 'a policy which seeks to relate pay to the nature of the work which an employee carries out and not to the capacity or ability-to-pay of his employer' (Meidner, 1978, p. 7).[3]

The originally stated LO objective was for differentials to be established by job evaluation exercises. However, this goal became replaced in practice by the simpler approach of reducing wage differentials via a policy geared towards helping the lower-paid. In the decade after the publication of the LO Report wage settlements generally combined a percentage increase with provisions for a minimum flat rate increase. This gave the lower-paid sectors larger percentage increases, thus permitting some narrowing of percentage relativities between sectors (Robinson, 1974).

The LO was clearly concerned to avoid a situation in which wage policy produced standardization of wages at a level sufficient to enable all existing producers to stay in business. This would generate 'excess' profits in some areas whilst providing a subsidy to low-efficiency employers that was not regarded to be in the long-term interests of their members. In this, as in some other areas, the trade unions and the employers were not in accord. The SAF wanted to make the general wage level low enough to be acceptable to even the least profitable areas, generating more generous profit margins elsewhere and thereby keeping all its members happy (Robinson, 1974). The trade unions, however, were strongly opposed to such a strategy. Instead they favoured the creation of a high-wage, high-productivity economy and believed that the solidaristic wage policy could act as a catalyst of structural change, speeding up the transfer of workers from low- to high-productivity sectors and thereby enhancing economic performance. This transfer of labour, it was thought, could be expedited, and the implicit loss of employment combated, by an active labour market policy.

The main purpose of the Swedish social corporatist strategy has been the maintenance of full employment and an equitable income distribution (Lundberg, 1985), with these to be achieved through a very close cooperation between a strong trade union movement and employers' organizations. The trade union movement, in the so-called Rehn–Meidner model, would achieve its objectives in return for promoting a wage structure that would avoid inflationary wage competition between different groups.

An active labour market policy was seen as the most appropriate way to overcome bottlenecks in labour supply. Indeed, this policy was supposed to perform the role of wage differentials in balancing labour supply and labour demand. Labour market policy was seen as playing a central part in enabling the economy to adjust to shortages in a less inflationary way than would otherwise be the case. In addition, via retraining and other policies, it was supposed to deal with the unemployment-generating implications of the LO strategy of 'equal pay for equal work' which, as discussed above, implied wages greater than those that could be sustained in the weaker sectors.

The active labour market policy is coordinated by the National Labour Market Board (AMS). This is a typical tripartite corporatist body in one way, but it is exceptional in composition (trade union representatives are in a majority) and in its employment of many union activists. It is, in fact, a prime example of how the Swedish labour movement aspired to transform traditional state bureaucracies into vehicles for social reform (Kjellberg, 1992).

The policy has a number of tiers: labour exchanges (with very low case-loads per member of staff), training programmes, and wage subsidies if workers have not been placed after six months. Only after this process has been gone through are workers entitled to unemployment benefit. This system is stringently administered and is certainly not open-ended. Those whose entitlement is exhausted, however, have the right in law to up to six months' work in the public sector (mainly with local authorities in construction or the caring services) which acts as the employer of last resort. It is a very important, but insufficiently emphasized aspect of the Swedish system that there was a perceived 'right to work' rather than a 'right to income' as such (Delsen and van Veen, 1992).

What is more widely recognized and commented on is the way in which the Swedish active labour market strategy has avoided the situation reproduced in the UK and other leading countries whereby two-thirds of total labour market spending is 'squandered' on unemployment benefits. Sweden's labour market policy has not, in fact, produced a higher proportion of GDP being spent on such measures. Only the composition is different. In Sweden around 70 per cent of expenditure under this heading is spent on training and job-creation measures. Sweden thus has spent her money on skills and jobs; the UK on the other hand has spent hers on maintaining the unemployed (Korpi, 1989; Delsen and van Veen, 1992).

BEYOND WELFARISM: THE SOCIALIZATION OF INVESTMENT

According to the original model, investment was to be left to the private sector. Although profits were to be highly taxed, 'excess' profits put into special 'investment funds' or 'renewal funds' were to receive tax exemptions thereby encouraging investment and training. The principal objective of these investment funds, however, which date back to 1938, was not so much to stimulate investment in any ongoing way, but to function as a counter-cyclical weapon. Also, given the historical volatility of private sector investment it might be felt that the original formulation of the model did not contain a sufficient socialization of investment.

Moreover, socialization of investment helps resolve the essential dilemma facing trade unions under regimes of wage restraint. If they exercise moderation in their wage claims, thereby protecting profitability, the benefits accrue to their employers. Whilst, of course, enhanced profitability *might* lead to increased domestic investment and a growth in the number of jobs and/or greater security of employment. On the other hand it might not – there are no guarantees. Furthermore, in the absence of stable long-term relationships between workers and employers there may be very acute problems of suspicion and mistrust. Thus, systems which tax profits and use the proceeds to finance capital accumulation (under the workers' control) can be seen as the necessary *quid pro quo* for wage restraint (George, 1993).

Certainly one of the most interesting, and controversial, modifications of the Swedish model was the creation of wage-earner funds. This was initially proposed in 1975 by an LO working party chaired by Professor Rudolf Meidner. Under the Meidner Plan wage-earner funds were to achieve a *partial* socialization of the means of production, with title to ownership being transferred gradually not to the state but to the trade unions.

A modified version of the Meidner Plan eventually became law in 1983. This plan proposed a system of five regional funds which would receive revenue from a 20 per cent profits tax and a 0.2 per cent supplementary state pensions levy from 1984 until 1990. The funds were self-governing and independent of each other and were run by boards appointed by the government but with a majority of members who represented the interests of employees. The funds were obliged to invest in the Swedish risk market (they were not allowed to buy shares in foreign firms) either via share purchase or the provision of risk capital to cooperatives, and were charged with pursuing the objective of meeting the interest of long-term capital accumulation in the Swedish economy and with providing an annual payment to the state pension fund equivalent to a 3 per cent rate of return. By the end of the 'trial' period (1990) the funds owned about 5 per cent of total stock market value, making each fund of similar size to a medium-sized private institutional shareholder. The funds were abolished by the Conservative government in 1991 (George, 1993).

The main economic policies embedded in the Swedish model have been seen as being very much within the spirit of the post-Keynesian paradigm (Arestis and Driver 1984; Arestis, 1986a). However, as has been noted, one policy in particular, the wage-earner funds, aroused excitement amongst those who regarded the socialization of investment to be of paramount importance as the backbone of post-Keynesian economic policies. This policy, challenging as it did the premise of private control of the investment process, was seen by many as constituting a major and extremely significant extension of the Swedish model since it involved 'an important element of collective ownership of capital, making a clear departure from the traditional, welfarist strategy of Swedish social democracy' (Pontusson, 1984, p. 71). Moreover, the potential of such a policy to stimulate investment and promote a more equitable distribution of income and wealth was strongly emphasized.

Furthermore, some post-Keynesians referring to the famous analysis of Kalecki, argued that wage-earner funds and the growing socialization of investment offered the possibility of reducing the sociopolical constraints on achieving and maintaining full employment (Arestis, 1986a). Kalecki (1943) argued that there would be considerable opposition by the 'industrial leaders' to full employment achieved by manipulating government expenditure. This would be so because of '(a) the dislike of government interference in the problem of employment as such; (b) the dislike of the direction of government spending (public investment and subsidizing consumption); (c) dislike of the social and political changes resulting from the maintenance of full employment' (p. 423).

Under the wage-earner funds scheme, it was argued, things should change. There should not be dislike of government interference and manipulation of government expenditure to achieve full employment since the wage-earner funds scheme, with its emphasis on and aim of stimulating investment, would be compatible with government involvement and indeed might reduce the scale of government expenditures required to achieve full employment. Wage-earner funds, it was argued, could provide, in theory, the investment necessary for lasting full employment with government spending being required only to subsidise consumption (through family allowances, old age pensions and the like). Furthermore, the ability of private capital to act on their dislike of the sociopolitical changes normally associated with the maintenance of full employment could be mitigated by the strengthening of the position of the working class via the growing industrial muscle of their trade unions as shareholders (Arestis, 1986a).

THE DISINTEGRATION OF THE MODEL?

The ability of corporatist economies like Sweden to survive the post-1973 problems that beset the work economy has been well documented. For example, the work of Bruno and Sachs (1985), Soskice (1983), Newell and Symons (1986) Calmfors and Driffill (1988), Calmfors and Nymoen (1990) and Rowthorn and Glyn (1990) has shown that corporatism was associated with a relatively low 'misery index'[4] and 'sacrifice ratio'[5] and with favourable employment performance and unemployment–real wage and inflation – output trade offs compared with non-corporatist countries. Moreover, via its active labour market policy, Sweden was able to keep its unemployment (especially long-term unemployment) rate, and therefore the hysteresis[6] effect, low. At the end of the 1980s the Swedish unemployment rate was only 1.5 per cent. Even at its peak in 1983, the Swedish unemployment rate was only 3.5 per cent (Ferner and Hyman, 1992, Table A.7, p. xlv). Indeed, it was only in the early 1990s that the unemployment rate reached double figures.

Sweden also performed well judged by the much vaunted criteria of labour market flexibility. For example, the Beveridge curve, showing the relationship between the unemployment rate and the vacancy rate (a frequently used indicator of the degree of labour market flexibility) shifted outwards in most European countries in the 1970s and 1980s, whereas in Sweden it remained fairly stable. Further, real wages were reasonably flexible and Sweden, again unlike most other countries, combined a high degree of functional flexibility with a low numerical flexibility[7] (Delsen and van Veen, 1992).

Despite these undoubted successes, however, it is clear that Sweden has suffered from relatively high labour costs, deteriorating labour productivity and rising inflation; and, significantly, a very substantial increase in unemployment in recent years. As has been well documented,[8] the 'Swedish model' came under increasing strain in the 1970s and 1980s and these strains caused certain fundamental modifications to be made to the model.

On the trade union side, the necessary unity of interest and purpose was eroded in the 1970s and 1980s. The growth of service sector employment led to the growth of white collar unions and the LO's dominant position in the movement became usurped by the white collar union confederation TCO/SACO. As the main architect of the 'Swedish model' has commented, the white collar unions were neither as politically committed as the LO unions, nor were they as attached to the idea of centralized bargaining (Meidner, 1993).

Accelerating pay competition between trade union groups replaced wage restraint and the public sector took over the role of wage leader, thereby undermining a vital element of the original 'Swedish model' (Kjellberg, 1992). Moreover, white collar unions were only concerned with solidaristic norms for their own members, and firmly opposed reduced wage differentials *between* white collar and blue collar workers. So even on the workers' side the support for centralized wage settlements and the narrowing of differentials was fractured.

On the employer's side, the increased international competitiveness and the rising real wages in the second half of the 1980s stimulated doubts about centralized wage bargaining and generated a growing interest in greater 'flexibility' at local level. Swedish private capital increasingly saw the traditional 'Swedish model' arrangements as no longer being compatible with their best interests and, with the lifting of financial controls, Swedish firms were free to seek better profit margins (and lower labour costs) elsewhere (Kreisler and Halevi, Ch. 11, this volume). Furthermore, no doubt fuelled by the 'demonstration effect' of countries like the US and the UK, taxpayers in Sweden and elsewhere in Scandinavia began to express opposition to a regime that required relatively high marginal tax rates.

In retrospect it seems as though the devaluation of the Kroner in 1982 brought only temporary relief and concealed growing problems of low productivity and relatively high production costs (Delsen and van Veen, 1992). Certainly whilst the performance of the 'Swedish model' has been good in the post-Second World War period, especially in terms of keeping unemployment rates low, it is clear that, along with virtually every other economically advanced country, performance has faltered in the late 1980s and early 1990s.

Furthermore key features of the model have been modified or, apparently, abandoned, and this has led some to speak of the effective demise of the 'Swedish model' as it has traditionally been understood (Kjellberg, 1992). In particular, the breakdown of the key feature of centralized bargaining has been emphasized, with employers showing a growing unwillingness to depart from local pay settlements.[9] Moreover, the trade unions have displayed a reluctance to restrain wage claims despite a deteriorating economic situation (Peterson, 1987).

Significantly, too, the solidaristic wage strategy has been compromised as workers' pay increases have increasingly reflected the profitability of their firms via local productivity deals and profit sharing. There is no doubt that the move to local bargaining has been accompanied by widening wage differentials (Delsen and van Veen, 1992; Kjellberg, 1992). Certainly the trade union movement itself seems to have fundamentally reformulated its solidaristic policy. Following the 1989 Metall Report, the talk now is of 'solidaristic work' and 'good jobs.' The 1989 Metall Report, 'Solidaristic Wage Policy for Good Jobs', focused on the need to eliminate the polarization between a relatively small proportion of stimulating jobs and a large (and growing) number of monotonous and physically stressful ones (Kjellberg, 1992). Metall argues for wage differentials to be accepted and used as incentives to encourage workers to improve their skills. Brulin and Nilsson (1991) have proposed a new 'Swedish model' where the trade unions accept decentralized bargaining whilst employers accede to union influence on work organization and local pay determination.

Also, the much vaunted wage-earner funds were disbanded by the Conservative government in 1991. Despite the fact that the wage-earner funds were restricted from growing larger than 5 per cent of total share capital, were subject to the same market disciplines as normal financial institutions and were required to make annual payments to the state pension fund, fevered arguments about a quick move to a command economy, the imminent collapse of the stock market and the burgeoning power of the trade unions (in fact the trade unions never acquired more than 4 per cent of the voting rights in any enterprise) seemed to have been influential. Thus, despite the progressive nature of Swedish politics since the 1930s and the successful adoption of the 'Swedish model' in the period after the Second World War, there was insufficient political support to sustain the wage-earner funds. Certainly it is apparent that the Swedish employers have been, and continue to be, hostile to any 'socialization' of investment.

THE LESSONS OF THE SWEDISH EXPERIENCE

It does seem as though some of the most central features of the classic 'Swedish model' have been fundamentally restructured (dismantled in fact does not seem too strong a term) in the face of a complex confluence of socioeconomic and political changes in the 1980s and early 1990s. This, however, is not to suggest that lessons cannot be learned from the Swedish experience or that all corporatist arrangements are doomed to failure. It certainly is not the case that we have to conclude that New Right policies are preferable or inevitable.

As has been seen, the evidence of the period after the Second World War suggests that corporatist institutions can improve macroeconomic performance and produce progressive distributional changes. Workers and owners have competing interests and if they are not satisfactorily coordinated in some way then problems will ensue. For example, it is clear that a refusal to accept cuts in profit margins in conditions in which wage increases (unaccompanied by corresponding improvements in productivity) are being successfully pursued can lead to an inflationary spiral. In the postwar period we have seen two main alternative ways of dealing with such distributionally based problems: either some sort of 'accord' between capital and labour is struck (as in the corporatist countries) or, effectively, the workforce is 'disciplined' through unemployment (see Chs 6 and 9, this volume). The latter, it hardly needs to be said, is an extremely economically and socially wasteful way of combating inflation. The main lesson here then is surely that the former is preferable to the latter.

For a long period corporatist arrangements proved successful in improving the wage–unemployment trade-off and they seem to have done this largely by reducing 'insider' influences on wage levels. The evidence of the 1980s in both the US and the UK seems to suggest that the decentralized wage bargaining so beloved of conservative economists and politicians in fact increases the influence of intrafirm productivity and profit trends and allows workers to 'rent-share' where their employers operate in imperfect product markets. That is, under decentralised bargaining 'outsider' influence is restricted; meaning, of course, that the impact of unemployment on wage inflation is restricted. The end result can be, as in the UK in the 1980s, that real wages can continue to rise even in circumstances where unemployment is high and rising and in which trade union power is significantly reduced (Metcalf, 1993). This situation prompts two important questions. Do we wish to have bargaining systems that require 3 million (or more) unemployed in order to curb wage inflation? Or do we wish to try to find institutional arrangements that connect wage setting to 'external' economic conditions and effectively substitute consensus for open conflict and the necessity of using unemployment as a socioeconomic weapon?

Other obvious lessons can be drawn from examining the Swedish experience in contrast to that of countries with neo-conservative regimes like the US and the UK. Perhaps the most emphasized are the benefits of the active labour market policy and the 'right to work' principle (Layard, 1989; Delsen and van Veen, 1992). Certainly the advantage of spending money on training and maintaining people in work over paying huge sums in unemployment benefits seems fairly clear.

Nevertheless, it is evident that there are limits to the extent that one country can copy or 'import' the socioeconomic arrangements of another. Certainly the example of Australia warns against any simplistic attempts to import the 'Swedish model' (see Kriesler and Halevi, Ch. 11, this volume). In fact, it helps emphasize a most important point, namely that there are no 'models', in the strict sense, to follow at all. Indeed the experience of Sweden itself shows quite clearly that there are no 'answers' to socioeconomic problems that apply to all societies for all time. Any given set of institutional arrangements can cope with a certain amount of economic, social and political change – but only a certain amount. It is not surprising therefore that the scale of economic and political changes that have beset the world economy would eventually have some impact on Sweden. The mutation of the 'Swedish model' therefore, in retrospect, is understandable and is not, in itself, something that should throw dissenting political economists into deep despair.

There are no master 'blueprints' that can be followed. This is one of the most important lessons of the Swedish experience. Life is not that simple, and what has happened in Eastern European countries reminds us of the potential disasters that can follow such a simplistic and dogmatic approach. Bearing this in mind one can see the significance of Jonzon's argument that there is no 'Swedish model' that can be accepted or rejected, brought or sold. There is simply an approach founded on dedicated and innovative hard work (Jonzon, quoted in Delsen and van Veen, 1992). What is needed is more innovative hard work to combat simplistic and wrong-headed approaches based on deregulation and market forces *and* to develop socioeconomic institutional arrangements that might enable the operationalization of the key principles and values found useful from the experience of Sweden and other countries.

What the Swedish experience also shows us is the ongoing difficulties that face the socialization of an investment project in even the most advanced of the welfare capitalist economies. In Sweden, clearly, there was not the social or political basis for an experiment in even partial socialization. As Pontusson pointed out, various features of the Swedish economy and society were not propitious to an experiment of this kind: public ownership of industry has always been very small, economic planning has never been undertaken, state intervention in production has not taken place (except in the labour market), capital markets have never been manipulated by the state, and the financial system has remained fundamentally dominated by the big private banks (Pontusson, 1984). Certainly events subsequent to the introduction of the wage-earner funds were never likely to enhance the prospects of success.

A major lesson of the experience of post-Second World War corporatism is thus not just that socioeconomic arrangements cannot usually be imported from other countries with any degree of success; but that, even *within* a country, it may not be possible to extend and develop particular institutional arrange-ments. However, we would argue that the lesson of Sweden's experience with socialization of investment in the 1980s is not that the wage-earner funds were a bad idea (on the contrary, as argued above, they can be seen as having a key potential role in corporatist strategies) or that they produced adverse economic results; but rather that the Swedish labour movement failed to build the necessary political support for such a project. Such radical change was not sufficiently supported by previous reform of the socioeconomic system and it was at odds with the prevailing political trends. Its re-emergence in more propitious economic and political circumstances, however, is neither impossible nor undesirable.

Discussion of corporatist arrangements inevitably focuses on the concepts of consensus and cooperation. Talk of 'consensus' and 'harmony' between capital and labour, however, can sometimes become overblown and lead to misun-derstanding. In Sweden, like everywhere else where some sort of accord has been achieved, firms have gone along with certain policies, even accepted certain restrictions on their activities and inclinations, because they have been constrained to do so or persuaded that this is, for the time being, the best they are likely to achieve. There has been no consensus with private capital in the sense of winning 'hearts and minds'. It must be remembered that the Swedish employers took the initiative on centralized wage bargaining in the 1950s because of a hard-headed view of the potential gains to them of wage restraint and the 'peace obligation'.

Moreover, during the heyday of the 'Swedish model' the SAF (the employers' federation) was 'restrained' within the corporatist arrangements by a dominant social democratic party (carrying all the appearance of a 'natural party of government') and by a strong, and unified, trade union movement enjoying a historically and internationally unique level of trade union density (Kjellberg, 1992). Since the 1970s, with growing economic pressures, periodic bouts of conservative government, and a divided trade union movement, we have seen them less constrained than in earlier years.

In Sweden as elsewhere 'consensus' is a type and degree of contrived coop-eration achieved between instrumentally oriented groups with conflicting interests. The achievement of consensus, as we have seen, can never be easy or permanent – even in Sweden. If they are to avoid the crude excesses of neo-conservative 'solutions', the difficult task that faces all advanced industrial countries is to build a set of achievable institutional arrangements in which an operationally significant amount of cooperation and trust can be fostered.

Given that the cooperation of powerful private interests is unlikely to be anything other than conditional and temporary – and this after-all is perhaps the most important lesson of the 'Swedish model' for social democratic progressivism – this is unlikely to be a prize that is easily won.

NOTES

1. In 1987 the model was adjusted to take account of a third sector, the 'public sheltered' sector. See Delsen and van Veen (1992, p. 90)
2. The hypothesis consistent with this type of behaviour by the unions is the 'real wage resistance' one common in the literature (see, for example, Arestis, 1986b).
3. It has also been viewed as 'a step towards equality by giving a lower percentage rise to higher-paid workers in the annual wage bargain with the employers' (Linton, 1985, p. 27).
4. The 'misery index' is the rise in inflation plus the slowdown in real GDP. The Okun 'misery index' is the sum of the inflation and unemployment rates.
5. The 'sacrifice ratio' is the cumulative rise in unemployment divided by the fall in inflation. In the depression of the early 1980s corporatist economies disinflating from a position of double-figure inflation experienced sacrifice ratios in the range 1:1 to 4:1, whilst non-corporatist countries suffered ratios between 4:1 to 7:1. See Dawson (1992).
6. Hysteresis models of unemployment take the equilibrium rate of unemployment to be path-dependent, i.e. the actual level of unemployment affects the equilibrium rate. Some economists have tried to explain the pattern of European unemployment by utilizing the hysteresis concept and drawing on insider–outsider models of the labour market (Blanchard and Summers, 1987). As regards the long-term unemployed in particular, if their skills and motivation declines and/or employers cease to regard them as serious candidates for employment then they cease to have any impact on national wage levels and any increase in their number may serve to raise the long-term equilibrium level.
7. Functional flexibility refers to the labour force acquiring a wider range of skills. Numerical flexibility, of course, refers to changes in the size of the workforce (see Atkinson, 1984).
8. See for example Myrdal (1980), Lash (1985), Lundberg (1985), Peterson (1987), Rehn and Viklund (1990), Kjellberg (1992) and Wise (1993).
9. If, however, there was to be a substantial reduction in unemployment, then decentralized bargaining is unlikely to be effective in restraining wage inflation (note the experience of the UK in the 1960s). Here we are likely to see a deterioration in the wage–unemployment trade-off. See the discussion in the following section.

REFERENCES

Arestis, P. (1986a), 'Post Keynesian Economic Policies: The Case of Sweden', *Journal of Economic Issues*, September.

Arestis, P. (1986b), 'Wages and Prices in the UK', *Journal of Post Keynesian Economics*, Spring; reprinted in M.C. Sawyer (ed.) (1989) *Post Keynesian Economics*, Aldershot: Edward Elgar.

Arestis, P. and Driver, C. (1984), 'The Policy Implications of Post-Keynesianism', *Journal of Economic Issues*, December.

Atkinson, J. (1984), 'Flexibility, Uncertainty and Manpower Management', Institute of Manpower Studies, Report 89, Falmer: University of Sussex.

Blanchard, O.J. and Summers, L.H. (1987), 'Hysteresis in Unemployment', *European Economic Review*, vol. 31, February/March.

Brulin, G. and Nilsson, T. (1991), 'From Societal to Managerial Corporatism: New Forms of Work Organisation as a Transformation Vehicle', *Economic and Industrial Democracy*, vol. 12, no. 3.

Bruno, M. and Sachs, J. (1985), *Economics of Worldwide Stagflation*, Cambridge, Mass.: Harvard University Press.

Calmfors, L. and Driffill, J. (1988), 'Centralisation of Wage Bargaining', *Economic Policy*, vol. 3, no. 1.

Calmfors, L. and Nymoen, R. (1990), 'Real Wage Adjustment and Employment Policies in the Nordic Countries', *Economic Policy*, vol. 5, no. 2.

Dawson, G. (1992), *Inflation and Unemployment*, Aldershot: Edward Elgar.

Delsen, L. and van Veen, T. (1992), 'The Swedish Model: Relevant for Other European Countries? *British Journal of Industrial Relations*, vol. 30, no. 1.

Ferner, A. and Hyman, R. (1992), *Industrial Relations in the New Europe*, Oxford: Blackwell.

Henley, A. (1990), *Wages and Profits in the Capitalist Economies: The Impact of Monopolistic Power on the Macroeconomic Performance in the USA and UK*, Aldershot: Edward Elgar.

George, D.A.R. (1993), 'The Political Economy of Wage-Earner Funds: Policy Debate and Swedish Experience', *Review of Political Economy*, vol. 5, no. 4.

Kalecki, M. (1943), 'Political Aspects of Full Employment', *Political Quarterly*, vol. 14. Reprinted in E.K. Hunt and J.G. Schwartz (eds) (1972) *A Critique of Economic Theory*, Harmondsworth: Penguin.

Keynes, J.M. (1936), *The General Theory of Employment, Interest and Money*, London: Macmillan.

Kjellberg, A. (1992), 'Sweden: Can the Model Survive?', Ch. 3 of Ferner and Hyman, (1992).

Korpi, W. (1989), 'Can We Afford to Work?', Ch. 20 of Bulmer, M. et al. (eds), *Goals of Social Policy*, London: Unwin Hyman.

Landsorganisationen (1951), *Trade Unions and Full Employment*, Stockholm: LO.

Lash, S. (1985), 'The End of Neo-Corporatism? The Breakdown of Centralised Bargaining in Sweden', *British Journal of Industrial Relations*, vol. 23, no. 2.

Layard, R. (1989), 'European Unemployment: Cause or Cure?' Discussion Paper no. 368, Centre for Labour Economics, London School of Economics.

Linton, M. (1985), 'The Swedish Road to Socialism', Fabian Society, no. 503.

Lundberg, E. (1985), 'The Rise and Fall of the Swedish Model', *Journal of Economic Literature*, vol. 23, March.

Marglin, S. and Schor, J. (eds) (1990), *The Golden Age of Capitalism: Reinterpreting the Postwar Experience*, Oxford: Clarendon Press.

Matzner, E. and Streeck, W. (eds) (1991), *Beyond Keynesianism: The Socio-Economics of Production and Full Employment*, Aldershot: Edward Elgar.

Meidner, R. (1978), *Employee Investment Funds: An Approach to Collective Capital Formation*, London: Allen and Unwin.

Meidner, R. (1993), 'Why Did the Swedish Model Fail?', *Socialist Register*, London: Merlin.

Metcalf, D. (1993), 'Industrial Relations and Economic Performance', *British Journal of Industrial Relations*, vol. 31, no. 2.

Myrdal, H.G. (1980), 'The Swedish Model – Will It Survive?', *British Journal of Industrial Relations*, March.

Newell, A. and Symons, J. (1986), 'Corporatism, Laissez-Faire and the Rise in Unemployment', Working Paper no. 853, Centre for Labour Economics, London School of Economics.

Peterson, R.B. (1987), 'Swedish Collective Bargaining – A Changing Scene', *British Journal of Industrial Relations*, vol. 25, no. 1.

Pontusson, J. (1984), 'Behind and Beyond Social Democracy in Sweden', *New Left Review*, no. 143.

Rehn, G. and Viklund, B. (1990), 'Changes in the Swedish Model', in G. Baglioni and C. Crouch (eds), *European Industrial Relations*, London: Sage.

Robinson, D. (1974), *Solidaristic Wage Policy in Sweden*, Paris: OECD.

Rowthorn, B. and Glyn, A. (1990), 'The Diversity of Unemployment Experience Since 1973', in Marglin and Schor (1990).

Soskice, D. (1983), 'Collective Bargaining and Economic Policies', Manpower and Social Affairs Committee (MAS 83), no. 23, Paris: OECD.

Wells, J. (1993), 'The Economy After Ten Years: Stronger Or Weaker?', in N.M. Healey (ed.) *Britain's Economic Miracle: Myth or Reality?* London: Routledge.

Wise, L.R. (1993), 'Whither Solidarity? Transitions in Swedish Public Sector Pay Policy', *British Journal of Industrial Relations*, vol. 31, no. 1.

11. Corporatism in Australia

Peter Kriesler and Joseph Halevi

This chapter deals with the question of corporatism in Australia. At the outset it should be noted that economists tend to pay very little attention to the conceptual meaning of the term 'corporatism', which has a much wider dimension than a purely economic one and originates from a complex historical process. This is particularly true for the issue of corporatism as it is meant today. Hence the second section will deal with the evolution of the notion of corporatism. Since corporatism is a wholly European phenomenon, the section will be concerned with experiences emanating from European countries. The evaluation of the corporatist project will be conducted by identifying two forms of corporatism. The first pertains to the interwar period, while the second refers mostly to the system of industrial relations in place in the Scandinavian countries as well as in Germany and Austria. Its existence dates from the end of the Second World War.

As far as Australia is concerned, reference to Europe is essential. Indeed, Australia has had – and still has – a number of institutional arrangements bearing a strong resemblance to the interwar conceptions of European corporatism. More importantly, however, postwar corporatism has become an explicit reference point in the Australian trade union movement during the 1980s. The manner in which corporatism has been incorporated into the Australian economy is examined in a later section, after which attempts are made to evaluate the implications of corporatism for the Australian economy.

TWO CORPORATISMS

Up to the early 1970s, anyone with a minimal political culture would have associated the term corporatism with fascism, and would have agreed that the elements of corporatism present in the postwar period in Europe represented a form of continuity with the fascist regimes of the interwar years. Not surprisingly, therefore, a regular stream of studies on corporatism flowed from Italy, France and from the small, but intellectually powerful, German critical thought. Gradually, during the 1970s, a different conception emerged. This was related to a notion of industrial relations based on strong and centralized unions having an institutionalized role in their respective societies.

The first of the two variants of corporatism (henceforth M1 and M2 corporatism) also gave unions an institutionalized role. However, this role was based on the physical elimination of the pre-existing, autonomously structured, socialist and communist labour organizations. In the M1 framework, industrial relations are governed, principally, by the Ministry of Labour. The unions become, therefore, instruments of mediation and of implementation of the directives springing from the ministry. The juridical and technical forms of M1 corporatism are characterized by a system of arbitration tribunals which, on one hand, absorb the bulk of the energy of the functionaries of the official unions, and on the other, put the unions in a subordinate position. This is so because the bodies envisaged by corporatism M1 are staffed by lawyers and 'experts' of all sorts, i.e. by social figures belonging to the classes for whom corporatism is a political instrument necessary to anchor the position of the working class at the bottom of the social hierarchy.

Fascism did not invent corporatism, nor did it devise its juridical form. In Europe, corporatist ideas are found first and foremost in Catholic social thought. In countries where Catholicism strongly influenced, directly and indirectly, the formation of political parties corporatism became a central component of a political and economic discourse in opposing the socialist movement[1] (Germany – Bavaria in particular – Austria and Italy are all examples of this). In Europe, M1 corporatism signified the elimination of the organizations produced by the history of the working class itself. In Latin America, especially in Argentina and in Brazil, it had a more ambivalent role. Corporatist forces in Latin America took from Italian fascism the notion that labour unions should be subordinated to the Ministry of Labour. At the same time, Latin American corporatism represented the institutionalization of the populist strands emerging from within the labour movement. Thus, as shown by Brazil's political history, corporatist institutions were used by labour leaders to expand their influence while the conservative forces used the same institutions to tighten control over labour organizations.

The above situation may be contrasted with M2 corporatism, which is essentially a postwar European phenomenon and remains confined to a relatively small number of countries. It builds upon, rather than rejecting, the autonomy of labour organizations *vis-à-vis* the state. But the term corporatism does not appropriately convey the character of class relations in the countries described as ruled by the M2 system.

The most important example of M2 corporatism is the Swedish system, which was based on the particular role of the metalworkers, connected with a profit squeeze notion of economic progress. The metalworkers would set the pace of wage demands, while the central union would ensure the spreading of those gains to the rest of the workforce. Sustained by appropriate state policies, such as retraining programmes and taxation policies, the weaker sectors would be induced to react to the profit squeeze by means of technological restructuring. The Swedish case can hardly be called a model, if by model we mean something that can be reproduced regardless of its historical specificity. It took nearly 20 years to materialize in the form of the famous Rehn Plan in 1951. It began to unravel in the mid-1970s,[2] precisely when sociologists and economists in the Anglo-American world started to consider it as a viable alternative model.

Austria and Germany are perhaps closer to a corporatist set-up, not so much because of the unions' strategic decisions, but because of the historical conditions which marked the evolution of class relations. In Austria, during the interwar period, corporatist orientations came from conservative Catholic forces who allied themselves with the fascist Heimwehr. This process was crowned by the corporatist constitution passed under the government of Chancellor Dolfuss in 1934. The stabilization of the Dolfuss regime was predicated upon the destruction of the social democratic movement, as shown by the military repression of the Vienna pro-democratic uprising in 1934. After the war, Austria underwent a long phase of occupation which lasted till 1955. In this period the Soviet Union pushed for the nationalization of heavy industries, while the British, thanks to the far-sighted vision of Bevin, pushed for a strong institutionalization of the reborn social democratic unions. This was done with the objective of limiting the power of the conservative – mainly Catholic – forces who did not shed their traditional corporatist orientations. Hence if, after 1955, the Austrian labour movement found itself endowed with a greater sphere of institutional influence, it was due to the limits imposed upon the traditional conservative forces of the country.

In Germany, by contrast, the unions found themselves, right from 1949, under the pressure of the old corporatist forces now under the umbrella of the Christian Democratic Party, CDU, and of its Bavarian ally CSU. As against the wide ranging reform proposals advanced by the labour movement in 1949, the CDU proceeded to shape the new Bonn republic on the principles of traditional corporatism adapted to a parliamentary regime. The two main aspects of this strategy were the links between the core firms and the state (Reich, 1990) and the notion of a social market economy. The latter is nothing but a prescription for a tight hierarchically structured society where the fruits of growth are supposed to be filtered from the top down. The hegemony of the CDU–CSU in shaping the institutions and the priorities of postwar Germany compelled the labour movement to accept the surrounding economic environment as expressed by the notion of social partnership developed by the DGB in the early 1960s.

The common characteristics of the Swedish, Austrian and German experiences in labour relations lie in the sectoral basis of trade unions, relatively centralized wage systems, and the existence of a significant cooperative sector, with its own banks and credit institutions, attached to the social democratic parties.

These three elements form the foundations of the politics of class compromise in those countries. Sociologists and economists became attracted by these experiences because, as the postwar boom ended, they appeared to show a greater degree of social equity and economic rationality than the purer forms of capitalism of North America and Britain. Economists have usually taken the first two of the above three elements as hallmarks of the postwar corporatist model M2, forgetting that – as Eduard Bernstein clearly realized at the beginning of the twentieth century – the creation and expansion of the cooperative movement was to act as a prime mover in the transformation of labour's politics from class confrontation to social participation.

There are some crucial problems in transforming M2 corporatism into a normative model. The main limitations arise because M2 experiences are all strictly determined by the nature of class and social relations prevailing during the formative years of each of the corporatist M2 experiences. In matters related to the political economy of the state in the postwar period, as well as to the institutional behaviour elicited by the appearance of economic crises, the historical specificity of each of these cases overwhelms the imputed normative value which, at any one time, can be ascribed to any of the above-mentioned experiences.

In Sweden, the labour movement gained the upper hand in 1932 and produced its Rehn model only after many years of social democratic government. This model governed Sweden's political economy for three decades; even the Conservative government of the 1976–82 period was not interested in undoing the institutional structure which sustained it. It is, therefore, understandable why its modification in the 1980s did not entail the outright abandonment of the goal of full employment. To undo it much more systematic forces had to be in operation. Those systematic trends gathered momentum during the 1980s. The core of the Swedish system is represented by the alliance between the large firms and the respective unions, which are structured by industrial sectors. Within the alliance the metalworkers played the crucial dynamic role. They set the pace for wage negotiations and imposed the criteria for achieving international competitiveness. The alliance worked as long as the international expansion of Swedish capitalism did not conflict with the creation of jobs at home. During the 1970s, however, some basic changes took place. For example, as will be discussed more fully later in the chapter, the share of industrial employment over total employment declined very sharply, more than in the other industrialized countries of Western Europe, with the exception of Britain. Of the two forms of corporatism, the inter-war variant – that is the fascist variant – is closer to attaining the status of a model in a legal sense. This is so because the juridical and technical norms regulating M1 corporatism were consistent with the declared objective of eliminating the socialist movement from the body politic and of relegating the working class to a subordinate position. Corporatism was, in this sense, genuine since it institutionalized a tight hierarchy of class relations without establishing any formal wage – productivity links or employment objectives. M2 corporatism is a hybrid collection of experiences resulting, mostly, from the postwar situation. Just as M1 corporatism was the expression of the political and economic crises of the interwar period, M2 corporatism was sustained by the determination shown by European governments in the first two decades after 1945 to maintain high growth rates. When this determination began to fade (as predicted by Kalecki in 1943) the parameters of M2 corporatism were also affected, including that of Sweden.

THE AUSSIES: NACH EUROPA UND ZURUCK

This brings us to the important question of where Australia fits into the picture. Given the importance of the Catholic church in the evolution of corporatism as well as its role in the development of Australia, it would be surprising if there had been no attempt to reproduce corporatism. In particular, the Catholic church has played an important part in both the union movement and in the Labor Party. In fact, during the McCarthy years, the vehement anti-communism of the church led to the split in the Labor Party which kept the Conservatives in power, at the federal level, until 1972.[3]

Australia's early history had elements of M1 corporatism without fascism. This early form of corporatism was centred on a number of policy imperatives. The most important of these was the general acceptance, from Federation until the early 1980s, of protectionism as a national economic strategy by all players in the economic and political spheres. In addition, until the 1970s, there was general agreement as to the nature of immigration policy.

European corporatism was explicitly taken by the Australian trade union movement as a reference point for reconstructing Australian industrial relations in attempting to develop a full-employment economic policy for the 1980s. Before this explicit adoption of M2 corporatism by both the federal government and the union movement, the unions maintained centralized control over the wage-setting process. In addition, for historical reasons, the process of arbitration of wage decisions was also conducted at a centralized level, with representatives of employers, unions and the federal government making their case before a federal court. This court set minimum award wages, which were also suggestive for the majority of workers who received over-award payments. As a result, labour relations were – and still are – governed by a system based on the conciliation and arbitration tribunals, the legal configuration of which bears a strong resemblance to the corporatist code formulated by the Italian nationalist jurist, and Mussolini's minister of justice, Alfredo Rocco. In these bodies unions are relegated to a subaltern role. The outcome of wage negotiations is decided on a pre-eminently legal basis in which judges and lawyers play a dominant role in what are, in fact, economic decisions.

The important point to note is that, despite the centralized wage system, the union movement before the 1970s did not have macroeconomic policy objectives. The high levels of employment in the postwar period meant that these were taken for granted so that union activity focused on the question of wages and conditions. This partly explained the lack of any discussion of the need for structural policies, which was reinforced by the fact that, with the important exception of capital goods and some final consumption goods, Australia produced nearly everything which it needed. In terms of the economic debate, it was argued that the main fetter on growth was the need to import financial capital and services.

Thus the conversion of the Australian unions to corporatism M2 is to be explained by two facts, one concrete and one idealistic. The material one is represented by the breakdown of the economic stability which allowed Australian early corporatism to survive, while the second is related to the explicit import of ideas derived on the basis of the Swedish experience.

The Breakdown of Economic Stability

For almost the whole period of 1949 to the beginning of 1980, Australia had a surplus in its trade account, while a substantial deficit on income and services led to a current account deficit for most of that time. Throughout that period, Australia had a net surplus on private sector capital inflows. This was put down to the country's relative youth, which was used to explain the scarcity of capital. The situation changed with the deregulations of the 1980s, which had substantial impacts on the domestic economy. Before then, Australia's economic growth had been based on the primary goods sector, while the manufacturing sector played a secondary role. Despite the substantial inflow of foreign capital, as well as direct investment by multinational companies, the secondary role of the manufacturing sector has not changed. This is because foreign investment in Australia was not dynamic; the domestic market generated levels of demand way below those of the expertise and technical level of those firms. The multinationals' aim was never to use Australia as an export base, but rather production was aimed exclusively at the small domestic market, so there was never any intention to generate economies of scale. Rather than being part of an overall production strategy by these companies, multinational investment in Australia was merely an attempt to exploit quasi rents resulting from domestic tariffs. Tariffs were unable to engender a local capital goods industry of specialized machine-tooling.

During this time Australia's growth rate, although allowing the maintenance of full employment, was nevertheless relatively low. This was due to the maintenance of the importance of the primary goods sector in the structure of the economy, initially related to Australia's ties to the UK, its main importer until the mid-1960s. The role was then taken over by Japan.[4] At the same time there was a switch from rural exports as the main category of exports to minerals.[5] Notwithstanding the fact that the Asian expansion absorbed some of the surpluses, this left exports in a weak position, at evermore unstable and deteriorating trend terms of trade.[6] That there has been no transition to a more sophisticated manufacturing export base, and no fundamental change from Australia's traditional reliance on raw materials and commodities exports is well documented. In addition, there are indications of a long-term decline, for at least 20 years, in the terms of trade, which is likely to continue for some time.[7]

When the full-employment period broke down with the collapse of the Bretton Woods system, and therefore the collapse of the fixed parity system, Australia was in a double bind over the future of exchange rate movements. Whatever the direction of such changes, there would be net negative effects on the domestic economy. The movement of exchange rates cannot be explained by equilibrium theory, as it is the result of disequilibrium capital flows. Given the peculiar nature of Australia's imports and exports, exchange rate movements are unlikely to lead to improvements in the balance of trade. As most of Australia's exports are primary commodities, they adjust more to changes in world income than to prices, so that they are relatively price-inelastic. Imports are mainly intermediate and final manufacturing goods. Demand for these is income-elastic, but will display asymmetry with respect to price elasticity. Due to the limited nature of import-competing domestic industries, there is a low supply elasticity of import replacement. As a result, a real exchange rate depreciation would hit the industrial base by increasing the cost of imported capital goods, without bringing forth domestic substitutes. So the likely impact would be inflationary.

A revaluation, on the other hand, would have a more ambiguous effect: it would hit the industrial base by increasing imports of consumer manufactured goods, whose demand is relatively price-elastic for reductions in price, while at the same time reducing the costs of imported inputs. In either case it is likely that the industrial base will be squeezed. This is because the industrial base is too weak to regenerate itself. Instead of becoming stronger during the 1950–73 period, the structure of the local economy became less adaptable as it still relied heavily on a declining primary sector. So it absorbed passively the negative effects of exchange rate changes. This may be contrasted with Sweden and Finland where active exchange rate policies were used to restructure the economy, e.g. by combining devaluation with retraining and investment programmes to retrain and re-equip the economy for new conditions, so making the economy more flexible.

Australia was affected by the changes of the 1970s on two fronts: first, the initial increase in the price of raw materials raised the cost of production, causing a cost-push inflation, as was the case in all other industrialized countries. This took place in an environment characterized by extreme competition in manufacturing products coming from South-East Asia and Japanese economic areas where development was showing much greater scale economies than anywhere else in the world. Second, since Australia's position in the world economy was determined by primary products, their increase in price crowded out the manufacturing sector. The main mechanism through which this occurred was the appreciation of the exchange rate which reduced the ability of the limited manufacturing sector to compete with imports. This influence was especially strong in the late 1970s and early 1980s, leading to de-industrialization. From a rational perspective increases in raw material prices and in the exchange rate should have helped modernize the economy as capital goods became relatively cheaper. Australia could have built a sophisticated and specialized industrial structure. However, as noted, the increase in raw material prices had the opposite impact via an overvalued exchange rate which led to serious contractions in the manufacturing sector rather than to expansion. The result was speculative gains in the raw materials sector, and a standard recession in the industrial sectors.

The crisis of the 1970s, just outlined, brought about the collapse of the division of tasks between unions, firms and the government which had dominated Australian economic life since 1945. According to this implicit arrangement, unions would be concerned with wages and conditions with no involvement in investment decisions, which were deemed to be the exclusive domain of management. Employment, on the other hand, was thought to be a matter for government policies. The Conservative governments of the 1950s to 1960s operated well within these parameters.

The crisis shattered this postwar consensus. During the first half of the 1970s Australia was governed by a very advanced Labor government under the leadership of Gough Whitlam. On the social plane it was the Whitlam government, rather than that of Hawke, which represented the first attempt to introduce elements of Scandinavian reformism, through the introduction of universal health care and free tertiary education. Whitlam also attempted to defend the bargaining power of labour by setting up, in a period of mounting economic difficulties, retraining programmes. It is safe to say that neither labour nor capital were in a position to respond constructively to the crisis. The former was still too fragmented in many craft unions and too locked up in a 'wages and conditions' mentality to shift its emphasis to social policies. The latter, by contrast, saw in the deliberate creation of a reserve army of the unemployed the most appropriate response to the crisis. From 1976 to 1983 Australia was ruled by a Conservative coalition which, while operating on the basis of traditional protectionist principles, attempted to discipline capital against labour through the use of the corporatist legal framework. The threat of the price justification tribunal was used in order to stiffen managements' resistance to unions' demands. This was coupled with the government threat to take unions to court in order to deregister them. Thus the institutional framework of mediation – which legally had many elements in common with M1 corporation – was turned into an instrument of confrontation.

Labor's ascendancy to power in 1983 was mostly due to the high level of unemployment (10 per cent) which set in from 1980 onward. Hawke stressed the idea of reducing unemployment with a policy based on compromise, in direct contrast to the confrontational policies of Fraser. The government's first task was to disentangle labour from capital and to create a climate where, to use a phrase by the then treasurer Paul Keating: "those who rule wages rule the country". The Accord constituted, in effect, the basis for both the disentanglement and the implementation of the second task. However, the Accord did not represent a sufficient condition: it did not reflect any specific union strategy, thereby appearing as a government directive. Furthermore its implementation required a consolidation of the multitudes of Australian unions into a smaller number of larger organizations, which became an explicit policy requirement. The only large organization which could act as a gravitational force was the left-wing Metalworkers' Union, not used to concerted forms of action.

In this context, the communist-led Metalworkers' Union was co-opted into the Accord platform as the crucial force which was supposed to provide the union-specific input to the policy framework.

The Import of the Swedish Model

It is important to realize that the introduction of the corporatist policy by the Labor Party occurred in two stages. On the political front, Hawke explicitly adopted a conciliatory and consensus approach to economic policy making as a reaction to the confrontationist regime of Fraser. Part of this policy, devised before the election of the Labor government in 1983, involved an agreement between the Labor Party and the union movement, subsequently called the Accord. The unions, under the leadership of the Metalworkers' Union, and after research into European models, published a document called *Australia Reconstructed* which explicitly proposed a Swedish-type corporatism with centralized wage fixing and an agreement with the government linking productivity and employment in exchange for wage indexation.

The underlying idea of the Accord was a commitment to full wage indexation and an alternative to the confrontationist polices of the previous Conservative government. The first Accord was aimed at achieving full employment growth without, at the same time, contributing to inflation, as the following extract from its introduction indicates:

It is extremely significant that the countries which have managed to fare better in this time of economic adversity, particularly by keeping unemployment to relatively low levels, have been notably those countries which have eschewed monetarism and have instead placed substantial importance on developing prices and incomes policies by consultation.

It is with this experience in mind that both organisations [the Australian Labor Party and the Australian Council of Trade Unions] have seen fit to try to develop a mutually agreed policy on prices and incomes in Australia for implementation by a Labor Government. Such a policy offers by far the best prospect of enabling Australia to experience prolonged higher rates of economic and employment growth, and accompanying growth in living standards, without incurring the circumscribing penalty of higher inflation, by providing for resolution of conflicting income claims at lower levels of inflation than would otherwise be the case. With inflation control being achieved in this way, budgetary and monetary policies may be responsibly set to promote economic and employment growth, thus enabling unemployment to be reduced and living standards to rise. (Statement of Accord by the Australian Labor Party and the Australian Council of Trade Unions regarding economic policy (1983), p. 160.)

In the early years of the Accord, the union movement had no explicit model of what they were trying to achieve, other than a general commitment to wage restraint and full employment, identified in this agreement. This brings us to the second stage of the Accord. In the mid-1980s the ACTU (Australian Council of Trade Unions) and TDC (Trade Development Council) sent a delegation to Northern Europe and Germany, to study their experiences and to prepare a report on the applicability of these experiences to Australia. The unfortunate upshot was that the specific history and social institutions of the Australian economy were ignored in the recommendations. Rather, they saw that the outcome of the Swedish case was desirable, and thought that to achieve the same results all that was needed was to implement the same policies, ignoring both fundamental differences between the countries and the changes in the world economy which undermined the Swedish and German strategies.

Australia Reconstructed, the report of the ACTU/TDC mission to Scandinavia and Germany, took the Swedish system, which was based on their metalworkers as well as the German retraining system, as the starting-point for an attempt to shift the Australian labour movement's outlook away from a purely wages and conditions approach. However, they did this without any realistic idea of the direction they were taking. In particular, two fundamental shortcomings of the blind absorption of the Swedish system must be pointed out. The first relates to the character of Australian unionism and to the role of the government, while the second relates to the evaluation of the economic situation in both Sweden and Australia.

The problem which led to the abandonment of the Swedish model as a policy option in the Australian case was the different union structure. In the European example, unions were sectorally based, so that union policies implied sectoral policies. In Australia, by contrast, unions were trade-based, and so crossed over many sectors. This meant that there was no logical benefit from union-wide retraining programmes as these crossed many non-intersecting skill requirements. In Sweden and Germany the capital goods sector was nurtured by capitalists independent of unions, and there are highly specialized technical skills schools. There is no equivalent in Australia, where education tends to be unrelated to skills. In Germany and Sweden the relation between the metalworkers and the capital goods sectors meant that there was an important related role for technical skills. In Australia, highly skilled tradesman *replaced* the capital goods sector, so skills, and hence retraining, were not attached to individual sectors. This makes the Swedish/German model of retraining inapplicable to Australia.

There was an additional consideration from the macro-side, related to the role of the government. In Australia, government policy was intentionally aimed at reducing the size of public infrastructure expenditure, which led to (cyclical) budget surpluses in the late 1980s, as shown in Figure 11.1. This does not appear to have been the case in Sweden.

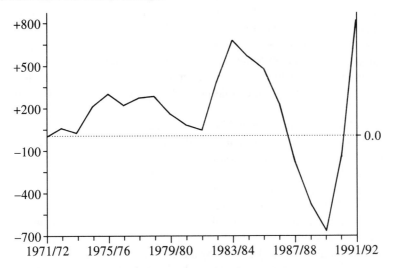

Source: Australian Bureau of Statistics and the Reserve Bank of Australia database.

Figure 11.1 Commonwealth budget deficit, 1971–92 ($m)

To understand the second aspect of the inapplicability of the Swedish model to Australia, we need to look more closely at what happened in Sweden. In a recently published paper Meidner (1993), the father with Rehn of the Swedish model, identified the failure of the Swedish experiment in two interrelated phenomena which occurred in the last two decades: the growth of white-collar employment and of the financial sector.

Unlike Germany, Sweden experienced a very steep decline in the share accruing to industrial employment. The concomitant rise of white-collar employment, Meidner argues, brought to the fore other types of unions which were politically neutral and not interested in centralized wage fixing. As a result, 'the homogeneous union movement became fragmented and conflicting interests dehabilitated LO's fight for egalitarian wage structure' (Meidner, 1993, p. 223).

Alongside this phenomenon the economic transformation of Sweden was no longer allowing the implementation of a profit squeeze strategy to sustain the egalitarian wage structure. The other side of the coin is that the more efficient firms obtained extra profits. As long as production was essentially domestically based and legal controls inhibited the free movement of international capital, profitable firms tended to reinvest the extra profits in the domestic economy. All this started to wane with the transnationalization of Swedish firms and with the lifting of financial controls. Today, Swedish capital is free from restrictions and can flow out of Sweden in search of better financial returns or cheaper labour. In Sweden, as well as in the UK, the decline in manufacturing jobs has not been compensated by the rise of services.

When Australian unions were studying the Swedish experience they were looking, in 1986, at something which was passing away, because it was not compatible with Swedish capitalists' interests. However one finds no hint in the Australian report of the dire straits in which the Swedish economy was finding itself.

The attempt to copy Sweden blindly could have been mitigated by a sober comparison with the Australian situation. In terms of the composition of employment, similar trends prevailed as in Sweden. Yet, in Australia's case, the rise in the service sector – mostly banking, finance and tourism – the decline in industry, and the formation of a plethora of small technologically primitive businesses (especially in New South Wales) did not mean the growth of another form of unionism. Instead, the shrinking of industry meant exit from unionism altogether. Thus, precisely when Australian trade unions were trying to counter the negative influences of the 1970s by means of the Accord and of a Swedish-inspired form of centralization, their social basis was being pulverized. The 1980s represent indeed a decade of sharp decline in union membership and in the social basis of centralized wage fixing: from August 1986 to August 1992, trade union membership fell six percentage points, from representing 46 per cent of full-time employees, to representing only 40 per cent (Australian Bureau of Statistics, 1993b).[8]

Structurally, Australia has been experiencing since the early 1970s a decline in the role of industry and a formidable expansion of finance. Unlike Sweden, industry in Australia has not played a dynamic role, as it was a passive importer of capital goods, often using already obsolete production lines. As a result of the industrial crisis in the 1979–83 recession, manufacturing began to be perceived as dwindling and sectors like finance and tourism were portrayed as being the saviours of the economy. The Australian Labor government *de facto* accepted this view, while deriving its stability from an agreement with a predominantly industrial union movement, soon to be marginalized.

The basic agreement between the Labor government and the union movement, the Accord, underwent many important changes as a result of the changing economic environment. So far there have been seven different versions of the Accord. The early versions were mainly restricted to agreements about the level of wage increases. Initially, full wage indexation was agreed on. However, Accord Mark 2 eroded this, as a result of the major depreciation of the value of the currency in 1985. The inflation rate was discounted for the effects of the depreciation, so that partial indexation resulted. It was the later versions of the Accord, from Mark 3 on, which explicitly included the M2 corporatism considerations derived from the Swedish model. As a result, elements other than wage setting entered into these later agreements, in particular measures aimed at inducing productivity growth, such as retraining and reskilling; as well as measures aimed at changing the nature of industrial relations, such as reductions in the number of unions, and a shift towards enterprise agreements.

These recent changes to the basis of the Accord agreement have had two significant effects on the labour market and on the potential of corporatism. The first of these has been the push to reduce the number of unions. This has been extremely successful, with the number of unions falling from 326 in June 1986 to 188 in June 1993 (Australian Bureau of Statistics, 1993a; 1993c). Although this has tended to increase the centralization of wage-bargaining decisions, it has not solved the fundamental problem of Australian unionism, which is that, rather than being industry or firm-based, they are occupationally based so that agreements within an industry or firm still involve many different unions. The other, more recent, policy push has had the opposite effect. This has been the attempt to decentralize the main elements of corporatism by the implementation of enterprise bargaining. In other words, instead of the main agreements affecting labour coming from an agreement at the economy-wide level, enterprise bargaining would break this down so that each enterprise would be required to enter its own agreement.

CORPORATIST POLICIES UNDER LABOR

Against this background, we can evaluate the corporatist policies of the Labor government since 1983, to see whether there has been the necessary change in the underlying structure of the economy to allow the return to full employment. However, instead of being concerned with long term questions of the structure of the Australian economy, the Labor government has been more concerned with short-run problems relating to maintaining steady macroeconomic performance so as to ensure electoral victory.

One of the main uses which the government made of the Accord was to legitimize a reduction of real wages, in return for a trade-off for higher growth and employment.

However, this did not lead to a strengthening of industry. Despite a substantial increase in corporate profitability during the 1980s, real fixed capital expenditure investment did not increase.[9] As a result, the gains from the Accord were short-term, with reference to employment during the 1980s, with no implications for long-term growth, employment or structure.

The fundamental problem with Australian corporatism is that, instead of being a basis for a programme of economic reform, with agreements not only in the labour market but also with both financial and industrial capital, the lack of involvement of capital has reduced its effectiveness. Instead of encouraging investment, the Accord has proved to be a way of reducing real wages in order to provide short-term gains in unemployment.[10] With no investment policy, there was no discussion as to required changes in the structure of the economy. As a result, the serious deterioration in Australia's current account throughout the late 1980s, meant that any gains were quickly reversed.

The lack of involvement of capital as part of the Accord may not have been important, if the Accord had succeeded in bringing a stable economic environment and encouraging investment. However, this has not been the case, due to the victory of financial capital at the expense of industrial capital. Further, the resultant 'level playing fields' view has led to reduced government involvement on the rationale that it would allow 'market forces' free play. However, all this has done is to reinforce the power and monopoly elements that already exist. Level playing fields only advantage those who already have power. The emphasis on market forces and (so-called) level playing fields is ideological rather than aimed at any real benefit to efficiency. Market forces are the sum total of different balances of power; they do not themselves guide things but are the outcome of processes at the decision-making level. So these forces represent the sum total of the relations of the market and the state, and are often the result of previous intervention. This is shown very well by the experience of many of the countries of East Asia (particularly Japan and South Korea) where the development of capitalism has been the result of deliberate intervention. In no way do their capitalist successes correspond to the blueprint of a free market. In Australia there has been a prevalence of those groups which call for a total hands-off policy, ignoring the implications for the domestic economy. For example, such policies will lead to further worsening of raw materials terms of trade, as strong countries like the US impose their conditions on Asia, as they are forced, increasingly, to rely on the export of primary goods. Australia cannot compete as an equal in such an arena.

Overall, what we see, then, is the tremendous importance of international factors for Australia's growth. This is backed up by historical evidence which shows a strong correlation between world economic activity and Australia's growth.[11] It is our contention that demand factors originating from overseas have provided the main restraints to domestic growth. In particular, the structure of the domestic economy limits its ability to respond to increased aggregate demand without incurring either domestic bottlenecks or balance of trade constraints. These constraints are reinforced by the nature of Australia's exports and imports.

This, coupled with the effects of financial and exchange rate deregulation, in turn reinforced short- and long-run balance of payments problems. The net effect is to augment long-run pressures which tend to reduce the size of the industrial sector. To combat such pressures, especially on the balance of payments, the government has attempted to reduce the level of domestic demand. The main instrument for this has been high interest rates, which also serve to maintain a high exchange rate. This has been reinforced by deregulation of both the exchange rate and financial markets. The cumulative effect is to make any long-term investment less attractive, and make the market more myopic. This has manifested itself in a decline in private fixed investment expenditure (except in building and construction), and a shift towards the acquisition of financial assets.[12] The deregulation of the exchange rate has led to greater volatility, which has had serious implications for investment. In addition, the deregulation of financial markets and high interest rates have led to a strong bias towards investment in financial assets, and to an increase in the number of mergers and takeovers as substitutes for investment in industry.

In Australia de-industrialization gave power (social and economic) to those sectors, like finance and recreational services, which are relatively free from the industrial base, and which have been motivated by the characteristics of the free market, i.e. short-term interests. In addition, both finance and recreational services have an extremely low proportion of union membership,[13] so that this structural change contributed to the decline in unionization of the workforce, discussed above.

One of the main consequences of deregulation of financial and exchange markets has been the massive increase in Australia's foreign debt, as indicated in Figure 11.2.

The size of the foreign debt has had significant implications for the current account balance. As can be seen from Figure 11.3, since 1983 the net incomes component has been growing, and has come to dominate the current account, being the main reason for its deficit in the early 1990s. Net income has been mainly determined by the repayments of foreign debt.

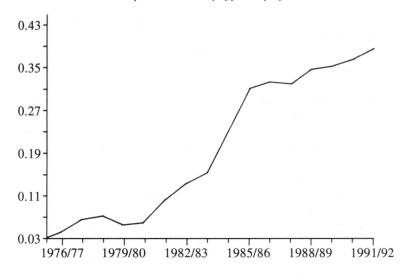

Source: As for Figure 11.1.

Figure 11.2   Ratio of net foreign debt to GDP, 1976–92

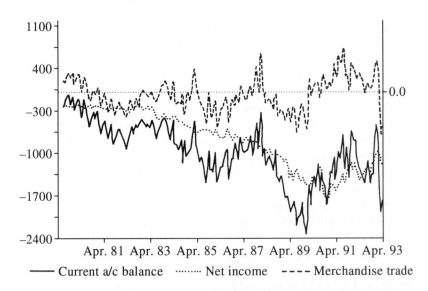

Source: As for Figure 11.1.

Figure 11.3   Australia's current account, 1981–93 (seasonally adjusted)

Thus we have a vicious circle, where the deterioration in the balance of payments has led the government to apply contractionary policy to dampen demand. However, the main instrument for contraction has been the interest rate, which merely accelerates the problem by reducing long-term investment and at the same time inducing capital inflows to keep the exchange rate artificially high.

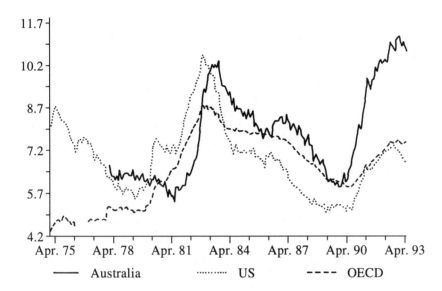

Source: As for Figure 11.1.

Figure 11.4   Unemployment rates, 1975–93 (%)

The failure of corporatist policies to lead to the desired restructuring of the economy has meant that it has also failed in terms of its chief goal: employment. Initially, Australia's record on the employment front, from 1983, was extremely good with respect to other OECD countries. However, as is demonstrated in Figure 11.4, this position deteriorated significantly at the end of the 1980s, when unemployment peaked at its highest level since the Second World War. The deterioration was the result of contractionary government policy specifically aimed at alleviating the current account problems identified above. In other words, corporatism in Australia has had little influence on the underlying structure of the economy, leaving it susceptible to the same international forces that have always dominated.

The one important macroeconomic variable which appears to have performed well in the early 1990s is the rate of inflation. Certainly there was a significant downward trend in Australia's inflation rate for much of the early period of the Labor government. However, this needs to be put into perspective compared to the inflation rates of her main trading partners. In this respect, Australia's performance only improved relatively, as a result of the *recession* and the consequent fall in aggregate demand, as is illustrated in Figure 11.5.

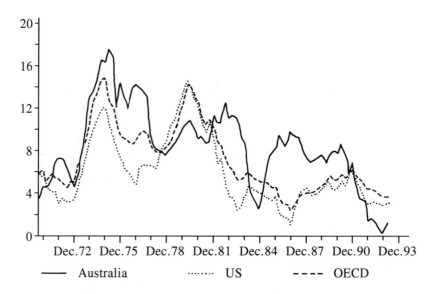

Source: As for Figure 11.1.

Figure 11.5   Inflation rates, 1972–93 (% change in CPI)

Although the relatively low level of inflation is a positive outcome, there are two important considerations which mitigate that result. First, the low inflation rate is associated with high social costs in terms of record levels of unemployment. Second, there is some debate as to whether the reduction in inflation is, in fact, permanent, or whether it is simply the result of a postponing of wage and price increases until recovery.

CONCLUSION

The above discussion has illustrated that the corporatist experiment has not been successful for the Australian economy. The Swedish model, and the main characteristics of M2 corporatism, on which the Australian post-1986 experience was based, were not appropriate for Australian conditions. The extent to which connections can be made between M2 Swedish corporatism and the Australian situation relates to the same forces which have undone the structural basis of the full-employment polity of Sweden, namely internationalization of capital and the spread of finance. The fundamental problem facing the Australian economy in the 1980s and 1990s was structural, based on the inadequacy of the industrial base. The declining world importance of raw materials, which had been the traditional base of Australian growth, meant that there was a need for other sectors to emerge. Partly as a result of policy, particularly deregulation, the emerging sectors of finance and recreation were heavily service-orientated, and undermined the basis of corporatism, which required a dominant union movement.

NOTES

1. In Australia the Catholic church has, historically, played a significant political role. Since the Second World War, it has been associated with anti-communist movements in the Labor Party. Hence there are important connections in Australia with M1 corporatism.
2. For reasons discussed below.
3. According to Professor Bruce McFarlane of the University of Newcastle, part of the agenda behind the split was an attempt to change the direction of the Labor Party in order to change its ideology into that of an agrarian corporatist culture.
4. See Foster and Stewart (1991) p. 11.
5. Ibid., p. 10.
6. See Gruen (1986), FitzGerald and Urban (1989) and Abelson (1989).
7. Ibid.
8. Peetz (1990) argues that structural change altering the composition of employment accounted for over half the decline in union density from 1980 on.
9. See Stegman (1993).
10. See Flatau et al. (1991) who argue that the Accord increased the influence of 'outsiders', particularly the unemployed, and, as a result, employment levels were higher that they otherwise would have been.
11. See Mclean (1989).
12. The evidence for these empirical observations can be found in Stegman (1993).
13. In August 1992, 28.4 per cent and 21.8 per cent respectively (Australian Bureau of Statistics, 1993b).

REFERENCES

Abelson, P. (1989), 'The sad truth about real commodity prices', *Economic Papers*, vol. 8, no. 3, pp. 92–8

ACTU/TDC (1987) *Australia Reconstructed: A Report by the Mission to Western Europe*, Canberra: Australian Government Publishing Service.

Australian Bureau of Statistics (1993a), *Labour Statistics, Australia 1991,* catalogue no. 6101.0.

Australian Bureau of Statistics (1993b), *Trade Union Members, Australia 1992,* catalogue no. 6325.0.

Australian Bureau of Statistics (1993c), *Trade Union Statistics, Australia June 1993,* catalogue no. 6323.0.

Bureau of Industry Economics (1989), *Information Bulletin 15: Trade Performance of Australian Manufacturing Industry,* Canberra: Australian Government Publishing Service.

Chapman, B. (1989), (ed.) *Australian Economic Growth,* Melbourne: Macmillan.

FitzGerald, V. and Urban, P. (1989), 'Causes and consequences of changes in the terms of trade and the balance of payments' in Chapman (1989, pp. 240–61).

Flatau, P., Kenyon, P., Lewis, P. and Rushton, A. (1991), 'The ACCORD, corporatism and outsiders in the labour market' in Johnson et al. (1991).

Foster, R.A. and Stewart, S.E. (1991), 'Australian economic statistics 1945–50 to 1989–90', Reserve Bank of Australia Occasional Paper, no. 8.

Goutevitch, P. et al. (1984) (eds) *Unions and Economic Crisis,* London: George Allen and Unwin.

Gruen, F. (1986), 'How bad is Australia's economic performance and why?' *Economic Record,* vol. 62, pp. 180–93.

Halevi, J. (1987), 'Corporatism', *New Palgrave,* vol. 1 ed. by J. Eatwell, M. Milgate, and P. Newman London: Macmillan.

Halevi, J. (1993), 'The Maastricht crisis' in P. Kriesler (ed.), Australian and European relations after Maastricht, CAER Paper no. 28.

Halevi, J. and Kriesler, P. (1993), 'Structural change and economic growth' in Mahony (1993).

Hennings, K.H. (1982), 'West Germany' in A. Boltho (ed.), *The European Economy: Growth and Crisis,* Oxford: Oxford University Press.

Hermele, K. (1993), 'The end of the middle road; what happened to the Swedish model?' *Monthly Review,* vol. 44.

Johnson, M., Kriesler, P. and Owen, T. (eds) (1991), *Contemporary Issues in Australian Economics,* Melbourne: Macmillan.

Kalecki, M. (1943), 'Political aspects of full employment', *Political Quarterly,* vol. 14, pp. 322–31.

Katzenstein, P. (1989), *Industry and Politics in Western Germany,* Ithaca, NY: Cornell University Press.

McLean, I. (1989), 'Growth in a small open economy: an historical view' in Chapman (1989, pp. 7–33).

Maddison, A. (1989), *The World Economy in the 20th Century,* OECD, Development Centre Studies.

Mahony, G. (1993) (ed.), *The Australian Economy Under Labor,* Sydney: Allen and Unwin.

Markovits, A. and Allen, C. (1984), 'Trade Unions and the Economic Crisis: the German Case' in Goutevitch et al. (1984).

Martin, A. (1984), 'Trade unions in Sweden: strategic responses to change and crisis' in Goutevitch et al. (1984).

Meidner, R. (1993), 'Why did the Swedish model fail?' *Socialist Register,* London: Merlin Press.

Peetz, D. (1990), 'Declining union density', *Journal of Industrial Relations,* vol. 32, pp. 197–223.

Reich, S. (1990), *The Fruits Of Fascism: Post War Prosperity In Historical Perspective,* Ithaca, NY: Cornell University Press.

Rowthorn, B. (1989), 'The Thatcher revolution', *Economic Papers,* vol. 8, pp. 1–23.

Statement of Accord by the Australian Labor Party and the Australian Council of Trade Unions regarding economic policy (1983), reprinted as Appendix A in Stilwell (1986).

Stegman, T. (1993), 'Aggregate investment and its sectoral composition: the failure of the restructuring policy' in Mahony (1993).

Stilwell, F. (1986), *The Accord and Beyond,* Sydney: Pluto Press.

Svenson, L. (1986), 'Class struggle in a welfare state in crisis: from radicalism to neoliberalism in Sweden' in R. Edwards et al. (eds), *Unions in Crisis and Beyond,* London: Auburn House Publishing.

Withers, G. (1987), 'Labour' in Maddock, R. and McLean, I. (eds), *The Australian Economy in the Long Run,* Cambridge: Cambridge University Press, pp. 248–88.

12. Economic development in the industrialized countries and the prospects for full employment*

Eileen Appelbaum and Ronald Schettkat

After a quarter-century of rapid increases in productivity and near-full employment in the main industrialized countries (the G7 countries plus Sweden), the last two decades have been characterized by slower productivity growth and higher rates of unemployment. In the 1960s the unemployment rate in these economies was about 2 per cent or even lower, with the exception of the US and Canada where approximately 5 per cent of the labour force was without a job. Twenty years later unemployment had risen to about 10 per cent of the labour force, and only Sweden and Japan still experienced unemployment rates of roughly 2 per cent (see Table 12.1). By the early 1990s even Japan and Sweden suffered from high or increasing unemployment. Today, industries experiencing high productivity growth are shedding workers in all the industrialized economies. What accounts for these dramatic increases in unemployment, and for the differences in the development of the employment to population ratio in these countries?

Economists' explanations for this dramatic increase in unemployment range from the impact of deflationary policies that reduce demand to the lingering effects of the negative exogenous supply shocks that occurred in the 1970s, and from structural shifts in technology or labour force characteristics that increase the natural rate of unemployment to institutional features of an economy such as the strength of unions, welfare state institutions, and unemployment insurance. Some of these explanations may capture part of the story, and exogenous factors have exacerbated the difficulties the industrialized economies have had in generating jobs and rising real wages. In particular, the excessively contractionary monetary and fiscal policies adopted by the UK, Germany and France, and more recently by Sweden have resulted in what Nobel laureate Robert Solow has termed 'Europe's unnecessary unemployment'. A different macroeconomic policy regime, however, would not be sufficient to restore unemployment rates to the low levels of the 1960s.

* Earlier versions of this chapter appeared in *Intereconomics* and *Wirtschaftsdienst*.

Table 12.1   Economic indicators, selected years

	Germany				Japan				Sweden				US			
	1963	1973	1983	1989	1963	1973	1983	1989	1963	1973	1983	1989	1963	1973	1983	1989
Employment trends, overall	100.0	100.3	93.8	103.4	100.0	114.5	124.8	133.4	100.0	106.0	115.5	122.1	100.0	125.5	148.8	173.2
Agriculture	100.0	61.2	40.6	32.1	100.0	59.0	44.5	38.8	100.0	58.4	48.4	33.6	100.0	74.2	73.5	70.1
Industry	100.0	97.9	83.5	84.4	100.0	134.4	136.9	144.2	100.0	95.1	84.1	87.6	100.0	118.7	118.8	131.6
Manufacturing	100.0	97.8	n.a.	86.6	100.0	130.2	126.9	133.9	n.a.	n.a.	84.1	n.a.	100.0	116.8	110.7	120.1
Services	100.0	115.3	133.6	148.6	100.0	133.4	164.9	183.4	100.0	129.0	162.2	177.6	100.0	136.0	176.2	211.1
Employment shares																
Agriculture	11.9	7.3	5.0	3.7	26.0	13.4	9.3	7.6	12.9	7.1	5.4	3.6	7.1	4.2	3.5	2.9
Industry	48.7	47.5	41.5	39.8	31.7	37.2	34.8	34.3	41.0	36.8	29.9	29.4	35.1	33.2	28.0	26.7
Manufacturing	37.7	36.7	n.a.	31.6	24.1	27.4	24.5	24.2	n.a.	27.5	22.3	21.9	26.6	24.8	19.8	18.5
Services	39.3	45.2	53.6	56.5	42.3	49.3	56.0	58.2	46.1	56.0	64.7	67.0	57.8	62.6	68.5	70.5
Employment rates (% of population 15 to 65 years)																
Employment overall	69.1	66.8	58.2	62.7	72.4	70.8	71.1	71.7	72.4	73.6	78.5	81.7	60.0	63.4	64.8	71.6
Agriculture	8.3	4.9	3.0	2.3	18.8	9.5	6.6	5.4	9.4	5.2	4.3	2.9	4.3	2.7	2.3	2.1
Industry	33.7	31.8	25.3	24.9	22.9	26.4	24.7	24.5	29.7	27.1	23.5	24.1	21.0	21.0	18.2	19.1
Manufacturing	26.0	24.5	n.a.	19.8	17.5	19.4	17.4	17.4	n.a.	20.2	17.5	17.9	16.0	15.7	12.8	13.2
Services	27.2	30.2	32.6	35.4	30.6	34.9	39.8	41.7	33.3	41.3	50.8	54.7	34.7	39.7	44.4	50.5
Other Indicators																
Labour force participation rate	69.6	67.5	63.6	67.4	73.3	71.7	73.0	73.3	73.6	75.5	81.3	82.8	63.6	66.6	71.7	75.6
Unemployment rate	0.7	1.0	8.4	7.0	1.3	1.3	2.6	2.3	1.7	2.5	3.5	1.3	5.7	4.9	9.6	5.3
Transfers/GDP (%)	14.4	17.1	21.3	20.4	n.a.	10.1	17.4	16.4	10.4	14.1	21.2	22.6	5.9	9.1	12.4	11.4
Taxes/GDP (%)	34.1	38.4	41.5	41.8	n.a.	21.3	27.1	30.2	32.2	41.0	50.7	56.7	27.0	29.3	27.9	29.2

Source: Appelbaum and Schettkat, 'Employment Developments in Industrialized Economies: Explaining Common and Diverging Trends', Discussion Paper FS I 93–313, Wissenschaftszentrum Berlin, Wirtschaftswandel und Beschäftigung.

We argue that the fundamental force behind the shift from full employment to unemployment is neither exogenous factors nor policy mistakes, but the endogenous development process itself. Our explanation rests on the fact that the price elasticity of demand for many consumer durables has declined over time as household wealth and the accumulation by households of these durable goods has grown. Our analytical model allows us to explain why the industrialized economies experienced a 'virtuous circle' of full employment and real income growth in the 1950s and 1960s, and why unemployment and low income growth have become problems in the 1980s. The core features of our model are the easily observable facts that productivity developments differ among industries and that the goods and services produced by these industries have different price and income elasticities of demand. These elasticities depend on levels of consumption previously achieved and on how large a quantity of each good or service is demanded at current prices, while current prices reflect productivity conditions in the various industries (for a more comprehensive description see Appelbaum and Schettkat, 1993).

In the discussion that follows, we show why productivity growth, employment, and income trends all developed so favourably after the Second World War. The theory we offer for these phenomena also explains why the highly industrialized economies no longer experience low unemployment. Furthermore, our model explains why employment rates (the employment to population ratio) in these economies have diverged since then.

We identify three distinct economic policy approaches to these employment problems that have been adopted by the industrialized economies:

- a low tax burden combined with other policies that allow high wage and income differentiation;
- active welfare state policies; and
- passive welfare state policies.

The US and Japan are examples of the first policy approach. Both countries experienced employment expansions in private services made possible by high wage and income differentiation and low tax burdens. In addition, the Japanese retained a high share of employment in manufacturing as a result of success in world markets, due in part to Japanese trade and industrial policies. Sweden provides an example of the second policy approach. Sweden experienced an expansion of employment in public services accompanied by low wage and income differentials, but also an increasing tax burden to finance public services. Finally, Germany and other continental European countries are examples of the third policy approach. These countries experienced employment stagnation, relatively narrow and unchanging wage differentials, a reduction in the employment to population ratio, and an increasing tax burden to finance income maintenance programmes.

After analysing employment developments over the last several decades, we conclude with a discussion of the principal policies which this analysis suggests can be effective in restoring full employment.

THE VIRTUOUS CIRCLE OF FULL EMPLOYMENT

The most important features of labour market trends in the industrialized economies up to the 1970s were low rates of unemployment, expanding employment in highly productive manufacturing industries, increasing incomes, and declining wage differentials. This virtuous circle of economic development, already apparent in the US in the 1940s, began in Europe in the 1950s. The positive correlation between productivity growth and employment expansion by industry provided the basis for the unprecedented growth in wealth of the industrialized capitalist economies.

Industries with high and rising productivity attracted labour by paying higher wages. Other industries followed and paid higher wages in order to compete for workers. Wage setting was mainly influenced by market forces. As is characteristic of a competitive labour market in full-employment equilibrium, wage differentials among industries tended to narrow and real wage growth by industry in each country tended to track the economy-wide increase in average productivity. As a result, wages grew slower than productivity in industries with above average productivity growth and faster than productivity in industries with below average productivity growth. Consistent with this, relative prices tended to fall in high-productivity growth industries and to rise in low-productivity growth industries.

With demand for goods and services price-elastic, markets for the output of industries with high and rising productivity tended to expand while markets for the output of industries with slow productivity growth tended to be stifled by the increase in relative prices. These developments are illustrated in Figure 12.1: productivity growth in sector 1 leads the demand for labour to expand in sector 1 and this leads the equilibrium wage to increase; employment in sector 2 – where productivity stagnates – declines. In the extreme, the demand for some services, such as railway porters or domestic servants, tended to be extinguished. At the high-productivity growth end of the spectrum, restrained wage growth allowed for an even quicker expansion of these industries. This process formed the basis for the famous Rehn–Meidner (or Swedish, see Meidner and Hedborg, 1984) model of industrial development, which was successful as long as employment in industries with more rapidly rising productivity expanded.

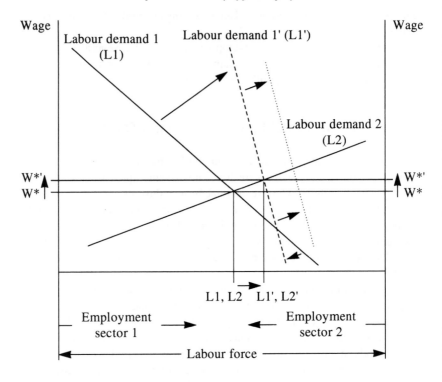

Figure 12.1   Price elasticity of demand for goods of sector 1 greater than 1

Industries with high and/or rising productivity were found mainly in manufacturing. Productivity increases and employment expansions were positively
correlated because three effects occurred simultaneously: (1) above average productivity increases allowed relative prices of manufactured goods to fall which,
because demand for manufactured goods was price-elastic, led to (2) an
expansion of demand for manufactured goods that more than compensated for
the labour-saving effects of productivity growth, and, because of the strength
of unions in this sector, led to (3) rising real incomes which were used to buy
the products of industries in this sector with high productivity gains. In Figure
12.1 this leads to a parallel shift of the labour demand function of sector 1. The
expansion of industries producing household durables became the hallmark of
this expansionary period. In this context, Keynesian demand management
policies, which pumped up income whenever private demand for goods and
services faltered, were highly successful. Rising income largely translated into
higher demand for manufactured goods, whose relative prices were falling, thus
reinforcing the endogenous growth process and obviating the need for more finely

tuned sectoral policies. Finally, productivity gains in this virtuous circle were driven by economies of scale as markets for mass-produced goods expanded. Thus, positive feedback effects from full employment and expanding markets in mass production industries led to further productivity gains and income growth as the scale of operations increased. In these circumstances, labour market effects of institutional differences among the industrialized countries were swept away by the market forces unleashed by a full-employment economy. This is confirmed by empirical analysis of the relationship between employment rates and institutions, which is not significant for the early 1970s but becomes quite significant by the 1980s (see Rowthorn, 1992).

THE END OF THE VIRTUOUS CIRCLE

In the 1970s and 1980s, diverging, labour market trends affecting employment to population ratios, unemployment rates, wage growth, and wage dispersion emerged in the industrialized countries. These diverging trends can be explained by institutional differences among these economies that shaped the responses to a new economic development common to all the countries: in contrast to the 1950s and 1960s, industries with high productivity growth experienced stagnant or even declining employment in absolute terms. That is, over the period since 1970, productivity growth in technologically progressive industries has led to a decreased demand for labour in these industries (as illustrated in Figure 12.2). It is industries with low productivity growth (sector 2 in Figure 12.2) that have experienced the most rapid employment growth. In countries with growing employment and a rising employment to population ratio, the employment of women in the service sector (which generally, though this is clearly an over-simplification, encompasses activities with lower and more slowly rising productivity) has expanded sufficiently to offset stagnant or declining employment in manufacturing. Countries which were not successful in shifting employment from higher-productivity goods-producing activities to lower productivity service activities experienced employment stagnation or only very small increases in employment, as can clearly be seen in the employment ratios shown in Table 12.1. This change in the relationship between productivity growth and employment growth marks a shift in the development of highly indus-trialized countries which is often, though imprecisely, described as the shift from an industrial society to a service economy. Now that employment growth depends on more rapid expansion of industries with lower productivity, insti-tutional features of the various countries have become important. Whereas the transition of labour from low-productivity, low-paying industries into high-pro-ductivity, high-paying industries is easily accomplished by market forces, it is difficult to imagine how market forces can manage the opposite shift.

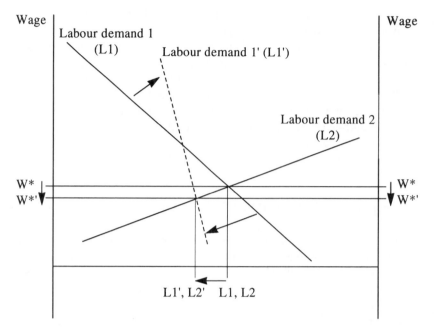

Figure 12.2   Price elasticity of demand for goods of sector 1 less than 1

At the heart of the change in the relationship between productivity growth
and employment growth is the change in the price elasticity of demand for
consumer durables from elastic to inelastic as most households in the industrialized economies have achieved ownership of these goods. While advances in
productivity in these industries still lead to reductions in relative prices, these
price reductions no longer lead to an expansion of the market for the products
sufficient to increase (or, in some cases, even to maintain) employment in the
relevant industries. According to OECD data for the G7 countries, manufacturing employment in the last two decades declined in absolute terms in Germany
and Italy, and as a share of total employment in all seven countries. The share
of the labour force employed in manufacturing declined by 17 percentage points
in Germany and Italy, by 10 percentage points in the US and by 6 percentage
points in the UK, France, and Canada. Even in Japan, manufacturing's share
of employment declined by 3 percentage points. Employment growth in these
countries, if it occurs at all, results from absorbing a growing proportion of the
population into employment in service activities.

Thus, such different countries as the US and Sweden have in common a high
share of employment in services and a high employment to population ratio.
These outcomes, however, are the result of completely different policies and

institutional settings. In the US the rapid employment expansion in low-productivity services was made possible by the expansion of marketed services which, in turn, was facilitated by high wage differentials. In Sweden, on the other hand, highly centralized and well organized labour unions successfully pushed for a solidaristic wage policy and low wage differentials, which did not allow private services to expand very much. Paying comparable wages to workers in both goods- and service-producing industries resulted in high relative prices for private services, which on price-elasticity grounds limited the market for these services. The Swedish solution to this difficulty through the 1980s was the absorption of a growing labour force through more rapid expansion of public services. As a consequence, the tax burden in Sweden rose tremendously, and this contributed in the most recent period to the decline of the Swedish model.

Both the US and Sweden successfully integrated an increasing part of their populations into the labour market, and in the US this was accomplished even though the population itself was growing. These countries represent respectively examples of employment expansion through wage differentiation and through active welfare state policies. A third pattern occurred in the continental European welfare states. Here, institutions such as social insurance and relatively low wage differentials limited the expansion of official employment in low-productivity activities. To reduce unemployment, these countries have undertaken deliberate policies intended to reduce the size of the labour force by encouraging early retirement and low female labour force participation rates. The result of these passive welfare state policies designed to maintain income via transfers while discouraging employment has been to increase the tax burden, albeit to a lesser extent than in Sweden. The low employment to population ratio, high tax burden, and high share of transfers in GDP shown in Table 12.1 confirm these results.

Even when the expansion of service employment occurs, however, it does not set a virtuous circle in motion. It is true that occupational segregation by gender has meant increased demand for women workers as service employment has expanded, and increased employment of women has led to the substitution of purchased services for the unpaid services of women in the home. But this has not generated positive feedback effects that contribute to rising productivity and rising wages. The reason is that, unlike most manufacturing industries, services that exhibit low productivity growth do not achieve economies of scale as their scale of operation increases. Hence an expanding market for these services does not translate, more or less automatically, into rising productivity.

Thus the old virtuous circle no longer operates. Deflationary policies have exacerbated the problems of employment and income growth, but expansionary fiscal and monetary policies are no longer sufficient to jump-start the economy and achieve acceptable income and employment outcomes. New approaches are necessary.

PRINCIPAL POLICIES PROMOTING EMPLOYMENT

Any theoretical model that represents the dynamics of economic development in a two-sector framework must miss many specifics of actual economic trends. Nevertheless, our simple model captures the main facts of economic development in the industrialized economies and suggests important conclusions for economic policy. Most important, our analysis makes clear that neither labour market regulation nor mistaken macroeconomic policies are the primary cause of 'de-industrialization' (the decline in the share of high-paying manufacturing jobs), or of employment problems generally. The root cause lies in the economic development process itself. In this light, the failed experiments with financial market deregulation and supply-side macroeconomic policies of the 1980s can be understood as misguided attempts to deal with problems that had resisted more conventional approaches in the 1970s. Current attacks on labour market regulations and social policy, should they succeed, will have no greater success in reviving manufacturing employment. Even policies to raise worker skills, improve manufacturing technology, and transform work systems in factories and mills – all of which are essential to raise living standards and to enable firms located in industrialized countries to remain players in markets for manufactured goods – will not reverse the decline in manufacturing's share of employment.

Manufacturing remains essential to the development of the industrialized economies. Even in the US, where manufacturing is a smaller share of both output and employment than it is in Sweden, Japan, or Germany, the US Department of Labour projects that real gross manufacturing output will increase from just over \$2.5 trillion in 1992 to \$3.5 trillion by 2005 (both measured in 1987 dollars). Manufacturing employment, meanwhile, which peaked in 1979 at 21 million, will continue to decline, falling from 18 to 17.5 million over the same time period (US Department of Labor, 1993). This change in the relationship between output and employment in manufacturing owes something to the deregulation of financial institutions and the increasing globalization of financial capital, and to the increase in imports from low-wage countries. Fundamentally, however, the decline in price and income elasticities of demand for manufactured goods in the wealthier nations means that the growth in demand for these goods in such countries has not kept pace with productivity gains. Manufacturing is important as the source of embodied technological change and for its ability to produce increasingly sophisticated goods, both of which are key to a nation's competitiveness. But the demand for manufactured goods no longer expands rapidly enough in the industrialized countries for output growth on this basis alone to lead to employment growth in this sector.

If there is to be an increase in employment sufficient to absorb a growing labour force and reduce unemployment, it will have to come in service sector industries. The key to higher wages and employment is a more rapid advance in productivity in services so that service production becomes more efficient and a wide range of services become relatively cheaper and more affordable. Rising productivity in service sector industries will lower the relative price of services, for which price and income elasticities are still high, and will greatly expand the market for these services and the number of service sector jobs. Unlike Taylorist mass production, which had limited applicability to services, the new high-performance work systems appear very promising in terms of their ability to increase productivity and reduce the cost of higher quality in service activities. It is by no means inevitable, of course, that changes in technology and work organization will occur, or that they will be translated into rising productivity and rising wages if they do. In the US the phenomenon of upskilling and downwaging is not unfamiliar in services, especially where women comprise a major part of the workforce. However, an increase in the bargaining power of workers in this sector, strengthened perhaps by the increasing unionization of women workers, will enable workers in this sector to share in the productivity gains via higher wages.

What policies, then, can succeed in promoting employment growth in the industrialized economies, and particularly the growth of high-wage jobs? Our analysis suggests that several principal policy approaches are available. Most promising are policies for raising living standards and developing markets in less industrialized economies where rising incomes can be expected to lead to a rapid increase in demand for manufactured goods; policies that promote product and process innovations in service activities where high relative prices stifle demand; policies that facilitate the development of new technologies to address articulated but unmet human needs (e.g., environmental technologies); and policies to expand public investment and collective consumption. We examine these policies below from the perspective of our model. We also examine the employment effects of high-wage dispersion, downward wage flexibility, and reductions in working time.

POLICIES TO RAISE LIVING STANDARDS

One way in which the immediate problems of saturated markets – markets in which increases in productivity lead to declines in employment – can be overcome and the demand for consumer durables and other manufactured goods can be increased is by raising the incomes of poorer households in the industrialized economies and of households in general in less developed countries. A 'Marshall' plan for Eastern Europe and Third World countries coordinated by the G7 nations, for example, will accelerate the expansion of world markets for goods produced by technologically progressive industries. Over the medium term, this may lead to increased employment in these sectors in the industrialized economies where much of the worldwide production capacity is presently located. Of course, world market share and jobs will depend on having a skilled workforce, modern facilities and work organization in consumer durable goods industries. Over longer time-periods, however, these industries will tend to locate in the developing countries, closer to the markets they are serving. At this point, it is hoped, other policies, which take time to have an effect on employment in the industrialized economies, may begin to show results.

In this context, trade policies to open world markets will raise employment and living standards in both high-wage and low-wage countries. Policies to reduce trade barriers have positive effects on employment in the trading partners, and are preferable to mercantilist policies that enable some countries to develop at the expense of others and only work in the absence of retaliatory actions by other countries to close markets.

PRODUCT AND PROCESS INNOVATIONS

Broad, basic innovations that lead to the development of a variety of new products and the creation of new markets around these products are another avenue for increasing employment in technologically progressive manufacturing activities. To achieve this requires policies that support the innovative activities of firms, and it may well be that individual firms or an industry within a particular country can capture the price-elastic demand for such new products. Then, further improvements in process technologies that raise productivity and reduce price will expand the market for this new cluster of goods and will expand employment in these new manufacturing sectors. Innovation policies are especially relevant in an open world market where countries compete on a global level.

To achieve a substantial employment impact in manufacturing, however, requires the development or application of a new basic technology, capable of creating a new Kondratieff cycle. Although it is difficult to imagine in advance which technologies can inititate such a cycle, the development of products that improve the environment may be such an area. Surveys in industrialized economies regularly show that a majority of the population cares about the environment and would like cleaner air and water and products that are environmentally friendly. More than innovation policy is required, however, for the development of environmental technologies. Since the environment is a public, rather than a private good, and it will be difficult to stimulate a market demand for environmental technologies, their development will rely either on public spending or on publicly mandated environmental standards for products.

In the latter case, environmental technologies will be incorporated into other marketed (private) goods (e.g. electric engines in cars). The demand for these technologies will be derived from the demand for products that will be consumed for other purposes, and thus may have limited employment-creating effects. These are enhanced, however, if environmental standards are set in a way that creates early obsolescence for privately consumed products (outlawing cars that do not meet rigorous emission standards), or if the public sector uses its procurement practices to create a market for such goods (requiring electric engines in cars purchased by a local municipality, for example).

While policies that support innovation have potentially important employment effects when breakthroughs that create clusters of innovations occur, innovations that are gradual improvements of existing products and/or substitutes for existing products will have only limited effects on employment. Japan and Germany may be regarded as countries that followed a policy of supporting innovations over the last two decades. But, as we observed earlier, both Germany and Japan, although very successful in world markets, did not experience employment growth in manufacturing industries in relation to the labour force, and manufacturing employment in Germany declined in absolute terms. In large part this resulted from the loss of employment in technologically progressive industries producing mature products for which demand in the industrialized economies is inelastic. This job loss accelerated as competition from the newly industrialized economies increased.

Thus, while it is important for the industrialized economies to follow policies that support product innovation, short of a new Kondratieff cycle such policies are not likely to be sufficient to expand employment in manufacturing. The discussion of ever shorter product cycles, translated into our framework, means that products move quickly from the price-elastic to the price-inelastic part of the demand curve. The computer industry, which is currently undergoing a severe shake-out, may be taken as an example of rapid market saturation, movements to price-inelastic demand, and continuous product innovations.

Process innovations, both the development of new machinery and the reorganization of work to achieve continuous improvements in efficiency and quality, have much the same limited expansionary effect on manufacturing employment. Such policies are necessary for manufacturing companies to maintain market share, but are not sufficient to increase employment in industries on the price-inelastic part of the demand curve. Failure to achieve continuous improvements in efficiency and quality is likely to prove disastrous for employment, however, as domestic producers would lose markets to competitors who had achieved such gains.

The exception are industries manufacturing goods for which demand is price-elastic, where improvements in efficiency that translate into price reductions do lead to an expansion of the market and of employment. Thus industries in which companies are innovative with respect to product technologies, process technologies, work organizations and corporate structure can experience significant growth in employment.

It is unfortunate that policies oriented toward improving production processes are focused on manufacturing, for it is in the production of services that the drop in relative prices that accompany productivity gains can be expected to expand the market and increase employment. As we observed earlier, the demand for services is highly price- (as well as income-)elastic – that is, demand is unsaturated and is very responsive to decreases in the relative price of services. As a result, productivity increases in these industries will lead to an expansion of demand and employment. The potential for productivity improvements in this sector is quite good. In contrast to old-fashioned factory automation, the new kinds of work organization and information technologies utilized in the production and delivery of goods in high-performance work systems appear to have wide applicability in many service industries. In the US, for example, purchases of computers and information equipment have been rising steadily for the last ten years. Purchases of this equipment now accounts for more than a third of all producers' durable equipment purchases. Computers, which were less than 1 per cent of the stock of equipment in both manufacturing and non-manufacturing industries in 1979, now account for nearly 5 per cent of equipment in manufacturing and nearly 7 per cent in non-manufacturing industries (US Department of Labor, 1993). In addition, the first steps towards transforming organizations into high-performance work systems, which began a decade ago in some manufacturing companies, have now begun to be taken in service firms. Despite the fact that many person-oriented services do not lend themselves easily to improvements in efficiency and have in the past registered stagnant productivity, the combination of microprocessor-based technologies and new work systems have begun to raise productivity in some service activities. Installation and repair services, information gathering and reporting services, accounting and design services, software development services, among others, have registered substantial performance gains as a result of work reorganization and process improvements. Evidence is accumulating that even in such diverse person-oriented services as hospitals and hotels reorganization of the delivery of client services can raise quality and cut costs.

The lesson from an earlier period of experience with manufacturing is that raising productivity in marketed services, and sharing the performance gains among workers, firms and consumers, is a promising way to raise wages and living standards while extending the market for such services and increasing employment. In the public sector, such efficiency gains reduce the tax burden associated with a given level of service.

PUBLIC INVESTMENT AND COLLECTIVE CONSUMPTION

Public investment affects demand and employment through several channels. It directly increases demand for manufactured goods and employment in manufacturing. The ability of domestic producers to capture this increase in demand, however, depends on (a) how competitive these firms are in world markets, and (b) whether government procurement favours domestic content. Public investment is likely to enhance productivity in domestic private sector industries. If higher productivity is passed along to consumers in the form of lower prices, this will expand the market for these goods. Employment effects will largely depend, however, on whether demand in the affected industries is price-elastic or price-inelastic – with favourable results if demand is elastic and unfavourable employment effects otherwise. The implication is that the indirect employment effects of public investment are likely to be largest if public investment spurs the development of new products or if it enhances productivity in stagnant but price-elastic service activities.

Public spending on services can also increase employment. If the hierarchy of needs hypothesis holds, we can anticipate a further shift of expenditures to services. Clearly there is a widely accepted need for more service provision in the industrialized economies, as indicated by the discussions of health services in the US and nursing care insurance in Germany. These person-oriented services, however, have been characterized by low productivity growth and, especially in the cases of long-term patient-care and child-care services, it is difficult to imagine that this will change. Given low productivity and low productivity gains in person-oriented services, employment expansion in these industries can occur in only two ways: relative wage reductions that keep the relative price of these services low, and public provision of these services (Scharpf, 1990). If wages in low-productivity growth, marketed activities rise in concert with those in high-productivity growth activities, the relative price of these activities will rise and demand for them decrease. This is sometimes referred to as 'the cost disease of stagnant services'.

Of course, if services are provided publicly or are publicly subsidized, then, in principle, a wage comparable to wages in technologically progressive industries can be paid without stifling demand. Day care provides a good example. If day-care providers are expected to have appropriate training in early childhood education and are compensated accordingly, very few households will be able to afford private day-care services. Public day-care facilities that operate like the public schools, however, can meet the need for day care while paying salaries comparable to those paid to other workers with similar education and training. But public services are financed through the tax system. Rising wages in public sector jobs will increase taxes if, like day care, these services are technologically stagnant. This is more easily accomplished when real wages in the whole economy are rising, but is burdensome for large numbers of taxpayers when real wages are stagnant or even declining. In addition, since public sector jobs are not mobile and jobs in the private sector tend to be footloose, the incentives for wage restraint are greater in the private sector. This may, as in Sweden, lead to relative increases in wages of public sector employees relative to those in the private sector, and may fuel a tax revolt. Finally, public provision or subsidies of services may create inefficiencies. These may not be larger than those of private sector firms, but there is no market to provide discipline or a correction, and the question of an effective public sector must be addressed directly in any programme for increasing public services.

WAGE DISPERSION

Alternatively, a wide wage dispersion can sustain the expansion of low-wage service jobs so long as there is a ready supply of workers to fill these jobs. In practice, this has meant the absence of a social safety net and the existence of discriminatory practices that limit the access of large numbers of women, minority group members, and immigrants to the high-wage sector. If the supply of labour to these low-wage jobs can be maintained, low wages in these services stave off the 'cost disease' while high wages in other occupations mean that there are people with sufficient discretionary income to purchase these services. However, should the supply of low-wage workers falter and demand for the services begin to outpace supply, wages will begin to rise. Then the resulting change in relative prices will tend to extinguish market demand tor these services as they become relatively more expensive, and to encourage the substitution of self-service activities. The demand for services is highly price-elastic, and increases in price have a strong effect on quantities.

A policy that replaces wage increases with public subsidies of low-wage workers through an earned income tax credit or other negative income tax scheme in order to maintain wage dispersion and relative price differentials can maintain low-wage employment, but only in certain industries. High-wage differentials create an incentive and a selection problem because workers are not willing to invest in training for low-paying jobs. In order to avoid negative selection in areas where skills are important, as in health care services or education, wages in these industries need to be not too different from wages in jobs in technologically progressive sectors with comparable skill levels. Given this dilemma for skilled services, the low-wage strategy seems to be limited to less skilled services. While a negative income tax may solve the price/wage problem of certain service industries, it will not solve the incentive problem for investment in human capital. Wide wage dispersion reduces the willingness of workers to invest in education and training, and leads to socially suboptimal levels of such investments.

DOWNWARD FLEXIBILITY OF WAGES

While downward wage flexibility would allow manufacturing firms that are on the price-inelastic part of the demand function to expand demand for their goods and would, in this way, preserve some jobs, the quantitative effect will be small. This is because price-inelastic demand leads quantities to react only mildly to price reductions subsequent to wage reductions. In any case, the employment effects of a decline in wages would be short-lived and would be wiped out by future increases in productivity. Firms will not be able to slow technological progress, and technological progress in industries on the price-inelastic part of the demand curve leads to reductions in employment even as prices fall and quantities of output produced increase. Moreover, a deliberate slowdown in productivity growth would damage a firm's competitive position in terms of price and, most likely, also in quality terms since product and process innovations are usually closely linked.

In fact, the wage restraint associated with less flexible wages may have a stronger positive effect on employment in firms and industries on the price-elastic part of the product demand curve. Here, wage restraint – in which wages rise more slowly than productivity growth – produces strong quantitative effects. According to a study of the impact of upward and downward wage flexibility in the US, wage restraint at the progressive end would have created more jobs in the 1970s than downward wage flexibility at the lower end was able to preserve (Bell and Freeman, 1985). The employment-creation potential of wage restraint policies (i.e. *less* flexible wages) is unevenly distributed. It is highest in firms at the price-elastic part of their product demand curves and it is low in firms at the price-inelastic part of their demand curves. However, a policy of wage restraint and too narrow wage differentials may also create microeconomic inefficiencies due to motivational problems (Freeman and Gibbons, 1993, Ramaswamy and Rowthorn, 1993).

REDUCTIONS IN WORKING TIME

Finally, if productivity increases in the technologically progressive sector are used to reduce average annual hours of work, rather than to increase wages, the effect may be to preserve employment in this sector. That is, the decline in weekly or annual hours of work can offset the labour-saving effect of productivity increases in this sector, at least until the next round of productivity increases. If, however, hours of work fall more rapidly than productivity, which would almost certainly be the case in the technologically stagnant sector and could occur in particular industries in the technologically progressive sector as well, then costs will rise, pushing up prices in the private sector and taxes in the public sector, and reducing aggregate hours of work and, perhaps, employment. This effect on costs and aggregate hours will be even more pronounced if wages rise with the reduction in working time.

Recent proposals for reductions in working time have focused on shorter hours as a technique for sharing income, rather than increasing the number of jobs. These plans increase employment by having workers share jobs, with each participating worker working less than full-time hours and earning less than full-time pay. The success of such plans depends on whether production in particular industries and occupations lends itself to job sharing, and whether workers are willing and able to take significant cuts in pay.

CONCLUSION

The problems of joblessness and/or stagnating or declining real wages that have persisted since the early 1970s in the industrialized economies have been viewed by economists and policy makers as something of a mystery. Long lists of complicating factors and special circumstances have been compiled to explain high unemployment in one country, slow growth in another, and severe wage competition in still another. But the fundamental forces at work have gone unrecognized, and serious attempts by political leaders to understand and address these problems have been lacking. Instead, workers have been counselled that they must 'adjust' to market forces beyond their control, must seek more training, and must wait patiently for recovery. Public policy interventions are seen as futile, or even counterproductive.

It should be evident by now that the employment problems of the industrialized world are not those of an ordinary business cycle. Our analysis of employment developments over the last two decades makes clear the common source of these problems, situates them in the development process itself, and points to a set of policies that can address them. This analysis challenges both the conventional views: on the one hand, that more austerity and less government will restore full employment and rising real wages; on the other, that traditional Keynesian pump-priming policies will do the trick. Reversing tight macroeconomic policies would go far towards eliminating 'unnecessary unemployment,' but would not bring the unemployment rate back under 4 per cent. Our optimistic conclusion is that the jobs problem, while difficult, is not intractable, and that the unemployment rate can again be driven down to its historic lows. What is required are policies that treat the systemic nature of these problems, and not merely their myriad symptoms.

REFERENCES

Appelbaum, E. and Schettkat, R. (1993), 'Employment Developments in Industrialized Economies: Explaining Common and Diverging Trends', Discussion Paper FS I 93–313, Wissenschaftszentrum Berlin für Sozialforschung.

Bell, L.A. and Freeman, R.B. (1985), 'Does a Flexible Wage Structure Increase Employment?: The U.S. Experience', NBER Working Paper no. 1604, Cambridge, Mass: National Bureau of Economic Research.

Carey, M.L. and Franklin, J.C. (1991), 'Industry output, job growth slowdown continues', *Monthly Labor Review*, vol. 114, November, pp. 45–63.

Franklin, J.C. (1993), 'Industry output and employment', *Monthly Labor Review*, vol. 116, November, pp. 41–57.

Freeman, R.B. and Gibbons, R. (1993), 'Getting Together and Breaking Apart: the decline of centralised collective bargaining. With special reference to Sweden', paper presented at the conference on Labour Contracts and Mobility, European University Institute, Florence.

Meidner, R. and Hedborg, A. (1984), *Modell Schweden. Erfahrungen einer Wohlfahrtsgesellschaft*, Frankfurt/New York: Campus.

Ramaswamy, R. and Rowthorn, B. (1993), 'Centralized Bargaining, Efficiency Wages, and Flexibility', IMF Working Paper, WP/93/25.

Rowthorn, B. (1992), 'Centralisation, employment and wage dispersion', *The Economic Journal*, vol. 102, May, pp. 506–523.

Scharpf, F.W. (1990), 'Structures of Post-Industrial Society – or – Does Mass Unemployment Disappear in the Service and Information Economy?' in E. Appelbaum, and R. Schettkat (eds), *Labor Market Adjustments to Structural Change and Technological Progress*, New York, Westport, London: Praeger Publishers, pp. 17–35.

Solow, R. (1994), 'Europe's unnecessary unemployment', *International Economic Insights*, March/April, pp. 10–11.

US Department of Labor, Bureau of Economic Analysis (1993), *Survey of Current Business*, August 1993, Table 5.8, p. 84.

13. European monetary integration and unemployment in the periphery

Keith Bain

The purpose of this chapter is to consider the impact on unemployment in peripheral regions/countries of economic and monetary integration in Europe, looking in particular at the possibilities for and desirability of institutional change. Our concern focuses on three areas: the attempt of peripheral countries to achieve the convergence conditions set down in the Treaty on European Union for membership of European Monetary Union; the impact of a single European monetary policy after EMU; and the possibility of financial fragility in peripheral countries as a result of economic and monetary integration.

Table 13.1   Per capita income in the EU (EU = 100)

Country	1960	1970	1975	1980	1985	1990	1991	1992
Belgium	95.4	98.9	103.1	104.1	101.6	102.6	103.8	103.4
Denmark	118.3	115.2	110.5	107.8	115.8	108.2	110.0	110.2
Germany	117.9	113.2	109.9	113.6	114.2	112.8	114.2	113.6
Greece	38.6	51.6	57.3	58.1	56.7	52.6	52.5	52.1
Spain	60.3	74.7	81.9	74.2	72.5	77.8	79.0	79.9
France	105.8	110.4	111.8	111.6	110.6	108.6	108.7	108.8
Ireland	60.8	59.5	62.7	64.0	65.2	69.0	68.9	68.9
Italy	85.5	95.4	94.6	102.5	103.1	103.1	103.1	103.2
Luxembourg	158.5	141.4	128.7	118.5	122.4	125.6	127.8	130.0
Netherlands	118.6	115.8	115.5	110.9	107.0	103.1	103.9	102.7
Portugal	38.7	48.9	52.2	55.0	52.0	55.7	56.3	56.3
UK	128.6	108.5	105.9	101.1	104.2	105.1	102.1	102.1

Source: Eurostat

First, however, we must specify what is meant by the term 'periphery'. The simplest approach is to make a distinction between 'core' and 'periphery' at national level, based on per capita income. In 1992 (as is shown in Table 13.l), four of the existing 12 members of the European Union qualified as peripheral on this basis since they had per capita incomes which were 80 per cent or lower of the European Union average – Spain 79.9; Ireland 68.9; Portugal 56.3; and Greece 52.1. There is a clear division between these countries and the group whose per capita incomes are around the European average.

However, within countries which do not as a whole qualify as peripheral there are regions which have per capita incomes sufficiently low as to be clearly part of the periphery. Although the most obvious example is Southern Italy, it seems reasonable to include as peripheral all regions within the EU which qualify for regional assistance under European Union rules.[1]

MEETING THE CONDITIONS FOR MEMBERSHIP OF EMU

As planned at Maastricht, member states will be able to participate in EMU if they meet four criteria of convergence:

- a high degree of price stability close to that of the three best-performing member states as regards inflation;
- a sustainable government financial position without an excessive budgetary deficit, defined as a maximum of 3 per cent for the ratio of the planned or actual government deficit to GDP at market prices, and a maximum of 60 per cent for the ratio of government debt to GDP at market prices;
- observance of the normal fluctuation margins provided for by the ERM for at least two years without any devaluation among the member state currencies; and
- the reflection of the durability of convergence in long-term interest rate levels, defined as a divergence not exceeding two percentage points from the nominal long-term government bond rates of the three best-performing member states as regards price stability.

The agreement does not, however, require that all conditions be fully enforced. The maximum government debt to GDP and budget deficit to GDP ratios are both described only as 'reference values' and countries may be able to join as long as their government deficits have not been censured by the European Council. Thus a realistic assumption would be that all countries allowed into the monetary union will have achieved the inflation, interest rate and exchange rate targets and have either achieved the budget deficit and public debt targets or have been judged to be moving sufficiently rapidly in the 'right' direction in terms of them.

However stringently the conditions are enforced, the peripheral countries must find themselves in one of two positions: either one-speed Europe – they have succeeded in meeting the convergence requirements and are members of the monetary union; or two-speed Europe – they have not done so and find themselves within the European Union but outside the monetary union. Let us take each of these in turn.

The Implications of the Convergence Conditions for a 'One-speed Europe'

We now consider what will be required in terms of economic policy if the peripheral countries are to meet the convergence conditions.

The exchange rate condition
To avoid devaluations in the run-up to EMU, countries will need to remove expectations of exchange rate depreciations and to do this will need to avoid current account deficits. Slower growth than the average of EU countries will be needed to reduce imports to meet this condition. The very least one can say is that the relative unemployment position of the peripheral countries is likely to worsen. As Ranci (1990), among others, has pointed out, even slow growth rates may not ensure an improving balance of payments. If cumulative chains are strong relative to neo-classical adjustment effects, current account performance may worsen. The response of conventional economists is to assume that private capital flows will then move in the correct direction and provide the basis for industrial development in low-income areas – a very suspect proposition which is discussed below.

The inflation rate condition
The ability of the peripheral countries to reduce inflation rates without experiencing high costs in increased unemployment depends on the strength of the credibility effect. On the assumptions that inflation is purely a financial phenomenon; and that workers believe both that the rate of inflation is determined by the rate of growth of the money supply *and* that the government has full control over that rate, the government's 'anti-inflationary' credibility becomes the principal factor in determining the future inflation rate.

The one practical problem with this argument is that there is an observable relationship between levels of employment (a real variable) and the rate of inflation, and that this relationship varies from one country to another. The response of modern economists is to acknowledge the role of labour market institutions in this relationship but then to argue that such institutions are only what they are in different countries because of different degrees of 'anti-inflationary credibility' of their governments! It follows logically enough that if previously high-inflation countries can produce low inflation in a manner which causes workers to believe that low inflation will become the norm in future, then labour institutions will change and all will be well. The unemployment–inflation rate relationship is argued to be a product of the low credibility of past governments. Thus, the nature of institutions is the result of a self-justifying belief and is subject to rapid change. For a clear statement of this view, which is discussed in greater detail below, see, for instance, Barrell (1992, p. 32).

However, all these propositions can be challenged and an entirely different view of the formation of institutions can be constructed which may help to explain institutional differences among countries rather more convincingly than through the anti-inflationary credibility of governments. Credibility failed to work effectively to bring down inflation at low cost in the period of EMS exchange rate stability in the late 1980s and early 1990s and there is little reason to believe that it will be of great help to peripheral countries in the future. Rather, convergence on low inflation in the EU will require strongly deflationary policies on the part of peripheral country governments.

Fiscal conditions

For peripheral countries to produce the primary budget surpluses required even to go close to meeting the Maastricht fiscal targets, large and rapid reductions in government expenditure will be needed. This is because the relatively narrow tax bases in these countries will make it difficult for them to raise tax revenues by a significant amount. The position will have been made more difficult by the gradual loss of seigniorage during the process of inflation rate convergence. With EMU, loss of revenue from seigniorage will again fall disproportionately heavily on peripheral economies. Seigniorage will accrue in the first instance to the European central bank. Although the bank's profits will be allocated in proportion to each national central bank's ownership of the ECB, this does not reflect the current division of seigniorage among EMS member countries. The peripheral economies tend both to be more cash-intensive and to maintain higher compulsory deposits by commercial banks. On both counts they will lose out.

The impact of the large cuts in government expenditure will ensure that the monetary union will start with a much greater unevenness in rates of unemployment across the member states than exists even at present. The absolute levels of unemployment will, naturally, depend on a variety of other factors which are difficult to forecast, including rates of growth of the US economy in the years leading up to the single currency; the nature of fiscal and monetary policy within the core EU countries and hence whether or not interest rate and inflation rate convergence have been on low inflation/high interest rates or the reverse;[3] any increases in overall rates of growth consequent upon the development of the single market; and the relationship between the EU as a whole and other countries resulting from the single market, the Uruguay round and developments in Eastern Europe. Even taking an optimistic view of these factors, it seems hard to believe that the peripheral countries will enter monetary union with anything other than historically very high unemployment rates. The unevenness of unemployment rates across countries immediately raises doubts as to how genuinely the term 'one-speed Europe' describes this set of possibilities.

Regional Problems in a 'One-speed Europe'

Formal balance of payments problems will disappear with the elimination of national currencies but these will be replaced by the extension of regional problems. The relatively low labour mobility despite the single market will ensure that the severe unevenness in unemployment rates across the union will remain for a considerable period at least. The absence of a unified fiscal policy with its associated automatic transfers from high employment to high unemployment areas removes another of the props of depressed regions within single countries. Further, the requirement of continuing low budget deficits in all member countries and the 'no bail-out' clause written into the ECB's constitution will reduce the ability of individual governments to boost employment through fiscal measures. The peripheral countries are fighting hard for sharp increases in transfer payments within the EU budget but core country acceptance of the need for such transfers is at best reluctant and it is difficult to imagine that the extent of these transfers will go close to matching those which would automatically occur within a unified federal budget.[4]

This all means that the solution of the regional problem will rest very largely on the movement of private sector capital towards countries/regions of high unemployment. We look now at the prospect for equalizing capital flows within the union.

The usual argument is that with freely mobile capital, and with the absence of exchange rate risk within the union removing one factor which would otherwise inhibit the flow of capital from core to periphery, capital will flow in the correct direction because of the lower wage rates in the periphery. These wage differentials, it is claimed, will be preserved by the downward pressure on wages in peripheral countries from high unemployment coupled with the tight EU-wide monetary policy.

However, the concept of low money wages as an attraction to capital ignores productivity differences among regions. Low labour productivity in economically backward regions may have resulted in the first place from a lack of capital and been aggravated by the hysteresis effects of high and prolonged unemployment. What is more, national collective bargaining has, in many cases, led to productivity differences among regions being greater than money wage differences, resulting in real costs per unit of output being greater in the less developed regions. This may well be one factor accounting for a tendency for the convergence of national economies within Europe to be greater in GDP per capita terms than the convergence among regions within countries.

Further, any cost advantages for firms investing in the periphery will be offset, at least to some extent, by the application of the common European policy on working hours and employment conditions. This probably explains the strong desire by the core countries for such a policy (and the hostility towards the UK for opting out of it) rather than any enlightened desire to protect the workers in peripheral countries. Overall, much depends on the balance between low costs on the one hand and low productivity aggravated by the hysteresis effects of high and prolonged unemployment on the other. In any case, industries for which wage costs are the most important element in the location decision now have an alternative within Europe in the form of Eastern Europe.

As well as a serious doubt about the prospect of capital moving in search of low wages within the EU, there are a number of other arguments suggesting that capital is more likely to flow from periphery to core than in the reverse direction.

First, prospective gains from the single European market seem likely to depend heavily upon the utilization of economies of scale. This will almost certainly involve rationalization of production and, during periods of rationalization, it is often large and relatively dated production units that tend to be the first to close. These are typically located in peripheral regions. Further, the decreasing reliance of manufacturing industry on natural materials has led to increased emphasis on the proximity of production units to final markets. Thus, it is suggested that there is an inevitable tendency for concentration to occur in core regions which both guarantee proximity to markets and immediate access to a range of supporting services. Footloose production and distribution units may also be drawn towards central areas. This will be reinforced by the typically less adequate infrastructure of peripheral regions.

Second, the progress towards the single European market may also produce job losses in peripheral countries from the closure of customs offices and, more important, from the attempt to enforce competition rules within the EU, both by opening up public procurement procedures and by forcing governments to reduce subsidies to local firms. Awarding government contracts to domestic firms has long been a hidden form of protection used to assist areas of high unemployment. Again, under EC competition rules, increasing pressure is being placed on peripheral countries to reduce subsidies to domestic industries. The rationalization forced upon these industries often occurs at the expense of the low per capita regions within the country.

A consideration of regional problems within EU countries provides little confidence in the proposition that private capital will flow principally from core to periphery after monetary union. If it does not, the notional balance of payments imbalances will be adjusted by income changes. Inequalities across countries will remain and, indeed, grow. Many regional problems are the product of political and social forces over long periods every bit as much as of economic factors. Thus there is no reason to believe that the economic relationship between, say, Germany and Northern Italy has any similarity to that between Northern and Southern Italy. This, however, merely opens up the prospect of the high-income regions of core and peripheral states converging in real terms to some extent at the expense of the sharp exacerbation of existing regional problems within member states.

In any case, capital flows in Europe since the full removal of restrictions upon them provide little comfort. The issue is clouded by the continued existence of foreign exchange risk within the EMS and by speculative flows associated with the uncertainties which have plagued the ERM but it is not possible to reject the Kaldor–Myrdal model (Myrdal, 1957; Kaldor, 1970, 1972) of cumulative causation with its bleak, long-run message for peripheral countries. This analysis is supported by the growth-pole and post-Fordist models, the financial implications of which are considered in Arestis and Palaginis (1993).[5]

This leaves us to examine the likely destination within the union of capital flows from outside the union. There have, in recent years, been significant absolute flows into perceived low-cost areas[6] of the union, notably in the form of Japanese direct investment. While this appears to offer some hope to the periphery, only a very small proportion of total flows of foreign direct investment into the EU has been into the peripheral countries. If anything, foreign direct investment has acted to widen the gap between core and periphery within the EU.

In any case, a good deal of recent foreign direct investment into the EC has been prompted by the single market process and the fear of 'fortress Europe'. The likelihood that this will continue depends on European and world trade developments and the extent to which profits from the investments are retained within Europe for further expansion. This will depend, in turn, on the ability of foreign firms to increase market share within Europe and on the rate of growth of the European economy. Given the attractions for European capital of rapidly growing markets elsewhere in the world economy, it is difficult to count on large and prolonged net inflows of long-term capital into Europe to act as the saviour of the European periphery. Further, the destination of capital inflow has been influenced by both the existence of pools of only recently unemployed skilled labour and the willingness of individual nation states to provide incentives of one form or another to the foreign companies (and these may be threatened by the demands of increased fiscal stringency). Recent experience, in other words, has often been the product of a number of particular local circumstances which may not be repeated.

The message, then, appears to be that a one-speed Europe is not a possibility on the assumption of a monetary policy conducted by an independent central bank operating conventionally to achieve low rates of inflation across the whole union. The notion that a monetary union involving all EU members would be a 'one-speed Europe' rests heavily on the assumption that real inequalities result from institutional inadequacies in peripheral countries – notably in wage-setting mechanisms in labour markets and in relative inefficiencies in public sectors and that monetary convergence would force institutional change.

In the case of the public sector, some faith has been placed in the privatization process as a means both of bringing about public sector deficit reductions and of increasing efficiency in the economy as a whole. However, although there has been an independent political motivation for undertaking privatization in some countries (most obviously the UK), in many cases the strength behind privatization programmes has increased sharply because it has been seen as a way of helping to achieve the Maastricht convergence targets. Thus it remains that much of the institutional change seen to be necessary to reduce real inequalities among members (or, at least, to prevent them from increasing) is seen as a planned by-product of the drive towards monetary convergence.

There are, however, three obvious areas of doubt. The first is whether large-scale institutional changes will indeed occur. It is possible to point to many examples of change within European labour markets including reduced membership of trade unions, increases in self-employment and in the number of part-time jobs and changes in wage agreements (such as the ending of the *scala mobile* in Italy). Yet these changes have so far occurred to a lesser extent in the peripheral countries. Further, it is not easy to establish whether the changes which have occurred would have done so in any case as a result of long-term changes in industrial structure or long and deep recessions. In either of these cases, future institutional developments are hard to predict. Again, the movement towards privatization, while probably continuing to gain strength in most economies, has so far been very uneven across countries.

The second doubt concerns the desirability of institutional change of the kind envisaged by free-market economists. Some changes may serve to provide the tighter links between pay and productivity increases which are regularly prescribed for higher-inflation economies. They largely work, however, through a change in the balance of power between employers and employees which carries with it a general worsening of the conditions of employment and a reduction in safety standards at work. The impact of such changes on worker morale and on longer-run labour productivity is, however, by no means clear. In any case, as we have already noted, the main impact within the EU would be a worsening of working conditions within core countries and much of this conflicts with the terms of the social chapter of the Maastricht agreement.

The final doubt relates to attempts to force the speed of institutional change. With the exception of changes brought about by cataclysmic events such as world wars, institutional change is the product of a complex of social, political and economic forces. The attempt by economists to raise inflation not only to the top of the economic policy agenda but also to the head of the list of social and political concerns, and thence to wish to bring about as quickly as possible any institutional change which appears to help in its defeat may reflect an ahistorical short-termism which fails to give sufficient attention to the relationship between economic growth and institutional change. But this may be both simplistic and circular! For many modern economists, 'credibility' has become a *passe-partout*, yet another way for us to avoid the complications posed by history and institutions.

TWO-SPEED EUROPE

We turn next to the case of a limited monetary union which excludes the peripheral EU countries. The implication of this would be that there had been inadequate convergence in relation to inflation and/or interest rates, the exchange rate had not maintained its central parity within the ERM over a prolonged period, or (most likely) targets for the budget deficit and/or public debt had not been achieved. The exact position of the peripheral countries would depend on how hard they had tried to meet the Maastricht terms. One possibility is that the country had not been willing to accept the necessary unemployment levels. In this case, the short-term position of the real economy could be reasonably strong, although long-term adjustments necessary to bring about competitiveness within a single currency system may merely have been postponed.

A second possibility is that the country had shown itself willing to undergo the 'necessary' pain but that the wage-setting and other institutions of the economy had not reformed despite the economic pressure to do so. Then, the economy would have been subjected to tight monetary and fiscal policies, unemployment would be high but inflation would not have been squeezed out of the system, and the country would remain uncompetitive in the absence of exchange rate adjustments. This would clearly be the worst case.

In both cases, however, exchange rate risk would remain and interest rates would include a risk premium to allow for this. Despite the risk premium, there would be a strong presumption that core country capital would flow largely within the core. The peripheral countries, still needing to adjust their balance of payments, would have to do so on current account and thus would need to cut domestic demand. Even the relative health of the real economy in the first of these two cases could not be sustained. High unemployment and the low level of capital inflow would damage confidence in the economy. Domestic capital may well flow towards the lower nominal, but seemingly more secure, rates of return in the core countries. Foreign capital would also more likely flow towards the core.

There would seem to be little prospect that, having failed to achieve the necessary conditions for membership of the monetary union at the first attempt, success would follow later. The possibility of later success is likely to be diminished further by developments in financial markets. Consider the position during the present period in which single market rules are having their effects on financial markets and institutions but prior to convergence and monetary union or during the period following the formation of a limited monetary union which 'temporarily' excludes the peripheral countries.

We assume here, following Arestis and Palaginis (1993), that banking sectors in the periphery are less developed than in the core, being at stage four of Chick's (1986) six stages of banking development.[7] We further assume that the ability of peripheral country commercial banks to compete in an integrated financial area is damaged by the implicit taxes resulting from the forced financing of large budget deficits (through having to meet higher reserve requirements and/or to hold a proportion of liabilities in the form of Treasury Bills).

Two consequences are possible. One is that the relatively low profits of peripheral country banks discourage the restructuring of the European banking system (Grilli, 1989a, 1989b) and the banking systems of these countries remain relatively underdeveloped with many banks continuing to be essentially regional. This would deny to peripheral countries efficiency gains which are meant to accrue as a result of the integrated financial market and would accentuate the already existing differences between core and peripheral countries. It may also increase the financial fragility of the peripheral countries since, if the EU is subject to asymmetric shocks, banks with a narrow base in a peripheral country will be more at risk because of their inability to diversify.

The second possible consequence (Gibson and Tsakalotos, 1993) is that restructuring of the banking sector nonetheless occurs, with core country banks taking over banks within the periphery. This may have a variety of consequences for the periphery, including the reduction of specialist regional advice and service within the periphery as the 'over-branched' peripheral banks are slimmed down in search of efficiency gains and better profit performance. The accompanying centralization of bank administration and decision making may also lead to a large reduction in available knowledge of the riskiness of potential borrowers. As we shall see below, this may further increase a tendency towards financial fragility. Alternatively, it may produce credit rationing, making it more difficult for small entrepreneurs to obtain funds for investment.

In either case, banking developments consequent upon the single market would appear likely to hinder the movement of peripheral countries into monetary union.

FINANCIAL FRAGILITY WITHIN THE EU

The concentration on the monetary policy role of the European central bank has gone together with the failure even to begin to give adequate consideration to other important central bank issues.

The most important of these is the need to police the entire banking system to minimize the potential for increased financial fragility with the possibility of financial crises which may severely damage the real economy. We have already referred to this scenario in the periphery consequent on asymmetric shocks. We can add to that the argument that a uniform tight monetary policy applied across the EU via reserve stringency is very likely to have asymmetric effects so that banking sectors are unevenly developed. Thus the European central bank itself may be responsible for increasing the financial fragility of the periphery and fail to appreciate the unequal impacts of a single monetary policy.

There is, however, a quite separate argument concerning the potential for financial fragility within the integrated European financial area. This arises from the increase of competition in the periphery and the inadequacies of the Second Banking Directive of 1992 and the Basle Capital Adequacy Agreement of 1988 (Gibson and Tsakalotos, 1993). This has as its starting-point Stiglitz and Weiss's (1981) model of credit rationing in a world with market imperfections. Here, risk-averse banks seek higher rates of interest on risky loans but lack the ability to identify perfectly the riskiness of borrowers. They realize that at some point higher interest rates will lead to a fall in expected returns through adverse selection and a tendency for the overall riskiness of projects they finance to rise as interest rates rise. Thus they engage in credit rationing.

Gibson and Tsakalotos, however, point to several cases where banks have not behaved in this way. They argue, rather, that in a competitive environment the concern of banks with their shares of the market in their traditional areas of business, combined with their wish to enter new areas in order to keep up with competitors, leads to declining risk premia, a reduced dispersion of risk premia between high-risk and low-risk borrowers and loosened credit limits. The consequences are excessive lending by banks to particular sectors and an excessive concentration of loans to a particular risk category by individual banks. Add to this the possibility that attempts to cut costs in order to maintain competitiveness might reduce the amount and/or reliability of information gathered about potential borrowers and an element of herd behaviour, and we have a greatly heightened financial fragility.

This argument applies particularly to the countries of the periphery given the small average size of banks in such countries and the lack of competition within the sector (due to government ownership of a significant part of the sector and/or a segmented market based on regional differences).

To the extent that restructuring in the banking sector produces banks which operate across a number of EU countries and in so far as the single licence aspect of the Second Banking Directive leads to competitive deregulation, the riskiness of the banking sector as a whole will increase and supervision on a national basis will become more difficult and less effective. This will place much greater weight on the effectiveness of international and/or EU supervision.

The principal instrument of international control so far devised is the Basle Capital Adequacy Agreement of 1988. It has been adopted by the EU but has been widely criticized as inadequate (see, for example, Llewellyn, 1992).

There are at least two messages here for the emerging European central bank. First, a common monetary policy for the union is very likely to produce asymmetric effects on different member countries because of the unevenness of development of banking sectors. Second, the need for a central bank which accepts responsibility for the supervision of and the stability of the European banking sector may be more important for the healthy progress of the single market than a common monetary policy and may, indeed, conflict with it. We run into a further difficulty here, of course. Effective supervision of such a large and disparate system necessarily implies rules and limitations on private sector behaviour – but how well does this fit in with 'the framework of free market principles' mentioned in the Maastricht agreement?

OTHER EU ECONOMIC OBJECTIVES

There are clearly many economic objectives for the EU beyond the desire to keep inflation low, ranging from faster rates of economic growth and improved European competitiveness within the world economy to greater regional balance. These are treated with varying degrees of seriousness by different governments within the union and the weight ultimately given to them may both influence and be influenced by decisions regarding the degree of European protection against the outside world, the shifting balance of the centre of the EU as its membership expands, the size of the EU budget and the political and social pressures exerted by high unemployment.

Our interest here, however, is in the significance of such objectives for the central bank and for EU monetary policy. Everything here depends on the extent to which the central bank is made independent of governments as we have assumed above and on the exact form of the objective function set for the bank. If the objective function is indeed a lexicographical one with inflation at the head of a list of objectives, interest shifts to the form of the inflation objective. Even if low inflation is given absolute priority, it remains that uncertainty regarding the links between growth in money supply and inflation, and between the interest rate and growth in money supply provides some scope for the central bank to take account of other elements of policy. Nonetheless, it is possible that it will be tightly constrained. Further, if fiscal policy is treated, as is implied by the Maastricht agreement, as no more than the hand-maiden of monetary policy, it is clear that expressed intentions and plans such as the Delors plan, which seem to give greater weight to the need to expand the European economies, will remain little more than words. European monetary integration will retain its deflationary stance and, as we have argued above, the real gap between core and periphery seems destined to grow.

THE FREE MARKET FRAMEWORK

This view of the likely common monetary policy is given extra credibility by the proposition in the Maastricht agreement that the ECB should operate within 'a framework of free market principles'. This seems to mean that the control of the money stock should be achieved chiefly through central bank influence on market rates of interest. As has been argued often enough in relation to the UK, and as has been shown clearly by the European-wide responses to Bundesbank changes to key German money market interest rates, the importance of the central bank within financial markets means that we are not talking about a situation remotely resembling perfect competition. Nonetheless the implication is that the central bank and, through the central bank, private sector financial markets are seen as providing control over the behaviour of profligate governments. Since the desire for a tight European-wide monetary policy requires the maintenance of a strong European currency against the dollar and the yen, interest rates will need to remain as high as international financial markets require to bring this about.

Thus the free market framework may:

- interfere with attempts of the periphery to overcome unemployment and encourage economic growth;
- increase financial fragility within the peripheral countries; and
- reduce the possibility of putting into place controls over commercial bank behaviour necessary for effective bank supervision.

CONCLUSION

In summary, the central argument of this chapter can be expressed as a rejection of the possibility of one-speed European union based on an independent central bank with the dominating objective of maintaining low inflation. Peripheral countries will either not be allowed to join at the outset and will later find it impossible to do so, or will, in the push to join, cause such damage to their real economies and financial structures that the real gap between core and periphery will have been enlarged and will continue to grow. And yet this should not be interpreted as a rejection of European monetary union but rather as a warning of the dangers to the periphery of the currently strongly favoured institutional framework and common monetary policy associated with monetary union.

The most obvious alternative is for the union as a whole to choose an objective function which gives much greater weight to increases in the rate of growth, reductions in unemployment and regional balance. This is unlikely to occur given the wide acceptance of arguments regarding the NAIRU and the impact of inflation upon it and of the importance of credibility as well as the clear German rejection of anything likely to weaken the monetary policy stance currently adopted by the Bundesbank.

Under these circumstances, the way ahead for peripheral countries seems to require an acceptance of their peripheral status and a willingness to cooperate to improve their joint position within the union. This does not simply mean rearguard action regarding the conditions under which new northern European countries will be admitted to the union or the size of transfers within the union budget. It requires a willingness to argue for a slower movement towards monetary convergence and, even after monetary union, greater freedom to operate independent fiscal policies to offset the likely asymmetric effects of a common monetary policy. It further requires that greater attention be paid to bank supervision and that free market principles should not be regarded as inviolable.

NOTES

1. This chapter deals with the existing members of the EU in 1994 although the argument would be little affected by the inclusion of Austria, Norway, Sweden and Finland. None of these qualify as peripheral as a whole but have regional problems, notably in relation to the Arctic regions in the Scandinavian countries.
2. During the transition to EMU, and in EMU itself, the fall in nominal interest rates necessary to meet the interest rate convergence criterion for EMU membership will reduce the cost of financing the budget deficit and thus reduce the size of the primary surplus needed. Nonetheless, the required reductions in deficit to GDP and debt to GDP ratios will be so great that it will not be possible to rely simply on reductions in the cost of financing the government deficit.
3. One does not have to accept the strong form of the proposition of German leadership to accept the dominance of the core countries. In policy terms this probably does, however, stretch only as far as Germany and France.
4. In any case, non-automatic transfers which must usually be justified by the development of infrastructural and other large projects may not have the same long-term benefits for residents of depressed regions. They are likely to produce relatively large boosts to small areas over limited periods but the effects will not be as widely spread and they may not predominantly employ local labour.
5. Similar effects can be obtained without reference to radical theories. For example, Markusen and Svensson (1985) show that in the case of product-augmenting technological change, factor mobility leads to factor trade and commodity trade being complements, rather than substitutes

as in traditional trade theory. Trade causes factor movements and these, in turn, reinforce comparative advantage, generating further trade. In the model, countries on average export goods in which they have a technological lead. As a result, prices of factors used intensively in those export industries rise. Then factors (notably labour and capital embodying technological know-how) move in response to the newly created international factor price differences. This movement allows further technological developments, expanding and preserving the initial technological lead, consequently generating further trade. In other words, capital flows *towards* the country with the technological lead (the core country) rather than in the opposite direction.

There has been a significant recent flow of funds into the economies of Eastern Europe but this may well very largely be in search of the once-and-for-all windfall gains associated with privatization at knock-down prices.

6. This includes investment in the UK, at least part of which expects cost advantages from the UK's social chapter opt-out.
7. Stage four is characterized by central bank acceptance of responsibility for the stability of the system but lacks financial innovations such as liability management and securitization which allow commercial banks to avoid the impact of reserve stringency and alleviate maturity mismatches (see Chick, 1986) for further details.

REFERENCES

Arestis, P and Palaginis, E. (1993), 'Financial Fragility, Peripherality and Divergence in the European Community', *Journal of Economic Issues,* June, pp. 657–65

Barrell, R. (1992) (ed.), *Economic Convergence and Monetary Union in Europe,* London: Sage.

Chick, V. (1986), 'The Evolution of the Banking System and the Theory of Saving, Investment and Interest', in P. Arestis and S.C. Dow (eds), *On Method and Keynes: Selected Essays, Victoria Chick*, London: Macmillan.

Gibson, H.D. and Tsakalotos, E. (1993), 'European Integration and the Banking Sector in Southern Europe: Competition, Efficiency and Structure', *Banca Nazionale del Lavoro Quarterly Review,* September, pp. 299–326.

Grilli, V. (1989a), 'Financial markets and 1992', *Brookings Papers on Economic Activity,* no. 2.

Grilli, V. (1989b), 'Europe 1992: Issues and prospects for the financial markets', *Economic Policy,* no. 9, October.

Kaldor, N. (1970), 'The case for regional policies', *Scottish Journal of Political Economy,* November, pp. 337–48.

Kaldor, N. (1972), 'The irrelevance of equilibrium economics', *Economic Journal,* December, pp. 1237–55.

Llewellyn, D.T. (1992), 'Bank capital: the strategic issue of the 1990s', *Banking World,* January, pp. 20–25.

Markusen, J.R. and Svensson, L.E.O. (1985), 'Trade in goods and factors with international differences in technology', *International Economic Review,* February, pp. 175–92.

Myrdal, G. (1957), *Economic Theory and the Underdeveloped Regions,* London: Duckworth.

Ranci, P. (1990), 'The EMS and the completion of the internal market', in Ferri, P. (1990), *Prospects for the European Monetary System,* London: Macmillan.

Stiglitz, J. and Weiss, A. (1981), 'Credit Rationing in Markets with Imperfect Information', *American Economic Review*, vol. 71, pp. 393–410.

Index